#74021

D0710689

Lot 12⁵⁰

My China Eye

Israel Epstein

MY CHINA EYE

Memoirs of a Jew and a Journalist

LONG RIVER PRESS
San Francisco

Published in the United States of America by
Long River Press
360 Swift Ave., #48
S. San Francisco, CA 94080
www.longriverpress.com
Editor: Chris Robyn
Cover designer: Tommy Liu

Library of Congress Cataloging-in-Publication Data

Epstein, Israel, 1915-
My China Eye : memoirs of a Jew and a journalist / by Israel Epstein.— 1st ed.
    p. cm.
ISBN 1-59265-042-2 (hardcover)
1. Epstein, Israel, 1915-   2. Jewish journalists—China—Biography.
3. Jews—China—Biography.   4. China—History—Republic, 1912-1949.
5. China—History—1949- I. Title.
PN5366.E67A3 2005
070.92—dc22

2005005132

Printed in China
10 9 8 7 6 5 4 3 2 1

TABLE OF CONTENTS

Chapter 1

CROSSROADS: WEST TO EAST

In the West the compass is said to point North. To the Chinese, who invented it, it is the "South-pointing needle." The dual view does not affect its ability to guide in all directions, but it does draw attention to the relativity of spaces and the concept of multiple polarities. To the acute and ancient awareness of the Chinese civilization, built even into their everyday language, is the unifying relationship of opposites. "How much" or "how many" in Chinese, is "much-little" or "many-few." The length of anything is its "long-short" relationship. More deeply, the beautiful and thoughtful Chinese word for crisis is "danger-opportunity," reflecting the dual nature of the concept and hinting at the potential to develop in either direction. As in real life.

From the Eurocentric viewpoint, China is in the "Far East." But continuing East from China one reaches California, which was to Europe the far West. And going westward from there gets one, at last, to the "Far East."

There we find a couple whose lives are linked together at a crossroads in time and space in the twentieth century. Their lives—from different geographical and social origins—were propelled forward in unison by the same currents which shaped the course of history.

That year was 1944. The place was Chongqing (Chungking), wartime capital of the republican Guomindang (Kuomintang) government in Western China. Elsie Fairfax Cholmeley was English, and from a family of landed gentry. I was a then a stateless Jew, born in Poland, brought up in China. We were married, and heading for the United States via her homeland, Britain.

In our way stood a veritable mountain of red tape. I needed a visa, hard to get when one is stateless. Elsie risked losing her own passport, even her nationality. Before the postwar British Labor government put an end to the male-centered legal barbarism, an Englishwoman marrying a foreigner forfeited her citizenship and was deemed to have adopted her husband's. But my lack of citizenship was the only argument for

Elsie retaining hers. First, however, even my statelessness had to be checked. "The man must have been born *somewhere!*" the consular official at the British Embassy in Chongqing muttered to Elsie.

I *was* born somewhere. In Warsaw in 1915. But where in twentieth century political geography? Warsaw had been, for almost two centuries, a part of Poland, which had fallen to the Tsarist Empire in a three-sided partition with Austria and Prussia. Only after my birth did Warsaw again become the capital of independent Poland.

Ethnically, moreover, I was not a Pole. Nor had I asked for Polish papers in the pre-World War II situation, when the country's government was semi-Fascist and anti-Semitic. One example was the segregated seating of Jewish students in its universities.

Finally a solution came. That same Polish regime (by then the government-in-exile in London), had an ambassador in Chongqing who had no use for my Jewish-ness, my politics, or me. So he was glad to certify that I wasn't legally Polish. This was an unintended favor to Elsie, allowing her to retain her British birthright. And for me, though a legal nobody—but with a legally British wife—I became eligible for a spousal visit to her homeland. On the condition, it was noted, that our visit was only a matter of a brief transit to the U.S. (to which we both had visas), so I wouldn't loiter in Britain.

There was bickering in the British Foreign Office, I was to learn from papers opened decades afterwards, about whether to allow me in at all. "No reason to," one official noted sourly. "Let him come," wrote another more blandly, because I was fresh from Yan'an (Yenan), the center of Chinese Communist activity, and might cast some light on the Chinese Communists' effectiveness in the still-ongoing war with Japan. Even though, went his words: "Epstein is, of course, *totally sold* on Yan'an."

For many years I used to tell of the troubles of statelessness as a joke, to show how benighted things had been earlier in the twentieth century. In its third quarter, the humor vanished. The ranks of refugees, more and more of them stateless, were again grimly increasing.

*　　*　　*

How did Elsie and I, though so different in origin, become a lasting married pair, and in China of all places? The answers lay not only in our story but in the twentieth century's own turbulent history.

It brought my parents, with me as an infant, to the Far East in 1915. They were from Vilna (Vilnius), at their birth Russian-ruled but later Polish-occupied and today Lithuania's capital. As Socialists, and Jewish ones at that, they had both been jailed or exiled for activities linked to the failed Russian Revolution of 1905, the peak period of their political lives. Then they became repeated migrants within Western Europe and finally to Asia. The winds of World War I deposited my father in Japan. By profession a bookkeeper, he had worked in Russian Poland for a firm trading with Western Europe. With the land route was cut by the German front, the sphere of commerce shifted to the Pacific, often through Japanese ports. So Father was sent to Kobe. In the meantime, the German army moved on Warsaw. To avoid family severance for years, Mother took me, via thousands of miles on the Trans-Siberian railroad, to join Father.

When Russia's Tsarist monarchy was overthrown in February 1917, father rushed from Japan to the Revolution's capital, Petrograd, to unite with old comrades. Russians and Russian subjects then living abroad were often very different from "white" Russians émigrés of later years. Anti-Tsarist, many flocked joyfully to their revolutionary homeland.

Thinking to fetch us back, Father asked Mother to move to Harbin, a city in Northern China along the on the overland route by rail. But after he came for us, the "White" revolt in Siberia severed the railroad. In the early 1920s, traffic was restored by the Soviet government. By then, however, differences between it and Father's Socialist faction (the Jewish Bund) had widened. Those tangles, objective and subjective, planted us in China.

From Harbin we moved to Tianjin, a "treaty port" city then divided into "concessions" (areas of foreign control), once imposed on China at gunpoint. Predominant were British and American influences—economic, political, military, and cultural. From the age of five, education in foreign schools made English my language of easiest use, and ultimately my medium in my chosen profession, journalism.

Yet the imprint of my parents' Socialist ideas, at odds with my colonial-type schooling, remained. They made me perceive as alien and immoral the glaring contrasts and injustices of China's domination by foreign powers. Moreover, in my generation, the Russian Revolution represented socialism. Its predecessors in 1905 and in February 1917, so real to my parents, became pre-history to me. Japan's encroachments and invasions of the 1930s and their attendant horrors, close and visible, awoke me to an ever-growing sympathy with the rising national-revolutionary tide among the Chinese people, shown both in armed action and in student demonstrations.

These were part of the global surge to resist the advancing world-wide menace of Fascism exemplified by the rise of Hitlerism in Germany and the German-Italian armed backing of Fascist rebellion against the Spanish Republic. Spain and China, the earliest battlefields against armed aggression by Europe's Fascist powers and their ally Japan, were perceptibly linked, stirring anti-Fascists everywhere to admiration and help. Had I been in Europe I would have fought for Spain with pen and tongue, and possibly gun in hand in the International Brigades. But being in China, where a revolution was in progress, I was increasingly drawn toward it and its leading core, the Chinese Communist Party. The newspapers and news agencies I worked for were, with occasional exceptions, Right Wing. My personal links, Chinese and foreign, were increasingly at the Left.

From 1929 well into the 1930s, on the heels of a boom trumpeted as promising endlessly increasing prosperity in the West, its "advanced" capitalist economies had dropped into deep economic crisis, with record unemployment. In sharp contrast was the fast economic growth of the Soviet Union, the only major country working for a halt to Fascism. Pro-Soviet sentiment extended far beyond the Communist movement. The realities of those times need recalling, having become old, vague history to those who have no memory of them.

Elsie, on the other side of the globe, was formed by the same historical climate. It brought her in her adult years to China in 1939. She had studied agriculture, then farmed in Yorkshire, and been bankrupted by the depression. Then she trained for, and found, a clerical job in London, which she lost. Joining the ranks of the unemployed, she felt as one of them, and sometimes joined in their protest marches. Experience, combined with earlier ideas drawn from her father, a liberal inclined to the radical views of William Morris, drew her to the Left. As a feminist she could have gone to the U.S. or the U.S.S.R., different as they were, not because her political views were as yet well defined, but because the status of women there seemed better than in contemporary England.

8

Later, chance and family connections threw her into a job with an international academic body, the Institute of Pacific Relations, and a subsequent world trip. On it she saw much of what then was termed the "colonial" world, now simply called the Third World. Later, while working in the IPR's New York headquarters with scholars of both the Right and the Left, she found the latter more enlightening and congenial. Among them she met Chinese citizens who impressed her greatly. They were, in fact, Communists, but secretly. If exposed as such, they could not, in the Chiang Kai-shek era of the Guomindang, have left China. In the West it would be difficult to find work in academia, but to remain in China would be to risk death.

With popular sympathy for China under Japanese attacks widespread, Elsie became active in the movement to boycott imports from Japan. In 1939, still with the IPR, she came to Hong Kong. There I met her among supporters of China's armed resistance and of the wartime Chinese Industrial Cooperative movement.

As a result of the blitz-attack on Hong Kong in December 1941 (on the same day as Pearl Harbor), Elsie and I found ourselves in a Japanese-run enemy civilian internment camp. Determined to escape, we succeeded, with the indispensable participation of three friends, one American and two British.

In 1942, on a perilous journey into inland China, came love. I was in the process of amicable divorce from my first wife, who was in America. With her, I had some common views, but our choice of paths differed. She wanted us to start a home and family in America, but I wanted to stay in, and with, China until Japan was beaten. Already in 1938 when my parents had migrated to America I had remained in China, a pattern opposite to the more typical one of the young men going first then bringing their parents over.

With Elsie we chose not only each other but the same road-map through life. We were married in 1943.

What took us out of China in 1944?

I had just returned from several months' reporting in Yan'an, the direction center of the Chinese Community Party, and other areas behind the Japanese lines which were wrested back from the invaders. There, we had seen not only a different way of national resistance to Japanese aggressors but the embryonic stage of a future China. About both, I wanted to write a book, not an easy think to do in Chongqing,

9

the seat of the Chiang Kai-shek government. All my dispatches had been required to go via Chongqing. It had not been easy to save them from mangling by Guomindang censorship to the most trivial details, despite my filing even for the *New York Times*. Fading away was the united front between the Guomindang and the Communist Party that had been formed to resist Japan. Chiang was hardly fighting the Japanese at all while awaiting their coming defeat by the Allied powers. Clearly he was hoarding his best troops and U.S.-supplied weapons for a subsequent war against the Communists, who had fought Japan incessantly and came to represent the national hope for a China free from her glaring current weaknesses and woes. This, too, was hard to write while in Chiang's territory in the shadow of impending civil war.

In May 1945, when World War II was won in Europe (though not yet in Asia), we were already in Britain, having, during the previous couple of months, experienced the last bombings of London by Nazi V-2 missiles.

In July 1945, in the last phase of the war with Japan, we arrived in New York. On our very first morning there, all newspapers front-paged the U.S. arrest of John Stewart Service—one of the best-informed and most open-minded young American diplomats in China. As a political adviser to General Joseph W. ("Vinegar Joe") Stilwell, the straight-talking, erudite and China-wise former commander of U.S. forces there, Jack Service had stood with his chief for cooperation against Japan alongside the Communist as well as the Guomindang forces. This advocacy led to the removal of Stilwell under pressure from Chiang Kai-shek. Following the death of President Roosevelt in April, the United States government chose to support Chiang under all circumstances, which meant he could prepare and wage his civil war. Most U.S. State Department officers in China had opposed this as bad for the United States, and for future mutual relations with China. For this, they were smeared in Washington as, in various degrees, "disloyal," incurring penalties ranging from transfer to posts as far from China as possible to being fired from government service. Prescience became punishable, prejudiced ignorance of the scene a merit.

It was part of a wider historic turn. Just as the Japanese invasion of China in the 1930s had signaled the real start of World War II, the U.S. decision to support Chiang in renewed civil war after Japan's surrender signaled the shift of U.S. and world politics from anti-Fascist war to

"Cold War." In fact, the defeat of Chiang, by Chinese for internal Chinese reasons, was inevitable despite all the arms and dollars with which the U.S. supplied him. It led, in American domestic politics, to the absurd, "Who lost China?" witch-hunt, as though anyone except the Chinese could own China once they mustered the strength to end the century of foreign domination, which by the late 1940s they had done. From the "Who Lost China?" outcry one can trace the earliest trappings of the McCarthyite blight which was to come. Internationally, it led to the efforts to "contain" and later "roll back" the Chinese Revolution, which animated U.S. involvement in the Korean and Vietnam wars. Only after 22 years, during which these ventures failed, were the first U.S. steps taken with President Richard M. Nixon's trip, towards state-to-state relations with the People's Republic of China.

History has its tides and Elsie and I were faced with another choice. In the five years we spent in the U.S., we tried to help Americans who opposed policies that flew in the face of unfolding reality. As in Guomindang China, this did not endear us to the establishment, and vice-versa. Though we were temporarily across the ocean, our energies centered no less on China than when we were there: first on arguing against the Truman administration's pro-Chiang actions, then on helping a campaign for U.S. "friendship, recognition, and trade" with the newborn People's Republic. In those early years Elsie and I made two crucial choices: the first was to leave China in 1944 to help the Western world understand the Chinese Revolution. The second was come back to live and work in the new China, which we did in 1951.

*   *   *

Before leaving Chongqing in 1944, we visited Zhou Enlai, who represented the Communist Party there within the long-tottering united front with the Guomindang. To re-live it for the post-World War II era, averting civil war and speeding national rebuilding from the ruins of the preceding devastating decades, the Communists were advocating a coalition government with the participation not only of China's two main parties but of smaller democratic parties and groups. Did Zhou really think such a coalition possible? We asked. "Yes," he replied without hesitation, "with or without *him*." The "him" clearly referred to Chiang Kai-shek. And "without him" that if Chiang chose war instead of cooperation, he would inevitably isolate himself from a very broad national consensus, including elements of his own party.

At a distance from China, sometimes with no means of communicating, we never forgot Zhou's remark. Borne out by what did happen between 1944 and 1949, it helped us, and our audiences abroad, to see the main trend in the intervening complex of events, culminating in the birth and growth of a China no longer, as for a century past, a football in the world arena but one of its leading players.

In 1951, we returned to China, in our last and fullest choice, to stay. And we did through weal, woe, trials and triumphs. Unlike "watchers" from the outside, we saw the international arena as it looked from within China. Considering our familiarity with both worlds, our perceptions might help others to a rounder view.

At the age of 90, I try to present in greater detail recollections of a complex life's journey in an increasingly interwoven world. Hopefully they may contain a few clues to a future bound to be more intricately interactive.

Chapter 2

ORIGINS

On the paternal side, my Grandfather, David Epstein, I was told, started life as a young student of Jewish Holy Scriptures but became a forwarding agent at the Vilna railway station in Lithuania, then ruled by the Russian Tsar. He married Haya-Kraina Baver, from a family of publishers of Hebrew prayer books and Talmudic texts used in many countries. Shipping these books worldwide broadened his contacts and knowledge since he had to write addresses and bills of lading in several languages. From letters received he learned something of events abroad. Though his income never exceeded the lower-middle level, he gained enough respect to become the gabbai (Elder) of a neighborhood synagogue. This status was symbolized on public occasions by a silk top hat, which impressively crowned his small height.

Grandfather and his wife presented many contrasts. He, short and stocky, moved and thought with deliberation. Grandmother, taller by a head, thin, swarthy, and handsomely aquiline, was decisive in speech and action (with a "Ministerial brain" one of her daughters recalled). But they lived in harmony and raised nine children—some tall, some average, and others diminutive—in two cases with spinal curvatures, probably the result of rickets.

Yet precisely those two, my father Lazar and his sister Rebecca, were outstanding in energy of mind, and grew into revolutionaries against the Tsar. Their organization was the Bund, or Jewish Labor Alliance, originally a section of the Russian Social-Democratic Labor Party, the Marxist group which later split into the Bolsheviks (Communists) and the Mensheviks (Socialists).

The Bund became their life. Dad, drawn in by an early teacher, served his party from the age of 12 or so. Tiny and humpbacked, he was not the type to be suspect of carrying secret revolutionary messages—which he did.

Able and warm-hearted, Aunt Rebecca, too, was a lifelong activist. She became a labor union functionary and, for a time in Paris, took courses at the Sorbonne. She was elected as a Bund member of the Vilna Jewish Community Council. Never married, but loving and concerned for children, she was incessantly involved in school and kindergarten affairs.

Ultimately, she would be murdered—buried alive—by the Nazis in the killing fields of Ponary near Vilnius. One believes that, even in line for grisly death, in circumstances designed to denude victims of all human dignity before the end, she stood as straight as her hunched back would allow, helping others.

Grandmother Haya-Kraina showed her mettle whenever the Tsarist gendarmes came to search the house for evidence against her son and daughter. She would hide incriminating papers where they could not find them. When her children were jailed, she would stride, head held high, with a basket of food to whatever prison they were held in, whether she would have preferred them to stay out of politics and jail was not the point: they were her children and she respected their choice.

At age 21, Father was a Bund delegate to the Seventh Congress of the Russian Social Democratic Workers' Party held in London in 1907. Including both Bolsheviks and Mensheviks, it was known as the Unity Congress because, drawing lessons from the initial great sweep of the 1905 Russian Revolution and the weight of its defeat, a last effort was made to heal the split between the two factions dating from 1903. Lenin was there, and Trotsky, and the still little-known Joseph Djugashvili (later called Stalin). So were the pillars of Manshevism: Plekhanov, Martov, and others, and fiery revolutionaries like the famous Rosa Luxembourg.

* * *

The Chinese have a proverb: "Withered leaves drop close to the roots of the tree"—in old age and in death one returns to one's origins. With Dad's Yiddish-educated East European Jewish generation this was hardly possible. The fruits were prematurely destroyed or scattered—the roots bloodily ripped out by Nazi genocide—or "ethnic cleansing"—to use a modern term sanitizing a murderous practice. So the surviving fruits did the next best thing: they fell close to each other.

When Father, past 90, finally had to go to an old age home in New York, he chose the one in the Bronx run by the Workmen's Circle, where there were many surviving old Bundists.

▲ *1*

10

12 11

13

14
15

16 ——————
         17 | 19
18 ——————

20

21

22

23

24

25

30
31

36

37

38

39

41

42

43

"I know you!" He was greeted on arrival by a contemporary already there. "I heard you speaking from a balcony in Minsk in 1906!"

Of our family who stayed in Lithuania and Poland a score perished in the Holocaust and only one remained alive—my first cousin Beba who survived a Nazi concentration camp for women. Just before Germany's defeat its remaining inmates were herded aboard a ship in the Baltic Sea to which a mine was attached. It failed to detonate. The women were rescued and taken to Sweden. In a long process cousin Beba made contact with my father in New York who brought her over to the United States. At this writing, she lives in Los Angeles, with her husband, children and grandchildren.

The only other survivors on my Father's side were his three sisters: Emma, Sonya, and Anna, and an older brother, Alexander, who went early to the Soviet Union. The sisters were all teachers. Alexander perished in a purge during the 1930s.

Another brother, Isaac, who immigrated to the United States before World War I, became a waiter in New Jersey and died there.

Isaac had no politics and floated out of the Jewish milieu. He lived largely among Italian-Americans, and was a *bon vivant* to the extent that his income allowed. Locally, he was popular—and a bit of a legend. So diminutive that he could hardly be seen behind the wheel while driving, the story was that when an empty car came rolling along, people said, "There goes Eppy."

When he died, nothing was found to indicate any desire to be buried in a Jewish cemetery. It is said that his devout Catholic ladyfriend insisted that this be done with the proper rites, so he would be at peace with his long-neglected God.

Mother's family was more prosperous, yet she too took the revolutionary path—to the Bund.

My grandfather on that side, Moshe Ebicz (later spelled "Ebitz" by his son in America), was a Vilna leather merchant.

A pious Jew, he was also affected by the "enlightenment" (Haskala in Hebrew). That nineteenth century trend in East European Jewry retained religious orthodoxy as a basis, but was open in various ways to modern thought. In later years, in China, I would find interesting parallels in its attitudes and timing to views of the Chinese reformers of the 1870s who wanted to acquire Western science and technology, heavy industry, national defense, and the like, while preserving their own Chinese (in their case Confucian) pieties and practices.

But there were also essential differences. China's "Westernizers" were officials, trying to save and adapt their feudal state. Jews had no officials and no state. So my maternal grandfather did not need to think about budgets, administrative systems, or armaments.

In religious life, a *mohel* (performer of ritual circumcisions) would advocate modernist practices by using antiseptic procedures instead of traditional, unsanitary ones (an old-time *mohel* would take the infant's penis in his mouth to stanch bleeding). So Grandpa Ebicz aimed at a measure of progress, but within the limits of the ghetto.

In temperament, the old man was also liberal, in fact happy-go-lucky. His many children—his wife bore sixteen, of whom seven or eight survived—were spaced over such a range that when the youngest were small the eldest brother was already earning and burdened by being the virtual paterfamilias. Mother recalled the eldest brother as the stern family disciplinarian while her father seemed kind and mild. Grandfather, was, in fact, unfair to his eldest son. When the latter was in his forties—and he himself in his 70s—he would grumble about his preoccupied and strait-laced first-born: "That *old man* bores me." Much more to his easy-going taste was the company of his younger offspring and his grandchildren. After Grandmother's death he scandalized most of the family by marrying again, the widow of a close friend. When World War II broke out he was 87, and still lively.

But not for long. The German occupation of Vilnius spelled his end. Was he asphyxiated in a Nazi gas chamber, or knocked to the ground by an SS officer, and, unable to scramble to his feet, kicked and left to die in the street where he fell like so many other old bearded Jews? Or did starvation and disease wither him in the ghetto? No eyewitness was found to tell the tale.

Grandfather's respectable merchant status, had, paradoxically, led indirectly to the first arrest of my mother, then only sixteen and his favorite child. The charge was engaging in revolutionary activity. She had just joined the youth organization of the Jewish Socialist Bund. Because her new comrades were from poorer families they had decided to hide their Marxist library in her home, which was thought to be less suspect. Soon an informer tipped off the Tsarist gendarmes, and my future mother was in prison, and within weeks on her way to exile in Narym, Siberia.

The exiles, in those days, traveled under convoy and by stages, *etapes* as they were called (in Russian borrowed from the French). They started their journey by train, continued by river steamer, then moved on by foot, spending the nights locked up in prisons along the way.

Mother was to recall her youthful ordeal less as miserable and more as exciting and enlightening. On the trail, and in Narym, she was in the company of revolutionary intellectuals, broad in knowledge, strong in conviction, which she saw as teachers. Most were much older than she. Some, like Valerian Kuibyshev, her senior by only a few years, were to become prominent in the U.S.S.R. He would, for a time, be at the head of the Soviet economy. After his death, a city named after him would become the country's temporary seat of government in World War II. Mother recalled him as a convinced, handsome, eloquent young man.

In the Bund organization, my father had been her superior. Though they had not previously known each other, he had taken her under his wing because she seemed almost a child. Also, as he told me decades later, she was sad and tearful: when he first saw her at youth reunion at a woodland resort near Vilna, she was despondent over the failure of her first girlhood romance.[1]

Though only five years older in years, my father had already been tested in the 1905 Revolution against Tsarist autocracy and had undergone the first of his five arrests. He traveled secretly as a Bund delegate to London. Now, going on a business trip (as a commercial employee) to Koenigsberg in East Prussia, he asked what he could bring back for my mother. A popular folding umbrella, she said, available in Germany but not locally. Koenigsberg would after World War II be ceded to the Soviet Union and called Kaliningrad.

By the time he returned, she was in prison, destined for Siberia. Upon learning that her barred window faced the street, he strolled on the opposite side, the umbrella over his head, to show her he had not forgotten.

Later, when she was in Siberia, they corresponded and he helped her to escape.

As Mother would tell it, he sent her a book—and a note commenting on its attractive binding. Taking the hint, she sliced it open, taking

[1]This resort, not far from Vilna, was Ponary, which in the Holocaust would become the Nazi killing fields for tens of thousands of the city's Jews.

17

apart the endpapers. On one side was a passport for her use (in those days such identity papers carried no photos and though the name was not hers the description could fit her). On the other side were some high-denomination banknotes, given to her by her father. Supplied with these, she managed one day to slip out of the area to which she was supposed to be confined—and kept on going.

That she could get away was due to several factors. She had been sentenced, like some other "politicals," not to jail or hard labor but to "administrative exile." A young girl, she had no "history" to warrant special surveillance. The local police inspector, responsible for several villages, was frequently off on circuit. Like many rural minor officials, he stood rather in awe of the intellectuals under his charge, and would ask them to help coach a son in mathematics, or another to help teach a daughter the piano. The exiles had virtually the run of his house—and even held political conclaves there while he was traveling. The police inspector's daughter was the same age as my mother and actually helped smooth her escape with advice on how to hire a horse cart to where she could board a riverboat. She encountered no difficulty. Mother had a document (in old Russia it was said that a human being had to have three things, "body, soul, and a passport"), and enough money to keep going. All the way by boat, road, and rail across Russia and over the border—as far as Paris.

She was happy about it all except for one reservation—would the inspector or his daughter get in too much trouble on her account?

In Paris, with the help of Bundist and other revolutionary expatriates, she found a job as secretary to the Yiddish poet Avrahm Reisin, went to museums and art galleries with Anatoly Lunacharsky—future Soviet Minister of Culture—a highly-qualified volunteer group tour guide, and generally expanded her purview. I still remember, from my childhood, already in China, browsing on the pudgy, abundantly illustrated *Petite Larousse* encyclopedic dictionary she had brought back, from which I learned some French and much else. France, incidentally, was not Mother's first experience in the West. At age 12 or so, she had been to London with her father who went on his leather business, and briefly attended an English school.

To Paris too, in due course, came my father, who in between had sat for a while in a Tsarist jail. Renewed acquaintance ripened into courtship. They vacationed in Switzerland, on Lake Lugano.

Shortly before the outbreak of World War I, they returned to Vilna, and married. And Mother, in line with their conviction that one must have a skill of use to people, trained as a midwife.

But that is another story.

Chapter 3

ELSIE

Of Elsie's background, there are some facts, from what she told me at various times, and from experience before our fates brought us together.

Her father was Hugh Fairfax Cholmeley (1864-1940), squire of the Yorkshire village of Brandsby, who inherited several farms but later in life had to sell most of them. For English country gentry, the family was not typical. As Roman Catholics they had for three centuries been barred from the civil and military careers that made their class in society a pillar of Britain's conservative establishment.

Though Hugh Cholmeley broke with Catholicism, to which the rest of the family continued to adhere, it was not to conform more to the prevailing social conventions, but to stray further. From his university days he tended toward radical views, often proclaiming them with a bright red necktie to shocking the prim and proper. A family story tells how a stuffy aunt ordered her doorman, if her nephew came so attired, not to let him in by the front entrance but to hint that he hop over the hedge and enter through the backyard. She was willing to see the young reprobate, but not to face neighbors' comments.

The young man himself, starting from volunteering at Toynbee Hall, which philanthropically helped London's poor, began to lean toward Socialist ideas. He came to admire William Morris and frequented circles that included, among others, Bernard Shaw.

Unconventional, too, in setting up his own household, he remained single until around forty, then married his gardener's daughter, Alice Moverley (1885-1953), who was to become Elsie's mother. But first he supervised her education, a la Pygmalion. Prior to the wedding, he sent her family out of the village to London where be bought them a home in the then still-rural suburb of Hampstead. So his freedom from conventions had limits.

As a squire, he was a paternalist reformer. He equipped his village with water taps and a public telephone, angering nearby landlords who feared that their tenants would want the same. To widen the mental horizons of his tenants, he built a small red-brick auditorium, "Cholmeley Hall," where they were expected to gather each Sunday afternoon to hear him read from that mouthpiece of liberal views, *The Manchester Guardian*. This was far less popular than the running water, as Elsie would amusingly recollect. After church in the mornings they would prefer to do something else. But to her father the editorial infusions might well have seemed a desirable antidote to a sermon. Though his ethics were Christian, he was not pious.

After renouncing Catholicism, Hugh Cholmeley himself attended Anglican Sunday services—it was the done thing. But he disliked the local parson, and so boycotted Brandsby church. Each week he drove past it in his pony trap with a loud jangling of bells on the way to the church in the next village.

This English eccentric, part Tolstoyan, part rebel, was artistic and musical. He had a good baritone voice and a repertoire of English and Italian folk songs, self-accompanied on the guitar. Music was part of his heritage to his daughters. Elsie learned the cello and her youngest sister, Rosamond (Ros for short), the violin—both performing with quartets of fair quality.

Rooted in Elsie's heart and memory were many old tunes of green, rural England some of which she taught me when our lives joined. In Chongqing we would meet another aficionado, Joseph Needham, head of the wartime British Scientific Mission, and future author of the monumental multi-volume, *Science and Civilisation in China*, a staggering academic work of global significance. He would bring his own guitar for sing-songs in our room.

Another thing for which Elsie thanked her father was his determination that his daughters, as well as his sons, should be educated. At that time, socially comparable young women were mostly rounded off for marriage at finishing schools. But he wanted them prepared to earn a living.

Elsie received her earlier schooling from a governess, and most of her secondary schooling from a public (which in England means private) school for girls at North Foreland on the Channel coast. She then studied dairy farming at Reading Agricultural College. Her youngest sister Ros was trained as a hospital dietitian at London University.

From Elsie's childhood and adolescence, I have only scraps of written evidence.

One is an undated letter she wrote at the age of 7 or so, addressed to Santa Claus:

> Dear Father Christmas,
>
> Please will you bring me a Bicycle and a large Doll in long clothes to take care of and a Book about Fairy Tales any kind will do and also I would like a pack of Beggar My Neighbour cards and a box of Paints and a ball to play games and catch with.
>
> Much love from Elsie Fairfax Cholmeley—if you cannot read the address it is 22 Montpelier Crescent, Brighton it is not at Brandsby.

Brighton, where the family moved to for a time, was where Elsie wanted her presents sent. Brandsby was the ancestral village in Yorkshire. Even so early she was definite and detailed in what she had to say, a characteristic she retained.

Two other letters are reminiscences, after she died, by former teenage schoolmates at North Foreland:

One wrote:

> I loved Elsie since I first met her. I knew she was something very special. She used to radiate goodness… In her company I felt a better person or wanted to be. Don't ask me why… Sometimes a single glance is enough to know people… I feel over-whelming gratitude for having known her—someone great in the real sense. So human and yet so pure.

The other recalled Elsie's funloving, and rebellious character. With three friends, including the letter writer:

> We were called the Four Musketeers for we were all anti-establishment…couldn't wait to leave the school & horrified the "goodies" most of whom wept at the end of the last term, unlike us who laughed with joy and had an illicit party.
>
> We called Elsie "Blossom" because when she had a cold her nose went pink. She always told us she was a farmer's daughter—when we supposed they had hams hanging in the kitchen Elsie got a real ham & hung it on a hook as a joke—she had a great sense of humour— although I hadn't seen her for all these years I'm sure she kept it until the end.

She guessed right, Elsie did.

Elsie's father's continued to influence her after she joined the working world, and the values he wished to pass on to her can be glimpsed from a letter to her when she was 25, job-seeking in London after a depression-era failure in farming:

Of the then most powerful British conservative press magnates, the Lords Beaverbrook and Rothermere, Hugh Cholmeley wrote caustically:

> They are both a bad lot politically. I think Rothermere is the worse villain, but I'm not sure. One of the two wanted a favor from [Prime Minister] Baldwin, a rise to the peerage and a place in the Cabinet for his son, and when refused attacked Baldwin out of spite.

On a more personal note, after suggesting that Elsie try to be a writer, he approved her expressed reluctance in terms, which cast light on both father and daughter:

> You are right about not being able to write unless you have something you want to say. All other writing is worthless even if people attain the art of writing about nothing...
>
> Which is one reason why you should read, cultivate ideas about topics of world interest and... interest yourself in important affairs, in human nature...
>
> With all great artists and writers, the higher they are in the scale the wider their interests... You will find poets like Shelley and Byron deeply & seriously interested in reform movements & even politics of their day: even painters like Michelangelo, Raphael, etc. had unsuspected intellectual & practical interests. William Blake, of all people, the mystical idealist, was deeply versed in political and social questions. And you can't get ideas worth having unless you take the trouble to go into questions thoroughly & not merely superficially, but the moment you begin to do that the ideas come fast enough...
>
> Then if you have the faculty of expressing them it is easy.

The writers he cited as models were progressives, and in the case of Shelley and Blake revolutionaries of their time. Blake had famously pledged:

> *I shall not cease from mental strife*
> *Nor shall the sword sleep in my hand*
> *Until we have built Jerusalem*
> *In England's green and pleasant land.*

Blake remained Elsie's best-loved poet. She tried to get every new edition of the powerful verse and art of this great eighteenth century visionary, from which we would often read together.

Closest to her father, Elsie talked with him the most, absorbed his thinking the most, and in practice went beyond him. Her childhood friendships among the tenants would last into old age. Her interest in cooperatives, which would lead her later to work with the wartime industrial cooperatives in China, also went back to Hugh Cholmeley. He had founded, in 1894, a decade before she was born, a co-op in Brandsby to help the farmers—with vans and other facilities—to transport and market their dairy products. After more than a century, it still exists.

Politically, in the early 1930s, father and daughter were sharply critical of the British establishment. Both read *The Week*, the radical newsletter edited by Claude Cockburn, with its informed exposés of reactionary and pro-Fascist trends in the upper world. But as the decade closed, the father, by then over 70, saw hope for "peace in our time" in Prime Minister Neville Chamberlain's appeasement of Nazi Germany. Elsie, though she never ceased loving her "Pa Cholmeley," was vigorously opposed.

Generally, Elsie's development was impelled by the same global spirit of the age as mine, far apart, as we were our geographical and social starting points. When worldwide post-1929 economic depression wrecked her livestock-farming in Yorkshire, she took a secretarial course in London but could find work only sporadically. Sympathizing with the growing mass of Britain's unemployed, she joined in some of their protest marches. Since jobs for women in England were even scarcer, and paid even less than those for men, she thought of moving elsewhere, to the United States or the Soviet Union where there was less sex discrimination.

Then, in 1935, came a surprising opportunity to travel to many countries. Though opened through upper-class connections of the family, it was to carry Elsie more decisively to the Left, and ultimately, to China, and me.

Elsie's father had asked influential friends if they could find something for her. One was involved in receiving a globe-trotting group from the Institute of Pacific Relations, an academic body which was international in scope but actually American-led. Its secretary-general, Edward C. Carter, was looking for a British addition to vary its image. Learning that Elsie was from a landed gentry family with a hyphenated-surname (Americans are often impressed by this) he thought she might be suitable. But first he wanted his wife to look her over. Elsie would later chuckle about how Alice Carter, while getting a permanent in a London

Beauty Parlour, gave her the nod. Tall, with good looks but not flaunting them, well-bred but direct and without airs, she seemed to the older woman to fit the role.

A financial snag intervened. Part of the travel expenses had to be borne by Elsie, but it was too much for her or her father. Only when a wealthy and affectionate aunt came to the rescue was the job hers.

Hired, she accompanied the IPR delegation through the rest of its tour—to Japan, China, India, Australia and New Zealand, all with local affiliate offices. She then joined the regular staff of the IPR's international center in New York, as secretary to its quarterly magazine *Pacific Affairs*, edited by the noted American Far Eastern scholar Owen Lattimore.

The unexpected and almost global safari widened her world. In India she saw the misery of the indigenous population beneath the panoply of Britain's empire; in China the back-breaking labor of the people harried by foreign and domestic oppression. In Japan, where the militarists were taking over, she met careful but determined opponents of this course—like the erudite Dr. Yasuo and the aristocrat Prince Kinkazu Saionji (the latter a Marxist who after the war was to live in Beijing and work to normalize the relations of the People's Republic of China with Japan).

In New York, and at an international conference of the IPR in Yosemite, California, she came to know two brilliant Chinese scholars working with the Institute, Dr. Ji Chaoding and Dr. Chen Hansheng. Both were Communists but not openly.

In 1937 Japan launched its full-scale invasion of China. In the United States, as elsewhere, opponents of aggression and Fascism took up China's cause. Elsie became an activist in the women's movement to boycott Japanese silk, used mainly for stockings in the pre-nylon days. Silk was the main export with whose proceeds Japan bought American oil, scrap steel, and other military essentials.

Elsie was also involved in the American Committee for Chinese War Orphans, as well as aid programs for the Spanish Republic (Spain and China were seen by anti-Fascists worldwide as fronts of the same cause).

Within the IPR she helped organize a union. Edward C. Carter, like many employers who are pro-labor until it comes to them, was hurt in his paternalist nerve. He began to regard Elsie, the well-born British

Miss he had hired, as ungrateful.

In 1939, Chen Hansheng and his wife Suzie (Gu Shuxing), by now Elsie's best friends, went to Hong Kong. Nominally they were engaged to work on publishing projects for the IPR; when in fact, they mainly went to assist Soong Ching-ling (the widow of Dr. Sun Yat-sen, leader of China's Republican Revolution of 1911) in mobilizing international support for China's anti-Japanese resistance, especially that of the Communist-led armies. In a wartime united front with the ruling Guomindang, the Communist forces were often deprived not only of military supplies but medical supplies as well.

Elsie had obtained a commission from the IPR to go into the interior of China to study traditional agricultural tools and methods. This, in wartime, proved difficult. Instead, under Chen Hansheng in Hong Kong, she worked in the International Committee for the Promotion of the Chinese Industrial Cooperatives, a movement to bring skilled workers and their tools out of the Japanese-occupied cities into areas of rural resistance. Elsie also collaborated with Chen on a newsletter about China's military and political situation, called *Internos* (later the Far Eastern Bulletin) using the pen-name Edith Cromwell.

It was in Hong Kong, and through common work in such efforts that we met. My first impression of her was of a pale, quiet blonde Englishwoman, topping me by a head, in her mid-thirties to my mid-twenties, hard-working, and not very communicative. She saw in me, as she later recalled, only a short, rather shy, youngster, with "long eyes that rolled upward" (they may have done because of her height). Any romantic interest was furthest from out minds. I was still married to my first wife. Elsie had her own social circle.

What first touched my heart was encountering her on a street in Hong Kong in mid-1941, her face drawn in sorrow, her blue eyes dimmed within dark circles. She had been, overwhelmingly, in love, in what she had told me later had been her life's high peak, not only of joy but also of seeming common understanding, only to have been deceived and rudely discarded.

I felt sudden, deep compassion for this woman, usually so self-contained, now surprisingly so vulnerable and stricken. Still, there was no thought or inkling that we would ever unite our lives.

On December 7, 1941 came the Japanese attack on Pearl Harbor, which ignited the Pacific War. Simultaneously, there were attacks on Hong

Kong. Elsie and I had met again in our pro-China relief volunteering. Apparently back on keel, Elsie had a new regular job, with the Chinese Currency Stabilization Board, a joint Chinese, U.S., and British undertaking to protect China's depreciating currency from collapse. She had joined it on the recommendation of old IPR colleague (and secret Communist) Ji Chaoding. Through a provincial-level and old family friend connection with the then Guomindang Finance Minister, H. H. Kung, Ji had become one of the Chinese representatives. In her new position, Elsie scandalized the British delegate, Hall-Patch, by siding not with the British but with the Chinese and American delegates, the progressive Roosevelt New Dealers, Manuel Fox, and Solomon Adler.

Amid the din of the 18-day Battle of Hong Kong, Elsie came more than once to see me at the *South China Morning Post,* where I was then working as a sub-editor. Each time she threaded her calm, brave way from Hong Kong's elite Peak area, where she had moved from her previous quarters to stay with a female friend, down sloping, winding streets where enemy shells were falling. She was, by then, doing war work, helping put out, together with progressive Chinese publicists, an information sheet called *Hong Kong War Express.*

Among the things we talked about was how to dispose of the papers of the Stabilization Board. As requested by Ji Chaoding in a note to Elsie before the leading group's hurried air-evacuation to Chongqing, we went to his room in the Hong Kong Hotel and, in its steel wastebasket, burned every scrap he had had no time to destroy. A more substantial part of the Board's documents, Elsie said with some wry asides, she and her Peak hostess had buried in a tin trunk under the manure heap of the latter's garden.

We further discussed how to keep from the Japanese the files of the Indusco (Chinese Industrial Cooperative) office, being destroyed by Elsie and her colleagues. And those of the China Defense League, some of which I helped my colleague, Liu Wugou, to burn.

These things done, we spoke of how, in the event of Hong Kong's inevitable fall, we could escape from Japanese vengeance, which for us, working closely with China's resistance, could be drastic. We understood that we would be helped to leave by the Communist-led underground, which had contingency plans for the evacuation of united front friends and activists. Yang Gang, the well-known writer, critic, essayist, poet, and literary editor of the liberal newspaper *Ta Kung Pao* (*Da Gongbao*), secretly a Communist, was to inform of us of the time and place.

In the chaotic days after the Japanese landed on Hong Kong Island after having seized Kowloon peninsula, we lost touch. Elsie, as she would tell me, became a volunteer nurse in the impromptu military hospital in what had been the cocktail lounge of the swank Hong Kong Hotel. Under doctors' orders, she did what she could for the increasingly crowded wounded laid side to side on the floor, some dying, some in agony. I could picture her—strong, tireless and caring—though, as she said ruefully, her medical training was limited to veterinary first-aid learned in her dairy-farming course at Reading and in practical farming afterwards. By now she showed no outward signs of the emotional distress I had seen earlier in the year. Her response was to act, not languish.

The arrangements for our evacuation fell through, because of the rapidity of Hong Kong's fall. When next we met, it was in the civilian internment camp set up by the Japanese at Stanley, a small peninsula on the southern side of Hong Kong Island.

Elsie arrived with the Peak contingent. The officially and socially prominent British inhabiting this exclusive locale, she said bitingly, had first petitioned the Japanese authorities, as between gentlemen, to be interned in their accustomed prestigious area. But they were, after some parley, refused and, since they were the last group to arrive at Stanley they received the worst quarters. On the other hand, being allowed to come by truck instead of being marched in on foot, they arrived with what in the internment camp was untold wealth: Simmons mattresses, trunks bulging with personal effects, food, and assorted loot for trading within the camp.

Elsie, not belonging to the Peak in any way other than geographically, came with them through the accident of having been the guest of a woman acquaintance there in the battle's last days.

Spotting her and her friend in one of the trucks, I helped to carry their luggage. Though short in stature, I had a strong back and strong legs.

We lived in different areas, she in the British and I in the American (as part of a pretended identity).

Common determination to escape, in order to dodge retribution for our work for China and to resume that work as soon as possible, brought us together. First in planning and, after further moves and perils, as a couple.

Chapter 4

HARBIN

Though my parents and I lived in Harbin, a city in the extreme north of China only from when I was two until I was five (1917-20), it is so vivid in my memory even at ninety.

Harbin's flavor was Russian, specifically, Siberian. Unlike most cities in China it had no pre-modern urban history but was a product of two decades of mushroom growth. Up to the end of the nineteenth century it had been a fishing village by the Songhua (Sungari) River, its name reputed to have meant, in the Manchu language, "a place for sunning nets."

Then came its boom-town urban birth, amid rapid railroad construction to serve the needs of an encroaching colonial power, Tsarist Russia.

The house where we lived was Russian in style, with wooden porches, set in a yard amid tall trees, a nesting and assembly site for cawing crows. The streets all had Russian names: Yamskaya (Post-Coach) and Artilleriskaya (Artillery) at whose crossroads our house stood. One echoed the pre-railroad form of transport in the area, the second the recent Tsarist military occupation. Among other reminders were streets caller Kazachya (Cossack), Zei'isk-Atamansksya (a branch of the Cossacks) and Politseiskaya (Police).

In Harbin, as in nearby eastern Siberia then, most roads were packed dirt in summer, with droshkies pulled by hairy nags plying for hire as taxis, and hard-packed snow in winter, when the vehicles for hire were horse-drawn sleighs with huge, curved iron runners.

Close to the house was the wooded Municipal Park (*Gorodskoi Sad*). Besides an onion-domed Orthodox chapel—its main building—it had plank-built kiosks for tea or cooling drinks, like the foaming kvas fermented from rye bread. Playing along its paths, I often encountered a human park fixture, its resident drunk (*pianitsa*), a fat, ruddy-faced old Russian woman encased in numerous skirts. Too vodka-sodden to stand, she would be sitting propped against a tree, or lying prone, asleep and snoring loudly. When disturbed by grown-ups she would growl and mutter curses. For small children she had bleary smiles, especially when we called her *babushka* (granny).

I spoke and understood Russian, although we ourselves were not ethnically Russian but Jewish, and proudly so, and our domicile had been Lithuania and Poland, as few Jews were allowed within ethnic Russia under the Tsars. Yet Russian language and schooling had been, for my parents' generation, the means to break out of the ghetto and to link with outside progressive thought. They read not only Pushkin and Tolstoy, and revolutionaries like Chernyshevsky, but, in translation, Rousseau, Voltaire, Emile Zola, Victor Hugo, Darwin, Herbert Spencer, and of course Karl Marx. They also came in contact with the anti-tsarist movement.

*　　*　　*

Harbin itself had shared in Russia's turbulent recent political history and, from her monarchy's last years, her revolutions. It was the hub of the Chinese Eastern Railway; a Tsarist-built shortcut in the major Trans-Siberian line linking two Russian areas but running through China's northeast (then termed "Manchuria"). Flanking it was a "zone" administered and garrisoned by Russia much as the Panama Canal Zone was run by the United States. Ante-dating the latter by a few years it had reputedly served as its model, a circumstance now forgotten.

Very differently from the Panama Canal Zone, however, a watershed change had occurred in the Chinese Eastern Railway Zone with Russia's Soviet Revolution of November 7, 1917 (October 25 by Russia's old calendar, hence known as the October Revolution). Only days afterwards, the zonal Russian garrison, following the example of much of the old army in Russia, hoisted the Red Flag. Within two weeks, on November 21, 1917, a local Soviet was formed in Harbin, on Lenin's direct instruction, comprising railway workers and staff as well as soldiers. On December 12 it displaced the zone's old administration. But by December 26, under Western and Japanese pressure, the insurgent troops were disarmed and repatriated by the Chinese warlord regime.

In the subsequent civil war in Siberia, the White armies, backed to various extents by U.S., Japanese, and Chinese governments, came to control the area. In Harbin, General Horvath, the old railway chief, and Admiral Kolchak, the self-styled "Supreme Administrator of all Russia" hatched the first White regime claiming nationwide legitimacy. For the Whites, Harbin became a supply and manpower base, and after their defeat by the Soviets, a mass refuge.

By my fifth year I was already dimly aware of such events, and particularly of my parents' political views and history.

After the February 1917 overthrow of the Tsar, half a year before the October Revolution, my father, then working in Kobe, Japan, had rushed back to Russia to greet the new order there. Mother, on his advice, took me to Harbin to prepare to go as well, by the direct overland rail link. Father traveled there to pick us up, but soon the civil war in Siberia cut the route. When it re-opened, years later, Father's Bund faction was increasingly at odds with the victorious Bolsheviks. So we all stayed in China.

The Bund, as I learned, then stood Left of the Mensheviks and Right of the Bolsheviks, neither with the Second (Socialist) International nor with the newly-formed Third (Communist) International. Father himself put much blame on the Second because its member parties had lined up with their respective capitalist governments in World War I, and because in post-war Germany its Social Democrats, after coming to power, had abetted the suppression of the Left wing Spartacus uprising and the murder of its leaders, Wilhelm Liebknecht and Rosa Luxembourg, both of whom Dad admired. The Third he could not accept for some of its disciplinary requirements for member parties. So for a time he favored the short-lived Vienna-led centrist group dubbed the "Second and a Half International." The White Russians considered him "Red," the Reds not Red enough.

Already as a child, often ill and kept indoors, overhearing much adult conversation I got used to political terms. Even my alphabet blocks had "B" for "Bolshevik" and "M" for "Menshevik," illustrated with images not of the usual nursery kind.

Though so small, I could not avoid the heat of Harbin's seething expatriate politics. At a children's fair in the City Hall, a Russian-Jewish journalist in his twenties, Alexander Cherniavsky, a reporter for the Left liberal daily, *Novosti zhizni* (News of Life), published by his father, came up to me and Mother as I was trying my fortune at a lucky dip. "How are you called, Uncle?" I asked, in the Russian phrase when asking a name. "I'm not called, I come by myself!" was his joking reply, so amusing that it has stuck in my mind ever since. A few days later the slender young man was a mangled corpse. White Russian officers spotted him at their public meeting and killed him as a "Jew Bolshevik."

This I heard told graphically by witnesses who came to our single room. There, too. I heard how White Cossacks under the Japanese-backed Ataman Semyonov were pulling Jews or suspected "Reds" off the trains at stations near the Russian-Chinese border—Grodekovo, Pogranichnaya and others—and stripping, torturing, bayoneting, and shooting them.

I was to hear, too, of the sadistic atrocities of the "Mad Baron" Ungern-Sternberg, also a Japanese-backed "White" who temporarily occupied Outer Mongolia, as it was then called, posing as a reincarnation to Genghis Khan. Death—as agonizing as possible—was his decree for suspected pro-Soviets, Socialists, liberals, and of course Jews in Mongolia's chief city, Urga (now Ulan Bataar). A favorite punishment was to cram victims into a wooden box in which they could not lie down, stand, or sit, with only an armhole though which they could reach for food. This was traditional Mongolia's most rigorous imprisonment, to which Ungern's men added a sadistic refinement that amused them: the food was placed just out of reach, and in Mongolia's sub-Arctic winter, when the outstretched arm froze solid, it would be snapped in half by one sharp blow with a stick, amid the howls of the victim and the laughter of his tormentors.

Decades later, in 1956, traveling though the Mongolian People's Republic when a new railroad, built with technology from China and the U.S.S.R., was inaugurated there, a Soviet newsman told me of Ungern's end. He had witnessed, as a youngster, the "Mad Baron's" public trial in Chita, Siberia, in 1921 after his capture by the Soviet army. In the dock, Ungern had lost all his arrogance. Sentenced to be shot, he died far more easily than his victims.

In my parents' circle, atrocities and pogroms were discussed with anger and sorrow, but not, in my recollection, with fear. They were seen rather as the last convulsions of an order doomed by history. Though the group was not Bolshevik, their sympathy in the civil war was totally with the Red Army.

Father, in fact, was once asked to take up a ministerial-level economic post in the Far Eastern Republic, the temporary Soviet-backed buffer state in which Communists, Socialists, and some non-party democrats worked in coalition to frustrate the Japanese-backed Whites, taking some advantage of the differences between the Japanese and American interventionist forces in easternmost Siberia.

Though Father declined the job, he went once to Vladivostok where he secretly met and was impressed by the Red partisan leader Sergei Lazo. Lazo was to meet a horrendous death. Caught by the Japanese, who turned him over to their Cossack hirelings, he was shoved, inch by inch, into a locomotive furnace and burned alive. Lazo became one of my childhood heroes.

We were familiar with the economic side of Harbin through Father's bookkeeping job, and through a Jewish family, the Beerbrayers, from whom we rented our room. Its elderly head, as I recall, was in the business of soybeans, of which Northeast China was then the world's top producer. He talked constantly of the prices of the beans, of jute sacks in which to ship them, and of bean cakes, the pressed residue after their oil had been extracted, which were exported as cattle feed. But his sons and daughters, and their friends who came to the house, were politically minded, despising business. Nadya, a tall girl with thick fair braids falling far down her back, would become an engineer in the Soviet Union. Her schoolmate, Gita Subbotnik would go to the United States and marry Irving Potash, a militant head of the Left-wing Fur and Leather Workers' Union and a leading member of the U.S. Communist Party.

* * *

Although Harbin was in China, my only childhood memory reflecting this was of a Chinese festival parade of dancers on stilts in colorful traditional costumes accompanied by folk music and the crackle of firecrackers. Weaving and twisting, they made their way through a celebrating Chinese throng. To me, four years old, the stilts seemed enormously high, and I had to look up to see even the bottoms of the dancers' feet strapped to them. And the performers—tall to start with like most northern Chinese—were doubly massive in their broad robes, towering over the heads of the crowd like giants from another world. For this spectacle, we must have gone especially to Fujiadian, the "Chinese quarter" of Harbin at that time. Indeed, it was a "Chinatown" in China! There were such abnormalities, in a number of her cities, in the century of colonial penetration of the country.

I recall no mention by my parents, though surely they knew of

33

them, of the contemporary historic events in China itself. The student movement, which began May 4, 1919, was stirring an intellectual revolution, and drawing the whole population into swirling protest against the imperialist re-partition of the country. Despite U.S. President Woodrow Wilson's announcement of the "self-determination of nations" as one of the aims of Allied victory in World War I, the Treaty of Versailles, which ended the war, did not bring to China, herself nominally one of those Allies, the hoped-for return of her territories and rights previously seized by the defeated enemy. Instead, the former colonial holdings of Germany in Shandong Province were handed over to Japan. Nor, of course, did any of the victorious "Great Powers" move to give up their own holdings or the humiliating foreign extraterritorial jurisdiction within China, as she had been led to expect and verily demanded.

The new Soviet Union alone did so, returning old Russia's "concessions" and related privileges. Hence the furious disappointment of Chinese with Western democracy, the burgeoning interest in Marxism and the Soviets, and the founding the Chinese Communist Party in 1921.

* * *

Under Tsarist domination, Harbin had developed in three distinct parts: the commercial Pristan (Dockside) on the bank of the Sungari river; the administrative Novy Gorod (New Town) with wide streets and massive civil and military institutional buildings, where the Chinese Eastern Railway and its occupied zone had their headquarters; and finally Fujiadian, the ramshackle and subordinate "native quarter" whose inhabitants were humbled into addressing any Russians as *Kapitan* (Captain).

In architecture the three sections differed. Novy Gorod was the monumental citadel of the burst of expansionist energy with which Tsarist Russia had laid the world's longest railway, the Trans-Siberian, and, in competition with the Western powers planted its springboards for what then seemed the imminent colonial vivisection of China. Tsarism had also grabbed as full colonies, in the free for all for Chinese lands at the turn of the century, the port of Dalian, Russified into Dalny (meaning Distant) and later called Dairen by the Japanese; and the naval fortress of Lushun, then known as Port Arthur. But these outposts of the Tsarist Empire proved short-lived, for the regime itself was near its grave. In 1905 its army was beaten and its main fleet sunk by Japan. And the Russian Revolution of the same year, though suppressed, proved to be a dress rehearsal for that of 1917, which ended imperial Russia. In the great flux of the twentieth century's first quarter, the new revolutionary Russia renounced the holdings and extraterritorial status in China it once shared with other foreign powers. And on the Russian side of the border, indeed deep in European Russia as well, units of Chinese workers fought in the ranks of the Red Army, in a revolutionary fraternity between the two peoples.

*　　*　　*

In Harbin I had the only fragment of Russian schooling in my whole life. It was in a kindergarten run by the ex-wife of Sergei Alymov, the revolutionary poet who wrote the lyrics of the famous song of the Red partisans of Russia's Far East. Thanks to her, and to Mother, I learned the Russian alphabet, and began to read at an early age. This preserved and increased my knowledge of the language although all my subsequent education from the lowest primary stage would be in English.

So much for the Russian influence. What about the Jewish? Religiously I felt none. Though both brought up in pious homes, my parents had long since become strong atheists. It was long before I even saw the inside of a synagogue (though Harbin had several I never set foot there). Nor was I taught Hebrew.

Not Zionist or Hebraist, they loved Yiddish as the then mass language of the common folk of the East European Diaspora, which at the turn from the nineteenth to the twentieth century had already developed a vital literature and its own press. But they never succeeded in teaching me Yiddish, as we were away from its home ground.

All this was early in the century, long before the rise of Hitler. The simmering political tendencies among the world's Jews were then three in number: The wealthy minority which were assimilated into society. Workers and part of the intellectuals were mostly Socialist. Zionists were still a minority. Religious fundamentalism was losing ground to them all.

*　　*　　*

In 1920, we moved from Harbin to Tianjin, another world.

35

Chapter 5

TIANJIN

After a little more than three years in Harbin we came to Tianjin (Tientsin). There I would stay for 18 years, have my entire education, such as it was, and grow up to work. In Harbin our world had been Russian. In Tianjin it was Western, mainly Anglo-American. So English became my language of choice and the easiest means of expression. Chinese was not a subject in the schools I went to.

Unlike the railway upstart Harbin, Tianjin was a centuries-old Chinese city. Yet in modern times it became a most graphic example of the creeping partition of China by a hungry pack of foreign powers, greater and lesser. In 1860, in the Second Opium War, Western naval guns had leveled its shore defenses, the Dagu (Taku) forts, opening the shortest way from the sea to Beijing. Thenceforth Tianjin was cut up into a patchwork of foreign administered and policed "concessions"—British, French, German, Russian, Japanese, Italian, even Belgian and Austro-Hungarian.

Hence the changing names of stretches of the continuous main road that ran through three such concessions—in the French, it was Rue de France; in the British, Victoria Road; in the German, while it lasted, Kaiser Wilhelmstrasse. The Japanese section had its Asahi Road, the Russian its Nikolayevskaya (for Tsar Nicholas II); Italy had Via Vittorio Emmanuele III for that country's king. Other streets were thus named, in a daily humiliation and insult to the Chinese, after foreign commanders who had warred against China, or diplomats who had dictated unequal treaties that shackled her: England's Admiral Seymour and Lord Elgin, France's Baron Gros, and the like.

There had also been, in the 1860s, a United States concession. Its quick abandonment used to be cited by Americans as proof of U.S. aversion to colonialism in China. A reply by Dr. Sun Yat-sen, China's first Republican president, was why, then, was this enclave never restored to China but handed over by the U.S. to Britain? Moreover, why, even without a concession, did the U.S. permanently station in Tianjin not only a naval vessel but also its 15th Infantry ("Can Do") Regiment. Among officers who served in this unit in the earlier decades of the twentieth century were such famous future generals as Dwight Eisenhower (who would become President), George Marshall (who would become Secretary of state), Joseph Stilwell (who would be a political victim of the shift from World War II to the Cold War); and such future figures in the Korean War as Matthew Ridgeway and John Deane.

Another question was why, when other powers forced unequal treaties upon China, the U.S. insisted on China granting it the same privileges, under the most favored nation principle, which, thus applied, made China the least favored nation? The answer was that in the nineteenth century Far East, the U.S. was not the military or commercial equal of Britain in the area, or the military equal of Russia. In insisting on the "open door" in their "spheres of interest," it was riding piggy-back on the aggressive policies of other nations, practicing what the U.S. writer Owen Lattimore wittily called "me-too" imperialism. Only after World War I did it become as powerful, then more so, pushing its way into the lead.

* * *

In 1920, when our family arrived in Tianjin, three foreign-ruled concessions had disappeared. The old Russian concession was returned to China by the new Soviet government. And those of Germany and Austria-Hungary were abolished after their World War I defeat. But five foreign-ruled enclaves remained, in full panoply.

We first lived in the Italian area, on Via Matteo Ricci, commemorating the famous sixteenth century Jesuit missionary to China. Next we moved to the ex-German, just off the former Kaiser Wilhelmstrasse, which, after the defeat of "Kaiser Bill," was not given a Chinese name, but became instead Woodrow Wilson Street, Ostensibly, it honored America's wartime president who proclaimed the self-determination of nations. In fact, it was a reminder of the post-World War I supremacy of the U.S. among the victorious allied powers. And it was a reminder of China's angry disappointment when Wilson assented to the handover of beaten Germany's colony in China's ancient province of Shandong (once home to Confucius), not back to China, but to Japan.

Finally, we moved to the British concession, on Parkes Road, named after a nineteenth century British invader of China, not far from the area's headquarters in the pseudo-Gothic turreted Gordon Hall, in flattery of the British officer General Charles "Chinese" Gordon who had helped loot and burn a magnificent Beijing palace of the Chinese monarchy, then helped the latter to bloodily crush the patriotic peasant uprising of the Taiping Rebellion.

My time in Tianjin, from 1920 to 1937, was terminated by the Japanese occupation, which first surrounded and finally was to engulf the concessions of rival powers.

Though the concessions all seemed torpidly quiet on the inside, the environment, near and far, during those years was very turbulent.

In China it included hostilities among warlords in the early 1920s; the nation's first anti-imperialist and anti-feudal political and military revolution in 1925-27; the counterrevolution in the latter year which precipitated the decade of the Guomindang-Communist civil war with its landmark Long March of the Chinese Red Army in 1934-35. In the meantime, Japan seized China's northeastern provinces in 1931, sparking the rise of China's resistance movement and leading to her all-out War of Resistance against Japanese aggression from 1937 on.

On the outside, the world economic depression began in 1929 with the crash of the hitherto booming United States stock market. Conspicuous industrial growth was for some years largely confined to the Soviet Union. Reaction in Europe gave rise to fascism. Nazi Germany and Fascist Italy intervened in Spain to crush her Republic, and in that country the Fascist and anti-Fascist forces of Europe clashed in arms.

Of all these factors I was increasingly conscious, and, together, they influenced my growth and life. Being in Tianjin at age 22 did not lead me out of China but rather out of foreign-dominated treaty ports and concessions into the heart of China and her people's struggles—a choice of a lifetime.

*   *   *

At age 5, my English-language schooling began, as pre-schooling, in the Catholic St. Joseph's Convent in the French concession of Tianjin. It was a school for girls, in which boys were allowed only in kindergarten—perhaps their male presence afterwards was deemed improper.

Each morning we faced a crucifix and intoned thrice, in unison,

"St. Joseph pray for us!" Any urchin naughtiness drew sharp raps on the skull by the signet-rings of the starchy nuns. Though taught in English we were rewarded, when good, by gilt-bordered mini-certificates inscribed *Billet d'Honneur* in French. For the glory of France, too, our whole school was once marched, in 1921 or 1922, to a special ceremony in the French concession's park, to see the visiting white-mustached Marshal Joffre, former commander of French forces in World War I, unveil a bronze victory statue of Jeanne d'Arc carrying a drawn sword.

At St. Joseph's I had an early whiff of theological anti-Semitism. A small Greek classmate remarked to me, without evident personal ill-will, that the Christ we saw on the crucifix had been nailed there by the Jews. As in all puzzling matters, I asked my father. He explained: Roman rulers did such things, not the Jewish people. Jesus, a Jew, Yehoshua, must have been executed for somehow challenging Roman supremacy. The mocking inscription on the cross, INRI, Latin initials for "Jesus of Nazareth, King of the Jews" couldn't have been put there by Jews.

The gospels said Jewish priests had egged on the Romans. Possibly. Most high priests, Jewish or otherwise, bowed before overlords, foreign or their own. That was one reason our family believed in no religion.

We did not attend synagogue, or fast on Yom Kippur, or keep a kosher or Passover diet, nor did I ever undergo *bar mitzvah*, the confirmation for Jewish males at the age of 13, when they are supposed to shoulder the moral responsibilities of adults.

But our atheist household was very Jewish indeed, in a secular way. Father and Mother conversed in Yiddish, which they loved. I had Yiddish lullabies lull me to sleep. From the Passover story, from my earliest childhood I knew Moses as the bold liberator of the Jews from slavery in Egypt, rather than as a religious seer. God or no God, we were not to worship the Golden Calf. At the Purim festival we ate *hamantash*, cakes stuffed with poppy seed to celebrate the doom of Haman of ancient Persia, who, according to the biblical Book of Esther, had wanted to massacre that country's Jews. Against invaders who oppressed us, we had constantly rebelled. Each *Hannukah* festival I heard again the thrilling story of the Jewish Maccabees and their patriotic revolt against the tyrant Antiochus Epiphanes. I was told too of the revolt led by Bar Kochba against Imperial Rome. When our own ancient kings strayed from virtue, our prophets' tongue lashed them without mercy (though, it must be said, it would be hard to find, among those prophets, any sympathy for the non Jewish natives of the land).

In the Diaspora, Crusaders sabered us, inquisitions burned us alive, pogroms pillaged and killed. Modern anti-Semites framed Dreyfus for treason in France, Mendel Beilis for alleged "blood guilt" in Russia. The Nazi Holocaust, the horror to end all horrors, was still to come.

Never did our family renounce or hide or slur over our Jewishness. I was never to change my name—Israel—to Isidore, Irving, or the like. Epstein was never anglicized into Stone, or Epworth. At the same time, I was never taught prejudice against non-Jews as such, but told of how many had opposed oppression and discrimination not only among themselves but against us. In France, Emile Zola aroused a nation to defend Dreyfus; in Tsarist Russia Tolstoy, Korolenko, Gorki, and Lenin denounced pogroms. Progressives, Socialists and revolutionaries everywhere stood with us. As progressive, revolutionary Jews, we should side everywhere with them, not with any reactionaries. This was the spirit my parents gradually instilled in me, was what being Jewish should mean. Neither inferior nor superior, but equal. Neither orthodox nor assimilationist. Theism we had discarded. Zionism was not our belief. But we had deep feeling, historical and social, for the Jewish people, and regarded the modern Jewish Socialist tradition as its height.

Somewhere in my early teens, I heard Father's reasoned critique of Zionism. His ideal was for Jews, of whatever country, to win equal status in harmony with, and participating in, struggles for progress by its entire population.

In a specifically Jewish state in Palestine he saw a danger, rather than a solution, for the Jewish people.

His points, as I recall them, were:

Palestine already had an indigenous population. A Jewish state there would inevitably have the character of a colonial settler state—anachronistic in our century and undesirable for the Jews as well as the local people; Situated at the crossroads of the three continents of Europe, Asia, and Africa, the land of Palestine had been fought over, and successively occupied, by a dozen empires over the centuries. It would continue to be fought over by "great powers."

A Jewish state in Palestine could not be strong and independent, but would be inevitably become tied, as an outpost or cat's paw, to one or another contesting imperial power.

These arguments he illustrated by many examples—ancient, medieval and modern. One thing he did *not* anticipate: Hitler's genocide.

Nonetheless, though Israel as a state is now a fifty-year old fact, the complications, as he perceived them, persist. Only in their solution, through co-existence and mutual development with the Palestinians and the Arab world, can it achieve tranquil development.

Though my parents never succeeded in teaching me much Yiddish, yet some Yiddish folk songs of the Jewish poor in Eastern Europe, often on my mother's lips, did stay with me. One, *Gegeben a pereneh* (I gave them a feather quilt) was the accusing plaint of a poor relative at a wedding of more prosperous family members. She had bought the best present she could afford but was still snubbed. "To be poor isn't good, to be poor isn't good," rang the chorus, "but let's not be ashamed of our own flesh and blood."

Politically, I knew the Yiddish anthem of the Bund, "Brothers and sisters of poverty and toil..." with its defiant refrain about the workers' red banner, dyed with their blood, waving in anger, summoning to battle.

Just as the Jewish Socialist struggle was seen as part of that of all others striving for a new world, so my store of such songs was multinational.

In Russian, I was taught *La Marseillaise* in its Revolution of 1905 version:

We shall sever ourselves from the Old World,
Shake off its dust from our feet,
Hostile to us are all gilded idols,
And hateful the palace of the Tsars.
We shall join with our suffering brothers,
To the poor and the starved we shall go,
Lay their curse on the doers of evil,
Arouse them to battle with the foe,

And of course I learned early to recognize, then to sing, the *Internationale*, the most rousing of revolutionary clarions.

* * *

These marks were already on my mind and in my feelings when, in 1922, I changed over to the small, community-run, Tientsin American School, which my parents chose as presumably the most democratic and least colonialist or parochial of the foreign schools. To my childish eyes so much there was entirely new. The portraits of Washington and Lincoln my parents could and did explain. One had led the Americans to independence, the other to abolish slavery. Both were revolutionaries, and in my parents' scale of values there was no higher term of praise.

But the American folklore characters in the frieze around my first schoolroom—Mother Goose, Brer Rabbit, and so on, were as inexplicable then to them as to me.

That British and other older foreign influences in China were being displaced by the American in the post-World War I balance of world political, economic and cultural power, was reflected in the expatriate communities in Tianjin, down to the children.

Juveniles like me who had never been to America were already undergoing long-distance Americanization, second only to that of actual immigrants to that country. American goods and brand names were flooding in. Following the long-standing example of American missionaries and business people, some families with no previous U.S. connections were ordering goods from Montgomery Ward, then the main mail-order suppliers across the Pacific.

American films already ruled the local screen, engrafting their values and images on us youngsters totally different in national backgrounds and, until recently, in language. David Griffith's *Birth of a Nation* spread its flagrant racism and prettification of the Ku Klux Klan. *The Kid*, with Charlie Chaplin and Jackie Coogan, spread laughter and humanism. I thrilled at seeing Chaplin, the homeless tramp, reading the New York Yiddish-language daily *Forward*, to which we subscribed, as he bedded down in the street (some of us concluded from this that Chaplin was Jewish, which wasn't so). Comedians Harold Lloyd and Buster Keaton had us in stitches. In films starring Rudolf Valentino we small boys hissed at the sentimental love scenes that sent girls and women into raptures. "Sheik," in current idiom, became the successor of "beau" and predecessor of "boyfriend." Lon Chaney froze us in *Phantom of the Opera*, forerunner of the horror film. Mary Pickford, Douglas Fairbanks, the Gish sisters, Gloria Swanson, and Pola Negri became familiar names and faces. Cliff-hanger serials, each episode stopping at a moment of mortal danger or stirring opportunity, made sure that the children would come trooping in for the next installment at the Biograph, Empire, and other local movie houses where matinee shows cost 10 cents.

To be sure, there were a few films from other sources, the French *Maciste* which in one release was paired with the English *Tarzan*, Lessing's *Nathan the Wise*, from Germany, even pre-October Revolution Russian movies with Ivan Mosjoukhine (Soviet films would come later). All these were silents, in black and white.

Sound would come, years later with Al Jolson in the sensational *The Jazz Singer*, and color much later still.

Aside from much mediocrity, kitsch, or trash, Hollywood did bring to Tianjin's screens some inspiring and thoughtful films. I still vividly remember *All Quiet on the Western Front; Little Man What Now; What Price Glory; The Case of Sergeant Grischa*, and *The Broadway Melody* with its songs like "Remember My Forgotten Man" and "Brother Can You Spare a Dime." These were in-depth works, sited to the times, re-examining World War I and its aftermath.

Soviet films of quality that reached us were *Road to Life*, dealing with the post-revolutionary rehabilitation of homeless waifs, *Chapayev*, about the complex political maturing of a legendary Red partisan hero of Russia's civil war, and Eisenstein's historic *Battleship Potemkin*, the last doubly impressive to me because of the placement of the 1905 Russian Revolution in our own family's past. Among slighter items, I was struck by *Seekers for Happiness*, about Jews in their new Soviet autonomous region of Birobidzhan, an experiment that seemed promising but wasn't.

Amid all this abundance, by contrast, I do not recall seeing even one Chinese film. None were shown in theaters attended by foreigners, though foreign films filled Chinese theaters.

In American productions, until the fairly conscientiously-done *The Good Earth* (based on Pearl S. Buck's novel, with Paul Muni and Luise Rainer as co-stars), Chinese were portrayed on film as either sinister (like Dr. Fu Manchu) or outright ridiculous caricatures. The one semi-positive Chinese character, detective Charlie Chan, was played by a Westerner, Warner Oland. Chinese-American actress Anna Mae Wong, though not lending herself to either stereotype, had only secondary roles, in a Western setting.

Movie-going was cheap then, especially for children, though theater costs included in-house musicians. I took in midday or afternoon matinees most weekends. The films provided tension: what was next in the serial? Villains could be booed, heroes cheered, mushy lovers—so they seemed to us—ridiculed. Since the films were silent we weren't hushed by people wanting to hear the words of the actors. Fun, too, was to be had, not only in on-screen antics but in off-screen mischief. From the cheaper balcony seats, we boys would aim paper airplanes, or darts tipped with used chewing gum, at the bald heads below.

At age 8, on my dreamy way to one movie one day, thinking of what I would see, I was hit by a passing car, breaking my left thighbone into three parts. In a way, this changed my life: unable to see films while spending months in bed making me an avid reader and, ultimately, a writer.

By contrast with the American dominance of film, live performances were, as a rule, European, and of top standard. Impresario A. Strok brought to Tianjin, as to other foreign enclaves in China, world-renowned violinists Heifetz, Kreisler, Elman, and Zimbalist, pianists Moiseyewitsch and Leo Sirota, singers like soprano Amelita Galli Curci and the famed Russian basso Fyodor Chaliapine, whom the Russian-speaking community idolized and came to hear en masse even at a what was to them a very stiff admission price. (For the Jews it was almost a ritual to attend, and a lift in dignity when the maestros were Jewish, as many were.)

Chaliapine I remember for his massive stature, white mane, and dramatic rendering, still electrifying even after he had outlived his voice, of "The Volga Boatmen," and "The Flea." Also, for a story I then heard about him and the famed Russian writer Maxim Gorki. As peasant youths, they had tramped together in old Russia, so poor that they actually did toil back-breakingly as "Volga boatmen" pulling barges upstream along the great river. At one town easier work beckoned—a local priest was hiring voices for his church choir. But after an audition, he picked only Gorki, not Chaliapine who would become one of the world's vocal greats. Not wanting to separate, the young friends went on as before.

In musical and artistic education in Tianjin—piano, violin and dance—Russian teachers held the field. Peggy Hookham, an English girl pupil at the Tientsin Grammar School, taught ballet by the Russian Mme. Voitenco, would one day shine internationally as Dame Margot Fonteyn.

I myself learned the piano, from age 8 to 14 or 15, from Mrs. Hohlachkina, who in the Petrograd Conservatory had had as her teacher the renowned Leschetitskaya. She put me on stage for three or four annual student performances to play, in particular, Chopin preludes, which I loved and in which she said I showed musicianship as well as technique. But other interests and exigencies were to take me away so far, and for so long, that, I now can't play at all—though I do retain some knowledge about music.

In cultural breadth the Western business community in the Tianjin "concessions" often lagged far behind us rag-tag East Europeans. Their typical interest, apart from business and socializing, was in sport. A close American friend and classmate of mine talked so much about major league baseball that soon I, with not a shred of knowledge about it, could soon also bandy names like Babe Ruth, Ty Cobb, Christy Mathewson, Rogers Hornsby, and the Brooklyn Dodgers, New York Yankees, and St. Louis Cardinals (who won the World Series one year, to my considerable interest as I had maternal cousins in St. Louis.) But when I mentioned the word "composer" in some connection, he asked, "What's *that*?" I explained, "Someone who writes music like Mozart, Beethoven, Chopin." Never having heard of them, he finally volunteered, "You mean like Paul Whiteman!" Then it was *I* who asked "Who?"

But a notable exception to such musical ignorance was my American school third-grade classmate and friend John Hersey, born in Tianjin where his father was a YMCA secretary. He knew his composers, studied the violin under a local Russian, and wanted to become a virtuoso. Though he shifted to literature, becoming a major novelist, he never lost his love of music. John's last work, *Antonietta* was about Stradivari's passion for the peak of his creation, a violin that was perfect.

Hersey, curiously enough, was to link his own move to authorship with my own turn to the written word while my shattered limb slowly mended.

As he wrote a half-century later: though "tiny" in size, I seemed "brilliant" with "a very high forehead" that resembled "a wonderful castle of thought."[2] Of this high flattering and exaggerated estimate I myself was quite unaware. But with this image of me it is little wonder

[2] John Hersey, "A Reporter at Large" *The New Yorker*, May 10, 1982.

that the traction rig over my sickbed at home was transfigured into a "magnificent machine" in which my smashed leg was "encased in plaster of Paris... elevated and attached to marvelous ropes, pulleys, weights" at the sight of which left him "burning with a wish to be Eppy." This "envy was unbearably compounded" when Tianjin's American-run daily *North China Star* described me, eight-year-old and bedridden, as "writing a history of the world" (which I fancifully told their gossip reporter I would like to do.) John, he later recalled, was determined to break his own leg and become a writer. To match me, he would do a Life of America's World War I president, Woodrow Wilson. Neither project, of course, materialized.

But John did become a writer of such quality, that if I helped prompt him, I shall be happy. His *Hiroshima* is a world classic of reporting, and of anti-nuclear activism. His *The Wall*, about the resistance in the Warsaw Ghetto, is a searing indictment of Nazism and high tribute to the Jews who fought it against impossible odds.

I wondered if it owed anything to his childhood impressions from when "on a seesaw in our yard one day, Eppy told me about the Jews. I had had plenty of Old Testament pushed at me in Sunday School, but it was Eppy who for the first time made vivid in my mind the story of that dispossessed and wandering race."

My voracious reading began, like my speaking, in Russian. Though without formal schooling in the language, my mother taught me to read it, and I never stopped. Quite early, I decided never to read translations from the Russian if I could get a hold of the original. This principle I followed with children's books, then with Pushkin, Lermontov and Tolstoy—beginning with his short *Prisoner of the Caucasus* and *Tales of Sebastopol* and ending with *War and Peace* (which I made a practice of re-reading every five years...discovering something new each time), *Anna Karenina, Resurrection*, and *The Kreutzer Sonata*. Later I went on to Dostoyevsky, Andreyev, and others, and still later to Lenin, Stalin, and many Soviet authors and publications. Most Russian works were borrowed from the good library of the Tianjin Jewish Club "Kunst," whose Cultural Committee was long headed by my father.

For English reading, too, I relied on libraries, myself owning few books. In the American School Library I regularly immersed myself in the copiously illustrated 20-volume "Book of Knowledge," then the children's encyclopedia *par excellence*, and the contemporary American juvenile magazines *St. Nicholas* and *Youth's Companion*. Here too I was first attracted to Washington Irving, Edgar Allan Poe, James Fenimore Cooper, Mark Twain—and unfortunately to Zane Grey, who wrote so much about warfare against the Indians—genocide presented as knightly adventure. When one teacher wanted Grey removed from the shelves, I joined in a boys' protest against her proposal and only afterwards understood that we were wrong and the teacher was right.

In the summers I visited two libraries in Beidaihe, the seaside resort we went to in the hot weather.

One belonged to the missionary community, but its children's items were un-Christian (more accurately, imperialist-Christian) adventure tales by G.A. Henty and the like, with a colonial mindset no better than Zane Grey.

Excellent, by contrast, was the vacation branch of the Peking Municipal Library which I used more as I grew older. From it I borrowed long works and I devoured them, though somewhat lazily: Charles and Mary Beard's *History of American Civilization*, Will Durant's *History of Philosophy*, critical-realist novels by Sinclair Lewis, Upton Sinclair, and Theodore Dreiser. In English translation from the French, Romain Rolland's "Jean Christophe," and translated from the German, books by Thomas and Heinrich Mann, Lion Feuchtwanger, Jakob Wasserman, and others.

But China, characteristically for the semi-colonial times, was not yet part of my reading or study (I could identify all U.S. states from their un-labeled, cut-out jigsaw puzzle shapes and recite the names of all American presidents forwards and backwards, but knew nothing of China's dynasties or provinces).

Yet China's realities were beginning to impinge on me, not from what I read, but from direct evidence.

Already before my teens, amidst the country's surrounding internecine wars and famines, I saw gaunt, ragged refugees flooding into Tianjin. Some begging tearfully for food, some offering to sell their children because it was better to have them be slaves than die of hunger. On a forever unforgotten winter morning, while going to school I came upon a boy of twelve or so, my own age then, crouching stiff and dead in a doorway where he had tried vainly to seek shelter from the freezing night wind.

In my fourth and fifth grades of primary school came the Chinese

Revolution of the mid-1920s, led by Sun Yat-sen, launched by the first united front between his Guomindang party and the Chinese Communists. Helped by Soviet advisers and arms, as agreed upon with Sun, it swept from its base in Guangzhou (Canton), winning widespread popular support with its pledges to defeat the motley foreign-based warlords, abrogate the unequal treaties forced on China by foreign powers in the past century, distribute land to the tillers and improve the political and economic status of urban workers.

Our family, rarely among foreign ones in Tianjin, saw this revolution as just and necessary. Moreover, Sun Yat-sen, for decades in friendly contact with European Socialists, was himself a Socialist in the eyes of my father, who, emphasizing the universality of his own ideals, had early told me that two of the world's great Socialists were Chinese, in modern times Sun, and, back in the eleventh century, the Song dynasty economic and social reformer, Wang Anshi.

And in April 1927, when Chiang Kai-shek turned bloodily against the revolution, which had made him its military commander-in-chief, Father told me it was not the first time such a thing happened, nor would it be the last—for dark, bloody treachery could also occur anywhere. General Cavaignac, commander in the French Revolution of 1848, had butchered its worker supporters when they claimed social as well as civil rights. General Gallifet, also in the name of the revolution-born French Republic had crushed the Paris Commune of 1871 in a merciless and indiscriminate massacre that spared no one. More currently, Italian Fascist Mussolini, an ex-Socialist, was dealing with his ex-comrades by assassination, flogging, and huge, punitive draughts of castor oil. But brutal suppression, Dad told me, could not stop history's long-term progress. He did not preach at me long-windedly, his remarks were brief but tied to real events, which I could later read about for myself in the context of his terse words.

So, drop by drop in my young mind, events and attitudes in China and abroad appeared in mutual linkage. I was learning to take sides, and be confident despite reverses.

In 1927, China's Revolution, to that point, reached its peak, and then failed. It was also the year of the execution in the United States of the Left-wing Italian workers Sacco and Vanzetti. There were worldwide protests because the criminal charges against the two were unproved and it was anti-Red hysteria that sent them to the electric chair.

In Tianjin, I pasted their pictures in my diary with my own young words of protest.

I also remember vividly, from my sixth or seventh grade days in the American school, how my hackles rose when a teacher sneered in class that the initials IWW stood for "I Won't Work." I knew differently. To me, the IWWs (or "Wobblies" as they were called), were the admirably brave members of the Industrial Workers of the World, a militant labor organization in the Western U.S. This view was passed on to me by my parents' and my friend, the burly and expansive Sam Bliwass, an ex-Wobbly himself who presented me with their "Little Red Songbook," perhaps the only copy then in China at the time. Sam, a Russian-Jewish-American, had done manual work throughout the U.S., including shoveling coal into the locomotive furnaces of trains running out of Sheboygan, Wisconsin. A Bundist before emigrating to the U.S., he had himself joined the Wobblies there, and also been involved in the Seattle General Strike of 1919. From him I first heard of Joe Hill, union organizer and song writer, sentenced to death and shot in Utah; Frank Little, another organizer, castrated and lynched by "Company" thugs in Centralia, Washington, and other unyielding victims in the struggle between capital and labor in the United States. They were workers and fighters for workers' rights. What quirk of fate finally brought Sam to Tianjin as a fur buyer, traveling to and from the U.S., I never learned. Nor do I recall, in our wide-ranging conversations about life and ideas, a single mention of his business.

Sam was particularly fond of Joe Hill's song: "Long-haired Preachers Get Up Every Night," telling working men to "Work and pray, live on hay" in order to be rewarded with "Pie in the sky when you die." With its final trumping punch-line: "THAT'S A LIE!" it helped to reinforce my atheism with Sam's brand. Unlike my father's intellectually arrived-at variety, it was born in blood and tears.[3]

Sam, as a small boy in a Jewish hamlet in his native Ukraine, had accidentally killed his little sister. She had fallen to her death from a swing he had pushed into motion. He had howled against God for let-

---

[3] Years later, American radical writer, Agnes Smedley, would feelingly sing this song, and, still later, so would the American seaman Parker Van Ness, with whom I formed a strong friendship.

ting it happen. Also, in the village *heder* (children's religious Hebrew school), he had been beaten by the rural Torah teacher for fidgeting instead of sitting still on his wooden bench. "How could I help it?" he cried out to me indignantly fifty years later. "The chickens belonging to the teachers wife were running loose and pecking at sores on my bare toes!" Why hadn't the all-knowing God known this, and softened the harsh teacher's heart? At first Sam was tortured by guilt every time he doubted God. Only in his late teens, with contact with revolutionary ideas, had his head cleared.

"So ooh-la-la, Old Top…" said Sam, using idioms picked up by American soldiers in France in World War I, "…things are plainer without any religion."

A similar homespun mental process was graphically described to me by a young Soviet Russian. As a village child, he had knelt and crossed himself in stark terror in every thunderstorm, begging God not to strike him dead for some fancied sin. The revolution had lifted that load from his heart by teaching him that thunder and lightning were natural phenomena, not signs of divine wrath.

* * *

In the late 1920s, Western powers once again poured troops into China, among them the Third U.S. Marines Division, which landed in Tianjin. The overall purpose was to fend off the Chinese Revolution of 1925-27 against feudal warlords and foreign imperialist control.

Of this revolution I remember, besides news in the papers, seeing black-uniformed police of the warlord regimes throwing down their rifles as they panicked outside their quarters in Tianjin's ex-German concession. In close pursuit of them were troops of the "Christian General" Feng Yuxiang, a warlord himself, then allied with the Revolution.

Nationwide, however, the revolution's apparently imminent victory was subverted when Chiang Kai-shek, its own commander-in-chief, turned on its Left-wing, in wholesale massacre of Communists and members of workers' and peasant unions.

The foreign forces assembled to check the revolutionary tide before it reached North China did not enter the fray only because their work had been done for them by China's own reactionaries.

Interestingly, in the U.S. contingent of the intended intervention, unease at being sent to uphold the decaying and corrupt warlords spread even to the high-ranking officers. General Smedley Butler, commanding the Marines in Tianjin, was an old-fashioned populist fed up with being used abroad to frustrate people's revolts against oppressors. Ten years earlier, General Graves, heading the U.S. intervention in Siberia after Russia's 1917 Revolution, had ended thinking better of the "Reds" he was meant to oppose than of the "Whites" he was sent to support. And in World War II, a decade after Butler, General Stilwell would find Chiang Kai-shek more interested in hoarding arms for future civil war against the Communists than in fighting the common foe, Japan, against which the Communists battled hard and effectively.

Ultimate policy, however, was not determined by these U.S. commanders, in whom some spark of America's own revolutionary tradition still burned. Only after retirement, did these three publish or leave strong criticisms of the aims they had been made to serve.

Pungently, General Butler summed-up his own career: spending 33 years and four months in active service as a member of the Marine Corps, from second lieutenant to major-general, and as a "high-class muscle-man for Big Business, for Wall Street... In short a racketeer for capitalism" helping make China and Mexico safe for American oil interests; making Haiti and Cuba and Nicaragua safe for banking interests; and making the Dominican Republic safe for American sugar interests.

Butler wrote that in those years he had "a swell racket" going, rewarded with honors, medals, and promotions. Looking back, he joked he could have given Al Capone a run for his money: the famous Chicago gangster only operated his racket in three city districts: the Marines operated on three continents.

*   *   *

That was the way things were in foreign-dominated Tianjin. How different from the early years of the People's Republic of China when a fair proportion of foreign children went to Chinese schools, and the frequent common language of children of different nationalities was Chinese. This was one of the signs of China's great change from inequality to equality.

Despite no teaching of Chinese and all the influences inseparable from the semi-colonial environment of those years, my parents' Socialist tradition counteropposed it, and its effect on the way I observed the things around me kept me from submerging into the foreign-dominated Tianjin way of life completely.

Also, I was getting closer and closer to Chinese reality.

After the events of the 1925-27 Revolution during my primary school days, came the impact on me of the Japanese seizure of China's three northeastern provinces in 1931, when I was 16 and already working.

Chapter 6

AN EARLY START IN JOURNALISM

As far back as I can remember, I wanted to be a journalist. Ours was a home with many newspapers, and the first joyful sight of my own words in print came at age 11 or 12, when a letter from me in Tianjin appeared in the children's column of the Yiddish-language *Forward* in New York (to which Father subscribed to for years and whose staff included many of his Bundist colleagues from pre-revolutionary Russia). My letter was in English—as was the whole children's section, because like me, the younger generation of immigrants couldn't write or read Yiddish. The column's editor, Gene Lisitsky, must have been pleased at hearing from so exotic a specimen—a Jewish boy in China.

At age 14 or 15, I was involved in the production of the Tianjin Grammar School annual, contributing a bit of doggerel in spoofing a schoolmate, and assisting in its editing and layout.

In the meantime, Father had bought me a rebuilt Underwood typewriter, then "engaged" me to help the commercial monthly he ran for a time, *The Oriental Fur Trade Review*, some of the contents of which were by non-English speakers, others poorly translated. I "contracted" to improve the language and Father to pay me the munificent wage of 12 "Mexican dollars" a month.[4]

In Grammar School, I won the essay and general knowledge prizes adjudged by Wilfred V. Pennell, editor of the British-owned daily *Peking and Tientsin Times*. A family acquaintance and neighbor, Pennell began to

---

[4] The Chinese silver *yuan*, at the time, was alternatively called the "Mex" dollar for interesting reasons of history. It was identical in weight and purity with Mexico's silver Peso, which was in turn a copy of the famed Spanish "piece of eight" (8 *reals*). From that coin—once a major medium of world trade, as well as object of piracy—the American dollar also traces its descent, hence the otherwise puzzling name "two bits" for the quarter-dollar. In Austria, once linked by Hapsburg dynastic rule with Spain, the "piece of eight" coin was called "thaler," which was Americanized into "dollar." When U.S. changed to the gold standard, the Chinese "Mex" silver dollar was pegged at half a "gold" dollar—hence my first wage was worth US$6.

think of me as a future employee. The reasons were two: I wrote easily and fast. And under the foreign-concession standards, I would be "local staff"—paid a sixth of the equivalent "home staff" (as well as double the Chinese staff). A further economy was that, for the locally hired, there was no paid passage or regular "home leave"—as there was for the staff hired overseas.

But as it turned out, my first, and brief, work in "grown-up" journalism was not in the English paper but on a Russian-language daily in Tianjin called *Utro* (Morning)—for which I interpreted Reuters and other news-agency reports from English. Unlike the city's two already established White Russian émigré papers, *Utro* was discreetly pro-Soviet. The editor was a Russian Jew named Lev Markovich Bihovsky, smooth-faced tweedy and suave. His wife—angular, severe, wearing thick *pince-nez* glasses was very much the administrator: sitting at the entrance she made sure no staff member was late (I got a bit of her tongue for this fault). The paper's sole typesetter, Rosenzweig, working entirely by hand, was massive, ruddy, and as slow-spoken as his fingers were fast—the first manual worker I knew who was Jewish. The flat-press printers were Chinese, the circulation a few hundred.

A frequent visitor, always with his Alsatian dog, was a bulky, middle-aged, hearty-voiced Russian named Skvortsov, working for *Angasta* (an acronym for "Anglo-Asiatic News Agency") a Soviet enterprise with a British partner named Hayton Fleet. Another caller was Waldemar Bartels, editor of the Tianjin's German paper, *Deutsch-Chinesische Nachrichten*. Wispy, moustached, thin, and frail, Bartels would die in World War II in a Japanese prison—charged with activities against Berlin and Tokyo.

It was in late 1930 or early 1931, when *Utro* folded and I was turning sixteen, that Pennell hired me for the *Peking and Tientsin Times*. It was owned by—and spoke for—the British-concession elite. Its editor from 1914 to 1930 had been H.G.W. Woodhead, a die-hard with a stony contempt for the Chinese, which most of them reciprocated. Pennell, his successor, personally had more respect—and even a liking for—the people and the country.

The two represented different generations of British journalists in China. Woodhead, arriving in 1902 on the heels of the foreign military suppression of China's plebeian-patriotic Boxer uprising, was formed in, and nostalgic for, the pre-World War I era. Pennell took shape in the changing post-war period. A glance at their careers may be historically instructive.

Although China had by 1912 changed from a monarchy to a republic, Woodhead thought the change a mistake. During the First World War, he strove to pull China away from her neutrality (which was in her interest) and into the conflict on the Allied side (which was not). For his efforts he was awarded the civic honor "Commander of the British Empire." He stood rigidly for extraterritoriality and other foreign privileges and had a to-the-bone hatred for China's national and social revolution (fiercely lampooning Sun Yat-sen, in his eyes a personification of both). Yet, be it noted, Woodhead was for some two decades, the compiler of the *China Year Book*, the thick annual volume regarded by most Westerners as *the* standard and most reliable manual on the country. Logically, he found positive aspects of Japanese imperialism in China— especially its installment of China's ex-emperor Pu Yi as ruler of Tokyo's puppet state of "Manchukuo." But Japan, once a client ally of Britain, had her eye on ousting British interests from China, and in World War II gave Woodhead a harsh taste of jail. Ultimately, he was repatriated in a prisoner exchange, a gaunt shadow of his former self.

Pennell, contrastingly, came in 1912, at age 21, to a China newly altered from monarchy to Republic. Joining the *Peking and Tientsin Times* in 1916, he remained until Pearl Harbor in 1941. In his editorship, he displayed occasional sympathy for the Chinese Revolution, for Sun Yat-sen, for Guomindang elements to the Left of Chiang Kai-shek, and sometimes for the Chinese Red Army. Unlike Woodhead, he took China's side against Japan. But in British politics he freakishly followed Sir Oswald Mosley all the way from the Left wing of the Labor Party to the British Union of Fascists: attracted by their advocacy of the "corporative state" favored by Italy's Mussolini, though not swallowing Nazi racism (Mrs. Pennell was, I think, Jewish).

For hands-on journalistic training, my job at the *Peking and Tientsin Times* was very useful. With 16 to 20 daily pages (including advertising and boilerplate), the paper had an editorial staff of only seven. I, by age 18, had read proofs, written headlines, done make-up, reported on local affairs from weddings and funerals to police and law court matters, and filled in as sports-writer and music and drama critic. When Pennell was unwell or out of town, I had even written "leaders" (editorials)—in which some of my already radical views showed.

In an early one during the Roosevelt administration, I asked, "Whose

New Deal?"—was it a move away from the economic system which had brought on the 1929 economic crash or an effort to save it? Commenting on "Technocracy"—another anti-depression nostrum—I criticized its ignoring of social forces. And in 1932 when the Machado dictatorship in Cuba was toppled by the then seemingly democratic sergeant Batista, I made a comparison with Russia's October Revolution which had also put former non-commissioned officers in command of its new army. This was of course short-sighted—as Batista would turn into another reactionary semi-colonial dictator—to be overthrown in 1958 by Fidel Castro. In 1933, I assailed Hitler, newly in power in Germany, in a "leader" that infuriated Tianjin's Nazis.

Pennell did not censor my articles. In 1934, when I married at age 19, he doubled my meager monthly salary—to $100 "Mex," or US$50 (still only a fraction of the pay of the most junior 'home' staff).

I began meeting with half a dozen young friends, Jewish, Russian, German and English, every week or so, to discuss Marxism and current affairs. We read the Socialist classics, Soviet publications, books like R. Palme Dutt's *Fascism and Social Revolution* and John Strachey's *The Coming Struggle* for Power. But, encapsulated as we were, I don't remember a single discussion devoted to China and her revolution—despite our general sympathy with it, our minds were abroad.

Nor, in my almost three years on the *Peking and Tientsin Times*, did I report or editorialize specifically on China. The closest I came was in reviews of the first books of two later well-known writers: *The Desert Road to Turkestan* by Owen Lattimore, and *Far Eastern Front* by Edgar Snow. With Snow, future author of the landmark *Red Star Over China*, I would soon develop a forty-year friendship. With Lattimore, too, I would have a long, though more sporadic, acquaintance.

Ultimately, however, my career at the *Peking and Tientsin Times* did not last very long: The business manager fired me after I was seen with an American Communist publication sticking out of my pocket. Pennell, in a letter of reference, wrote glowingly of my quick learning of the newspaper game, but covered himself with "Epstein's views are such as to suit a paper of liberal or radical views." This, in semi-colonial China, was a certificate of non-employability. So I never showed it.

After discharge from the *Peking and Tientsin Times* came almost a year of unemployment, during which I partnered, with an older friend, in a commercial translation service, mainly translating Russian into English, for which there was a demand by Tianjin's Russian-speaking business community. On my own, I also did some academic translations, which were published.

The longest was a treatise on medieval Mongol law (under and after Genghis Khan) by a specialist, the Russian professor V.A. Riasanovsky (later of the University of Oregon), which was printed first serially in the *Chinese Political and Social Science Review* in Beijing, and later as a book. Shorter was the economic-political pamphlet entitled *China and Silver* (China had just demonetized silver and sold the bullion to the United States) by M. Gurevich, a former instructor at Moscow University. Forty years later, I was intrigued to find a record of both under my name in the New York Public Library card catalog index.

This bilingual activity extended my vocabulary—Russian and English—in new directions. But neither I nor my partner did any translation from or into Chinese, which we could not read or write—again the encapsulation of concession life.

In spite of the colonial trappings, however, anti-colonial sympathies were moving me into siding with China and the Chinese in an increasing number of ways. One example was my resignation, together with Anne Burnett, a *Peking and Tientsin Times* colleague, from Tianjin's British Municipal Library—after a fight to get it to reverse its exclusion of Chinese patrons.

Despite its colonial official ownership, the library was well and widely stocked. There I had browsed endlessly in encyclopedias, and for years borrowed a wide variety of books and periodicals—of many political, literary and scientific schools, from Right to Left, from classic to modern and contemporary. I couldn't afford many books—but there I could find most of what I wanted. It had helped educate me and I valued it highly.

But, broad though its holdings were, its membership by-laws were the epitome of narrow-mindedness and colonial exclusivity: Chinese were not admitted. And at an annual meeting when Anne, who had grown up in China, demanded a change—and I seconded her, we found ourselves up against a stone wall. The objections were ridiculous and often insulting. Even a tall Eurasian affecting an Oxford accent, whose mother was Chinese, advanced such arguments as, if the books go to a Chinese home, who knows what germs they will pick up to infect us. After this meeting, Anne and I resigned and she organized an alternative "Bookworms Club," whose members lent books to one another—and met to discuss them. The one Chinese member was the young expert on Shaw and Brecht and future distinguished playwright, Huang Zuolin, known in Tianjin as Jolin Huang. Foreign members included two American YWCA secretaries, Lydia Johnson and Elizabeth Hiss, both progressive-minded.

Gradually but decisively, my own interest shifted towards events and trends in China, and to writing about them as sole themes for decades to come. My first ventures were freelance, mainly for publication abroad, often under pen-names because of my vulnerable stateless position. The earliest, a result of accidentally meaning a roving reporter for that paper, was a brief series in the *Philippines Free Press* in Manila, describing a personal trip in Japanese-occupied Northeast China (Manchuria).

Then I published a piece on the Long March of the Chinese Red Army in *The Nation* in New York, which stirred up a small hornets' nest, as will be told later, which a friend translated it for the Paris daily *L'Intransigeant*. Though I had no direct information on the Long March, I made a few errors: I could see by marking on a map the successive places in which the Chiang Kai-shek press reported the Red Army "defeated" or "annihilated," that it was still there and fighting its way forward. And I was already convinced, from history, that the Chinese Revolution, despite any reverses, was indestructible.

The piece in *The Nation*, unbeknownst to me, almost ran me into serious trouble. It set off a storm, and brought Edgar Snow vigorously to my defense. In early 1935 it was the center of an attack on "the liberal and radical press in America" in a Shanghai English-language publication by J. B. Powell, editor of the *China Weekly Review*, who was friendly to China but saw Chiang Kai-shek as her bright hope.

Snow's rebuttal, in a letter dated April 1, 1935 to the editors of both *The Nation and New Republic*, read in part:

> The missionaries are terribly depressed about your attitude and… plan to set you aright on the "Truth About the Chinese Reds."
> There is a bloodthirsty man-hunt on in North China at present to discover who is hiding under the name "Crispian Corcoran" for it is suspected that he is the vile beast who is misguiding you… I stumbled upon this young man… [and] found him a very brilliant alert journalist unquestionably responsible and… that it is my impression that his information is as reliable as

it is possible to get from the chaos in China today.

"Crispian Corcoran" was, of course, my alias, playfully contrived by combining the names of two fictional characters in my all too recent adolescent reading.[5]

Then along came another newspaper job in China. While translating and freelancing I became part-time "Our Correspondent" (with no personal by-line) of the *Peiping Chronicle*, an English language daily in Beijing—called Peiping then—which wanted to extend its readership to Tianjin. Though asked only to cover foreign social events, I sent in an investigative report (again anonymously) on Japan's systematic, politically motivated pushing of narcotic drugs (mainly heroin) among Tianjin's Chinese population.

The outlets were a horde of small shops, which sported the term *yang hang* (foreign firm) in their names. In return for handling the drugs, they were registered as Japanese-owned—which under the unequal treaties exempted them from Chinese law. Initially, they gave away, free, packages of secretly heroin-spiked cigarettes which created the habit—once hooked, the addicts had to pay. From the front, the shops sold anything, from candy to bicycles. Their back rooms were improvised dens. In a couple of these I saw rows of prone men greedily inhaling from cigarettes in which the tobacco at one end had been crumbled out and replaced by powdered heroin. To avoid spilling, they had to be smoked pointing upward. The slang name for them—"anti-aircraft guns," and for the heroin "white flour"—entered the local language alongside the wildfire spread of the addiction.

The dens catered mainly to working people (manual workers, petty clerks, some students), who were soon reduced to illness and beggary. Richer addicts indulged themselves at home, in more refined and presumably less lethal narcotics. The whole mechanism was reputedly rigged up by Japanese Military Intelligence—to help them in demoralizing sections of the people, recruiting agents and gathering throngs of drug-paid "supporters" for their schemes of separating northern China from the rest of the country.

---

[5] About Snow's defense, which may or not have been published by *The Nation*, I learned only 60 years later from his biographer, Robert Farnsworth, who came across carbon copies in the Snow Memorial Archive in Kansas City. That Snow never mentioned it in our long friendship was typical of his habit of doing much good and saying little about it.

The *Chronicle* (Chinese-owned though largely foreign-staffed) liked the reports—and made me another offer. Its news editor, Cecil Taylor, an Australian, was going on extended home leave—in those pre-air-travel days usually six months every three to five years. Would I fill in for him, including house-sitting in his domestic-staffed rented courtyard home in Beijing, during his absence? I would. Salary—although in the *Peking and Tienstin Times* it had been $100 "Mex" monthly, the *Chronicle* had paid half as much again for part time in Tianjin—so I asked for got $300, to which Zhang Mingwei, the business manager for the Chinese Guomindang owners, agreed. So in Beijing I was housed, and lived something like the general run of local foreign journalists and academics. China's ancient beautiful former capital (Chiang Kai-shek had shifted the government to Nanjing) was more to my liking than the Tianjin "concessions" and brought me closer to China, even though still through foreign sympathizers. Besides the Snows, there were not a few, mostly in their twenties and thirties, who were—or would be—prominent in China-related scholarship, journalism, and politics:

John King Fairbank, the future all-American pundit of China studies, was a student on a Harvard fellowship; Owen Lattimore would cover the gamut from academic writer, to President Roosevelt (Lattimore was appointed wartime adviser to Chiang Kai-shek), to being the viciously-targeted victim of post-war McCarthyism. The more flexible Fairbank would also be smeared but was able to maneuver his way out; Harold Isaacs, once intrepid in help to the Chinese Communist Party, had veered Left to Trotskyism, and was writing *The Tragedy of the Chinese Revolution* just when that revolutionary tide was turning toward victory, and Issacs himself would move Right into neo-Conservative academia; Ida Pruitt, China-born head of social work at the Rockefeller Institute's Peking Union Medical College, was to use her post to shelter underground patriots after the Japanese occupation, then give up her well-paid job at the Snows' behest to devotedly muster international support for the wartime Chinese Industrial Cooperatives, and finally become, until she died in her nineties, a staunch friend of the Chinese People's Republic.

Two others were colleagues on the *Chronicle*: F. McCraken "Mac" Fisher helped the editorial department alongside his regular job as a UP correspondent. Months earlier, he had supported the patriotic Beijing student movement of December 1935. After Pearl Harbor, he would become an official, heading the U.S. Office of War Information (OWI) in China. Post-war, he cautiously stayed in government service, feeling it more secure and quieter than journalism. Miscalculating on both counts, he was tarred by the McCarthyite brush, too slightly to be fired but sufficiently, despite his efforts to wipe off the stain, and thereafter kept in very minor positions out of the public eye and, absolutely, out of the China field.

Then there was Jack Belden, a man without caution or calculation, intense, passionate, a writer of major and burning talent, fresh off the ship on which he had worked his passage from the United States. Jack was laboring for a pittance as proofreader. After Japan's all-out invasion of China he became a front-line correspondent for the United Press, and later for *Life* magazine. No hanger-on of headquarters or social crony of officers, Jack would always head to places where ordinary soldiers fought and died, and share their dangers. After Pearl Harbor catapulted the U.S. into the war, he was in the grueling retreat from Burma under General Stilwell, a commander who shared weal and woe with the troops. Later, for *Life* magazine, he covered the Allied landings in Italy where he was severely wounded. Back in China in her renewed civil war which followed the end of World War II, he wrote *China Shakes the World*, a book ranking with Snow's *Red Star* as journalism and surpassing it as literature. Because McCarthyism smothered its sales, this fine work was less known. In the Cold War years Belden survived on odd jobs, including driving a taxi, and sometimes on unemployment or old age relief, until he died in Paris. A sad waste of a major American talent.

The *Peiping Chronicle* was interesting in structure and key personnel.

The aging editor, Sheldon Ridge, was a very different Englishman from Woodhead of the *Peking and Tientsin Times*. A veteran of teaching and journalism in China, he had stood up for her as early as 1915, when his denunciations of Tokyo's "Twenty-One Demands" ultimatum, intended to degrade China to a protectorate, had made him a target of Japanese threats. He was now grizzled and lamed (it was said by youthful injury as a Rugby player), and his editorial habits were peculiar. Caring little for what went on in the rest of the paper, he would type virtually non-stop, shut up in his own office, for about four days each week (often leaving the meals brought for him uneaten) then totter out, pale and unshaven, to the car that took him for three days of recuperation in Beijing's tranquil Western Hills. What he wrote, or selected for reprinting occupied the whole of the centerfold editorial double page—set in columns wider than the rest to ensure that no other copy would trespass on that sacred territory, which on weekends always carried a sermon by Ridge titled "The Quiet Hour."

But beneath Ridge's eccentricities there lay a bedrock of grit and loyalty. After the Japanese seized Beijing in 1937, he kept the paper going against many odds, personally delivering it to subscribers and buyers from his old black car, after newsboys and the post-office were intimidated by the ruthless invaders. If, after Pearl Harbor, he was interned by the Japanese he must have had an extra hard time of it. He died in Beijing in 1946, aged 70.

One Chinese member of the *Chronicle's* news staff was Y. C. Sun who also worked for Reuters and was hard put to make both salaries meet the needs of his large family (including half a dozen children). Another was Wang Gongda, called George, a mercurial, sharp-witted *bon vivant* who was close to the Guomindang. They did all the reporting on Chinese subjects. The foreign staff stayed in the office, sub-editing texts and layout in the pattern of the English-language press abroad.

The paper was supervised by its owners, the Guomindang, through its general manager, Zhang Mingwei. In technical matters, and handling foreign news-agency dispatches, the staff had some freedom, in domestic matters much less. This I found when dealing with one of the mendacious Guomindang reports about the civil war it was still waging against the Chinese Red Army, instead of militarily resisting the Japanese invaders. The official Guomindang news sources had repeatedly claimed that Mao Zedong, Zhu De (Chu Te), or other leaders had died (Mao was falsely rumored to be terminally tubercular) or been slain in battle. I headlined one such item, "Chu Te Killed Again"—and was soon informed by Mr. Zhang, who had earlier been friendly and complimentary about my work, that my services were no longer required, though he gave no specific reason. I don't remember if the offending quip ever appeared, or was noticed and killed before printing. But retribution was swift. Anti-Japanese slant was acceptable, even encouraged on the *Chronicle.* Criticism of the Guomindang's anti-Red crusade was not. Jobless again, I returned to the intellectually drab, commercial, parochial world of Tianjin's foreign concessions.

But Beijing could not but leave a lasting stamp on me, as on many others who lived and worked there, even briefly. Its buildings and layout recalled the heights and depths of China's ancient and modern history. It was so pulsatingly sensitized to all that went on in the country that even the most foreign of foreigners could not totally encapsulate themselves. Outwardly often serene, it could explode with youthful patriotic fervor galvanizing the whole nation, as in the then recent 1935 student movement, or produce visceral symptoms of the country's contemporary unease.

I remember how, cycling home through unlighted but familiar and normally quiet side-streets after a night shift on the *Chronicle* at about 2am, I was brought up short by the bayonet only inches from my face, of a Chinese soldier not normally present. Teen-aged and obviously a raw recruit, he had been posted there apparently to enforce an urgently declared curfew and expect trouble, the nature of which had not been explained to him, and was not disposed to take chances with anything looming out of the dark night. In fact he shook like a leaf, as did the weapon directed at me. I confess to being more frightened than even in later days amid real warfare. Little can be more unnerving than a fear-distraught boy soldier—finger on trigger, bayonet at the ready, both directed at you. To our mutual relief, we soon saw no reason for alarm, and both stopped quaking. It never could have happened, at that time, in Tianjin's concessions, insulated by administrative borders, and even more by cast of mind, from the convulsions of the China around them. So it had long been, but would not be for long.

Despite my not directly reporting on Chinese events even in Beijing, my stay there began my crucial turn from inconsequential writing mainly about, and for, the cocoon-like foreign communities to the subject of China as a whole, for a much wider audience, both abroad and among the Chinese.

Two publications to which I was soon contributing, were *democracy* (spelled deliberately with a small "d"), in Beijing, and *Voice of China* in Shanghai. Both had Chinese students and intellectuals as their main and most avid readers. Both were in published in English, edited by foreign sympathizers, and registered as foreign enterprises, and so were not subject to Guomindang censors. Both sprang up after the anti-Japanese student movement in December, 1935 which began in Beijing and spread nationwide, and the Xi'an Incident of December, 1936, in which Chiang Kai-shek was "detained" by two of his own commanders, the "Young Marshal" Zhang Xueliang, and another general, Yang Hucheng, who agreed with the students that, for national survival, the civil war between the Guomindang and the Communists should be stopped in favor of uniting against the ever-spreading military encroachments of Japan.

The monthly *democracy* was initiated by the Snows. It was the first to print statements by Mao Zedong brought back by Snow from his path-breaking trip to China's Red areas. Its editorial board, some of whom were also its volunteer writing and editing staff, included the talented New Zealand reporter and writer James Bertram, a Rhodes Scholar fresh from Oxford, who was in the process of writing *Crisis in China*, the best foreign contemporary account of the Xi'an Incident of 1936; Hubert Liang, Randolph Sailer, and Harry Price, professors respectively of Journalism, Economics, and Psychology of the prestigious Yanjing (Yenching) University in Beijing, all of whom had supported the student movement; Zhang Dongsong, a noted Chinese philosopher of the time, and John Leaning, a pipe-smoking young Englishman fresh from Labor Party and anti-Fascist politics at Oxford, did most of in-office editing, A prize catch from the Right of the political spectrum was Dr. John Leighton Stuart, President of Yanjing University. Subsequent historical events would make Stuart the last U.S. ambassador to China before the 22-year break in relations as a result of the U.S. support to Chiang Kai-shek.

In the mid-1930s, Stuart, though already long an admirer of Chiang, was for ending the Guomindang's civil war to suppress the Communists, and sympathetic to the growing demand among the Chinese for united resistance to Japan, though he hoped Chiang would be its symbol and head. Such was the moment in history that Snow and Stuart could both be on the Board of *democracy*, and its first issue carried an article by each praising, respectively, Mao Zedong and Chiang Kai-shek.

More than a decade later, in the new-born People's Republic of China, Huang Hua, a Yanjing student who had been a leader of the 1935 demonstrations and who would ultimately become new China's Foreign Minister, would convey to Stuart an invitation to come to Beijing as a guest of his former university and its alumni, by then many prominent in the Communist Party and new state. But while Stuart was not reluctant, the U.S. State Department would say "No" and thus break one of the few remaining avenues of contact.

Invited by the Snows, I was an activist for *democracy*. I wrote for it, assisted in its circulation in Tianjin, and by its last issue, before the Japanese seizure of Beijing in July 1937 killed the magazine, was listed on its masthead as an editorial board member—the very youngest, having just turned 22.

Financially, *democracy* was funded by the gaunt Reverend Spencer Kennard who, long before the term existed, was a veritable "Liberation theologian." A former missionary in Japan, he had run a religious pacifist magazine there, but been expelled by the militarists. Luckily for us, he came to China with an unspent portion of its contributed funds, about US$1,000—in the 1930s no mean sum—and with the determination to devote it to anti-Fascist purposes. Once published, *democracy* quickly caught on and was read eagerly by Chinese students and other patriots who knew English, as material it contained could not then appear in Chinese. The magazine was a thorn in the side of the Guomindang government, which urged the American Embassy to take action against it. And it alarmed the Japanese who attempted to buy up and destroy copies found on sale.

Helen Foster Snow, outstandingly active in *democracy*, has included a whimsical and interesting account of its origin and fate in *My China Years*, published in 1984 when she was already very old.

The lifetime of *Voice of China* was co-terminus with that of *democracy*, the first half of 1937. It appeared in Shanghai with the support of Soong Ching-ling under the editorship of two members of the U.S. Communist Party, Max and Grace Granich. It advocated the same course for China—a national united front against Japan. Through Chinese intermediaries in Tianjin, I was invited to write for it, too, and did so, under different aliases (as distinct from *democracy*, in which I used my own name. So far as I remember, neither I nor other contributors took any pay for our pieces. Through writing for these papers, and a brief visit to Shanghai, I eventually became known to Soong Ching-ling, though I did not yet meet her, much less have any idea that I would work with her in the decades to come.

Also associated with one or both magazines were Agnes Smedley, the revolutionary American writer who had been the accredited China correspondent of the once-liberal German paper *Frankfurter Zeitung*, and Rewi Alley, of New Zealand, factory inspector in the International Settlement of Shanghai. Agnes wrote for the *Voice* under the pseudonym Rusty Knailes and Rewi under several. Both, though not Party members, were close to the Communist underground, hiding in their homes

65

its secret emissaries and, in Alley's case, its clandestine radio station. Alley, after the Japanese invasion, would join with the Snows and Chinese promoters in launching the Chinese Industrial Co-operatives which drew workers and skills from the enemy-occupied industrial areas to become an important and progressive adjunct to the economy of industry-poor unoccupied China and Communist-led rural bases won back from enemy control. Among the English-speaking Chinese I met around the *Voice of China* were Zhu Bosheng, Zhang Ji and Cao Liang, Communist Party members although I did not then know it.

Zhu Bosheng, known to us as "Johnny Chu," was willowy and bespectacled, with the gentle, refined mien of a Chinese scholar. He was an erudite and devoted admirer of Chinese literature. But within that exterior he was an accomplished Communist underground operative, sometimes in the guise of a pleasure-loving and mahjong-playing dilettante among the politically powerful and the rich. So effective was his surface that he could long continue not only under the Guomindang but in the long period of Japanese occupation in World War II. If exposed, he would surely have been mercilessly tortured to death. But he survived, and in the future People's Republic he worked in cultural relations, a role for which he was well-fitted.

Zhang Ji, lanky and raw-boned, had studied to be a mining engineer at the University of Minnesota in the United States. There he had joined the U.S. Communist Party and volunteered for the Lincoln Battalion, the American contingent of the International Brigade fighting against the Fascists in Spain, where he was wounded and, while convalescing, contracted tuberculosis. I knew him later in Hong Kong but whether he survived World War II, I never heard.

Cao Liang, short, stocky, and round-faced, was a popular teacher in the Christian missionary-run Medhurst Academy, a secondary school in Shanghai. Also active in the underground, he instilled in his mainly well-to-do students a wish to actively oppose the Japanese invaders, which many later did, some becoming Communists. He was also a member, with Rewi Alley, of a small international group of men and women, including Americans, Germans, Austrians and others who met to study Marxism and helped the Chinese Communist Party. During the war, Cao went inland and worked under Zhou Enlai. Later, he was moved to Hong Kong, and, through a shipping company, helped organize travel to the liberated areas of many figures who would assume positions in the People's Republic.

Cao himself, however, fell on evil days in the early 1950s. His old superior in the underground, the daring and gifted Pan Hanian, who had become vice-mayor of Shanghai, was falsely suspected of renegacy, disgraced, and imprisoned. So were Cao and his wife who spent a quarter-century in jails and labor camps before they were cleared and rehabilitated—as was Pan, who in the meantime had died.

At one stage, Cao's cell-mate was Shen Zui, at one-time a prime "Communist hunter" in Chiang Kai-shek's secret police, who had once tracked Cao, hoping to catch, break, or destroy him as he had others. Released after a full confession and serving his sentence, Shen had been given a fresh start in the new society for his exposure of the evil web of old. But in the Cultural Revolution, he found himself jailed again, his pardon revoked, his freedom reversed. In dark despair he regained hope only through the example of his old intended prey, Cao Liang who had been jailed for no real cause far longer than he. Cao not only remained loyal to the revolution, but revived Shen's faltering faith in its validity and promises.

Ultimately freed, Shen wrote a memoir of this experience. Cao's release and full rehabilitation came later. He emerged confident and optimistic for the cause. In freedom, Cao and Shen remained friends.

* * *

Soon after my return to Tianjin, my unemployment ended with a job in the local bureau of the U.S. news agency, United Press (UP), then belonging to the Scripps-Howard newspaper chain. It was, at the time, a vigorous worldwide rival of the giant AP—Associated Press. (In later years, it would merge with the third major U.S. news provider, the International News Service (INS), a Hearst enterprise, to become United Press International (UPI).

Snow later sent Agnes Smedley, calling herself Mrs. Rogers, to see me in Tianjin. I had, by that time, read her *China's Red Army Marches* as well as her autobiographical *Daughter of Earth*, with "Mary Rogers" as its heroine. She asked me to contribute to *China Today,* a magazine of the Friends of the Chinese People in New York. It was the beginning of a long friendship in China and, subsequently, in the United States which lasted until her death in 1950.

democracy, though run by foreigners, gave me unprecedented contact with the Chinese Left. In Tianjin, an effort to promote its circulation led me to the Zhishi (Knowledge) book store in the city's French concession, secretly run by the underground North China Bureau of the Chinese Communist Party, then led by Lin Feng. Only a half-century afterwards did I learn of this from Ye Duzhuang, the noted translator of Darwin's works into Chinese, who had worked in the store. Lin Feng I was to meet in 1944. He would by then be the political leader of the Northwest Shanxi anti-Japanese resistance base established by the Eighth Route Army (the former Chinese Red Army) behind the front lines of the invaders, where I interviewed him at length on many aspects of the situation there.

It was through *democracy* that I came out of hiding politically, agreeing to be listed on the masthead under my own name. If my situation was risky, it was also exhilarating. Soon afterward were the more tangible risks of the battlefield. On July 7, 1937, when Japanese cannon suddenly began to thunder at Lugouqiao, also known as the Marco Polo Bridge just outside Beijing, I was within earshot of the nearby Western Hills—appropriately in the grounds of the Temple of the Sleeping Buddha so far as the oblivion to the imminence of the fateful storm was concerned. As so often during periods of protracted tension to which one has becomes accustomed, the flash-point seemed further away than it was. The winding up what had been a bucolic family vacation, I hurried not toward the scene of the clash of arms but back to my UP post in Tianjin. It was there that, as the wave of all-out Japanese aggression rolled on, that I started my years as a war reporter.

My personal baptism of fire came at July's end, running back and forth across Tianjin's old International Bridge (today called Liberation Bridge spanning the Haihe River). On the west bank were the quiet, "neutral" Western concessions, from which I filed my news dispatches. On the east bank, battle raged between several thousand well-armed Japanese invaders and some six hundred Chinese paramilitary police—the "Peace Preservation Corps"—with only rifles and machine-guns. Chinese regular troops had not been allowed in any part of Tianjin since 1901, under the foreign-imposed unequal treaty known as the Boxer Protocol, and had been excluded far beyond that by more recent "peacetime" capitulation by Chiang Kai-shek's government to Japanese diplomatic-military pressure. The bridge was within the fire-zone, but the whispering whine of rifle bullets did not convince me of the danger until I was chilled by seeing new corpses so recently vitally alive—like the "shapes of the dead in their crumpled disgrace" the British poet Siegfried Sassoon had written of in World War I. At the same time, the invaders were dive-bombing Nankai University, particularly concentrating on its library: books, along with patriotic students seemed the main object of their hate.

I long kept the record I made of a press conference at the Japanese headquarters. We foreign newsmen asked, "Why bomb the university?"

"Because, gentlemen, the outrageous Chinese are keeping troops there." The "outrageous Chinese" was the official stereotype used by Japanese spokesmen to designate, in English, all Chinese opposed to them.

"I saw no troops there," said one correspondent.

"But the buildings are very strong. The Chinese would use them."

"How do you know?"

"If I were the Chinese commander, I would use them."

"Is this any reason to bomb a world famous educational institution?"

"Gentlemen, Nankai University is an anti-Japanese base. We must destroy all anti-Japanese bases. Nankai students are anti-Japanese and Communistic. Always making trouble for us."

"But, Captain, it is the summer vacation, there are no students on the campus."

The Captain got really angry. "Gentlemen, I am a military man. I inform you that we are destroying Nankai University. It is an anti-Japanese base. All Chinese universities are anti-Japanese bases."

"Then the Japanese will bomb all Chinese universities?"

"You will please excuse me."

As for Tianjin's black-clad armed police, despite the fact that they had been far from liked by the people in normal times, their resistance was heroic, lifting spirits in the city and sobering the enemy with this proof of the breadth and depth of Chinese nationalism. Outnumbered and out-gunned, some defenders surrounded the Japanese unit at the rail station, and made a gallant attempt to destroy enemy planes on an airfield, not desisting until half their number was mown down. Such reckless courage dispirited the invaders. "We may all be massacred tonight!" the young English-speaking spokesman for the Japanese command said during the fighting to the assembled foreign press.

In the course of its resistance, the police unit was helped by a number of students and other young civilians. Many were shot by the Japanese, some simply on suspicion. In contrast to the tanned faces and varied wounds of the dead Chinese armed defenders—the students lay pale and shot in the head—plainly victims of execution. It was a fearsome sight but more still an infuriating one.

*   *   *

While fighting raged in Tianjin, another battle erupted at Tongzhou, only a few miles from Beijing. It was the "capital" of the made-in-Japan "autonomous state of East Hebei," rigged up by the Japanese after the Guomindang had signed the capitulatory Tanggu Truce with them in 1933.

There, another Peace Preservation Corps, organized by the Japanese themselves, rebelled against their masters, killing several hundred.

The Tongzhou regime had been touted by the Japanese as a shining example of what North China could be if all of it was "autonomous" under their patronage, so this revolt hit them particularly hard. In Tianjin, the Japanese spokesman complained almost hysterically, "Whatever their motive, the Tongzhou peace guards turned against the state which they had agreed to serve and the people with whom they had been connected by bonds of friendship only a few hours before!"

However, we who listened to him had already heard that the revolt came after the Japanese had disarmed a token force of Chinese soldiers still in the city, guaranteed their personal safety, then gunned them down defenseless. And this had proved too much for the "loyalty" of the puppet forces, among whom patriots had done some secret work, and who rose to avenge the butchery of Chinese like themselves, with whom they had often walked, talked, and smoked.

For the Japanese, the bitter sign was that they could not trust any Chinese to stop being Chinese on their behalf. The Tongzhou rebels having left the town and melted into the countryside, the invading Japanese army in Tianjin invited the foreign press to go and see the remains of their compatriots "outrageously massacred" and kept on display rather than immediately cremated as was the Japanese custom. Nothing was said about the previously slaughtered disarmed Chinese soldiers, whose corpses had been hastily removed.

Because of the incessant rain and summer heat, the body-viewing trip for the foreign press was called off by the Japanese themselves.

* * *

By the end of July 1937, the Japanese were in control of Tianjin with the significant exception of the concessions of Western countries. The large British-run area, mainly, became a haven for persons choosing not to live under Japanese rule. From it, via foreign ships and coastal ports not yet seized by the enemy, one could slip through to the unoccupied interior of the country. With the demand, to find living space in the concessions became difficult, and to buy steamer tickets much more so.

First, the Snows sent a few students to me, where I was to assist them in finding lodging. Then Ed himself, with Jim Bertram, came by rail from occupied Beijing, escorting an older group, two women and a man, who—I was told—were patriots wanting to leave. With neutral foreigners, they could be passed off as their employees or attendants, with less risk of detention or worse, from the Japanese gendarmes now posted in the train station.

In fact, the group was more distinguished—and faced worse peril— than I knew.

The older of the two women was Deng Yingchao, wife of Zhou Enlai, herself a senior functionary of the Central Committee of the Chinese Communist Party, secretly in Beijing in disguise for medical treatment of tuberculosis contracted during the Long March. Snow had known her when gathering material for Red Star Over China, then she had worn a uniform. With no idea that she was in Beijing, he failed to recognize her when, after the Japanese seized the city, she had walked into his home dressed as a fashionable urban lady (for the journey to Tianjin she was to change into the plainest of clothes).

The man was Wang Shiying, stocky, middle-aged and attired in Western dress. Described by Snow as a professor, Wang was a seasoned member of the Communist underground in the Guomindang-controlled areas.

The younger woman was Zhang Xiaomei, also a Party member and, as I learned much later, a sister of Deng Xiaoping's first wife who had been executed by the Guomindang. All used other names and I had no inkling of their true identity: that they were patriots needing assistance was enough. I put up Wang in the apartment of my then in-laws, American citizens protected by extraterritoriality, who were away for the summer. For the women a place was arranged in the Talati House, an Indian-owned residential hotel.

Snow asked if I could help book them on a foreign coastal vessel to Shanghai or other still un-invaded port. As it happened, I was looking for such a passage for myself, as my anti-Japanese writings were already no secret and, stateless, I was exposed to danger. Luckily, my father's business—which included marine insurance for export cargoes—was on good terms with the British shipping firm of Butterfield & Swire. By presenting the three as accompanying staff, I was able to get them on the same boat with me. The young English ticket agent did ask with a grin, "Sure they're not bandits?" Not much of a joke under those circumstances, but when I just grinned he inquired no more. He may even have enjoyed the thought of pulling a fast one on the Japanese who were pressing hard on the previously dominant Anglo-American interests in China and were the subject of increasing resentment.

Without a hitch, we boarded a launch on the British concession side of the Haiho River and chugged down to Dagu at its estuary, where a Shanghai bound coaster was standing well out to sea. As we weighed anchor, a swarm of Japanese landing craft appeared, bringing troops for the growing invasion of northern China.

Let them come, I remember thinking. The Chinese nation was at last rising in resistance. Easy as the aggressors found it to arrive, they would be hard put to extricate themselves and were bound finally to be expelled in defeat, though it would not be soon. My seasoned co-passengers must have thought the same, not just out of youthful enthusiasm, but with their long experience of victories over odds.

None of us got to Shanghai. On our second day out, the ship's radio brought news of the large-scale Japanese attack there, on August 13, 1937. The captain announced that, after stops at Yantai (then also known as Chefoo) and Qingdao, where there was still no fighting, he would head straight for British-ruled Hong Kong—where none of us wanted to go.

My Chinese companions disembarked at Yantai, entrained for the rail hub of Weixian in Shandong Province, and made their way, as I was to learn, to Xi'an and later Yan'an. I disembarked at Qingdao and went to Nanjing to join the UP office there.

For many years, both before I knew the background facts, and after, I did not speak about this episode. Neither, to me at any rate, did my traveling companions. I did see Deng Yingchao again in 1938, from a distance. She accompanied Zhou Enlai, who represented the Communist Party in its then developing anti-Japanese united front with the ruling Guomindang. But her appearance and circumstances had changed so much from those in Tianjin that I made no mental connection. Neither did Zhou Enlai, whom I met as a correspondent, allude to the matter, though I suspect he must have known because he helped me very much in my news work through subordinates who kept me up to date on many wartime developments.

It was only in 1973, in the third decade of the People's Republic, at the ceremony in which a part of Edgar Snow's ashes were laid to rest on the Beijing (formerly Yanjing) University campus where he had long ago taught and helped the student movement, that Deng Yingchao came up to me and recalled our link in 1937, forty-five years earlier, making sure that all around us could hear. At that time, the Cultural Revolution was still going on, and one can imagine why she chose this time to speak and, moreover, what it meant to me. In 1985, on my 70th birthday, she brought up those old events much more publicly, and they first appeared in print.

Wang Shiying I had encountered much earlier, after a seven-year gap, in 1944 in Yan'an. I was part of the Sino-Foreign Press Group to the Northwest, the first break in the Guomindang news blockade of the Communist-led areas since its re-imposition in 1930—in the second year of China's war with Japan. Some of us foreign newsmen were getting ready to witness and report on the guerrilla warfare in the Shanxi-Suiyuan anti-Japanese base of the Communist-led Eighth Route Army behind the front lines of the Japanese, from whom the area had been wrested. The senior member of the army's general staff who was assigned to lead our expedition looked hard at me and exclaimed in surprise, "Weren't you in Tianjin?" In the gray-uniformed cadre I did not recognize the Western-dressed "professor Wang" Snow had brought to me. I too, had matured from the lad of 22 he had once known. We were to talk much of what had happened in between.

Zhang Xiaomei, after Liberation, was to head the Women's Federation in Beijing.

Both Wang and Zhang, however, would not survive the Cultural Revolution—a sad waste.

Enough has been said to know that in 1937, though I was still not fully conscious of it, history's stream had already turned me from external observation of the Chinese Revolution to involvement that would increase for the rest of my life.

Chapter 7

WAR REPORTER IN NANJING

As it turned out, my move out of Tianjin led me not away from the war but deeper into it. Unable to land in Shanghai, I was assigned by UP to Nanjing, China's wartime capital.

Already on the train to Nanjing, I had a taste of what it felt like to be bombed as a target, not as witness to a spectacle, as the raid on Tianjin's Nankai University had been. It would happen to me hundreds of times thereafter.

On my first night in Nanjing, in the UP office, where I slept, I was awakened by the thudding vibration of bombs and roar of anti-aircraft guns. Crisscrossing rays from defense search-lights and multicolored tracers probed for enemy planes. Glued to the sight from the window, I forgot the danger. Only when I ventured outside and saw the dead: some horribly blown apart, some whole but killed by the blast, did the reality take hold.

With time, I learned to sleep through night raids—between hourly phone calls from the UP China head office in Shanghai, I would cat-nap. Never again would I be kept up at night by fears or worries. I might go to bed with them, wake with them in the morning, but in between I slept. It was unsought but useful conditioning for many future alarms and perils.

At first Nanjing was bombed only sporadically. Japan was still alternating intimidation with feelers for an armistice, by which she meant China's surrender. Her international go-betweens were German diplomats, her internal ones were Chinese defeatists and traitors. In September, after these overtures failed, came an ultimatum and intensified air attacks, some raging constantly for days and nights. I particularly remember clearly intentional hits on a large Red Cross hospital filled with local and frontline casualties. The real target was morale in the city and to tell all concerned that, even if maimed and under treatment, they could still be blown apart in their beds.

I saw soldiers who were victims of internationally-prohibited weapons: mustard gas had pitted their flesh with cheese-like holes, which penetrated agonizingly ever-deeper. Of Japanese chemical warfare I was to see more proof elsewhere. Disease-spreading biological weapons were also being tested in China, spreading deadly ills like plague and anthrax.

Nanjing's people were uncowed. Whenever an enemy bomber, downed by defending fighter planes or anti-aircraft fire, plummeted earthward trailing flame and black smoke, or exploded overhead into a hail of charred fragments, exultant crowds would rush, heedless of danger, to the crash scene. Once I saw Soong Mei-ling (Madame Chiang Kai-shek) clambering over the wreck of a fallen bomber. As head of the Aeronautical Commission, she seemed on the job. Courage she did not lack.

But, characteristically for the center of Guomindang power, popularly organized war services like those in Shanghai were not noticeable. In military and bureaucratic Nanjing, proud of its massive new buildings and broad boulevards, emergencies were attended to by smartly uniformed police and gendarmes. At each air raid alarm, they cleared the streets and ordered people into freshly-built public shelters. Flimsily constructed, little more than roofed trenches, these gave some protection against shrapnel and flying glass but none against direct hits or even near misses, even by light bombs. Cars and trucks, camouflaged with tree branches, were parked in the shade along the roadside.

In central Nanjing, at first glance, there seemed none of the plain, threadbare, patched, often ragged townsfolk then so visible everywhere else in China. Yet I soon spotted them, living under culverts or in makeshift sheds in empty lots where the poor neighborhoods had once been, tucked half out of sight behind the façade of metropolitan construction, or banished to outskirts still "undeveloped."

Even so, the bombs seemed to seek out the poor. Invaders try to preserve the most opulent, most livable places for their own occupation. Where there are shacks as well as palaces, the bombs usually fall on the shacks.

Gradually, however, the social atmosphere was beginning to change. Previously there had been two Nanjings. One was the arrogant new capital with its wide avenues, trimly tailored white-gloved officers, conceited and indolent high officials in Packard cars, and portly, brisk businessmen in expensive American-style suits. The other, more and more marginalized, was the city of the original inhabitants. Now every enemy plane shot down was a victory for all, particularly the poor who had suffered most, and for the war refugees, who brought with them from their devastated, abandoned homes the deepest hatred for the invaders.

On September 18, 1937, the sixth anniversary of Japan's 1931 armed seizure of China's northeastern provinces, wartime Nanjing saw its first citywide popular demonstration. Students from Beijing and other recently-occupied cities were permitted to agitate openly for firmer national armed resistance. The capital's powerful radio station broadcast, for the first time, the "March of the Northeastern Volunteers," with its clarion, mobilizing words:

> *Arise, all ye who refuse to be slaves*
> *With our flesh and blood we build our new Great Wall*
> *The Chinese nation faces its greatest danger*
> *Millions with but one heart, braving enemy gunfire*
> *March On! March On! March On! On!*

Months before, when I first heard it in Tianjin, it had been banned in Guomindang-ruled territory. Today it is the national anthem of the People's Republic of China.

In that complex September, too, I attended a performance by a drama group of the Beijing and Tianjin Student Union, newly arrived from the lost cities to tour the battlefronts. Their short, agitation "Living Newspaper" items and one-act plays were based on their own recent experiences. "Defend Lugouqiao" depicted the war's outbreak at the Marco Polo Bridge; "Night in Beijing" told of the production of an underground news sheet after the occupation; "Big Drum" was a patriotic call in the strident beat of authentic peasant music: an early and stirring experiment in the use of folk arts for current issues, later so important in China's wartime culture.

The war we watched onstage was punctuated by the real war offstage—power-diving Japanese planes and the thudding of bombs:

"At Lugouqiao…" a singer chanted to this accompaniment, "We heard the guns of the enemy." An explosion, very close, rocked the building. "Hear the rage of the foe!" he responded. "Let nothing stop us until we have driven him into the sea!"

Among the audience were some fairly high-ranking officials, of whom Propaganda Minister Shao Lizi was one. Their cars waited outside, ready to head for the concrete bombproof shelters available to them. But they too stayed in their seats, though one nervously kept putting on and taking off his hat. Even the plainclothes security, ever on watch at such gatherings for "subversive elements" did not seek cover.

Yet, behind the signs of the new, the all-too familiar past still loomed.

Wanting to interview the students' leader, I took down his address. When I looked for him there a day or two later, a girl from the troupe told me, "He's at the gendarme headquarters." Summoned on the pretext that the Student Union was unregistered, he still had not returned.

Such was the mixed scene in Nanjing then. On the one hand were defiance of Japan and signs of the united front for national resistance. On the other, the old authoritarian arrogance; the knee-jerk functioning of agencies of suppression was still in place. Things were better than before: the detained students might have been held indefinitely, tortured, even secretly killed. Now they were often out in a week.

Unfortunately, even this moderate thaw would continue only through the war's first year.

* * *

Under the united front agreement with the Guomindang, a resident delegation of the Communist Party had come to Nanjing. There I first met its representatives openly. Though its presence was legal, its location was kept secret from inquiring newspapermen by Guomindang bureaucrats loath to adjust to the new political situation.

Setting out to see real-life Red Army Long Marchers, I expected stern-faced veterans, worn and hardened by a decade's grim struggles, perhaps difficult to converse with.

What I found instead was a gangly, bespectacled intellectual in what looked like a student's blue uniform, not much older than the average post-graduate, speaking English and Russian, and a handsome, smiling officer dressed in khaki. Both were younger and more relaxed than I could have imagined, and spoke willingly, putting me entirely at ease.

The civilian introduced himself as Chin Bangxian (also known as Bo Gu), former chairman of the Northwestern Chinese Soviet Government, and the officer as Ye Jianying, former Chief of Staff of the Chinese Red Army. (Today, knowing that Bo Gu had been at sharp odds with Mao Zedong, and demoted for errors in leading the Long March, I marvel all the more at the recalled absence of tension).

The notes I made at the time have perished. My UP dispatch on our discussion hasn't. It read:

> Refuting the suggestion that their party has 'surrendered to the Guomindang,' Chinese Communists maintain that their own Marxist principles dictate the fullest cooperation, both during the war and the subsequent period of national reconstruction, with the government that for ten years tried to exterminate them, and slaughtered so many.
>
> The national struggle against Japan, they believe, is revolutionary in nature. Marxist theory, they say, differentiates between the nationalism of oppressor states and that of oppressed peoples fighting for national liberation. The former is regressive, the latter progressive. Furthermore the Communists believe that the country-wide struggle against Japan will teach every Chinese to connect his personal fate with wider national issues, and therefore aspire to take a hand in the political shaping of a new democratic China. They advocate mass organization based on this new consciousness of the people.
>
> This view has caused the Chinese Communists to make the struggle against Japan the cornerstone of their activity and agitation. Apprehending that the intensification of social strife at this juncture might throw the propertied classes into the camp of peace [meaning compromise] or even the arms of the Japanese, Chinese Reds are now advocating the cooperation of all classes in the interests of the war. Having adopted this policy, they are branding traitors those opposed to such cooperation. To them, the use of revolutionary slogans and traditions to create a state of disunity that would facilitate the victory of the imperialist Japanese is the lowest form of political trickery, and they denounce as Trotskyites all those who try in this way to break up the national united front of all classes and parties which they advocate...
>
> Communist leaders have assured me that their party has not been, and will not be dissolved [as was urged by the Guomindang –I.E.] Its members are giving everything to the anti-Japanese struggle not because they have 'reformed' but because they consider it is their duty, as Communists, to do so.

*   *   *

At the time, the three-month pitched battle for Shanghai was continuing heroically, but not saving the city. In it, the lives of many of China's best equipped Guomindang-led troops were lost, leaving a huge vacuum for the Japanese to press on into.

Simultaneously, the Communist-led troops of the former Chinese Red Army, reorganized under the united front into the Eighth Route Army, waging the mobile and guerrilla warfare they had developed, won the first Chinese victory of the war at Pingxinguan, along the Great

Wall far to the north. Equipped with little more than rifles, they recovered rural areas originally seized by the Japanese, and increased—instead of lessening— their own numbers. For them the vacuum to be filled was the enemy's own rear. There they inspired and organized new armed forces, including peasant militia auxiliaries, villagers fighting on their home ground, which soon came to outnumbering the core of uniformed troops.

Strategically, the Guomindang thought in terms of the Chinese regular-army vs. the Japanese regular army. In that confrontation the Japanese with their better weaponry—on land, sea, and air—had the inevitable advantage, as was proved in Shanghai. The Communists in contrast, reckoned in terms of Chinese armies plus armed people on their own soil vs. the Japanese army on invaded soil. In that confrontation, the Japanese were outnumbered and surrounded, and could be ambushed, outmaneuvered and progressively eroded. This was shown at Pingxinguan.

The Guomindang, with its class fear of arming and empowering the common people, minimized the impact of Pingxinguan, and at first simply tried to talk it away. Madame Chiang, at a Nanjing press conference, answered "No" to my question about the battle having been won by the re-named Chinese Red Army.

But by mid-December, after the fall of the capital had followed that of Shanghai, even Chiang Kai-shek himself acknowledged that the basis of China's prolonged resistance was no longer to be found in Nanjing nor in China's great cities and towns, but in the villages and in the countryside, amid the fixed determination of the people.

To state this was one thing, to act on it was another. The Communists, with their long support of, and by, the peasants, were able to rally that great latent force which Chiang's government, which had long fleeced the rural population, neither dared nor knew how to do. It did temporarily invite Ye Jianying and other Communists as instructors in guerrilla warfare, but only to give technical training to its existing troops. To satisfy the condition that such warfare must be waged by the armed people as well as the regular military ran counter to its ruling-class interests.

By mid-November, with Shanghai lost and the Japanese advancing westward, the evacuation of Nanjing began.

I was reassigned by UP to Wuhan, the interim capital upstream on the Yangtze. The government-chartered ship I took was designed for a few hundred passengers but carried 3,000. Officials of medium rank were squeezed four or five into a two-bunk cabin. Humbler functionaries crammed the lower-class cubicles and decks. In the steerage, wounded soldiers lay piled across each other, chattering with fever, pain, and cold.

I bunked down in the ship's tiny post office, together with a Guomindang representative from the Chinese community of Madagascar, and his seven-year old daughter. The child kept lustily singing "The March of the Volunteers," so widely had the song now spread.

The vessel was so crowded that a deck passenger was jostled into the rushing river when trying to urinate over the side. Luckily we were not bombed as the weather all the way consisted of fog, rain, and sleet, and was so bone-chilling that a ray of sunshine would have been welcome even with the added risk.

Had I not left then, I might have, like my young UP colleague Weldon James, gone via the American river gunboat, U.S.S. Panay, which might have seemed safer, but was in fact was bombed by the Japanese with many casualties. The surprise attack—a shock with the two countries still at peace—triggered sharp tension between Tokyo and Washington, but it did not halt profitable U.S. sales of scrap iron and oil needed by Japan for her war.

A similar, though less damaging, air attack on the British naval craft, H.M.S. Ladybird, drew an even milder reaction from London. Japan was deliberately trial-signaling, "Out of my way." The low-key response might have led her to conclude that Britain and America could be pushed aside, reacting only with aggrieved complaints.

Nanjing fell on December 13, 1937, to Japanese troops who subjected it to a wholesale orgy of rape and slaughter. Some 300,000 disarmed prisoners and unarmed civilians were systematically exterminated—roped together and machine-gunned, thrown into the Yangtze to drown, beheaded, buried alive, used for bayonet practice, and slain in unconceivable ways. Among American eyewitnesses I knew were Professors M. Searle Bates and Lewis Smythe of Nanjing University, George Fitch of the Y.M.C.A., and *New York Times* correspondent F. Tillman Durdin. Even the German businessman John Rabe, prominent among the Nazis in China, was shocked into acts of protest. He chaired a foreign-run safety zone committee and wrote an unsparingly revealing report to Berlin for which he was reprimanded—the German-Japanese alliance was in the making.

Records made by resident foreigners, including Rabe's long-secret diary, plus contemporary news reports, letters, and photographs stand as unassailable proof of the Nanjing holocaust. First-hand Chinese evidence aplenty, adduced in the post-World War II trials of leading Japanese war criminals, secured death sentences for the main perpetrators. Yet even today, Japanese Right-wing apologists seek to minimize or deny what happened. On the other hand, some Japanese participants have come forward to attest the grisly facts, and voice repentance.

* * *

At that time, foreign media coverage in Nanjing consisted of the AP, AP, and the *New York Times* from the United States, Reuters from Britain, TASS from the Soviet Union, and German news agencies. In general, all, including Germans still not replaced by out-and-out Nazis, favored China against Japan, and were mutually friendly. Some of long-term or temporary bachelors, including me, ate together in Durdin's apartment, where there was a piano he often played while we sang in chorus.

Before the bombing got too bad, we would sometimes dine, Dutch-treat, in Chinese restaurants, a favorite one located in the Fuzimiao (Confucius Temple) area featuring a soup said to have been kept simmering for centuries in the same frequently-replenished pot, like the steak-and-kidney pie in the Cheshire Cheese coffee house in London, fancied by Fleet Street journalists. Since none of us could be everywhere at once, we shared much of what we saw, except for real scoops, which we would send out first and talk about later. If an alarm sounded while we were eating outside, we would jump in our cars and drive back to our respective offices.

Among our group of foreign newsmen-residents the most colorful was the jovial, square-built Vladimir Rogov of TASS. In his mid-thirties, and of Cossack origin, he had been illiterate until the age of twelve, gone to school and university after the revolution and attained erudition, both in his first specialty, economic geography, and in Chinese. Incidentally, Russian newsmen, of whom Western reporters were apt to speak slightingly for their inadequate knowledge of English, were not assigned to China unless they knew Chinese, whereas the vast majority of the Western ones did not. Convivial and humorous, Rogov did not at all fit the model of Soviet people among foreigners. Powerfully built, when I, a new and poor driver, ran a wheel of the UP car into a ditch, he jumped out, put his shoulder under the chassis and lifted it back to the road.

Among the "visiting firemen" was Lord Killanin, a young red-haired Irish peer, sent out not so much for his journalistic record as for the attractiveness, for some readers, of his title. Actually, he was modest, although an East European acolyte who accompanied him invariably addressed him as "M'lud." What would be notable about Killanin is that, in the distant future, he would become chairman of the International Olympic Committee.

Another visiting newsman of aristocratic background was Sir Anthony Jenkinson, with a hereditary baronetcy going back to the sixteenth century, when an ancestor of the same name was one of England's earliest envoys to Russia rumored to have carried back to England a fruitless proposal of marriage from Tsar Ivan (the Terrible) to Queen Elizabeth I. Lanky and very tall, with a small face, he was fresh from the university, and like many students of that time, inclined to the Left. Years later I would work for the Allied Labor News, of which Jenkinson would be a founder and outspokenly anti-imperialist chief editor. To us he was just "Tony." One of his accomplishments was as a yachtsman; once he sailed around the Caribbean with Leicester Hemingway, brother of Ernest, to write about Right-wing dictatorships then prevalent in the region.

Among the more or less permanent foreign fixtures in Nanjing to whom we went for news, beyond the usual round of government departments and embassies was William Henry Donald, so long established that some called him "Donald of China." An Australian and veteran of journalism (he had been a war correspondent at the time of the Russo-Japanese war of 1904-5) he was in 1937 an adviser to Chiang Kai-shek as well as Madame Chiang. A year previously, he had attracted international attention by helping in the settlement of the Xian Incident in which Chiang had been detained by his subordinates to be released only through the intermediacy of the Chinese Communist Party's Zhou Enlai after Chiang's promise to halt civil war and resist the Japanese.

I, in my 22-year-old brashness days after I arrived in Nanjing, went

83

to ask Donald if he could fix a one-man interview for me with Chiang Kai-shek, which none of the older correspondents there had had. Donald, parrying, led me on to interview himself. For more than an hour over tea and cakes, he regaled me with stories, told self-effacingly, of how much he had done for China. Naming each one, he told me of the Chinese honors and decorations he had invariably declined, when they were offered and turned down by him. Never have I heard modesty boasted of in such detail.

The facts were probably accurate, Donald was not a bluffer. And it must be said for him that he was genuinely for China against Japan. In 1940 when defeatists in the Guomindang tried to resume civil war while leaning toward a capitulatory peace with Japan, he quit his adviser's post of many years.

The rest of his story is incredible. On December 7, 1941 he was out in the open Pacific off the China coast on his own small yacht, sailing, as was his favorite relaxation, with his Chinese secretary, Ancie Lee. Here the Japanese Navy, scouring the open seas, picked him up. Asked his name, he gave it accurately. Seemingly, he was a prize catch, for the famous Australian adviser to China's great leaders was certainly on Japan's "most wanted" list. But he was supposed to be on the mainland, or in Hong Kong, or on a visit somewhere abroad. Never did the Japanese Navy captain, nor, as it proved, Japan's entire intelligence network, expected to find him plying out on the open sea. Put ashore, he was handed over for confinement, again registered in his own supposedly coincidental name, placed in a Japanese civilian interment camp in the Philippines, and again not identified with "Donald of China." Freed when Japan surrendered in 1945, he later died peacefully in bed—of cancer—in Hawaii.

Chapter 8

WUHAN

The move from Nanjing to Wuhan was a retreat geographically. But many felt it marked an advance politically and morally (in my experience the two are inseparable).

After the fall of Nanjing, China was plunged into its deepest crisis. But "crisis," we shall remember, is in Chinese denoted by two linked characters: the first "danger," the second "opportunity."

Wuhan's face was turned toward opportunity, the latent ability of the nation and people to unite, survive, and win. That confidence, in turn, built self-respect, not just national, but in both individual and mutual outlook.

The "Wuhan mood" of hope, in Guomindang territory, would have a short life of only a few months. Yet it would long be remembered and missed, almost lovingly, not only by Chinese but by foreigners who experienced it, including most of the resident correspondents writing in English from Agnes Smedley on the Left to those of the major media-middle and Right-wing.[6]

People who were progressively inclined did not, by then, just miss Wuhan but were looking for the center of national hope elsewhere. They became more aware of the Resistance bases led by the Communist Party, mainly in territory wrested back from the enemy in guerrilla warfare in areas behind the lines of Japanese occupation. Moreover, knowledge of Communist policies and successes, long blacked out by Guomindang censorship became generally available in the much freer atmosphere as compared to Nanjing. In Wuhan, in 1938, the first and best year of the united front of China's two major parties against Japan, bookstores publicly displayed works on the Long March and China's

---

[6] A group photo of these "Last Ditchers," as they called themselves, most of whom stayed in Wuhan till the last moment, showed Agnes Smedley; U.S. officials Naval Attache Evans F. Carlson, Assistant Military Attache Frank Dorn, and Embassy Secretary John Davies; correspondents F. M. ("Mac") Fisher, Jack Belden, and A. T. Steele; British writer Freda Utley, and, in the picture with them, Chinese Communist Party official Zhang Hanfu.

Red Areas, both by Chinese and by foreigners such as Snow's *Red Star Over China*. Writings by Mao Zedong and other long-proscribed Chinese Communist leaders—particularly those proposing a strategy for the war with Japan—were openly bought and discussed, after years in which the very possession of such literature could cost one's head. Young people were the most eager to read and respond.

Flocking into Wuhan were not only officials from Nanjing but professors, students, and progressive editors and writers from intellectual centers such as Beijing and Shanghai. They set up in the city many liberal and Left-wing publications which, in quality and vigor, were preferred by readers to the official and semi-official output of the Guomindang, or of conservatives and aesthetes having no bearing on the burning questions of the day.

The Communist party itself, outlawed and hounded during a decade of civil war, had in Wuhan a much more prominent presence than in Nanjing. Its official delegation in Wuhan was bolstered by the usual presence in the city of the Party's vice-chairman, Zhou Enlai. Officially the office of the Eighth Route Army, it was in fact a plenipotentiary in all wartime relations with the Guomindang. There, on one visit, I had a "scoop" interview with the fiery Ye Ting, appointed through bi-party negotiation as the commander of a second Communist-led army, the New Fourth.

In Wuhan, too, early in 1938 the Communist Party brought out its first legal newspaper in Guomindang-controlled territory since 1927, the *Xinhua Ribao* (New China Daily), national, not just local, in scope. Its founding was a public affair, participated in by many non-Communists, and which I attended. Despite intimidation of newsboys and other Right-wing attempts to impede or stop this daily paper, including an obviously staged riot, its sales and reader base grew.

Although the Guomindang kept all government ministries in its own hands, Zhou Enlai was made vice-head of the Political Department of China's entire army—a recognition of the relevance of the fighting methods of the Chinese Communists forces, and particularly of implanting political motivation in the troops in the war to save the entire nation. Under Zhou, the Department's Third Section, which released information and built public morale, was headed by the Left-wing writer Guo Muoruo. Guo, freshly returned from ten years of political exile, had done major political work in army of the 1925-27 Revolution during the first historic period of Guomindang-Communist co-operation, against reactionary warlords and their foreign imperialist backers. His reappearance on the political scene was a reminder of the victories achieved in that cooperation, and the national defeats that followed its sanguinary split in 1927, both of which Wuhan had vividly witnessed.

Working in the Third Section were many intellectuals, Communists, and other progressive patriots. From this channel, and through it from Zhou Enlai, I had much help for my work as a correspondent.

In short, the Wuhan feeling of opportunity arose because, confronted by Japanese aggression, Chinese were no longer fighting Chinese but again beginning to unite for the country's independence and future. And in Wuhan too (actually the tri-cities of Wuchang, Hankou, and Hanyang) earlier in the century, the 1911 Republican Revolution had started, bringing an end to dynastic rule in China. Many in this city still carried the positive memories of efforts for national unity and advancement. That too was a factor in its mood of opportunity. Expressive of the new Spring was the collection of poems by Guo Muoro, himself a major poet, entitled *Wuhan Hope*.

Moreover, by contrast with Nanjing, which had ossified into a bureaucratic-military excrescence, Wuhan was an industrial hub where the working class had much political and organizational experience both of high triumphs and of grim setbacks. There, China's labor unions, under Communist leadership, had achieved their peak of influence and strength in 1926-27, when they had been the main force in the mass takeover of the former British concession, the first Chinese place to be recovered from foreign rule since such enclaves had been implanted during the mid nineteenth century. There too the workers' movement had survived warlord suppression as early as 1923, and been crushed for years after the Right-wing Guomindang anti-Communist massacres of 1927. But now it was rising again.

As one sign of the changed atmosphere, Wuhan, on May Day 1938, celebrated its first international festival of labor in eleven years. A mass audience of workers in its main park heard, also for the first time in a decade, a speaker of the Communist Party, Wang Ming, then still was the party's top leadership. Wang, at one time dogmatically Leftist, was now equally dogmatic for the united front with the Guomindang, which he saw not as a partner but as a leader.

* * *

Most important of all, Wuhan carried the rising flame of optimism sparked by the small-scale but cumulatively considerable advances against the Japanese invaders by the Communist-led former Red Army forces (now comprised of the Eight Route Army and the New Fourth Army). It offered proof that the revolutionary impulse had not only survived all adversities—as in the Long March—but was at work in the vast countryside in effectively counterattacking and wearing down the invading enemy, despite the loss of the cities.

In those areas, it was the Chinese and not the Japanese who were advancing: slowly but with infinite long-range promise.

The Guomindang armies, besides being poorly led, were organized for pitched battles and the defense of fixed positions. In such contests the better-equipped, better-trained Japanese, backed by a much stronger industrial machine, had the upper hand.

The Communist-led armies, by contrast, waged guerrilla and mobile warfare in the wide rural or semi-rural spaces between the main Japanese garrisons, where the enemy was spread thin. Large expanses of mainly rural territory were thus turned into liberated bases behind the enemy lines. Regular army vs. regular army, the invaders had the advantage. But as invading regulars vs. the defending *and* counterattacking *irregular* army, the Japanese were often outnumbered, outwitted and beaten, with part of their weapons and equipment captured by Chinese forces who thus armed themselves.

That a poorly-armed force which had popular appeal and support could frustrate a well-armed one which lacked these qualities had previously been proved by the Chinese Red Army in ten years of civil war when it beat back Chiang Kai-shek's "extermination campaigns" and captured so much of his equipment. Moreover, the Long March had shown, on epic scale, how a forced retreat could become a victory.

Of the sympathetic foreign eyewitnesses of the 1927 revolutionary days in Wuhan (when so many foreigners were antagonistic), only one remained there in 1938, the American Protestant Bishop Logan W. Roots. Zhou Enlai, who had known this fair-minded and sympathetic old man a dozen years earlier now reached out to him again. Soon the spacious home of Bishop Roots became a united front outpost. Left-wing foreign house guests there included Anna Louise Strong, who had also seen Wuhan in 1926-27 and then gone, and Agnes Smedley, long on the side of China's Revolution. This won for the Roots house the joking nickname, among local foreigners, of "Moscow-Heaven Axis." Having little to do with Moscow, despite Anna Louse Strong's then permanent residence there, it did become a social bridge between China's Communists and Wuhan's foreign officials, civil and military. One could meet, having tea together on its lawn, Zhou Enlai or other members of his entourage and U.S. diplomats like Jack Service, and the U.S. military attaché Evans Carlson.

I met Carlson during my first weeks in Wuhan, in December 1937. He was a tall, lanky, pipe-smoking American with a craggy profile and quiet deep-set eyes, wearing a sheepskin-lined leather jacket and shouldering a rucksack. He had come to see me, bringing me a note from Edgar Snow who described him as a strongly pro-Chinese, anti-Japanese U.S. Marine Corps officer who wanted to see for himself the resistance against Japan by the Communist-led Eighth Route Army. Would I, wrote Snow, steer him to the Wuhan office of the Communist-led Eighth Route Army, to which he had a separate recommendation from Snow?

I took Carlson to see General Ye Jianying and Dong Biwu, who were just settling in before Zhou Enlai arrived. They contacted Yan'an and soon arranged for him a journey to the guerrilla bases behind the enemy lines.

Returning, Carlson aired his enthusiasm about what he had seen. One channel was through his official reports. These were supplemented, as not generally known until many years afterwards, by letters written directly to U.S. President Franklin Delano Roosevelt at the latter's request when Carlson was sent to wartime China. As it happened, he had come to know the President as a friend from a preceding assignment as commander of the guard at the "summer White House" at Warm Springs, Georgia, where Roosevelt spent much time for reasons of health.

In Wuhan, on his return from the guerrilla fronts, Carlson also spoke of his impressions publicly. At a gathering of foreign newsmen, missionaries, and others, I heard him describe the Eighth Route Army as the most combat-effective force in China, the most motivated in war and the most democratic both in its own ranks and in relations with the people. He lauded its commander-in-chief, Zhu De, through comparisons from American political and military history: "humble as Lincoln, militarily brilliant as Lee, and tenacious as Grant." By contrast, he quoted with outrage the chilling words of Jiang Tingwen, the general leading the Guomindang troops already blocking not only military supplies to the Eighth Route Army but medical aid for its wounded in battle against Japan. Far from disowning these actions, this anti-Communist die-hard had growled to Carlson, "Can't you understand. We don't care if they die. We want them to die."

These experiences changed Carlson himself. Before China, he had been filled with prejudices against anything that smacked of the Left (he had been part of the U.S. armed intervention against the national hero Sandino in Nicaragua). Now he admired the spirit and effectiveness of China's Communists, coming closer to Americans of like mind. From Edgar Snow's eyewitness descriptions of these forces, which he had already heard before the war in Beijing, he had carried away the strong impression that they could and would play a vanguard role in Chinese armed resistance to Japan—the country he saw as the future enemy of the United States as well. From then on, therefore, he considered them important as a future military help to America against a common foe. And, in the Eighth Route Army he met Agnes Smedley, who deepened his mind on socio-political "whys" and "wherefores" he had not hitherto considered. Back in Wuhan, Carlson helped Smedley to collect medical supplies for the Eighth Route, and helped both Snow and Rewi Alley to promote the Chinese Industrial Cooperatives.

Carlson's new outlook would not change but develop. In World War II he would win wide fame, emerging as the highly-acclaimed Pacific theater commander of the famed Marine Raiders whose training and indoctrination he would base partly on his experience in the Eighth Route Army and whose battle-cry: "Gung Ho" came from this work-together motto of China's democratic Industrial Cooperatives. That President Franklin Roosevelt's eldest son, James, served under him in battle was a measure of the President's appreciation of Carlson.

And in his final years, he was an outspoken leader of American opponents to Washington's ill-starred backing of Chiang Kai-shek in the latter's renewed civil war against China's Communists.

Among Wuhan's unofficial foreign residents, there was also an upsurge of sympathetic interest in the Communists' war record and policies. While travel was still relatively free, Frances Roots, the Bishop's daughter, led a group, mainly American missionaries and young people, on a trip to Communist General Zhu De's Eighth Route Army head-quarters in southeast Shanxi Province, where they too were deeply impressed. Some were later to participate in the progressive movement in the U.S. itself. An older member of the group, Ralf Sues, a Polish former official of the League of Nations, wrote a book about this journey published and much read in America, called *Shark's Fins and Millet,* whose title contrasts one of the most expensive Chinese banquet dishes with one of China simple, basic food staples in a symbolic representation of the life-styles of the Guomindang and the Communists, respectively.

From abroad, in those same months, a delegation of the International Student Federation traveled through Wuhan to Yan'an, where they had interviews with Mao Zedong and other Communist leaders. The American delegate Molly Yard, born in China in a missionary family, was to head, decades afterwards, the National Organization of Women (NOW), the chief champion of womens' rights in the U.S.

Among Wuhan's Chinese people in 1938, one felt a vigorous identification with the international fight against fascism. Especially strong was the sense of solidarity with the only other armed struggle then being waged against Fascist aggression: the defensive war of the Spanish Republic against Franco's reactionary military rebellion backed with troops and arms by Hitler's Germany and Mussolini's Italy.

In Nanjing, the patriotic anthem, "Arise, you who would not be slaves" had burst forth after having been banned there for years, much like, as historians record, *La Marseillaise* had reappeared in Paris in the Franco-Prussian war in 1870, after long having been outlawed by the restored monarchy and Napoleon's empire. In Wuhan in 1938, adding an international dimension was a new Chinese song "Defend Madrid!" born of the feeling that China and Spain were linked fronts.

Many people knew who La Pasionaria was, and knew the defiant Spanish Republican slogan "No Pasaran" (They Shall Not Pass). In the ranks of the International Brigade in Spain were a hundred or so Chinese who, living in the West, had volunteered for it. From the other direction, I briefly met in Wuhan, on his way from the Spanish front, the devoted and highly skilled Canadian surgeon, Norman Bethune, en route to the Eighth Route Army's bases behind enemy lines, where he would set up a field service for its wounded and end up dying at his post, earning a lasting reputation in China and a famed eulogy from Mao Zedong, read throughout the country. Along the same track came the distinguished Dutch documentary film pioneer, Joris Ivens.

Accompanying Ivens from Spain, was the renowned Hungarian (later American) war photographer Robert Capa. Later, as the Spanish Republic went down in tragic defeat, a score of International Brigade doctors came from internment camps in France to serve an anti-Fascist front once again in China.

In April 1938, coming from Wuhan in its most hopeful mood, I witnessed the first victory by Chinese regular forces over the Japanese since the war began, a victory that brought that mood to a peak, sending a thrill throughout China. It was won at Taierzhuang, on the border of Jiangsu and Shandong provinces. While Guomindang troops fought on the spot, Communist guerrillas, far to the north, cut the communication lines of the Japanese to obstruct enemy reinforcements—in useful united front cooperation.

I went to Taierzhuang in most congenial and instructive company. There was the Joris Ivens film team, fresh from embattled Spain, where they had made a then well-known documentary, *The Spanish Earth*. In China they were in the process of creating another, *The Four Hundred Million*, which was equally effective and was narrated by the American film star Fredric March. It would include Taierzhuang, which they witnessed directly, and material from the Communist-led guerrilla fronts, where the Guomindang would not allow them to go, but where they sent a camera to a local operator who managed to send the scenes back. Also in our group was Evans Carlson, fresh from Communist-led guerrilla zones behind the Japanese lines. From Guo Muoruo's Third Section came Cao Liang, whom I had met first in Shanghai at the *Voice of China*, now a teacher at a missionary-run school, and secretly a Communist. From the Guomindang Ministry of Information there were men of another type: One was an official photographer who tried to dictate what should be filmed, and duplicated what was filmed with his own camera for censorship purposes. And the top "handler," comically, was comfortably stout Theodore Du, a former YMCA choir master, brevetted as wartime Brigadier General, but so unwarlike that two stations before the railhead to Taierzhuang, he rushed over, alarmed, to say, "We can't go on, I've just learned that a Japanese shell fell here *yesterday!*" To get us to turn tail would have suited him, and probably his immediate superiors. But, having already been in places where shells and bombs rained down on the same day, and would do so tomorrow, we shrugged this "warrior" off. The whole combination of circumstances reflected the complexity of China, official and unofficial, in wartime transition.

In the main, the stage was still upbeat, and more and more so as we approached the front. At strategic Xuzhou, the regional military headquarters at the intersection of two main rail lines, we interviewed its commander, Marshal Li Zongren, who did not belong to the core body of Chiang Kai-shek's troops but to the provincial army of Guangxi Province. In the courtyard of his headquarters was a dense crowd of peasants moving to the war front; the nearer we got to Taierzhuang, the higher the morale. Xuzhou, thirty miles away and strategically located at the intersection of two of China's main railroads, was the regional headquarters and the target of the Japanese offensive. From it we could already hear the thudding of cannon, and on its station platform lay dying soldiers who could not survive until evacuation to the further rear. Yet the city streets, surprisingly, were full of optimistic life. Fresh patriotic posters covered the walls. Troops and local recruits marched constantly. But civilian life also continued actively. Newsboys cried out the papers' headlines. Men carrying sandwich boards advertised plays and films. Student propaganda groups performed spontaneous skits outdoors, and in the parks where women took their children. Despite bombings people seemed more confident than in still-distant Wuhan, where there were worries about the effects of a breakthrough to Xuzhou. Here it was expected that the foe would be thrown back.

General Li Zongren, heading the war zone with its 300,000 troops, was a trim, light-boned, energetic southerner who had brought with him a large local force from his multi-ethnic home province near the Vietnam border. At the Headquarters gate, we jostled through peasants bringing pigs to feed the soldiers. The general ascribed explained the popular support, in an area where Guangxi's dialects weren't understood not only to overall patriotism but to the prohibition of compulsory unpaid requisitions.

Closer to Taierzhuang, after a half hour by train, we trudged to the advance command post of General Sun Lianzhong, a typical massive Northerner, his rugged face unshaven, his voice hoarse from sleepless fatigue in the preceding two weeks' fighting. But amid the still-heard sounds of war, peasants were working in the spring-green square fields.

The next day we crossed to Taierzhuang by a pontoon bridge rigged across the ancient Grand Canal. Amid the ruins lay the dead: many soldiers, a peasant man carrying a goose, which now lay dead just beyond his prone, outstretched arm. Nearby, the driven-out Japanese had cremated their own dead, using iron-spring beds as a bier that they had dragged into the open, sometimes able to complete only half the grisly work before they fled.

Chi Fengchen, commander of the Chinese 31st Division, which, in a bloody hand-to-hand street fight, finally dislodged the invaders from Taierzhuang. Chi was slim, keen, and, in his mid-30s, young for his rank. In an unorthodox move, he had changed from his combat fatigues to slacks and a leather jacket. Seventy percent of his force, he said, had fallen in the previous months; both in sporadic fighting and in the final bloody encounter. Outside the city wall, half shattered by shelling, stood the remains of four Japanese tanks, disabled and abandoned.

A characteristic of the Taierzhuang campaign was that it was fought chiefly by "gray" troops—then the Chinese term for units not belonging to Chiang Kai-shek's carefully-groomed elite units and much less well-equipped. Brought together from far-flung and remote provinces, despised and viewed as expendable by Chiang's top command, they proved brave and fearless in the face of certain death.

Geographically, this showed a wide-reaching national spirit. In that sense, much of the country participated. Chiang's core troops, hoarded as the key to his power, took part only from afar, with artillery, and that used sparingly.

Highly placed Japanese spokesmen, shocked by their reversal of fortunes at Taierzhuang—and that at the hands of "secondary" troops, resorted to their favored way of dealing with setbacks: they denied for days not only that Chinese had won back Taierzhuang, but that the important rail link at Xuzhou, of which Taierzhuang was an outpost, had ever been a Japanese goal in the campaign, which of course it was—and continued to be.

On April 29, 1938, three weeks after the land victory at Taierzhuang, spirits in Wuhan were further raised by a triumph in the air—above the city itself. I watched it from atop a nearby building. The swarm of enemy planes was met in the skies by a squadron of Soviet nominally volunteer fighter pilots who had recently come to Wuhan's defense. Within a short time a score or so Japanese aircraft were shot down with a minimum loss for the defenders.

The Taierzhuang victory was memorable for several reasons:

After the loss of Beijing, Shanghai, and Nanjing, it was the first large recovery of a town in the enemy's possession.

It greatly encouraged confidence throughout China and the world in the determination of China and the Chinese people to fight and their ability to win.

Internally, it was acclaimed everywhere—in the Guomindang ruled rear, in Yan'an and the liberated areas, in the occupied areas and among Chinese overseas—and also by friends of China all over the world. Many who had wavered in their trust that China could fight on—including official quarters abroad—ceased to waver so much. To the Japanese aggressors their check at Taierzhuang was a shock, and to their troops' morale a severe blow.

The armies that fought in Taierzhuang, coming from all parts of China, were in high spirits. Against the background of so many disasters in the war's first year, they fought bravely and tenaciously until victory. The direction at the levels of the Military Area (Li Zongren), the intermediate level (Sun Lianzhong), and in the town itself (Chi Fengchen), was sound. It must be kept in mind that the political climate was relatively favorable—Guomindang-Communist cooperation was at its brief height. The Communist-led forces, which had won the victory at Pingxinguan, which preceded Taierzhuang, helped the latter by attacking the transport lines of the Japanese from North China.

On the other hand, time was to show that Taierzhuang and its immediate vicinity could not be retained in the face of later Japanese counterattacks. Xuzhou fell to the enemy soon after and Wuhan and Guangzhou within a few months.

Under the then circumstances, the promising and inspiring local triumph could not be followed up by strategic dispositions for fighting the whole war—there was no increase of mobile and guerrilla warfare on the regular front but only in the liberated areas. Cooperation between China's two major parties, in the year that followed, was not strengthened but weakened. The Guomindang did not, and could not, have the vision of Mao Zedong in his programmatic work "On the Protracted War" with its view of the three stages of resistance to Japan and how to ultimately move from the defensive to the offensive. This required a force based on and incorporating the strength of the whole people. But Chiang Kai-shek was already showing a disposition to hoard his own forces, habitually not committing them against the Japanese,

but keeping them for future use in civil war to secure his own power—
against the people.

A truer picture was given by a verse found on the body of a Japanese soldier:

Four hours we fought and took Tianjin,
Within six hours Jinan was ours,
This little village Taierzhuang,
Why does it take so long to fall?

Taierzhuang, did not then fall but was held and won by the Chinese. What plunged was the faith of Japan's army in its own invincibility. However, the morale of the aggressor troops was far from broken. On our way to the newly-recovered town through a seemingly bare field, a wounded Japanese soldier left alone in a shell hole covered by a blanket, shot at us repeatedly until at last killed by our armed escort. Since he could have escaped notice as we passed, his was a deliberate "suicide of honor" by a man deeply indoctrinated by the Japanese army. He must have been convinced that falling into Chinese hands meant a cruel death or, if he survived as a prisoner, a disgrace to the emperor and eternally to his own memory and family in Japan. Pity, said one of our Chinese companions, that none of us could speak Japanese—to try and coax him out.

Carlson recalled, from his own recent experience, that in the battle-zones led by the Chinese Communists, such work was regular and organized. There he had met captured Japanese soldiers who not only stayed alive—including some who at the onset tried to kill themselves or provoke their Chinese guards to kill them—but gradually changed their whole outlook. Told they could go back to their own units or stay, they chose the latter. More, some became convinced that China's war was just and Japan's was bad for the Japanese people as well as for the Chinese—and undertook perilous yet effective publicity: yelling into a megaphone within earshot of their own former units, as devoted to their new perceptions as they had been to the mystique of the Emperor.

* * *

Despite the Taierzhuang victory, the Chinese front in the surrounding territory began noticeably to unravel in late May 1938. Xuzhou, within a few weeks, fell to greatly augmented Japanese forces.

Then, when the invaders began to drive towards Wuhan, Chiang Kai-shek ordered the opening of dikes on the Yellow River to put a raging flood across their path. Not stopping the enemy for long, it also drowned countless villages and hundreds of thousands of Chinese. This again was in sharp contrast with the Communist-led areas. There only the enemy devastated villages and fields, while the people strove to preserve them intact or, if lost, to recover and rebuild them. Hence, after Taierzhuang, the difference between the two battlefronts, not just in tactics, but in basic outlook, stood out more sharply.

Politically, the Right-wing and capitulatory forces within the Guomindang, temporarily dormant but not reduced, came back onstage. Their ranks had grown through the return from seeming exile in Europe and elsewhere of Wang Jingwei, the Guomindang's vice-chairman, together with a number of his clique. The softly handsome Wang was a political chameleon, like an actor changing roles. In 1926-27 he had headed the revolutionary united front government in Wuhan in opposition to Chiang Kai-shek, then, like Chiang, massacred the Left, and contended with Chiang unsuccessfully for power in the reactionary camp. Traveling abroad, he had flirted with Mussolini and the German Nazis. Yet when he reappeared in Wuhan in 1938 it was in the disguise of a patriot eager to join in the war with Japan. The lieutenants he brought on his coat-tails, Chen Gongbo and Zhou Fuhai, were even more adept at color-change. They had been among the twelve delegates at the founding Congress of the Chinese Communist Party in 1921, then moved through the Left wing of the Guomindang to its Right wing. Installed in the wartime government in Wuhan, both held, successively, the post of Minister of Information. Both were to bolt with Wang into the Japanese camp in 1940, and die as condemned traitors: Zhou in prison, Chen by execution, after Japan's defeat.

My personal memories of all three were not pleasant. Wang's handshake at public functions was boneless, lifeless, and soft as a marshmallow. The dapper, womanizing Chen, once a student at Columbia University, seemed always to be acting. He, and the bespectacled Zhou Fuhai, when among reporters, noticeably seemed to cozy up to those speaking German or Japanese.

Also, in this complex period, there was a major defection from the Communist Party. Zhang Guotao, a Central Committee member since its 1921 founding, and for a time even of the Executive Committee of the Communist International, slipped into Guomindang territory alone (even his personal guard did not accompany him). A careerist, he had a long habit of appearing Left or Right depending on the issue. Gradually, personal ambition emerged as his chief motive. During the Long March he had split the Party's political and military ranks, ultimately leading the Fourth Red Army, which he commanded, to near-annihilation by Muslim warlords in far Western China. There he had hoped to seek safety near the border with the Soviet Union—by contrast with the troops under Mao Zedong who marched instead toward the battlefield with Japan. After defecting, he held various positions under the Guomindang, some nominally high but none with authority, and, after the founding of the People's Republic, fled first to Hong Kong and then to Canada, where he died.

*　　*　　*

One of my side trips from Wuhan in 1938 was to Changsha, capital of Hunan, the home province of Mao Zedong. There I saw a simple but significant token of the undying spirit of the revolutionary mid-1920's: surviving despite murderous repression. In other Chinese cities the rickshaw pullers were apt to race to please their customers. In Changsha they would at most go at a fast walk. Their frequent retort to passengers urging them to go faster was to lower the vehicle's shafts, saying, "Get out and run yourself!" This was the heritage in health protection and dignity of a victorious strike, many years before, of the once strong and militant Rickshawmen's Union, although the organization itself was long crushed.

*　　*　　*

Wuhan's role as temporary wartime capital ended in late October 1938 when it, too, fell to the Japanese. At the top level of the Guomindang the drift toward the Right increased, and even though Chiang Kai-shek made new declarations of resistance to Japan (especially after Wang Jingwei's flagrant treason), there was no clearing out of the capitulatory elements still within the coalition. But at other levels, the positive mood of the earlier months persisted.

Among the foreign press in Wuhan, I myself did not become a

"Last Ditcher." In July 1938 I was transferred to another major Chinese city—and Japanese objective: Guangzhou, known abroad in those days as Canton. Becoming a key front, and fiercely and continually bombed, it was at last captured by the Japanese in October, the same month as Wuhan.

It was in Guangzhou where I became a true "Last Ditcher," not in name but in fact, witnessing the city's fall, and having to scramble out of the ditch afterwards.

Chapter 9

GUANGZHOU

Guangzhou was both a high point and a low point in the Guomindang-ruled area in wartime. High in popular courage under long-sustained Japanese bombing and the persistent threat of invasion; Low in quick disintegration at the top despite loud official pledges to lead in resistance. Once the enemy landed and began to advance, officialdom there ran out on the people.

In five months in Guangzhou, June to October 1938, I saw it all: The worst of the terror bombings; the subsequent resurgence of popular organization, and finally the evacuation and fall of the city. At the short-lived front, following the enemy landing, I observed some military causes for the speedy collapse. Trying to leave the occupied city, I witnessed, for days in the countryside, the spread of Japanese control and the reaction of the rural population.

That famed southern city, when I arrived in mid-summer, was the last top-level Chinese seaport not yet seized by Japan. It had faced foreign assaults and threats since the Opium War of the 1840s, and consistently fought back. From the turn of the nineteenth to the twentieth century, it had been a cradle of two of China's modern revolutions, that led by Sun Yat-sen which by 1911 finally toppled China's ancient monarchy, and that of 1924-27, which strove heroically to free China from control by foreign powers externally and by feudal warlords internally. From the vicinity of this metropolis came most of the "Overseas Chinese"—emigrants to Southeast Asia and the Americas, intensely eager for progress in their ancestral areas and in China as a whole.

From my first day there the people of Guangzhou, shorter and slighter than their compatriots further to the north, impressed me with the ebullient energy reflected in their limber bodies, burning black eyes, and quick, loud speech. What would pass for unusual excitement elsewhere was here considered the normal tone of conversation.

Also, Guangzhou in 1938 was ablaze with patriotism. Daily Japanese bombings were accompanied by enemy taunts, by radio and leaflet:

"Why doesn't your government send planes to defend you?" But in Guangzhou mass demonstrations would demand that China's government *not* send those planes, but keep them for the defense of Wuhan— the country's provisional capital. Such was Guangzhou's national spirit.

For weeks before I arrived, the Japanese had been using the crowded city as a training ground for their young and raw bomber pilots. On my second day there, 2,000 civilians lay dead along the Pearl River waterfront. Each flight of enemy planes was not large, but they came in constant relays. On June 6, there were 1,500 more corpses. Direct hits turned men, women, and children into unidentifiable shreds of flesh and bone. Quivering wounded people sobbed, pinned down by fallen concrete.

On some consecutive nights, even when fewer bombs were dropped, planes droned overhead ceaselessly, to murder sleep. Around the clock, weary crowds stood on the banks of the creek bordering the British and French concessions, at whose bridges foreign armed guards prevented entry. The terror from the air over Guangzhou was then unparalleled except by Hitler's fliers over Republican Spain. The aim of the Japanese was to demoralize Guangzhou by terror.

But the city's did not crack or bend. Volunteer Red Cross and firefighting squads, and young Boy Scouts, worked unflinchingly under the bombs. Essential services were kept functioning. Newspapers appeared regularly. At numerous outdoor meetings, young and old contributed funds for resistance, the women often donating gold ornaments and family jewelry. Tea houses, the beloved day and night resorts of the Cantonese, stayed full. Movie theaters showed, endlessly, the same American films (the suppliers in Hong Kong refused to risk replacements). On June 6, London-based artist Jack Chen, son of a one-time Chinese Minister of Foreign Affairs appointed by Sun Yat-sen in the revolutionary Guangzhou of the 1920s, gave an exhibition of anti-Fascist art in a building at whose doors many people had been killed the same day. Guangzhou's mayor was among the large crowd in attendance. There was promise, in the atmosphere, of the upsurge of popular organization the city would witness in months to come.

As in Wuhan and elsewhere, I quickly found the congenial, to me, milieu of progressive intellectuals and students. In the young staff of the *National Salvation Daily* (Jiuwang Ribao), edited by Xia Yan, commentator, playwright, and a pioneer of modern Chinese film; and Shang Zhongyi, a former professor of Beijing University, were its avuncular seniors—though themselves scarcely out of their thirties.

Closely associated was a group of young woodcut and poster artists and cartoonists whose militant placards were often seen in the streets or displayed at meetings. I asked Miao Yifan, a slim, serious student aged 19 or 20 who was going down to the coast menaced by the Japanese, to do a story for UP when he returned. But he never did, dying on his way of the cholera raging there. The book I wrote many years later, *The Unfinished Revolution in China*, was dedicated, among others, to this eager student patriot.

In mid-June the raids temporarily subsided. Attention, both domestic and international, shifted to the Japanese drive materializing against Wuhan. To obstruct this, on June 10, Chiang Kai-shek had opened the Yellow River dikes. Blocked by flood, the Japanese did not stop, but switched their route to the Yangtze valley, using land, naval and air forces—and poison gas.

Some Guomindang units were let down by decadent generals. When the Japanese attacked the river forts at Matang, the commander was away feasting in town. Its defense leaderless, this key strongpoint along the Yangtze fell in a day—and Japanese warships moved easily through its reputedly impassable boom which proved as shoddy in construction as its defense in organization.

Then, for a few weeks, the enemy advance was slowed. In part by stronger stands by regular forces under the Guomindang. In part by an upsurge of guerrilla warfare in the enemy's rear areas by the Communist-led Eighth Route Army (in northern China) and New Fourth Army (on the lower Yangtze). The cumulative effect was to reduce the pressure of the Japanese on Wuhan and limit their ability to move reinforcements there.

International factors also played a part.

Feeling for weaknesses along the Soviet frontier with occupied Northeast China, Japanese troops at Zhanggufeng (not far from Vladivostok) were thrown back so vigorously that a Tokyo spokesman could find nothing to talk about except the weight of Russian artillery fire, and the Japanese soldiers' difficulty in bearing it, let alone winning it.

Foiled in northward probing by land, the General Staff in Tokyo turned toward the more promising alternative of naval and amphibious attacks on the Western powers' positions in the Pacific. On the principle of "a soft answer turneth away wrath," Tory-ruled Britain flirted with a new division of spheres of influence in China with Japan. In Wuhan, Wang Jingwei urged better relations with Germany and Italy—potential mediators of a capitulatory Sino-Japanese "peace." This was in tune with the gathering tide of appeasement of Hitler fascism by Britain and France, already apparent after the German seizure of Austria months earlier, and before Czechoslovakia was cast to the wolves in the Munich Pact signed on September 30. This in turn emboldened the Japanese to strike at Wuhan and Guangzhou simultaneously.

* * *

On October 12, 1938 the Japanese grab for Guangzhou began with a beachhead landing at the isolated coastal village of Hachong. No resistance was put up by an archaic local general called Mo Xide. Mo was a *poseur* known for the ferocity of his military airs and training methods. He, together with his cronies, was also known for his involvement in the smuggling of tungsten ore to Hong Kong, and, ultimately, to the Japanese. In the Cantonese pronunciation, Mo's full name sounded like "Mock Hay Duck," which he was thenceforth dubbed in English conversation by irreverent foreign correspondents. For his non-performance in defense, he was arrested and court-martialed. But in the meantime the enemy, from the first bridgehead, and promptly followed by others, landed hammerhead armored columns in quick succession. These, with strong naval aircraft cover, partly punctured, partly outflanked and often destroyed the Chinese deployments in their path. Huizhou, east of Guangzhou, was levelled by bombs which a British engineer there described as falling "at the rate of ten seconds each for two bloody midday hours."

Inside a week, the Japanese were at Guangzhou's door. During a bizarre twelve-hour night taxi tour of the front, I, together with two other newsmen, found myself first accompanying the spearhead of a momentary Chinese advance, then darting back to dodge a fast counterstroke by the enemy.

Initially, for 30 miles or so, moving eastward from the city, we saw only large-scale movements of Chinese troops, parade-ground in precision and with no signs of battle. Finally, we came abreast of dozens of Chinese Vickers Whippet light tanks accompanied by motorcycles and a long hearse-like vehicle serving as a staff car. The officers inside proposed that we follow behind. But we moved on beyond them.

Then, suddenly, we met motorcycles and foot soldiers hurrying in the opposite direction. They shouted that Japanese tanks were straight ahead and had machine-gunned some unaware buses. The hearse, and we, turned tail. Soon we were amid a reverse movement of Chinese mechanized units and heavy artillery, suggesting that no stand would be made, probably due to successful Japanese outflanking.

Back at our hotel, we decided to go to the front again the next morning. Instead, the front came to us, with a rumble of numerous tanks along the Pearl River. From further off we could hear the blast of dynamite, as important sites were blown up by the last departing Chinese troops. Civilians were also fleeing.

Venturing deeper into town I found twenty Japanese tanks clanking, unhindered, along a main thoroughfare, leaving, as tokens of their passing, only some bullet-ridden walls and the crumpled bodies of four civilian men, one girl and one soldier, and two bullet holes in the American flag outside the YMCA. Overhead, Japanese planes droned as they circled low.

At the day's end, Japanese armor dominated the roads into Guangzhou which, only the night before, we had seen swarming with relatively well-equipped and mechanized Chinese troops. Those that survived did not retreat through the city but along by-paths on either side of the Guangzhou-Huizhou road.

We, the casually taxi-borne newsmen of a few hours earlier, had in fact been close to sudden death. The Chinese unit with which we had traveled until 4 a.m. was decimated before dawn by dive-bombing planes (on the pattern of the "Stuka" Nazi aircraft in Spain) and the tanks that followed. The desperate battle of men against machines began at 5 a.m.

In the city during the day we chanced on a California-born Chinese battalion commander, to whom we had given a lift the night before. Now haggard and out of uniform, he said he had not at first believed the talk of Japanese tanks down the road because his orders had been to take up a position in a supposedly second line of defense further ahead. What follows is his account, which I have put into quotation marks because, though I no longer recall it word for word, I do remember vividly its sequence and spirit:

"But we never saw any second line. Instead, we received a new order that each unit should operate independently, signifying a Japanese break-through. An hour afterwards, the Japanese planes discovered us. Keeping under cover as much as possible, we at first didn't reply to the machine-gunning, but after some men were killed their furious comrades opened fire.

Then the Japanese determined to wipe us out. First six tanks advanced on us. We knocked out four. Then about fifty Japanese planes came in waves. Our soldiers propped up anti-tank guns on improvised bamboo tripods to hold them off. But after Japanese had dropped about three hundred small bombs, those guns were out of action. Men were blown high all around me. By noon, only 275 were left out of our 500. We destroyed our heavier arms and came here cross-country. Now I'm trying to find out which way our headquarters went."

In Guangzhou, in the meantime, the spirited rallies that continued almost to the last, in some cases with distribution of rifles to civilians, gave way to mass exodus, people carrying what possessions they could and leaving the rest, more in a last gesture of defiance than in panic.

* * *

In retrospect, just before and after the Japanese landing, mass morale in Guangzhou remained high. Even a day or two before the enemy entry, there were huge mobilizing rallies, and brave-sounding speeches by top officials. In fact, as distinct from their audience, the latter were preparing for a quick getaway. Neither in the city nor its environs did they appear to have left a presence or substitution. For the moment, the people were left in confusion. Afterwards—and their patriotism was shown mainly by their own evacuation, more complete and rapid from Guangzhou than I had seen elsewhere. Hundreds of thousands of its citizens simply refused to live under the Japanese yoke.

Only later would armed resistance around Guangzhou take shape—in the East River Column and related guerrilla formations, under Communist leadership.

* * *

That this movement was not organized, and did not gel into previously prepared cells of resistance in the outskirts, was a result of the unseemly flight of the political and military authorities out of the city.

From October 27 to 31, American freelance cameraman Rey Scott and I tried to make our way out of the fallen city and toward Hong Kong, but failed and had to retrace our steps. Back at the Victoria Hotel within the British Concession, I wrote a UP dispatch which, by a standing arrangement, it was still possible to send via Naval radio, through the transmitter of the U.S. gunboat anchored in the Pearl River:

> Have just returned from four days in No Man's Land during which I witnessed a Japanese landing at a hitherto untouched river port, was subsequently chased by three Japanese planes and bombed for 45 minutes, and walked and boated a total of 80 miles.

Scott and I had tried to get out by way of back creeks and by-paths in order to bring out the first pictures of the Japanese occupation. The Japanese were blocking the delta waterways with constant aerial surveillance, patrols by armed launches and landing parties of a hundred or so men each at key points.

However, they had not yet penetrated far by land, and a 20-mile radius around Guangzhou was a virtual no man's land with the Chinese authorities gone and the Japanese army not yet arrived.

In ten or so villages we passed through, the inhabitants were spiritedly discussing two questions: first, what to do when the Japanese arrived, and second, how to keep from being swept away by the flood of refugees.

In a suburb of Foshan consisting of one mile-long street, armed civilians had driven a small Japanese force back toward the railway station. A typical solution for dealing with refugees was to give them one meal and move them along.

Blue–clad village self-defense militia wearing sashes denoting their function carried rifles and Mausers, checking up on travelers and defending their homes. But alongside the effective small-scale organization was an almost complete absence of communication and coordination. Some villagers only ten miles from Guangzhou steadfastly refused to believe that "real Japanese" had entered the city. Even those who had resisted the Japanese in nearby Foshan insisted that they had repelled only Chinese traitors masquerading under the Japanese flag.

There seemed to be no Chinese troops in this area. The only evidence of more widespread organization was in one village where a score of reticent student-type youngsters, eager for every scrap of news we could give them about things we had experienced. They seemed to be planning to assume leadership of the scattered defenders of the countryside, still doubted the fall of Guangzhou but were unable to find confirmation from refugees who had left it before the enemy entered.

On our way, Japanese planes dropped bombs close to our hired sampan, seemingly suspicious of anything that moved. Once, a Japanese patrol launch passed within ten yards without noticing us two foreigners—Scott and myself—crouching under the matting roof.

We had with us two Browning .45 pistols lent by the U.S. gunboat, at Rey's request, for protection from robbers. But it would have been fatal to attempt to resist the Japanese with them.

Ultimately, increasing obstacles forced us to retreat back to Guangzhou. From there I finally sailed to Hong Kong as a passenger on a Standard Oil Company launch: The West would not be at war with Japan until Pearl Harbor, more than three years later.

As a final service to Guangzhou's patriotic Chinese intellectuals, I brought, in two large tin canisters, a full set of the *National Salvation Daily (Jiuwang Ribao)* entrusted to me by its editors—which I returned to them when they themselves later got to Hong Kong.

*   *   *

During my stay in Guangzhou, Soong Ching-ling, the highly principled and revered widow of the "Father of the Chinese Republic," Sun Yat-sen, came to the city twice. Her presence at this life and death juncture for the people and nation was deeply meaningful because she had lived and worked in the city in two previous important periods in China— Sun Yat-sen's struggle to maintain the momentum of the Revolution of 1911 which overthrew China's ancient monarchy, and in preparation for the Revolution of 1924-27 against foreign control and feudal warlordism.

On her August 1938 visit I did not see her, but transmitted through the UP a statement she then made, which clearly expressed her key outlook. She had said:

> I have returned to Canton for the first time in 12 years...to see for myself the spirit with which my own people—the Cantonese—have withstood the savage Japanese bombings...
>
> China's strength lies in her people. The war which the Japanese are waging in China is one of total aggression—no distinction between military and civilians. The only effective answer is total resistance... Without general mobilization of the entire people, China cannot win.
>
> Even after a year of war this is not sufficiently understood. Many offi-

cials tend to rely more on foreign powers… When the international situation seems against us as when Germany recognizes 'Manchukuo' or there are rumors of Anglo-Japanese negotiations, they say in despair all is lost. When there are indications that South China will be invaded, that the British and Japanese are at odds… or when Japan provokes the Soviet Union on the border they say, 'The foreign powers must now intervene and we are saved.' This is the attitude of a weak and semi-colonial state which can only survive by depending on others. It shows lack of faith in the power of the people— the only thing that can and will save China… The extent to which we can mobilize our own people and resources will determine whether we win. Not that we do not desire foreign aid… For all help given to us, we are grateful.

To the people of America, I wish to say: Your sympathy is with China, but many bullets which kill our soldiers at the front, and the bombs that have fallen upon the defenseless population of this city were made of American scrap iron. Japan's economy is dependent on the United States. These facts should be put clearly before the American people.

Prophetically, two and a half years before Pearl Harbor, she added:

Today Japanese planes burn your oil to bomb us. Tomorrow they will be over the Philippines and Hawaii. You are building a navy to defend yourself against a menace which unscrupulous American business helps create. What are the American people going to do about this?

My first personal meeting with Soong Ching-ling was during her last visit to Guangzhou, on September 18, 1938, the anniversary of the Japanese seizure of Northeast China in 1931—a searing memory of national humiliation. But on that day in Guangzhou, the day blazed with defiance and courage. At night, tens of thousands of civilians paraded through the streets with burning torches. If enemy warplanes were sighted on the coast, they could reach Guangzhou within fifteen minutes, but even that did not deter the people. With them in the front rank marched Soong Ching-ling in calm determination. This was my earliest, indelible sight of her—though I had long known her by reputation.

Within the next 24 hours, we met and talked. The meeting was a group comprised of both Chinese and foreigners whom Soong Ching-ling had called together because she knew they denounced the Japanese bombings. She was inviting us to form a Guangzhou branch of the China Defense League, founded by her in Hong Kong. The League's task was to mobilize support abroad, with medical and other supplies, for China's armed resistance—and in particular its most effective element, the guerrilla warfare that was recovering so much land from the enemy. I was included in this group for my reporting of Guangzhou's ordeal. Also because she knew of my contributions to *Voice of China*, the patriotic English language journal she had sponsored in Shanghai.

A day or so later, she had asked me to come along when she met with the Indian National Congress Medical Mission organized by Jawaharlal Nehru, now bound for the front. The mission included the valiant young Dr. Dwarkanath Kotnis, who would take over the work of Dr. Norman Bethune.

The Guangzhou Branch of the China Defense League never got properly started, as the city quickly fell to the Japanese. But my association with Soong Ching-ling, the China Defense League, and her other undertakings was to last more than four decades and be a determinant factor of my subsequent life. Ultimately, I was to undertake, at her request, the writing of her biography to be published after her death, in 1981, in which she was named honorary President of the People's Republic of China, the only individual ever to hold this title.

Chapter 10

HONG KONG

Japan's seizure of Guangzhou ended my first period of war reporting, and soon after I went to Hong Kong. There I would spend more than a year working with Soong Ching-ling to publicize and enlist worldwide support for China's cause.

The change proved a watershed in my entire life. Hong Kong, an old-style "crown colony" of Great Britain since its seizure from China in the Opium War a century earlier, was outwardly tranquil and distinct from the turmoil of war which raged in the countryside only miles to the north. Its façade, not surprisingly, remained Victorian, redolent of the nineteenth century, and very different from the jungle of concrete, steel, and glass that would sprout after World War II. Administrative buildings and financial houses were of brick and stone, festooned with columns and balconies, weightily representing the old imperial, monied power of British interests.

On the hillsides, lush, green, and semi-tropically wooded with sturdy banyans and scarlet-blossomed bougainvillea, stood many bungalow-type houses for the colonial officials and wealthy Chinese. The main commercial thoroughfares, along the harbor, could just as well have been in London. The narrow streets branching from them teemed with petty shopkeepers, peddlers, and artisans plying their trades like those existing for centuries in China's southern cities. On the reverse side of all the above was a jumble of slums and shanties, the abodes of the working poor.

In Hong Kong's governance, 95 per cent of the inhabitants, who were Chinese, had no legal status. Nor indeed did the foreigners, even Britons outside official and military service. For there were no elected bodies: all authority stemmed from the governor appointed from London. But among the population, overwhelmingly Chinese and including many wartime arrivals, political directions reflected those of the mainland. In short, the colonial pattern slept intact, cheek-by-jowl, with China's desperate struggle for survival.

Most importantly, Hong Kong, at that time, was the only remaining main conduit between the outside world and the locale of the China war.

* * *

After leaving Guangzhou I was discharged by UP. Once Guangzhou fell, and then Wuhan, UP seemed to judge that China's resistance would crumble. It reduced the number of reporters from the Chinese side of the lines, but not the Japanese side where it expected the real story would be. Not negligible was the fact that newspapers in Japan were the main Asian buyers of news from UP, while a top American executive in the Far East, Tokyo bureau manager Miles Vaughn, was said to have invested heavily in Japanese Imperial War Bonds.

And who was more eligible for firing than me since I was "too pro-Chinese" and not employable in the occupied areas. Moreover, I was cheap to let go—being locally hired, with no contractual claim on severance pay, repatriation passage, and other "home staff" privileges.

To me, this separation was less an end than a beginning. Soong Ching-ling quickly asked me to join the Central Committee of the China Defense League in Hong Kong. My function was to edit and produce its English-language publications. This work—volunteer and unpaid—became my key motive for staying in the colony. A job with a local daily paper, obtained soon after, provided me with bread and butter.

What made Soong Ching-ling start the China Defense League in Hong Kong, and not elsewhere? War-torn inland China was suffering from two blockades. One blockade was by the Japanese invaders who controlled the coast. Another, rapidly developing, was the Chiang Kai-shek government's ban on supplies—even medical supplies—getting through to the anti-Japanese forces and bases led by the Chinese Communist Party, as well as a gag on news of their military and political successes.

The League's task was to puncture both blockades, ensuring that no sector was unfairly deprived of access to outside, or of the right to have its voice heard.

Hong Kong—a seaport then still open to most of the world—was the best "window" for such an effort. Soong Ching-ling, in consultation with Zhou Enlai, went there and helped made it a channel for support from anti-Fascist forces throughout the world, and from the overseas Chinese community abroad. This was intended to strengthen the united front of China's two main parties and its entire people in fighting the invaders.

To be the pillar and soul of that undertaking, Soong was irreplaceably fitted by her history, firmness of principle, and magnetic personality. She was respected throughout the world as the widow of the leader of China's Republican Revolution. Equally, she was known for her undeviating devotion to China's patriotism and unity in the name of progress, her purity of motive, and her personal incorruptibility. Her warm personality enabled her to make deep friendships, Chinese and foreign, and unite people of varying views on points of common interest. She could hold her own among the world's most famed and powerful leaders, yet her modesty could make the youngest and humblest feel at ease with her.

Our China Defense League committee in Hong Kong was small, vigorous, and young. Soong Ching-ling, then age 45, was regarded as its mother figure. Liao Chengzhi, important as the Hong Kong representative of the Communist Party and its anti-Japanese armed forces, was 30. The other members were in their thirties or late twenties, while I, the youngest, was just turning 23. Around Soong Ching-ling and this small core was a large and varied circle of volunteers, who, because of her prestige, were available at her every call.

Politically, especially in its first two years, the sponsorship of the League and its support groups abroad was also very wide. Soong Ching-ling secured, as its first president, her brother, T.V. Soong (Soong Ziwen), a high-ranking Guomindang official. In the United States, the honorary head of the China Aid Council, which sent funds through the League, was the mother of President Franklin Delano Roosevelt.

In her relations with co-workers within the League, Soong Ching-ling was thoroughly democratic. Though a nationally and internationally-known figure, she treated all as equals. Whatever the job—from typing letters in the office, to packing crates with relief supplies, she did her share of the work alongside the rest of us. At meetings she chaired, everyone felt free to voice suggestions and opinions, before she gave hers, or after. Chinese members saw the fight of their own nation for survival as part of the worldwide struggle for progress against regression and aggression. Foreign members upheld the Chinese people's resistance to Japan as part of the worldwide anti-Fascist cause.

In Hong Kong, I shared an apartment with Donald Allen, an American teacher also in his twenties, who as a volunteer helped the League, the Industrial Cooperatives and other anti-Fascist causes. Once we invited Soong Ching-ling to a home-cooked lunch. But our joy when she readily accepted was immediately followed by alarm as we had no tablecloth, and so instead substituted a clean but quite obvious-looking bed sheet. After we had eaten and talked about League and other matters, she thanked us, and then asked archly: "Which one of you sleeps under this cloth? Tell me before I go." We all laughed together. That's how she was: strong willed and an indomitable fighter, yet relaxing and a pleasure to be around for those much younger.

In 1939-40, the work of the League grew fast. Contacts were established with progressive China-aid organizations abroad, foreign sympathizers, and overseas Chinese communities.

From many parts of the globe came monetary contributions of money and relief goods. Donations were also made by foreign seamen who passed the hat among their shipmates, bringing the cash to our office, and went off with sheaves of our literature to distribute. For every gift, large or small, Soong Ching-ling herself signed the receipt.

Transport of supplies to the mainland was still possible. Truck and ambulance convoys were sent in through French-controlled Vietnam. Field hospitals in the resistance areas—mainly those behind the enemy lines—were organized, following the example set by Dr. Bethune. As authorized by the anti-Fascist International Peace Campaign, they were named International Peace Hospitals. Nurseries and kindergartens were set up for war orphans and children of parents who had sent them away while remaining behind at the battlefront or in occupied areas.

Assisted projects in the Guomindang areas included the Medical Relief Corps of the Chinese Red Cross, and in both the Guomindang and Communist-led areas, the Chinese Industrial Cooperatives. In the latter, workers, especially refugees from the Japanese-occupied cities, were organized in self-employed, self-managed, self-salaried productive units to meet the urgent needs of many localities for civilian consumers, as well as those of the armed-struggle—such as army blankets and, in the guerrilla areas, weapons.

These co-ops were pioneered by an international group composed of Chinese patriots and foreign friends. Among the latter, Edgar and

Helen Snow did much to publicize them internationally, and Rewi Alley worked indefatigably in the field. Soong Ching-ling, who lauded co-operative economic forms, as an embodiment of Sun Yat-sen's Principle of the People's Livelihood, consented to be honorary chairwoman of the International Committee for Chinese Industrial Cooperatives set up in Hong Kong, and patronized various activities on their behalf.

* * *

In Hong Kong, the China Defense League organized fund-raisers and bazaars, with donations coming from two sources—the working population, and prosperous enterprises, both Chinese and foreign. For both sources, the name of Soong Ching-ling was the catalyst which drove the successive campaigns. Though openly liberal in her views, she had such prestige that the governor of Hong Kong, Sir Geoffrey Northcote, felt it incumbent on him to attend functions sponsored by her.

In China's politics, much attention was thus paid, when, in the fight against Wang Jingwei's treasonous defection to the Japanese, Soong Ching-ling appeared with her two sisters: Soong Ai-ling (Mrs. H.H. Kung) and Soong Mei-ling (Madame Chiang Kai-shek), for the first time in many years. In April, 1940, the trio went to Chongqing in a demonstration of solidarity for resistance to Japan and in opposition of Wang's capitulation.

In the same period, as a tribute to the China Defense League's reputation for incorruptibility, the "Friends of the Wounded," an organization headed nationally by Madame Chiang, designated the League as auditor of its fund-raising drives in Hong Kong.

Yet, in China, the united front that had seemed so promising in the Wuhan period was unraveling dangerously by the close of the decade. In June 1939, in Pinjiang, Hunan Province, two staff members of the representative office of the Communist-led New Fourth Army were shot and four others were buried alive by Guomindang authorities. A mass protest meeting in Yan'an demanded that such things never occur again. However, cases of sabotage of the united front multiplied in various parts of the country, including armed incursions into Communist-administered bases. That they were not accidental but systematic was indicated by the publication and issuing, to Guomindang military and civil officials, of "Regulations for Control of the Alien Party." Anti-

Communist provocations included disguising Guomindang agents and gangster groups as Eighth Route Army soldiers to create the illusion that the Communists trafficked in opium. The Communist-led forces, meanwhile, reiterated that the Guomindang soldiers were simply "roaming" the Japanese-occupied territories, not fighting the enemy there.

Factual rebuttals made by Mao Zedong, Zhu De, and other leading Communists, stressed the need for cementing, not disrupting, inter-party unity. Nonetheless, the Guomindang continued its accusations and insinuations, which in time would harden into mantras repeated without end, and without proof. Even years later, when permission was finally extracted from the Chongqing authorities for foreign reporters (including myself) to visit the areas led by the Communists, these charges were dinned into us before the journey. In months of travel in the "accused" regions, we found no basis for them in fact.

* * *

Hong Kong, in 1939-40, had its own pressures. Britain's ambassador to China called on Soong Ching-ling, urging that she refrain from political comment, especially her criticism of the Guomindang authorities (the advocacy did not accord with the personal views of the envoy himself, but he had his orders from London). And both earlier and afterwards, the Hong Kong government was very nervous about angering Tokyo. In the Chinese language press of the colony, explicit references to Japanese aggression and war atrocities were not allowed (the forbidden adjective was replaced with an "X"). For Britain's own imperial reasons, Hong Kong's people could not be referred to in the Chinese press as *Zhongguo ren* (Chinese), but only as *Hua ren* (of Chinese origin). And Hong Kong's censors banned plain-spoken films on the war in China, for example, the China Defense League was unable to screen Joris Ivens's first-hand documentary *Land of the Four Hundred Million* made during our trip to Taierzhuang.

* * *

While work in the League focused on the politics and warfronts of China, my local newspaper job, although also serving China's interest, was in the midst of Hong Kong's long-preserved colonial milieu. Soong

Ching-ling, knowing that I needed paid employment, asked Morris ("Two Gun") Cohen, her husband's former Canadian (though London-born) bodyguard, who knew Hong Kong well and actually held the rank of Brigadier General in the Chinese Army—earning his nickname for his pistol-shooting skills—if he could think of a preferably journalistic publication. He did: The *Hong Kong Daily Press*, the oldest English-language paper in the colony, founded in the 1850s or so and for several decades prestigious, had fallen on hard times. Part-sold to the Guomindang it was being geared to promote China's cause against Japan. Amid internal squabbles, it needed a new editor. With her recommendation, I applied.

Next came an interview with the Guomindang official in charge, Yu Hongjun (known as "O.K. Yui"), an ex-mayor of Shanghai. In Hong Kong he headed the Guomindang's "Central Trust" which was financing the paper. Suave and English-speaking Yu was an alumnus of the University of Michigan and had himself been a reporter before entering politics under the patronage of the eldest and youngest Soong sisters, Soong Ai-ling and Soong Mei-ling, respectively. Yu seemed satisfied with my journalistic experience, and not put off by my youth. Nor had the united front against Japan soured sufficiently to warrant rejection of a recommendation by Soong Ching-ling. What mainly counted was that I was on China's side. Not negligible, too, was my willingness to take a salary far below that of editors of rival English-language papers.

The *Hong Kong Daily Press*, I discovered, was a riddle and a riddle in a bit of a shambles at that. Its typeface fonts were worn and long unchanged, and its printing inferior to that of its competitors. Who really owned it was a mystery. Part of its shares (referred to as "debentures"), were held by Colonel Murrow, a ruddy-faced, white-haired scion of its founding family. Not a journalist, he had returned to head the family paper after a lifetime in the British army in India. Another block of shares had been bought by the Guomindang government. A third shareholder could be the key—in alliance with either the British or the Chinese holdings—to control the property. But where was it? Dormant and inoperative in the forgotten, moldy trunk of some dead or senile Murrow relative? Or acquired and secretly held by one of the disputing Guomindang factions until the time came to outmaneuver the other?

Discounting this risk, the faction backed by Yu was crowding out the other in a creeping siege—desk by desk and chair by chair. Soon I was in charge, with a small staff—a young Scottish sub-editor named

MacNider, two senior reporters—a journalistically professional British-Chinese Eurasian named Alec Greaves, a tall intelligent Sinhalese whose surname, Jansz, harked back to the seventeenth and eighteenth century Dutch occupation of Sri Lanka, and a self-effacing young White Russian whose name I have sadly forgotten. Also there was a large bony American woman signing herself A.W. Hyer (I never knew her first name) who ran the shipping news and personal arrivals and departures column, and did not hesitate, on occasion, to jovially address me—though her junior in years, but her superior as editor—as a "futump" with no hint of respect. I took it in stride since she did her job and was not an intriguer. No Chinese, as I recall, served on the editorial staff—only on the printing and business side—a situation typical in Hong Kong then.

Our big headache was circulation. We were—and it showed—far poorer than our British-owned competitors, the *South China Morning Post*, *Hong Kong Telegraph*, and *China Mail*. One day, I checked the streets to see how our paper was being sold by the middle-aged women who were Hong Kong's equivalent of newsboys. Seeing only rival papers draped over their forearms, which was their method of display, I asked one, "Don't you have the *Daily Press*?" "Sure," she said, dragging out a copy from the bottom of her stack.

"Why carry it there?"

"To keep the sweat from my arm off the *Post*," was her crushing answer.

Despite all disadvantages, we put some real work into the *Daily Press*, and not entirely in vain.

Our editorials, many written by me, were often straight-talking and spirited, with a sting that sometimes attracted notice.

We denounced continuing Japanese aggression in China and criticized Western—in particular, British—tendencies to appease it, both before, and especially after, the 1939 outbreak of war in Europe.

While the front against Germany was for months idle in what was called the "phony war," we criticized the temporarily rising advocacy of a Western switch to an "alternative front," a transparent code word for intervention against the Soviet Union—then engaged in a border war with Finland flanking nearby Leningrad.

When the turncoat Wang Jingwei clique set up a pro-Japanese puppet "Republic of China" government in Nanjing, we castigated not only the open treachery of the act but also the scheme to turn China's national war into a civil war, glossing over foreign aggression, and enabling other powers to pledge ostensible neutrality while in fact moving towards granting belligerent status to the Wang regime, as was virtually done in Spain with Franco. Similarly we flayed Japanese Premier Konoye's sudden seductive talk of peace which was related to overtures by Wang Jingwei for reconciliation with Chiang (under the auspices of Japan). In relation to all such maneuvers, we called for support of Chiang's anti-capitulatory stance.

And even though the paper was Guomindang-owned, I managed, editorially, to occasionally mention the guerrilla war led by the Communists, including, by name, the resistance bases behind enemy lines—a rare occurrence in Hong Kong's English-language press, even though there were some references in the news columns.

With regard to distorted accounts of the situation in China percolating from the Japanese-occupied areas, we polemicized with the *Reuters* Shanghai office for presenting as fact what they should have, at most, reported as rumor.

At all times, we called for foreign support of China's resistance to Japanese invasion as an essential sector of the multi-national struggle against Fascist aggression, and under no circumstances a "side issue" once Europe became a theater of war. On such matters I had almost nightly phone conversations with Jin Zhonghua, the progressive editor of the Sing Tao daily, one of Hong Kong's most popular Chinese papers. Often our editorial interpretations ran in parallel.

*   *   *

Stateless, and in Hong Kong legally on sufferance, I depended for extensions of stay which had to be applied for every two months, on backing by the China Defense League's honorary secretary, Hilda Selwyn-Clarke, who pulled some weight as the wife of a senior official of the colony—its Director of Medical Services. But I also had, as head of an old-established newspaper, a position bound to be respected, and as such was invited to the briefings given by Sir Geoffrey Northcote, the Governor, for heads of the English-language press. There we heard the official viewpoints and were served with sherry and barley water.

Old Colonel Murrow was seldom in the office. But late each night, when MacNider and I were struggling to "put the paper to bed" in our printing house, he would call boozily and wordily from his club, always beginning with "How are things going over the-ah?" Once I could not refrain from impatiently cutting him off with, "Please let us get on with our work!" Obviously considering his nightly call a bounden responsible duty, the old Colonel felt outraged and complained to Yu, who had us up in the palatial Central Trust office to smooth the waters. "No one has ever spoken to me like that," the Colonel harrumphed. After I said I was sorry I'd been curt but we had really been in a rush, honor seemed satisfied. The Colonel, showing no further anger, called each night as before, though with less garrulousness. His main other sign of concern for the paper was an inevitable monthly inquiry, "Have we paid the troops?"

A more meaningful crisis loomed when the staffs of our rival papers in Hong Kong came out on strike. It might have been seen as a heaven-sent opportunity for us to increase sales. But I, taught from childhood that strikes should be supported, proposed to the staff that we stop work in sympathy. In Hong Kong, such things were "simply not done" by an editor (in Guomindang China they could be considered criminal). Also, I must admit, I did not draw much response from our rather tame staff. Though the issue soon faded with the strike ending, I had definitely blotted my Hong Kong copybook.

The scrapbooks in which *Daily Press* leading articles were painstakingly pasted-up by my friend Liu Wugou of the China Defense League are near-miraculously still in my hands after a half-century of turbulent ups and downs. Leafing through them I recall nostalgically the energy of my youth, which they reflect.

Work on the newspaper, done tensely from dusk to past midnight, did not tire but left time for many other things. Besides the publicity of the China Defense League, I edited a pamphlet or two for the Hong Kong Promotion Committee for Chinese Industrial Cooperatives. Also, I completed my first book, *The People's War*, about events observed in China in the first two years of defense against Japan. Published by Victor Gollancz in London, who had brought out Snow's *Red Star Over China*, it was abundantly—and on the whole favorably—reviewed: Soong Ching-ling endorsed it thusly:

> ... Different from any other foreign work on our war of Resistance because it relates its analytic first hand account of the struggle to past history and future prospects.

Edgar Snow called it:

> Superb war journalism written with sympathetic understanding of China's hopes.

Although it wasn't in my own eyes deserving of such praise, I felt it to be a creditable effort for a very young newsman, and one done at high speed (the final 40 pages of manuscript, as I recall, banged out on the typewriter during one overnight stretch).

Not bargaining for royalties, thinking only of getting the material out, I was paid by Gollancz just £35 (after taxes) for the almost 400-page book. Then, quite literally, it underwent a test of fire: the London warehouse where most of the copies were stored by the publisher was bombed by German aircraft. Luckily, a few did get sold, and I still find *The People's War* quoted in books and references dated a great many years after. A stroke of good fortune, ironically, was that a photostat "pirate" edition was quickly "published" in Shanghai—in the foreign concession area known as the "International Settlement." That enclave, until the outbreak of the Pacific War two years later, was still exempt from the surrounding Japanese occupation, but because of its isolation, very eager for news of the struggle elsewhere. Thus, more copies became available, not only to others but to me in Hong Kong to meet friends' demands for gifts. Otherwise, after the ten or so gratis copies that Gollancz allowed me, I would have had to buy others at a price an underpaid writer simply couldn't afford. Only the cheap reprints fitted my meager purse.

That made me, perhaps, the world's one author glad to have his work pirated. But in those circumstances, "piracy" was hardly the word. Firstly, China had stayed out of the international copyright convention, membership in which would have been hard on her, so few were her books sold elsewhere, so many the ones she needed from abroad for readers and students (and, as we have seen, even authors) who could not afford the price of imports. Secondly, people in the Japanese-occupied areas hungered for books on China's continuing resistance as a primary source of morale. Mine, besides being inexpensively reprinted in English, was put into Chinese almost instantly, segments being distributed to several translators working simultaneously, and the product circulating both legally (in the International Settlement) and through the underground in enemy-held territory. Strictly on those terms, "piracy" was beneficial to the cause, even patriotic.

More quietly, I worked on the English-editing of translations of Chinese Communist Party documents under the aegis of Liao Chengzhi, son of one of the Guomindang's early revolutionary martyrs, the San Francisco-born Liao Zhongkai and his brave and talented wife, He Xiangning. Young Liao, after his father was assassinated by Right-wing elements in the Guomindang in 1926, had become a Communist, and in 1938-41, Head of the Eighth Route Army office in Hong Kong as well as a leading member of the China Defense League. He was every inch alive, likable, many faceted, and multilingual. He was fluent in Chinese, Japanese (he had been born in Japan and partly educated there) and English (from early life in Hong Kong), and held on to a smattering of other tongues. History had formed him as a revolutionary. In 1925, as a middle-school teenager he had marched with his sister Cynthia (Liao Mengxing) in Guangzhou in the anti-imperialist parade machine-gunned by British and French troops from their concession enclave in what went into history as the Shakee Massacre. After the reactionary murder of his father a leader of the Left-wing Guomindang, he joined the Communists, gone abroad, and worked among Chinese students in Japan and among Chinese sailors in the International Seamen's Club in Hamburg. Returning to Shanghai, he was arrested by Chiang Kai-shek's secret police, but was later released on the cognizance of his Guomindang-veteran mother. Slipping out of the city, Liao made his way to the Chinese Red Army on its Long March and almost perished in factional struggle when Zhang Guotao (who was later to defect to the Guomindang) held him hostage as part of an attempt to wrest Party leadership from Mao Zedong.

Artistic and humorous, he was an accomplished painter and a strikingly imaginative cartoonist and raconteur. His friends called him "Fatty" for his almost invariably easygoing and relaxed demeanor, but underneath was a strong-as-steel core, forged and tempered through many flames. In Hong Kong in 1939, during a temporarily tranquil interlude, I saw it reflected when, as we left a taxi together, I accidentally slammed the heavy door on his thumb, leaving it crushed and bleeding. He made no sound, wrapped a handkerchief around it, and, a smile never leaving his face, waved off my profuse apologies. Nor did he ever refer to the matter again, though for weeks afterwards his injury, which must have hurt badly, remained coal-black under and around the nail. A true Long

Marcher, I like to call him, inured to shocks and pains compared to which this one was trifling.

The documents Liao gave us for translation were chosen by Yan'an for international circulation. They included Mao Zedong's classic long essay *On Protracted War*, which outlined, validly as the coming years proved, the expected course of the war with Japan and the strategy to be adopted. Clear and persuasive, it was a true masterwork, helping shape events as well as explaining them. Other papers dealt with the growth and risks of Guomindang-Communist friction. Still others discussed internal Party policies in the argument with Wang Ming, trained and promoted in Moscow, who seemed concerned more with pleasing his mentors there than with the actual situation in China.

These and other translations from Yan'an, done in Hong Kong, were published and circulated worldwide, sometimes from there, sometimes from Manila. One of the local translators was the young author Ye Junjian, later a distinguished novelist. On the "polishing" of the English, I worked with my housemate Donald Allen, who had joined in inaugurating the China Defense League branch in Guangzhou, and, after the fall of the city, come to Hong Kong. Don, it turned out, was a member of the American Communist Party—not strange at that time, since it was at its peak in terms of membership (100,000 or so) and influence.

Don, Ye, and I, in our rented apartment on Hong Kong's Robinson Road, worked on the texts, typed them on stencils and mimeographed them to be sent out pre-publication or for reprinting abroad. Later we were joined by Molly Beckman Tallentire, who had worked with Don in the mutual-welfare International Workers' Order (IWO) in New York.

Somehow, with all this, we also found time to edit an English-language translation of the Yan'an-recommended *History of the Revolutionary Movement of China*. We also managed to edit several issues of *Chinese Writers*, presenting a variety of contemporary work by Chinese authors, translated into English by the talented and sensitive Ye. All three of us were keenly interested in literature and met occasionally with Chinese novelists, essayists, and poets then in Hong Kong—from Mao Dun on the Left, to modernist Dai Wangshu, Ye Linfeng, and others of different traditions but now inclined to join the United front. We also met with patriotic artists like Ye Qianyu and Ding Cong, and met frequently with Chinese editors and co-workers of *Chinese Writers* such as Feng

Yidai, his wife Zheng (known as "Anna May Cheng"), and Yang Gang of Ta Kung Pao.

It was in this period in Hong Kong that I offered, and had accepted, my first contribution to the *New York Times*, dealing with China's new literature and art, which was printed in its noted Book Review section. Years later, I was to write for the *Times* its first series of first-hand reports from the Communist-led areas of China.

The translation of political documents, organized by Liao, was ultimately under the control of Zhou Enlai. From 1939 on, during the ups and downs of the cooperation of the two parties against Japan, Zhou headed the Communist Party's military and political delegation in Chongqing, and simultaneously the Party's South China Bureau.

Being the highest representative of the Chinese Communist Party and areas at the center where all foreign embassies in China were located, Zhou was also, in fact though not in name, the party's foreign minister.

* * *

In late spring of 1940, my first stay in Hong Kong came to an end. An old friend, the New Zealand author and journalist James Bertram, became available to take over the China Defense League newsletter. And Don Allen and others were still there to help with the translations.

As for the *Hong Kong Daily Press*, it was in any case a stop-gap job—I had no wish to be a long-term editor in the then British colony.

So I decided to join my then wife, Edith, in Chongqing where she had arranged work for me in the international radio station. We two had been apart so much that our marriage was fraying at both ends, though, as one-time school sweethearts, neither of us was yet ready to give it up.

Most of all, I had been out of direct touch with what was going on inside China for far too long and yearned to go back.

Chapter 11

A LONG WALK THROUGH THE COUNTRY

In 1940, the border between Hong Kong and the mainland was sealed by the Japanese, leaving no overland way to start a journey toward Chongqing. To go by air was too expensive, and offered no view of conditions en route, which I eagerly wanted. So, along with a temporary traveling companion, a young Chinese artist named Chen, I chose to start by sea, then go inland. The nearest landfall free of Japanese, Shayuchong, just a sandy beach with a wooden jetty, was only a few hours away by small steamer. It lay on the inlet of Daya Bay (also called Mirs Bay) to the northeast, and had once been known (as had much of the south China coast) for pirate alcoves. Currently, it was sometimes used by the China Defense League to slip in relief supplies. Power over the area technically belonged to the Guomindang. But to the latter's discomfort, a Communist-led guerrilla detachment, the East River Anti-Japanese Column, joined by many student patriots who had come from overseas Chinese communities, was beginning to organize there.

Our co-passengers were some overseas Chinese families from Southeast Asia coming to visit their home villages a short way inland. One foreigner, Father Pilenga, was a massive middle-aged Italian Catholic priest with a mission in same area. He invited me to taste his homemade wine and cheese, which was served up by women parishioners. Interestingly, among the teenagers and young children who flocked to gather round us, some seemed to resemble him.

Our way inland was along narrow footpaths, with our luggage carried on shoulder poles by hired porters. The whole party of thirty or forty was guarded by a few lackadaisical police called "Peace Preservation Corps," armed with old rifles or Mauser pistols. This force, we later learned, was more on the look out for "Reds" of the East River Column than for agents of Japan.

Our first overnight stop was at a board-built inn, divided into tiny cubicles, each with a bed for two occupying half its cramped space. Tired, everyone soon slept, but not for long. Around midnight a shot rang out close by. In an instant, a score of robbers dressed in black varnished silk jackets popular in Guangdong, rushed in. The young man—Mr. Chen— and I were ordered to turn over our money, and in particular a gold ring the robber insisted I must be carrying, but wasn't. Ignoring my denials, he hammered my kneecaps with the butt of his Mauser pistol. Finally he left, taking our money, but was soon back, not with a pistol in his hand this time but instead a Chinese kitchen cleaver! Gruesomely, I could picture how this common utensil could be used if all else failed. Again he demanded the non-existent ring. Luckily, a shout from a neighboring room, seemingly hailing the discovery of a greater haul, sent him running there to get his share.

As he was leaving, young Chen, who had so far taken everything meekly, boldly grabbed the bandit's sleeve, "You can't go off with this foreigner's identity papers!" he declared, "How can he travel on without them?" Pausing for a moment, the brigand held out my wallet. From it we took not only the pass but a Bank of China traveler's letter of credit, with no objection from our apparently illiterate visitor. Warming to the fray, young Chen challenged him further: "We've given you *all* our money. How can we pay for breakfast tomorrow?" At this, the thief handed us each a ten-*yuan* note (he had taken a few hundred). Once the robber had left, young Chen burst out, beaming with national pride. "You see, in China even our bandits have a conscience and listen to reason!"

The next morning, there were no robbers, only complaints from their victims to the Peace Preservation Corps. And the Italian Father, hearing our tale of woe, came through with advice. On reaching Huizhou, the county town, I should see the local general, Xiang Hanping, who would make good the monetary loss because it was "bad face" for such things to happen to a foreigner in his bailiwick. Indeed, General Xiang did just that, with courtesy, especially when I showed him my "To Whom It May Concern" credential from Soong Ching-ling. Young Chen had a supplementary explanation: Hadn't I noticed how much a couple of the robbers, despite their changed apparel, looked like our "Peace Preserver" protectors? No wonder General Xiang was so accommodating—but if that fact was mentioned he would lose face doubly. Since he had made generous amends, who would be so boorish as to embarrass him?

Our journey's next phase was uneventful until we reached Shaoguan, temporary capital of Guangdong Province. Our way there was partly by riverboat, on which we met another Catholic priest, this one French, with a long beard, miserably afflicted with bacillary dysentery which, he wailed bitterly, had attacked him despite the strictest care to eat nothing in China that was raw or unboiled.

Cockily, I boasted to him that, having lived in the country for decades, I had eaten hundreds of supposedly unsanitary street snacks with no ill effects. Vengeful fate must have overheard; the next morning, I exploded with the same complaint, as did young Chen. Reaching Shaoguan, on the recommendation of my Guangzhou American acquaintance Ed Lockwood of the YMCA, we went straight to the London Mission hospital, where we passed two miserable weeks. With antibiotics still hardly known, the heroic treatment was to purge us, already dehydrated, with large doses of Epsom salts. It worked, although we quickly lost half our weight. I, moreover, developed malaria and an inept quinine injection hit a nerve in my leg, which left it numb for years to come.

While ill, I telegraphed my wife Edith in Chongqing. Alarmed, she asked Hugh Deane, the China correspondent of *The Christian Science Monitor*, just out of Harvard, and who was reporting on the southern provinces, to look me up in Shaoguan. Hugh and I were to remain friends for six decades.

Still weak and shaky after leaving the hospital, I bade young Chen farewell and started with Deane for Chongqing, again on foot. From a listless dehydrated bag of bones, I quickly recovered my appetite and gained weight. Seemingly, there was no better cure for my condition than waking at dawn and tramping some 90 Chinese li (about 30 miles) before dusk, with an hour for a roadside snack and a brief rest in between. The walk was also full of interest. Going north from Shaoguan into Jiangxi Province, we passed through the former bases of the Chinese Red Army, which had embarked on the Long March in 1934. Despite Guomindang efforts to wipe out its traces, many of its military and social slogans were discernible on the walls. Deep and favorable were the popular reminiscences we heard in low-voiced conversations. A cook in a roadside restaurant told of how Red Army chief Zhu De had eaten in his place—he was "approachable, not at all like a general."

In Ganzhou (now Ganxian) prefecture in southern Jiangxi, Deane and I interviewed its head, the stocky Chiang Ching-kuo (Jiang Jingguo), son of Chiang Kai-shek, returned after many years in the Soviet Union. There, as a student in the late 1920's, he had publicly denounced his father as a blood-stained reactionary. Now, reconciled with him, he still spoke of, and carried out, some urban reforms, including support for the Chinese Industrial Cooperatives in his area. Before long, however, he would be arresting co-operators and hunting down Communists like most other Guomindang officials. In Moscow, as I would learn much later, young Chiang had studied together with Deng Xiaoping at the revolutionary Sun Yat-sen University. They had stood side by side at roll calls, being the two shortest in the class. Decades later, Chiang Ching-kuo would become president of the Guomindang regime on Taiwan, succeeding the father he had once disowned.

Moving on through Hunan Province, Hugh Deane and I comically experienced the unfamiliarity of rural China with things outside. "What are *those*?" we heard one peasant asking another at the sight of Deane, standing well over six feet, and me barely reaching his shoulder. "Must be foreigners," replied another. "Why is one so tall, the other so small?" "He's a *young* one," came the confident reply.

The rest of our journey, part by bus, part by the one of the few short stretches of rail still in Chinese hands, ended at Jinchengjiang—a bottleneck whose ramshackle inns were packed with impatient travelers waiting for scarce road transport, and dubbed by us the world capital of bedbugs which marched on sleepers in the inns in battle formation and leaped down on them in mass "paratroop" jumps from the ceilings.

After Jinchengjiang, one was lucky to get a seat on a truck, usually atop piles of cargo, which could be comfortable, if bales of cotton, or painfully bruising, if metal or heavy machinery. Then, one got to hilly, misty, and impoverished Guizhou Province, home to several ethnic minorities, in an area traditionally known for the "No Threes: No three *li* of flat land, no three days without rain, no one with three yuan in his pocket."

Further toward Chongqing lay the notorious "72 bends" of mountain road, flanked by numerous precipitous edges with nothing but a sheer drop to the canyons and crevices below. Here also one saw the horrors of Chiang Kai-shek's conscription system—press-ganged peasants in various stages of starvation tied together by their necks to prevent desertion. Those too weak to trudge ahead were left to die on the road. Over one body—gruesomely flattened into the road by previous vehicles—our truck was driven as though to do so was normal. Officers of units in which these unfortunates were listed would continue to collect, and pocket, their pay and rations long after their deaths.

In Chongqing, re-united with Edith, I rested for a week in a missionary-owned bungalow she had rented on the misty south bank of the Yangtze, then went to work she had arranged for me, in the Chinese International Broadcasting Station XGOY.

Chapter 12

CHONGQING

The move from Wuhan to Chongqing was a retreat in every respect. This hill-girt river port far inland up the Yangtze was semi-feudal and mercantile. Dominated for decades by local warlords it had been far less affected by changes in China's modern history than the seacoast. Nor was any basic progress brought about by its becoming the country's provisional wartime capital. Coming at a time when the Guomindang regime was itself regressing from the brief progress in Wuhan, it added the weight of the national government bureaucracy and military dictatorship to that of the trammels already existing locally in a gradually hardening reactionary hold.

For a brief initial interlude, this turn was not apparent. In 1939, Chongqing's first year in its new role, two tests were met relatively well. One was the desertion of Wang Jingwei and his followers to the Japanese camp, which did not cause a split in the government, as the majority, centering on Chiang Kai-shek, reaffirmed its commitment to resistance. At this time, when I was still in Hong Kong, a certain improvement in the united front atmosphere made it possible, for example, for the three Soong sisters to travel to Chongqing in their fist political activity together in many years. In the same season, Chongqing experienced its heaviest enemy bombings, with consequent devastating fires, which did not, as the foe intended, shake the determination of the government and the inhabitants—a test well passed.

It was on the heels of these trends that, early in 1940, I came from Hong Kong and began work in official International Broadcasting Station, XGOY. In that atmosphere it was still possible for someone to work, who, in Hong Kong, had once worked in the China Defense League.

Three young Americans on the station's foreign staff—Melville Jacoby, Theodore White, and Betty Graham—had gone off to work in major American media. While the station was looking for replacements, my then wife Edith, who was already in Chongqing, applied successfully to have me fill the gap in improving the language of English scripts and, when required, announcing in English.

Usually we broadcast from a booth in the yard of the International Publicity Department, where the Foreign Press Hostel was also located. When bombings were frequent or severe we were moved in trucks to the deeply-buried, concrete-reinforced transmitter site at Shapingba outside the city and did our work there.

On average, in early 1940 when I arrived, most of the working staff were patriotic, seeing their posts as battle-stations in the war which China must ultimately win.

But the environment was already fraying. On the Guomindang-held front, fighting with the enemy became increasingly sporadic and rare, although official communiqués pretended otherwise. And discontent with things in the rear was rising, as well.

This was forcibly brought home to me during my early days at work. Watching a Japanese air raid with a group of junior colleagues from a slope in the open (we did not always go into shelters), I was shocked to hear one exclaim, "Damn, missed it again!" How could anyone openly regret an enemy miss? I'd never heard such a comment in Nanjing, much less in Wuhan. And why was there no objection from the others?

"It didn't fall on Kung's residence," someone coolly explained to me. These young people's hatred for the invaders was undoubted. But so was their growing detestation for some top officials of the Guomindang (though they themselves included members of that party). Living far below their pre-war standard, and getting poorer as inflation increased, they were particularly bitter against profiteers from the national calamity. Fat, smooth-talking H. H. Kung, in charge of national finance for the Guomindang, was clearly a loathed symbol.

Soon after, at the Foreign Press Hostel, where I was lodged, I ran into an instance of this almost within earshot of Kung himself. Having donated a modern toilet, bathtub and shower to the building, he had arrived to inspect it, and hear due thanks from its residents. Yet the armed policeman at the gate of the Press Hostel found it possible to growl to me, patting his pistol that he wished he could use it on Kung, who arrived with his own retinue of bodyguards. Against Chiang Kai-shek even a mild criticism could have meant jail at the very least for an ordinary Chinese. Cursing Kung was obviously less risky. It may even have been considered a useful lightning rod to deflect popular anger. And Kong's very unpopularity could ensure his pliant subservience, in financial and other matters, to his master, Chiang, who was also his brother-in-law.

* * *

In fact, during my year in Chongqing, from early 1940 to spring 1941, the situation there and in the Guomindang areas as a whole was going downhill fast. Warfare against Japan languished. Repression and corruption worsened. The danger of civil war grew from occasional reactionary provocations to a nationwide threat. Even the regime's propaganda officials were grumbling disgustedly. Peng Loshan, head of the radio's English service, an ex-YMCA secretary, and previously an uncritical booster of the Guomindang, said to me sadly, "I'm tired! In 1938 when we gave our news and publicity over the radio, we believed it ourselves. We were inspired. The work seemed easy. Now, too often, we know we are talking nonsense."

Higher up, his chief, Hollington Tong (Dong Xianguang) was grumbling in similar terms. Tong remained keenly nostalgic for the atmosphere of active resistance to Japan and growing national unity which took shape in Wuhan. Moreover, he did not relish many of his new duties in Chongqing. When his department was ordered to doctor the English translations of items appearing in the Chinese press which it distributed to resident correspondents, to make the wording more acceptable abroad, he privately warned some of the foreign reporters not to be fooled but to use their own translators, and tipped them off to file dispatches early in the morning before his immediate superior, the Minister of Information, would wake and decide the day's censorship problems.

Internationally, with war proceeding in Western Europe, getting any China news into the papers was very difficult, especially as there wasn't much of it. The period was one of those epitomized in the alleged instruction of the UP to a China correspondent to send only "world-shaker" stories, and those to "shake in under fifty words." So the "queerness," in the strange sense, of "things Chinese" was re-invented. U.S. media centered for days on a tale, that during the Lunar New Year, eggs in the country could mysteriously be stood on their small ends. As to why, questions were posed to eminent scientists, including Albert Einstein.

In Chongqing, trust in the Guomindang was steadily dwindling among the foreign press people. Although very few had Left ideas, what they heard from the Communist Party about the general situation of the country repeatedly proved more truthful than government presentations.

This was especially true at the time of the Guomindang's backstabbing attack on the New Fourth Army in January 1941—an arrant civil war provocation which could benefit only Japan. Virtually all the correspondents, doubting the Guomindang version, sought the Communist Party's account—which they trusted more. Notable, too, was a press reception given by the British Ambassador, Archbald Clark Kerr, who spoke of hopes that China would remain united, and asked Gong Peng, representing the Communist daily *Xinhua Ribao*, to sit beside him as he spoke—a clear indication that Western governments, at that juncture of World War II, were also apprehensive of the outbreak of civil war in China and wanted to show their attitude in many ways.

The Communist Party, on its part, had taken a number of precautionary initiatives to make sure of understanding abroad. Already before the South Anhui Incident, Anna Louise Strong, about to leave Chongqing after a short visit, told me about a confidential background briefing given her by Zhou Enlai—in anticipation that such an attack might happen—to publish in the United States if and when it took place. Preparatory information had also been conveyed to Edgar Snow—who was then not being admitted to China by the Guomindang—to be made public when necessary. In Hong Kong, similar material had been supplied to the China Defense League led by Soong Ching-ling. In these ways the news blockade was broken.

In Chongqing, the American correspondent Jack Belden, who had visited the New Fourth Army not long before and come away full of respect for its anti-Japanese struggles, staged a one-man demonstration, shouting with tears of rage that the Guomindang generals were murderers—and that the Guomindang information agencies were lying to cover up murder. He did this right on their own compound, where the Press Hostel was located, and told other newsmen what he himself knew about the New Fourth Army.

Big-hearted Belden indeed had a passion for truth. From our early days in Wuhan I remember his admonition to me to be more perceptive and less didactic: "Eppy, if you talked less and listened more you might learn something," he taught me. And I have since tried.

In Chongqing, the strongest and most dramatic reaction to the attack on the New Fourth came from Zhou Enlai himself. When Guomindang censors crossed out all reference to it in the Communist Party's newspaper, he was on the premises, and instructing that the resulting blank space on the front page be kept open, where he inserted, in his own calligraphy, a brief, passionate denunciation. If anyone was arrested, he insisted, it should be him. As he was the Communist plenipotentiary for the inter-party relationship, any such action by the Guomindang would mean their taking the full responsibility for breaking the anti-Japanese united front, which they would hesitate to do.

On its part, the Communist Party's top leadership in Yan'an rejected the government's order dissolving the New Fourth Army, which it placed under the authority of its own reconstituted Revolutionary Military Committee, which in turn appointed new leaders for the force, in place of its commander Ye Ting, who had been wounded and taken prisoner in the attack, and vice-commander Xiang Ying, who had been killed.

Internationally, in March 1941 the government of Nazi Germany was to record in its archives a conversation between its Foreign Minister Von Ribbentrop and his Japanese counterpart Matsuoka in which the latter said that he was "in personal contact" with Chiang Kai-shek and "knew him and trusted him."[7]

After the New Fourth Army Incident, the environment in Chongqing became more stiflingly reactionary than ever before in the course of the war. Many progressives and democrats made their way to Hong Kong where they could speak their minds. I myself had already

---

[7] Document Aufz. RAM 1941 (dated March 21) of the German Foreign Ministry seized and published by the U.S. Government after World War II. The date indicates that in January 1941, when Chiang Kai-shek launched his intendedly exterminatory attack on the Communist led New 4th Army, these contacts were already in place. One can also infer that the mutual understanding between Chiang and the Japanese had its bearing on subsequent developments. Months later in 1941, after Nazi Germany's invasion of the Soviet Union which initially seemed irresistible, Chiang was widely said to be playing with the idea of joining the Axis powers once the Germans took Moscow, and, in harmony with their "Anti-Comintern Pact," launch an all-out civil war against China's Communists. But the Germans never did take Moscow, and their repulse there, leading later to their crucial defeat at Stalingrad, put an end to Chiang's speculation on an Axis victory.

arranged to go back to my China Defense League tasks there. No longer did I find it possible, as I had in past years, to work for both Guomindang-owned and Left-leaning media against the common foe, the Japanese invaders. Not after the New Fourth Army Incident, with Guomindang publicity actively incubating a new civil war.

In 1940-41 the situation in Chongqing and in the Guomindang areas was deteriorating. Serious warfare against Japan had virtually stopped. Repression and corruption were worsening. The threat of civil war grew. In my work as a correspondent, just as I had done in my first period in Chongqing, I got my most reliable news from Zhou Enlai's office, sometimes directly and often through Gong Peng and others of its members who kept in touch with the international press.

One major characteristic of Zhou Enlai was his tirelessness in his work. At one discussion with foreign reporters I found him looking so ill and exhausted that I suggested he needed rest. His response was an angry glare, the only departure from his usual cordiality with me.

Another characteristic was his magnetic charisma. At gatherings of intellectuals, young and old, he sometimes appeared unheralded, and was so unobtrusive that he could stand unnoticed at the door. As soon as he was seen, however, he would become the center of animated, deeply meaningful conversation for the duration of the occasion.

Still another was his approach to the united front, even at its most frayed edges. Once, at a height of our press battles with Hollington Tong's censorship—he told me quietly during a brief handshake at a public reception not to bait Tong too sharply. Whether he was making a political distinction between Tong and the latter's more reactionary superiors; or simply warning me not to mark myself as too Left, I did not know—in either case the hint was thoughtful.

It was instructive and impressive, too, to see Zhou among his own comrades in the Communist delegation—here the atmosphere was that of a family. Whether with its top personnel or those lower down: cooks guards, messengers, and the like, his air was that of an equal—he ate, sang and relaxed with them. Even though, where work was concerned, he was known to be demanding down to the last detail, of others as of himself...

Zhou was a song of a man. A man of grace, of principle, of duty, of inner strength. In future he would become China's "beloved Premier." Because he was beloved long before he was Premier.

Chapter 13

ESCAPE FROM HONG KONG

By 1941 I was back in Hong Kong. On the eve of the Japanese attack on Pearl Harbor, and the simultaneous attack on Hong Kong, I was working at the *South China Morning Post*. At the same time I was running, as a volunteer, the publicity work of the China Defense League.

The "balloon went up," as the attack was termed in Hong Kong, on the morning of December 8, 1941 local time (where it was still December 7 at Pearl Harbor). I was awakened, in the sagging spring bed of my rather tatty lodging-house in Kowloon, pretentiously named "Baron's Court," by the thud of bombs and "ack-ack-ack" of anti-aircraft fire. Though familiar with such sounds, I didn't believe another war had begun. My first fuzzy thought was that it must be maneuvers. So it had been three years earlier in Beijing when the boom of Japan's cannon at the Marco Polo Bridge had announced her all-out war on China. Unwelcome truths are slow to penetrate.

While knowing that Japan was bound to go for Hong Kong, I had not thought it would be so soon. The mood of the city was very much similar. While it was true that aircraft shelters were being built, contractors, sub-contractors, and sub-sub-contractors were making huge "cost-plus" money out of the goings, part of which went to the pockets of bribed colonial officials. In Hong Kong's press, these scams and their attendant sex scandals and suicides, made bigger headlines than signs of the approach of war.

Canadian troops had arrived to reinforce the original British and Indian garrison, but on a scale not suggestive of imminent danger. When the assault began, much of their equipment had not yet arrived: the Japanese got there first.

The Canadian soldiers hated the political atmosphere of colonial Hong Kong, especially the ban on enlisted men going where officers ate and drank. "Let the Queen defend the fucking Empire," I once heard them yell on the cross-harbor ferry. Nonetheless, they were to fight the Japanese bravely, and would be slaughtered in large numbers when sent

135

into battle still insufficiently armed and unfamiliar with the terrain.

From history, I knew that Japan's military were expert at surprise attack, making war before declaring it. They had done so in their first assault on China in 1894, in the Russo-Japanese War of 1904-05, and for that matter in China throughout most of the 1930s. But precedents don't really prepare one for new realities.

Before the attack, my daily routine had been to cross the harbor from Kowloon where I lived to Hong Kong Island for my job with the paper. After the attack, I hurriedly moved to my workplace, sleeping on one of the desks. I also kept in contact with the China Defense League. Soong Ching-ling had left on the second day of fighting. But the League office had become the temporary home of one of its workers, Liu Wugou, her father, the famous poet and Left wing Guomindang elder Liu Yazi, her mother, and small son. They were all fleeing from Kowloon, which was the first area to fall. In off hours I too went to the League office amid Japanese gunning from across the bay, to help Liu Wugou burn numerous papers.

Simultaneously, I was in sporadic touch with other Chinese progressives and the foreign friends sympathetic to the cause, many of whom were moving from place to place so as not to be spotted by the invaders.

As defeat loomed, I too decided to vanish from view to avoid arrest by the Japanese. Though not categorized as an "enemy national," being neither American nor British, I was in fact worse off: a known personal foe, stateless, and unprotected by any government or international convention. For years I had written against the Japanese militarists and worked with Chinese patriots resisting them, so they had grudges to settle with me and could do so unceremoniously.

In consultation with Yang Gang, a "disappearance" was arranged for me with a rescue to follow. Liao Chengzhi, then the Chinese Communist Party's representative in Hong Kong, made an anonymous telephone call to the offices of the *South China Morning Post*, telling them that he had seen me blown up by a Japanese shell in Hong Kong's Wanchai district. The story was credible because the bombardment there had been fierce, and it was an effective screen for getting me away.

Unfortunately, this tale got to my parents, now in America, via a hearsay dispatch printed in the *New York Times*. Needless to say the news caused them dire grief at the loss of their only son, and as it turned out, it would be months before I could show up again, alive.

After the report of my death, I went with Yang Gang to a Chinese house where a friend of hers, Dr. Wu, was living. There it was decided that I should to go under an assumed name to a hospital from which I could be smuggled to the East River Guerrilla Area. To be hospitalized, one had to be wounded, so Dr. Wu made a rip in my leg through my trousers, which resembled the effect of shrapnel. It wasn't dangerous or even painful because he expertly avoided disabling damage to tissue and cut me under local anesthetic. With my jagged and bleeding wound I limped to the nearby Queen Mary Hospital.

Margaret Watson, the head nurse whom I knew from China war relief work, admitted me. I couldn't use my own name, so signed in as "Alec Stevenson," allegedly an American missionary who had arrived in Hong Kong from the interior of China just before the attack. My home town I gave as Sigourney, Iowa, where I had never set foot but which I had heard something from a friend born and raised there.

When Hong Kong's surrender took place, I was already in a ward among military and civilian wounded. Among them, I encountered varied and instructive reactions to the developing events. A British regular army officer, shot in the arm in the battle in which he had undoubtedly fought bravely, was standing by me at a hospital window on the morning after the collapse. Suddenly, among the white flags, we saw a gasoline depot explode in flames. I expressed joy at this sign of popular determination to keep war supplies out of enemy hands. The officer, to my surprise, disapproved. "If the Japanese had surrendered to us, we wouldn't want them setting fire to their dumps. It's against the rules." To him war was a kind of game, though a bloody one, among gentlemen. Civilian resistance seemed illegal, even immoral. The massacres by the Japanese in China and the Nazis in Europe hadn't changed his established views.

Far form such fight-by-the-book concepts was the view of an Irish-American merchant seaman, Ray O'Neill, in our ward with a bomb fragment in his back. When the fighting broke out, he had come ashore and volunteered for war work. Could he drive a truck? He could. So he was signed on to do this but they still had no truck for him to use.

Seeing a brand-new truck in the window of an automobile showroom, Ray decided for himself that it was needed, and he proceeded to drive the vehicle through the glass window into the street, reporting to the British officer in his depot, "Here's our truck." Instead of praise he got a reprimand: "It doesn't belong to us, and we can't take it without the government buying it." Ray could see no point in such quibbles during a life-and-death fight, and he used that truck to carry ammunition to the front-line troops. That was how he got his wound and into hospital.

Already while in the hospital, I had been within a narrow squeak of serious trouble with the Japanese, since it wasn't long before the hospital wards were checked. Anyone they deemed sufficiently recovered was marked for removal to internment camps if military or civilian camps if civilian. My wound was healing too quickly—despite repeated efforts to force it open with my fingers—for me to keep staying in the hospital, from which my escape was planned.

A Japanese army doctor, his officer's sword dangling at his side, asked me, at my bedside, about my bandaged leg. "Bomb fragment," I said. "Can you walk?" he asked. "No." I answered, though I could. Luckily he didn't require me, as he did others, to show him the injury.

Half an hour later, out of bed and walking along the corridor, I heard a noise and saw this same Japanese army doctor striding along about ten paces behind, with all his sword straps, buckles, and scabbard clanking at his side. I began to limp as hard as I could. Lucky again, he hurried passed me without so much as looking at my face.

After he was out of sight, I heard a peal of laughter erupt from a wounded Briton standing in a nearby doorway. "Silly bugger," he cackled. "You're limping on the wrong foot."

Finally, I resumed hoped for my soon-to-be-arranged escape. Dr. Wu had managed to transfer into my hospital. Yang Gang also came, as a nurse's aide, although untrained. They told me of arrangements to bring out other foreign friends. Could I, they asked, get hold of a Red Cross armband with a Japanese seal? Wearing one, some captive personnel of the hospital were allowed to go into town to make needed purchases.

The plan was for me to put an armband on, walk the past the sentry post at the hospital entrance, and proceed around a corner where I was to meet a Chinese man also wearing such an armband. He would guide me to a boat which would go to one of Hong Kong's smaller outlying islands, and from there to the East River Guerrilla area.

I did get an armband through Hilda Selwyn-Clarke of our China

Defense League committee, who was working in the hospital as an auxiliary nurse. Wearing only a set of hospital pajamas, I also needed clothes, which had been taken from me when I was admitted. My escape was set for one Sunday morning. I told the nurse in the ward that I wanted my clothes. "But you haven't been discharged," she objected. I argued that I was well enough to attend church services (which were held in the hospital), but didn't feel right doing it in pajamas. Accepting my excuse, she brought my things.

While still in the corridor, I kept the armband in my pocket, to avoid curious questions close to the main exit. A British missionary named Short, who was administering the hospital, stopped me with, "Where are off to?"

"Just to get some air and maybe to buy some smokes." I replied. But he planted himself resolutely in my way. Doubtless he may have been warned by the Japanese that if any patient got away he would he held responsible. So, there was my Chinese contact waiting outside, and me inside unable to get out—cut short by...Short!

On my way back inside the ward I managed to tell Yang Gang. She later brought word: try again tomorrow, same time. The next day I got to the front entrance, only to find the entire driveway filled with trucks and swarming with Japanese soldiers and discharged patients, ready to head off to the internment camps. My contact was a few minutes' walk away, but I simply couldn't reach him through this maelstrom. So this whole escape plan failed.

Days afterwards, toward the end of January 1942, all patients were moved to the civilian internment camp at Stanley (Chek Chue in Cantonese). I was still registered as Alec Stevenson, and from Stanley there I still hoped to escape. In the meantime my alias could protect me, as an ordinary internee among 3,000 others, but only until the Japanese found out who I really was. Sooner or later they would doubt me, and with no identity papers they could probe and probe. Time was of the essence: the escape couldn't be put off too long.

An advantage was that not too many other foreign internees in the camp would know me, since in Hong Kong I had associated mainly with Chinese and was not well known in the foreign enclaves. Still, I was sure to be recognized by a few, even with the beard I was growing. I had only one razor blade, kept secretly since my hospital days, for slashing my wrists if all other options failed. Outside aid was now unlikely, and my Chinese friends might not be able to get in touch with me in the camp, or even know where I was.

Luckily, I found foreign friends inside as determined to escape as I was, and mostly for similar reasons: involvement in China's cause against Japan.

In the American bachelor quarters I was billeted—accidentally but conveniently—in the same room as Parker ("Dutch") Van Ness, whom I knew from his work for the Chinese Industrial Cooperatives. Originally a seaman, he had been an active member the International Longshoremen's and Warehousemen's Union, then led nationally by Harry Bridges and in Hawaii by Jack Kawano, his personal friend. When war came he had a temporary job as a mechanic at Hong Kong's Kai Tak airport.

I quickly told him I wanted to escape. So did he, he confided, and the sooner the better, because he had fired on attacking Japanese troops, and if found out could be shot out of hand as a civilian non-combatant joining in the fighting.

Also assigned to our room (for four) was Ray O'Neill, my impulsive truck-driving hospital ward-mate. Should we keep him in the dark? Difficult. Better to include him, I thought, and Van Ness soon concurred. Ray's already-proven fearlessness and his sailor's experience would both be assets in getting away from Stanley by sea, the only way out. He agreed readily. His genuineness was beyond doubt. Our only worry was that his ebullience might violate necessary caution.

Also in Stanley Camp, was, of course, Elsie, of whose whereabouts and even survival I hadn't been sure in light of recent events. I told her how our Chinese friends had looked for her. She said she had been part of another projected escape, which had failed as well. If there was a chance to break out on our own, she would take it. From then on she was active in our scheme.

In the British part of the camp, Elsie had met an Englishman, F. W. Wright, working in the Chinese Customs Service, who told her of his own wish to get out. His wife was Chinese. He spoke Cantonese, which none of us could do, and which would be an asset with the local people. As a Customs man he knew all water routes around Hong Kong. We agreed to Elsie's sounding him out, separately since none of us knew him. Wright was willing. We didn't think it wise to tell him the whole background: our previous links with Chinese friends on the Left, or even my real name, but when it came to how exactly to get away he was in on all our discussions.

Stanley Camp, at the time, was luckily not under heavy Japanese guard. Its inmates were civilians: mainly women, children and the elderly. Most of the younger males had joined the Hong Kong Volunteer Corps whose members were now held elsewhere—as prisoners of war. We didn't worry the Japanese in terms of being a security risk. Perhaps they were doing too well in the war to be concerned. As they rapidly overran Asia and the Pacific, Hong Kong was left far to the rear in their wake while their troops and administrators were needed closer to new theaters of action.

Stanley formed a tiny peninsula of sorts, surrounded on three sides by water and connected to the southern part of Hong Kong island by a narrow strip of land. All they then did about Stanley Camp was to march a patrol, parade style, with stomping boots and firearms shouldered, around its perimeter. You could time it when the formation reached a given point, it would not be back the other way for 20-25 minutes.

Inside the detention area there were no Japanese, only Chinese traitors whom they used as supervisors. Control was largely by written threat. One signboard read: "It is forbidden to look out to sea. Whoever does so may be SHOT." And another read: "Don't approach the barbed wire or you may be SHOT."

How to get away? At first we thought of swimming out, in stages, islet by islet. This reflected our resolve, not realism. We, like other inmates, were weakening physically. The diet was a poor ration of rice with a sauce containing about an ounce of meat or fish per portion. Doctors among the internees figured we were taking in only about 700 calories a day.

Suddenly, a new and better possibility unfolded. Van Ness, peering at the nearby seashore despite the warning, had glimpsed a boat leaning up against a bathing hut, half concealed by bushes. The beach had been used by pupils of St. Stephen's School, which had become part of the camp. The boat, the only one not removed, had apparently been left there as derelict.

That same night, Van daringly slipped down for a closer inspection. The boat was just a hulk with huge gaps between the boards from being too dry for too long. It had a centerboard (drop keel) but nothing else—no rudder, oars, mast, or sail. But Van judged that, if we could somehow improvise those accessories, it could carry all of us in a pinch. The gaping boards, he suggested, would tighten after some time in the water.

From then on our effort was to devise some means of propulsion plus containers to carry fresh water. Our intended objective was Daya Bay and the Guangdong East River Guerrilla Column.

For one oar, we got hold of a paddle used to stir rice gruel in a big pot in the camp kitchen. The other we made crudely from the abandoned door of a bombed-out house. These treasures we brought into the room where Van Ness, O'Neill, and I were living, together with an older American seaman named Clarence Huber. We had to tell him what we were working on each night. And we invited him to escape with us. A middle-aged family man, he said he couldn't take the risk. But he wouldn't snitch: "Just tell me when you leave, I'll be absent and have an alibi." From then on he helped with some of our preparations even though he wouldn't join in our flight. And he prepared his alibi by offering to go out to play cards, which he would do when we escaped.

With some extra room in the boat, we considered who else we might help get out. In consultation with Elsie, we decided on old Morris ("Two Gun") Cohen, though with his age and bulk he could be more passenger than participant. We had reasons for considering him. First, although tied closely to the Guomindang he was always personally helpful to Soong Ching-ling and to her work in Hong Kong, in both the China Defense League and the International Committee for Chinese industrial Cooperatives. Second, he had already been tortured and threatened with death by the Japanese gendarmerie, and probably would not survive another round of such treatment. Third, whether he came with us or not he would not inform on us: he wasn't that kind. But Cohen declined our proposal. He was too old, he said, would slow our getaway, and if our boat tipped over would probably drown, as he suffered from phlebitis and leg cramps. His decision proved wise: a few months later he was allowed to go back to Canada in an exchange of internees between the warring sides, mediated by the International Red Cross.

We worked like squirrels. We made a second set of paddles. We tore out a map of Hong Kong from a book in library of St. Stephen's School. We filled an empty 5-gallon gasoline tin with water and sealed it. We also managed to find a small compass.

Van Ness, in bold night forays to the beach, buried these objects, one by one, in trenches dug in the sand by the British when they were defending the area. It was only necessary to push in more sand, which, unlike soil, left virtually no sign of having been disturbed.

Van Ness was the real hero of the undertaking. Every time he went down to the beach he risked his life. He not only hid our gear but brought back needed information, taking a rough measure, with his fingers, of the rings on the boat so we could build a rudder. He even reported the name with which its former owners had christened the craft—the *Vanda*. We joked that it was enough like "Van" to show fate at work. Van recognized and faced every difficulty and danger. Once determined on a course, he carried it out, untiringly and unflinchingly. He was an American worker of the best kind.[8]

*　*　*

Before the Japanese attack on Hong Kong, because I was in the colony on sufferance, I had to ask the police each month or two for a prolongation of stay. Usually I was referred to a Sgt. Youe of the Special Branch (political security) whose manner was cold and reluctant. From within Hong Kong, my repeated applications were backed by the China Defense League (through Hilda Selwyn-Clarke), and later by the two newspapers that I successively worked for, *The Hong Kong Daily Press* and the *South China Morning Post*. On the personal side, I cited the need to wait for an answer to my application for a visa to the United States, made at the U.S. Consulate-General in Hong Kong, sponsored from New York by my then wife Edith and my father in New York, both U.S. citizens. To guarantee my eventual departure, I was required to deposit my trans-Pacific passage money with the police. Even so, each prolongation hung by a hair—until my last encounter with Sgt. Youe, under

---

[8] For many years afterwards I lost track of Van. Till 1978 when our friend Joan Hinton, who works in Beijing, ran into him while speaking for the U.S.-China Friendship Association in Jacksonville in, his native Florida. Van, active in the organization, mentioned me and Elsie. Joan on her return to Beijing gave us his address, and we wrote. A few years later, when Elsie and I were visiting my father in New York, I phoned Van and he came up to see us. He had two tall sons by then, Karl and Mark, a non-coincidental resemblance with Karl Marx.

In 1992, when I saw Van again with his wife Renee, he was already over 80—but lean and keen as before and as firm in his socialist faith.

Japanese bombardment. Then he gave me back my money and said, "Now you can stay as long as you like."

The fortunes of war had turned us both into captives of the Japanese, and Sgt. Youe was one of the few Stanley internees who knew me as Epstein, not Stevenson. Though I didn't think he would volunteer the information to the Japanese, I did doubt if he would withhold it under questioning, especially if the British alien registration files passed intact into the hands of the Japanese gendarmes.

I asked Youe one day if those records had been burned, but he shook his head dismissively as though I was making an improper suggestion. Whatever they chose to keep from enemy hands, I suspected, would not necessarily include files on suspected alien "Reds," toward whom British and Japanese official views did not much diverge.

But I wondered: did Youe in some way give the cue for a further incident? In March 1942, I was accosted in the camp by another interned officer of the Hong Kong police, one Inspector W. P. Thompson, whom I hadn't known by sight. "You're a journalist?" he said, more as assertion than query. Waving aside my denial, he made a proposal. With another person, he was escaping the following night. The route would be through the New Territories along which food and other needs had been cached by British troops prior to the war. He was allowing me to accompany him on the condition that I obey his instructions as leader of the attempt.

Here was a dilemma. Thompson's route might indeed be the best. And I very much needed to get away before a Japanese comb-through of my identity.

But what about my own group of escapees? If Thompson's breakout came first, the hitherto lax camp security would surely be tightened, and my friends would not likely make it out.

Gathering our group I told them, without specifying that Thompson had talked to me. If they agreed to sail the next night, I would reject Thomson's offer. They all agreed to immediate action.

On grounds of health and uncertainty, I said "No" to Thompson, who, having no inkling of our plan, may have merely thought me a fool or a coward.

Both escapes took place the same night, though at different hours and by different routes. Both were successful—but no one was able to flee Stanley afterwards.

Thompson's plan had long puzzled me. Did Youe tip him off that I must be anxious to leave? Did he want a journalist along to write up his exploits as his companion in the adventure, as Mrs. Gwen Priestwood eventually did after they escaped?

Only after reading about Thompson's exploits in a book published two decades later did another possibility suggest itself. Knowing my Left affiliations, did he want me along for the possibility of contacting the Communist-led guerrillas operating around (and secretly within) Hong Kong?

Thompson eventually made it to Daya Bay to set up a private scheme for the escape of more civilians from Stanley. Guomindang disapproval of his actions was so strong that the British Embassy was obliged to agree that Thompson should leave China and not return. This episode served to exacerbate the already difficult relations with the Nationalists over the Communist connection to the BAAG, the British Army Aid Group, later established inside China.[9]

[9] Ride, Edwin, *British Army Aid Group BAAG, Hong Kong Resistance 1942-45*, Oxford University Press, Oxford, 1981, p.58.

Chapter 14

THE VOYAGE OF THE *VANDA*

On March 18, 1942 we escaped from Stanley. After dark, our group: myself, Elsie, Van Ness, O'Neill, and Wright, made our way to a ridge overgrown with shrubs and trees alongside the road that ran around the camp's perimeter. Below the road was the forbidden beach surrounded by barbed wire, and below that the sea. Along the road the Japanese patrol of twenty or so men would tramp on its regular circuit. We sat in the bushes waiting for them, then, as they passed, we waited as they went forward another couple of hundred paces before we stole quietly across the road and down to the beach. There we lay prone beside the barbed wire before cutting it with a pair of wire cutters we had taken. We uncovered our goods in the sand where Van had bravely hidden them, placed them in the boat, then heaved and dragged the boat into the water.

As soon as we started to use our makeshift paddles we discovered the sea to be heavily phosphorescent, flashing with cold but revealingly bright light at every stroke. As we learned only later, the same unpleasant surprise had chilled other sea-borne escapees from Hong Kong though not from our camp:

> We could only stand and stare in agony. The water was full of brilliant phosphorus. Every dip of the bow, every sweep of the oars would be visible many miles away.[10]

Though we were all experiencing a feeling of elation, sound as well as light threatened to betray us. Down the slope, we had dropped a metal container, which rolled and clanged loudly. Fortunately, no one seemed to be within earshot. While still close to shore, we sighted a promontory where a Japanese patrol craft was anchored and occasionally swung its searchlight.

[10] Proulx, Benjamin, *Underground from Hongkong*, New York, 1943, E. P. Dutton & Co., 210-11.

If caught on the beach, we would almost certainly have been beaten senseless at the very least. If spotted in the water, we would have been machine-gunned on the spot. But all we thought of was how good it was to be out. That we were young, with hope easily outdoing apprehension, must have been one reason.

We did get past the Japanese patrol sloop, and luckily no one seemed to have noticed those phosphorescent flashes. Yet, our roughly-fashioned rudder did not fit in its mounting. Our sail improvised from two blankets couldn't be hung. Soon one of our handmade paddles snapped. Though it floated, the boat was taking in water, and we were furiously trying to bale out the water which was seeping in the darkness under our feet. Unable to steer, we couldn't head where we had planned. So we decided to make for nearby Lamma Island to the west, which was sparsely populated, and make the most urgent repairs to our escape craft. We planned to stay sheltered on the island during the day, then take to the sea again at nightfall.

No such luck. As we approached, we found the shores perilously rocky, with no secure place to land the boat. Apart from Van Ness, who rowed, we all continued to bail water like mad. We were tired. I was so woozy that after a while I was bailing water into the boat instead of out of it, and was promptly called "an idiot." But we made jokes too: "We're bailing ourselves out of jail," was one we laughed over.

Our closest brush with death was not with any enemy. In the dead of night, in open water, a huge dark shape swooshed past only a few meters away. It was a junk, most likely smuggling something past the Japanese, and of course running no lights. The *Vanda*, with us in it, weighed less than a ton, the junk at least 50 tons. Any collision would certainly have finished us off. By the time fear came, the danger had passed. Still another menace loomed: virtually adrift, we could easily have been swept up by currents out of coastal waters and into the vast Pacific with no telling of where we might end up, if anywhere.

But we kept on. At daybreak, we tried to get near the tiny dumbbell-shaped island of Cheung Chau, where we thought we might find landfall unobserved. Instead, we saw on the shore some new concrete pillboxes built by the Japanese, so again we rowed away.

What would we say if the enemy caught us? Light-headed, we decided to pretend to be Germans out fishing: since the Germans were friends of the Japanese, we thought they might simply leave us alone.

Sheer fantasy, since none of us spoke German, or even remotely looked to be out fishing. The men now had a several-day-old beard, and my beard, camp-grown for disguise, was even longer. We were all wet to the waist from the water that kept seeping into our boat. A sorry sight.

We finally landed on Lantau, actually the largest of Hong Kong's many islands but in those days the least developed. It was a forced decision as a Japanese patrol craft hove in sight, chasing a suspicious-looking junk under full sail. If the chase turned to us, things would end badly, so we made for shore and hauled our boat up on the sand, doing nothing more to conceal it than to draw it up into some bushes as far as our strength allowed.

Dead tired, we collapsed on the beach and slept.

The first thing I saw upon waking was a ring of the island's fishermen standing around us. They looked down at us lying there and talked among themselves. Wright, who knew Cantonese, said they knew we must be escapees. We hemmed and hawed, not knowing whether to confirm or deny anything. Their tone was friendly, but we could not stay there, they said, and they led us up away from the beach to the bushes. Then, using their hands and bare feet, they smoothed the sand so no one could see where we'd been lying or where the boat left tracks. Behind the line of bushes was a gully where they told us to lie low. "Any Japanese around here?" we asked almost immediately. Only occasionally, they answered, from a station on the main settlement of the island. So, we were not to come into their village, where the enemy might come by surprise or have informers. They told us to wait until they returned, and left us sitting in the gully.

We knew also that the consequences to these villagers, if it were discovered that they had helped us, would be severe. As we sat there, we believed more and more that they had no thought of actually turning us in, which could mean a reward instead of punishment. It felt wonderful to know that. They were poor people, and worse off for the war. How much worse, we realized when they brought us some food, what they themselves were eating, just sweet potatoes boiled in water. They hadn't, they said, seen rice for a long time, having run out of it weeks before.

Soon we learned that one of the older fishermen had been a seaman on British and other foreign vessels, including, at one time, those of the "banana fleet" of the United Fruit Lines plying between Central

America and the U.S. Ray O'Neill had also sailed under United Fruit. The smiles exchanged over this link of worker solidarity made things easier.

The person who took charge of us was a tailor from the village. He said he would go on with us to unoccupied territory, and we all agreed. We talked about where to go next, and how. They didn't ask us for any money. We had very little, a couple hundred Hong Kong dollars among us, which we offered to share. At that time, the "usual fee" for being smuggled out of Hong Kong was from five hundred to one thousand dollars per head, with even higher prices for the hazards of conveying persons requiring special precautions because they were sought by the Japanese. Yet, here we were, unable to give more than 20 or 30 dollars each. It was no sort of money to risk one's neck for. These plain and poor Chinese villagers, unforgettably, weren't out for money but were patriotic sons of their great and ancient nation.

They fed us several times, keeping us safe in the small gully for two days, while out departure was planned. After two nights they put us on a fishing boat, with an awning under which we could hide. Heading for Daya Bay (our preferred destination) would be too risky, as it would have required us to go counterclockwise around much of Hong Kong island where there were still numerous patrols. So we chose instead to cross the Pearl River estuary and make for Macao, which, as a Portuguese colony, was technically neutral in the war.

At the jetty on Lantau from which we left there was a small shrine honoring Matsu, goddess of the sea and the "patron saint" of Chinese fishermen, who would burn incense and pray for safety before embarking. The skipper of our boat and his young son who was about twelve, who was his sole crew, made an offering before the shrine piously. Then all of us, including the tailor, piled aboard and we set off. To be less visible, we hoisted no sail, being propelled only by the large single sweep-oar at the rear.

It was dark, and we virtually hugged the shoreline in an attempt to be less obvious to patrol craft. "What if the Japanese see us?" we asked the young boy. "We have this," he said, scooping away some straw on the bottom of the boat to reveal a rifle.

Once we were clear of Hong Kong, we ate squid, caught from the boat fresh out of the sea, tough and chewy but with a flavor ambrosial to our long-deprived taste buds. It was cooked over a charcoal pan on board, carefully shielded to throw no light.

At about 4 a.m., before the first glimmer of dawn, we slid into the fishing harbor of Macau—the rear harbor, not the main harbor used by the regular shipping trade. There it was crowded with hundreds of small craft, all trying to avoid (or escape from) the Japanese-controlled waters. When we had moved in among all those boats it was impossible to tell which had just arrived and which had been there a long time.

As our boat edged alongside some small steps leading up to the quay, we saw the blurred shape of a single policeman walking on shore, and heard church bells. Macau, largely Catholic, was greeting the Sunday morning with many carillons.

We continued to hide under the boat's awning until the policeman had passed out of sight. Then, our captain and the tailor motioned for us to go. We thanked them hurriedly and scrambled ashore, with our extra clothes in sandbags under our arms, and started walking along the waterfront nonchalantly. Suddenly a small, dark, round man came briskly toward us. After one look he said, "Hey, are you folks from Hong Kong?" Clearly an American, he introduced himself as Father Paulus, a member of the Catholic Maryknoll Mission, headquartered at Ossining, New York.

With our bedraggled looks, what else *could* we be? So we did not argue the point but asked him the way to the British Consulate, which was now certainly the only official Allied representative body along the Asian Pacific coast from Vladivostok in the Soviet Union practically down to Australia. All the others were in territory held by the Japanese.

"Come along with me," said the rotund Father. "But first I have to say Mass in the Carmelite Convent."

"We don't want to be seen," we countered.

"Don't worry," he assured us, "those nuns are under a vow of silence." We accompanied Father Paulus to the Mass. As we sat in the pews, Ray O'Neill, Irish and brought up in the church, went down on his knees, although he had previously shown no sign of piety.

The morning sun was still low in the sky when, after Mass, we called on the British Consulate. That functionary, named Reeves, was still in his dressing gown, and rubbing his tired eyes when he came to the door. But he soon turned animated when he saw us. I recognized him, having seen him before in Wuhan in 1938 at the British Consulate there, but he did not seem to recognize me, and when I gave my name as

Alec Stevenson I realized he probably did not remember who I was.

"Come in, come in! Has anyone seen you?" Not really, we told him, just the nuns sworn to silence, and a few people along the quay in the grey dawn.

"If anyone has seen you in Macau, it'll be all over the city. Have no illusions." Then he disappeared into the next room but we soon heard him on the phone, talking excitedly: "Hello? Hello? You know what I've got here? Five people straight from Hong Kong! Yes, they may have news about your family."

We did of course know who was interned at Stanley Camp and who wasn't. There were a lot of Allied nationals from Hong Kong in Macau from before Japan's invasion. Some had just come for a few days' gambling. Some were British wives who, when the authorities insisted that they leave Hong Kong, decided not to go home but to this nearby neutral enclave. Now, all were stranded here for the duration of the war, while their loved ones back in Hong Kong had become prisoners of Japan.

We told Reeves: "We want to go on from Macau so we'd better lie low." This he brushed aside, "Nobody goes anywhere from here, you're stuck until the war ends, so forget about leaving."

What Reeves told us about the local political situation was not comforting. There were two factions in the Portuguese administration. The Governor was on the side of the Allies, while the Chief of Police, named Lobo, was pro-Japanese. Macau, with its population suddenly quadrupled by refugees, could now bring in food only through the Japanese lines. If the Japanese wanted anything all they had to do was threaten to cut off provisions. We saw with our own eyes a horrific portent of that disaster: meager food rations were being issued to long lines of people who were too weak to stand and were on their knees. Anyone carrying food, even one raw fish, was liable to be set upon by mobs of crazed, starving children, who would seize it and stuff it into their mouths. Reeves darkly muttered that there were already reports of cannibalism.

Worriedly, the Portuguese had already given to the Japanese most of the cotton in their warehouses, and all the petrol for the sole plane which constituted the Macao Air Force. The implication was clear: if the Japanese asked for us, we'd be handed over too.

To calm us, Reeves said, "I'll talk to the Governor to try and get you some disguise registrations, not from Hong Kong." He took Wright with him.

Elsie, I remember, was supposed to be an Austrian, Elsa Maurer, and was put in a high-class hotel, the *Buena Vista*. Awkwardly, among its few residents was the chief Nazi officer in Macau. She, the reputed Austrian, knew no German and had to dodge him.

Wright, because he was British, and Van Ness because he was ill, were put up by Reeves in a spare room in his house. O'Neill and I (as Alec Stevenson) stayed in a humble flophouse with a high-flying name: the *Aurora Portuguesa*.

As for money, Reeves said he'd try to help. But every Allied refugee in town, he explained, was trying to borrow money from him. All he could do was to sign IOUs on behalf of the British government which might or might not be honored. He had tried to reach London for funds, but it was hard to communicate or collect remittance. Once time when a coded radiogram arrived, he rushed into the receiving room to decipher it. Soon he came out sputtering sarcastically, "…In view of the disturbed condition of the world, members of His Majesty's Foreign Service are requested to travel with as few effects as possible, and not ship furniture." Such was the first message after all his waiting.

Reeves' advice to us was self-contradictory. Sometimes he'd say, "Don't go around together, you're too conspicuous." And other times, "Don't go out alone, it's safer to be together."

On the pleasant side, Reeves took us out for our first post-escape beer. I shall never forget the delicious bursting of its every bubble on my tongue, since almost nothing with any taste at all had passed our way much, since Hong Kong's fall months before.

Elsie, in the final stage of the Hong Kong battle, had been given a Chinese address in Macau by Sa Kong-liao, a progressive Chinese journalist. Just in case, he said, we ever had to escape through the Portuguese colony. Once far from our minds as we had anticipated a different getaway route, it was now a straw to clutch at.

The address belonged to a physician named Tang. Elsie and I, the only ones who had this tip, set off looking for him. But the street name given to us proved hard to locate, possibly she wrote it down incorrectly. After some searching, we at last knocked on a likely door which was a doctor's office. The receptionist asked what our trouble was. Elsie said her stomach hurt and was let into the consulting room while I twiddled my thumbs outside. When she asked the doctor for help to get out of Macau, as suggested by Sa, he said, "It's my *brother* you need to talk to." We were duly introduced to the "brother," named Chen, who looked like the typical Chinese intellectual, and we guessed that he was a school teacher. He said, "Yes, we can arrange it. We know some people who are engaged in smuggling and the like, but they do take people out. They don't want any money, they're patriots."

He then told us that such an effort was already underway to take out a Mr. Wierink, who used to be the Dutch merchant consul in Guangzhou, and his wife. The pair, stranded in Macau, would be moved to unoccupied China at the request of none other than…Reeves.

We gulped. Reeves who had told us categorically that there was "no way out" of Macau? He might have wanted to take as few risks as possible lest he lose this connection. When we saw Reeves again we said nothing about it.

Given the circumstances we couldn't ask him for assistance in our departure, nor even for a loan of money we might need. So we mentioned carefully to Father Paulus and his Maryknoll colleagues, whom we visited now and then, that we might have a chance of going back into the China and would like to borrow some money which we could repay there to whoever they wished. They agreed to our proposal, as there were Maryknoll missionaries inside China to whom they had been trying to get funds. Thus, we got a couple of thousand Hong Kong dollars, not a large sum, but one that they thought worth risking.

Another difficulty was that one couldn't carry anything like luggage in the streets of Macau, because no one was traveling and it would attract notice. When we took the problem to the smugglers, they posed an interesting solution: they said they would come to our inn posing as second-hand goods merchants who wanted to buy our clothes and belongings. Many refugees were already selling their personal property when their funds ran out. Once the "deal" was done, the goods would be placed on the boat for us.

A vociferous haggling session was staged in the yard of the Aurora Portuguesa. Kibitzers gathered to watch and contributed the usual advice: "Don't sell it so cheap," or "Too much for that junk." At the end we had "sold" practically everything we had brought, even the blankets we had used for sails, and were left only with the clothes on our backs, bewailing that we'd let things go for a pittance because we were so hard up. A normal Macau scene.

There were further complications: Up until now, Ray O'Neill had been a model of courage and sobriety all through our escape, bearing up admirably despite a piece of shrapnel above the kidney which the hospital in Hong Kong hadn't taken out. But once in Macau he began to imbibe, heavily. Cadging drinks at various bars, he would talk carelessly and return at night in an uproarious mood. Once he even grabbed the iron fence around the Japanese Consulate and rattled it hard with both arms, shouting, "You bastards! We're going to China to join the guerrillas to fight you sons of bitches!" With his ailments and ranting, he could be a peril to us all in our departure routes which would take us through occupied territory before we reached the interior of China. Our escorts simply would not risk this. So we left him in Macau to be treated for his wound and be taken out another time, which was some months afterwards.

Late one evening, moving like dim shadows, we were guided to the waterfront where we descended to a little boat and were rowed to an anchored junk in whose hold we waited a couple of hours in pitch darkness. The wait was for Dutch Merchant Consul Wierink and his wife who were late because at the last minute he insisted on bringing a considerable amount of baggage including a pair of steamer trunks. Unlike our few items, this must have involved incredible maneuvering on the part of the smugglers to pass unnoticed.

Our Chinese escorts were grumbling about the nuisance, but the pair had to be helped just the same. The delay might have been life-threatening: an arrangement had been secretly made with puppet guards (Chinese working for the Japanese) stationed on a headland we had to pass just outside Macau, to let our boat through at a certain hour. We had to pass by at the exact time as specified because it would be the only way to identify the ship in the dark. If we reached the headland too early or passed by it too late, we would be fired on. So tension increased until the tardy couple arrived at last with their effects. Wierink himself never let go of a cardboard tube which contained his accreditation as Merchant Consul.

Wierink was fair, large, heavy-set and outwardly stolid, his anxiety only apparent from a slight twitch in his eyes. His wife, a dark and vivacious Austrian Jewish woman apparently traumatized when Hitler took over, was visibly distraught.

It was with them and their stuff that we had to be taken, out of the hold and down a rope ladder in complete darkness into what was called a "snake boat," a very long craft like a dugout canoe. It had several oarsmen, with whom we shared benches. At the stern another stood erect, wielding a kind of sweep as a rudder, and chanting to synchronize the rowing—a combined steersman and coxswain. We reached the headland late, and were fired on, bullets swishing over the water. Just then, Mrs. Wierink decided she must wear a hat and, from her bag, brought out a white had which stood out vividly in the moonlight, and we couldn't get her to take it off. Determined and physically strong, she sat bolt upright with her head held high. That the rowers couldn't help bumping it with a thud each time they brought their oars forward didn't seem to upset her.

When we were shot at, our man at the stern did not duck for cover. Standing taller than ever, he ordered "Row closer, row closer!" and once within earshot of our attackers shouted a password, adding some curses as an afterthought. The shooting stopped.

We had run the gauntlet. Peace was restored.

Once we had cleared Macao, we soon disappeared into the darkness of the West River (Xijiang) delta. Along its network of little canals and streams we zigzagged until we stopped at a village. Besides our two "snake boats," we had a small boat like a pinnace, bearing the brother of the chief of our smuggler-protector. In the village there were armed guards who, our escorts explained, were supposedly puppets working for the Japanese, who seldom came to this area. As our escorts explained further, they were actually not pro-Japanese at all but only pretending to be. At the time, we had to be satisfied with that explanation.

Staying overnight in this village, we found its people were very friendly. Walking over to one of the so-called puppet soldiers we looked at his gun, a rusty World War I relic. He apologized for it, then he took us into an old temple, and uncovered some very business-like looking rifles, saying, "These are for when we need them."

The next morning we got into three other boats—shallow-draft river craft grouped in formation, which we would call our flotilla. The first, small and mobile, was for reconnaissance. The second, larger boat carried some cargo as well as all of us. It had an awning under which we could hide by day. The rear boat, similar in size to ours, held some of the village guards, wearing puppet uniforms and carrying rifles and at least one machine gun. It was much like the world, we remarked: diplomacy and intelligence-gathering were up front, as the preferred way to the goal. Backing it was armed force, which could used as a deterrent or, if necessary, as a lethal weapon.

It would take almost a half-century to clear up for me the "mystery" of our smugglers and their background. In 1991 I received a letter from a man who had met us at the end of our escape. He was a young teacher and a journalist named Zhong Hua, which is pronounced very similar to the word for "Chinese." Following Liberation in 1949 he had become a leading staff member of the nationally-popular Guangzhou Evening Daily, and in old age retired.

He told me that Zhao Qisiu (Jiu Keiao in Cantonese) the leader of the organization that took us to safety, was originally a merchant who indeed did much smuggling. But he was also a patriot and, after the war broke out, organized a local anti-Japanese armed force. The Chinese Communist Party, deciding to draw him into the united front, sent cadres to observe and work with his unit. Zhao proved consistently anti-Japanese, progressively inclined, and cooperative.

Zhong Hua was already an underground Party member. By profession a teacher and editor of a local news sheet, he finally became Zhao's secretary, and helped him to develop a force led by the Communist Party. Zhao, from his smuggling past, had an extensive waterborne communications network and could pass through Japanese and puppet-controlled effectively. He set up a new trading firm in Macao, where Mr. Chen (Dr. Tang's "brother"), through whom we made the connection, was his fellow townsman and friend. Doctor Tang, well regarded in Macau, was still living there, in retirement. Zhao, however, had died of illness. After the war he had received an award from the British government for help in and around Hong Kong, to the Allies at war with Japan. This may have accounted for his link with Reeves.

What I learned in 1991 cast new light on what happened in 1942. After the failure of our first attempt at escape from Hong Kong, with Party aid, we had thought that we were entirely on our own. But through Sa Kong-liao's tip to Elsie about Macao, and, our contact through Chen with Zhao's "smugglers," we were again aided by the Party, though we did not know it. In fact, most escapes by foreigners and Allied efforts around Hong Kong depended on the Communist-led resistance.

It was like China's legendary "Monkey King" Sun Wukong. Sitting on the Buddha's hand, he had boasted that with gigantic somersaults he could whirl his way to the furthest limit of the Universe. The Buddha said, "try it." Sun leaped until he reached five huge pillars which he thought certainly marked that limit, and wrote his name "Kilroy-Was-Here" style, on the middle pillar. "Did you reach it?" asked the Buddha. "Sure," said the Monkey King proudly describing the five heavenly pillars he had visited. The Monkey King watched in amazement as the Buddha raised his hand, and on his middle finger was the Monkey King's name. One can leap within history, not outside it. In China's case, history then was the anti-Japanese resistance and those who were its most active element.

Chapter 15

CHONGQING REDUX

My second spell in Chongqing was during the Pacific War, when China no longer fought Japan alone but had Western powers as allies. This should have improved fighting morale in China's official wartime capital. But instead it hatched reliance on the United States defeating Japan while Chiang Kai-shek and his Guomindang cohorts conserved their forces and hoarded arms received from abroad for subsequent civil war against the Communists. At least one offshoot of the U.S. government, however, was involved in civil war preparations by the Guomindang.

The "Sino-American Co-operation Organization" (SACO), linked to the U.S. Office of Strategic Services (OSS), and U.S. Naval Intelligence (ONI), trained Chiang's secret police in "third degree" interrogation, including torture, for use against suspected Communists and sympathizers. U.S. Air Force General Claire Chennault, an ardent partisan of Chiang Kai-shek, favored such activities. General Joseph Stilwell, commander of U.S. Forces in the China-Burma-India Theater, fiercely opposed them. Stilwell stood for joint military action by U.S. and Chinese troops, including those led by the Communist Party, in fighting Japan.

Ultimately, Stilwell was politically outmaneuvered by Chiang and his coterie, both Chinese and American, and recalled from his post. The decision was mistakenly made by President Roosevelt who probably would not have taken it if he could have foreseen its fateful consequences. For it set the United States on a course which led, after Roosevelt's death and the end of World War II—both in 1945—to involvement in China's subsequent civil war on the side of Chiang Kai-shek; attempts to subvert instead of recognize the newly-formed People's Republic of China; ill-starred U.S. military interventions in Korea and Vietnam; the rupture of relations with China for over 20 years to the detriment of both countries, and to issues which still bedevil these relations, such as the question of Taiwan.

The Guomindang's policy in 1939-45 included more than refraining, where possible, from battles with Japan. It included allowing substantial military desertions (57 generals with their troops) to the Japanese-created Chinese puppet government headed by Wang Jingwei. Employed against the "Reds" by the Japanese, they would ultimately return to the Guomindang fold for similar use.

"Sitting on a mountain and watching the tigers fight," was how Communist leader Mao Zedong would ironically describe Chiang's role in his period. The "tigers" were the Japanese invaders on the one hand and China's Communist-led forces on the other.

In 1942-43, the Japanese military in China, having little to do on the quiet front facing the Guomindang, concentrated their strength and ferocity on drives intended to exterminate the rural Communist-led resistance bases. Their renewed, savage approach became known as the campaign of the "three alls" (kill all, plunder all, destroy all). But the terrorism did not break the back of these bases. On the contrary, they proved able to arouse new multitudes of peasants to throw themselves into armed resistance and into a remarkable "production movement" equally necessary to foil the foe. Literally, the soldiers' militia and auxiliaries, fought with one hand on the gun and the other on the plow, spinning wheel, loom, and similar simple implements to produce the necessities of life. In hellishly difficult conditions, the bases strengthened their roots not only for survival, but for coming expansion. Japanese spokesmen and media increasingly referred to the Communists as their main and most frustrating foe in China. And the resistance bases, with each hardship overcome, perceived themselves (and were perceived by others) to be the Chinese nation's pillar of hope. This feeling, born in 1937-38, in the war's early phase, was all the stronger now that such grim adversities had been overcome.

The increasing contrast between the Guomindang and Communist-led fronts was also noted by the governments of China's Western allies. In the light of their perceived long-term interests, they did not favor the Communists. But as a factor for victory over Japan, they could not overlook the growing contribution of the Communist-led forces.

As for my own work situation, I made it to Guilin after the escape from Japanese internment in Hong Kong. Hollington Tong, in Chongqing, telegraphed me an offer of renewed employment working on publicity matters for Guomindang interests. This put me in a dilemma: To refuse outright would leave me with no place to go. To accept would leave no chance for me to write about my own views. I cabled Edith, by then back in New York, to try to get me a prompt appointment as a foreign correspondent in China. Luckily she got one, from Allied Labor News, a newly established agency supplying world news to the trade union and Left press. Their radiogram in hand, I could tell Tong, with thanks, that I was already engaged, with a foreign press accreditation. ALN paid infinitesimally, but I had my independence and could make ends meet with the aid of sideline jobs. I soon got one with the Chongqing branch of the U.S. office of War Information, (OWI) a new wartime outfit which much later would become the U.S. Information Service (USIS). Heading the branch was "Mac" Fisher, once my colleague at the *Peiping Chronicle*. Putting out a daily news bulletin (radioed from Washington) for the Chinese press took me only three or four hours, and paid my habitually moderate living expenses.

*   *   *

Personally, the big shift in my second Chongqing period was my marriage in 1943 to Elsie, who was to remain my wife for over forty years. I was the insistent one: Elsie long demurred, thinking she was too old (she was nine years my senior).

We were wed following my divorce from Edith, my sweetheart from my Tianjin schooldays and my wife since I was nineteen.

Though Edith and I were still on good terms and mutually helpful to each other, we had lived separately for years, and our aims were different. Hers was to set up a family, mine to report from China's war front. So we were heading for a parting of ways. I would go on to a life with Elsie, to whom I had become tied through our escape, and through similar life-plans. Edith would remarry in the United States where she would busy herself with teaching, support of progressive causes, and with her new husband, whom she had met through association with wartime relief for China, have children and grandchildren. Despite all permutations, our two families would remain warm friends.

Reflecting legalities in two countries, the United States and China, and their mutual relations, were the special circumstances of our divorce.

It was history's first involving a foreigner with former extra-territorial rights to occur under Chinese laws. Edith, an American citizen, was the defendant—after consultation I sued her for desertion, as she had been absent, since 1940, in the U.S. Prior to 1943, such a case would have had to be heard in an American consular court in China, under the extraterritorial jurisdiction many foreign powers had extorted from the country. In that year, however, with China allied to the U.S. and Britain, the exemption of their citizens from Chinese law was formally relinquished.

Interestingly, even under Guomindang, the divorce law in China's modern civil code law books was more enlightened than America's. It recognized as a major motive, mutual consent, which the courts in New York, where Edith resided, regarded as smacking of unacceptable connivance, preferring to act on lurid evidence of adultery, real or invented. We chose desertion as the grounds, since it was a cause accepted by both countries, as was still required.

This litigation, reflecting contrasts with the past, would also have its ties to the future. My lawyers were Shen Junru and Sa Qianli, both eminent Chinese jurists. Prior to the war, they had been vocal and influential advocates of armed resistance to Japan when the Guomindang was still reluctant, and had been jailed, with five others, in the then famous case of the "seven gentry" of the National Salvation Movement. In wartime Chongqing, they were still kept out of official posts and favor, and had to eke out a living on their legal fees, which were meager, as clients who could pay well avoided them, and those who used them could pay little if at all. But after he founding of the People's Republic, though neither was a Communist, these patriots would be held in high honor, Shen becoming its first Chief Justice, and Sa a Cabinet Minister.

Even less formal than the divorce, and easier to legitimize under Chinese law, was my marriage to Elsie. In a stationery store we bought a marriage certificate illustrated with a pair of ducks, a symbol of nuptial constancy. This we signed with two friends as witnesses. Then, as required when there was no public ceremony, we put an announcement in a newspaper.

* * *

After Elsie and I were married, we lived at the Chongqing Press Hostel. It was square of shack-like structures, some single-story, one with two floors, rapidly put up on the campus of a former elite middle school, whose original brick buildings had become the offices of Hollington Tong's International Publicity Department. Our flimsy walls were of white plaster applied over crisscrossed bamboo laths. When Japanese bombs fell nearby, the plaster sometimes blew out, and would leave us in wicker-like "cages" easily seen through. Temporary repairs were done with the hostel's abundant supplies of "green sheets"—the daily releases issued by the International Publicity Department. But neither green sheets nor plaster could cut out the sounds everyone could hear of whatever went on next door—clacking typewriters, conversations (political or ribald), loud parties (stag or mixed), and love-making (marital or otherwise).

We had a one-story shack. Each structure had a window and a door opening out into the courtyard surrounded by leafy banana trees that never yielded fruit. When drinking got heavy a correspondent could show his strength by tugging them up by the roots. Sturdy Robert "Pepper" Martin of UP once set a record by uprooting a whole row of banana trees without a pause).

When Elsie came up from Guilin I could get her a shack near mine, on the strength of her being a publicist for the Chinese Industrial Cooperatives. We spent much time, when free or working together, in my shack or hers, and when a shack next to mine could be found, she settled there. After marriage we knocked a gap between them, in which we installed a charcoal pan stove to warm both.

All ceilings were made of white paper laid over bamboo lattice. Overhead, the Chongqing rats, huge and reputed to feast on kittens, would frolic, urinate, and sometimes put a forepaw or foreleg through the wet paper. At night they would occasionally descend. While Elsie slept, one gnawed some hair from the side of her head. Straw-colored and very soft, it must have seemed ideal for lining a nest. The rat worked quietly and carefully; and only upon waking the next morning did Elsie find herself shorn.

For light we had a tiny bulb, sometimes 25 watts and sometimes, when we couldn't get that, only 15, with a homemade paper shade.

For the entire Press Hostel, with its score of rooms, there was only one flush toilet and one bathtub, both of smooth gray cement with pebbles inlaid and polished flat, like terrazzo. These facilities, which we used in turn, were the gift, as already described, of Guomindang Finance Minister H. H. Kung.

* * *

Apart from my paid job and Elsie's work in the Chinese Industrial Co-operatives, we resumed our voluntary work in the China Defense League. After the December 1941 Japanese attack on Pearl Harbor, and on Hong Kong, Soong Ching-ling was on one of the last planes to leave the colony. She flew to Chongqing, and it was there, in August 1942, that she reconvened the League, after several months of disentangling herself from the uncomfortable hospitality of her highly-placed sisters, and arranging for a private residence apart from theirs which was closely guarded but all but inaccessible to her friends.

Difficulties in getting the League started and working were greater than they had been in Hong Kong. We had no office, and so had to gather in her living room. We had no access to printing facilities, so we sent out publicity by hand with friendly travelers to be published by support groups abroad. But there were also comparative advantages: Chongqing was the wartime capital, with high-ranking diplomatic, military, and relief agency representatives from the Allied countries, as well as the press corps representative of major Allied media. All of these would be inevitably drawn toward Soong Ching-ling's stature as an uncompromising advocate of internal unity against Japan and opponent of civil war. The Guomindang could not isolate or censor the widow of its own founder, Sun Yat-sen, whom it semi-deified, while departing from his example and principles. Moreover, in Chongqing there was a representative of the Communist Party, Zhou Enlai, whom the Guomindang could not prevent Soong Ching-ling from meeting. Under these circumstances, some portion of relief funds from abroad were obtained for the Communist-led areas and actually reached them.

The China Defense League enhanced its own profile locally and internationally. Among its volunteer helpers one could find the wife of an allied ambassador as well as some younger officials of the foreign diplomatic establishment. Some of the latter participated in benefit performances, including an international concert and football tournament for victims of the devastating wartime famine in Henan Province, which the Guomindang largely ignored, but the Communist-led area in Shaanxi Province helped by organizing temporary homesteads.

Among the foreign military missions, Soong Ching-ling made a firm friend of General Stilwell who not only spoke Chinese but had a higher opinion of China's common folk than of the gilded upper strata. Stilwell, after successfully advocating the sending of a U.S. Army observer group to the Eighth Route Army to ascertain its role in fighting Japan, and, if possible, heighten its effectiveness with military aid, authorized the aircraft flying to Yan'an to carry medical supplies to the Eighth Route Army, on one occasion ordering the widening of an airplane door with a blowtorch to accommodate X-ray equipment.

Across the spectrum of the Allied military community, Soong Ching-ling gained popularity from the invitations she extended (not only to officers, to whom social life in Chongqing had previously been confined, but to NCOs and privates as well) to her home and to benefit dances and fundraisers. In the breadth of her united front outreach she was unmatched.

Soong Ching-ling never ceased to focus attention abroad on the Guomindang blockade of medical relief and other supplies of the Communist-led areas. In one strong statement, "A Message to American Workers," which I was proud to have sent out through Allied Labor News, she urged the U.S. labor movement to insist "that the products of its efforts and the gifts it makes be equally distributed to every force in China, wherever situated, that is actively engaged in operations against Japan—and to no force that is otherwise engaged." Further she denounced "the threat of civil war by which some reactionaries are preparing to destroy a democratic sector of our struggle...the guerrilla base in North Shaanxi and behind the enemy lines where the labor movement is fostered and encouraged and many detachments of armed miners and railway workers cooperate with the guerrilla forces to pry Japan loose from her main continental base in North and Central China."

This statement, and her angry references to the discriminatory line on one side of which China's wounded and sick were deliberately denied access to medicaments, infuriated the Guomindang.

Recorded by U.S. diplomat John S. Service in his official dispatches are Soong's defiant remarks about the "childish lecturing" she was subjected to when Guomindang War Minister He Yingqin, its Secretary-General Wu Tiecheng, and others came "to belabor me," she told a friend. "They refused to admit facts, only kept reproaching me for appealing to lift the blockade." Mentioning to Service that her brother-in-law H. H. Kung had asked worriedly, "if they would intern you if you kept talking?" she said she had told Kung she would welcome it.

* * *

In a favorable turn in the Guomindang front at the end of 1943, Changde, in Western Hunan Province, was re-taken from the Japanese by ground troops supported by U.S. Air Force planes. I witnessed the battle, and after reported on the deliberate devastation of the town by the Japanese troops:

> When the history of this war comes to be written, much investigation will be devoted to the question of why men of the Fascist Axis armies did the unbelievable things they did. Some case histories engaging their attention will come from the devastated city of Changde. They will ask why Japanese peasants, who revere rice as the fruit of back-breaking labor and the stuff of life, not only stole rice from the Chinese peasants, not only fed it to horses but also used stores of rice they could not remove as a favorite latrine spot.
>
> They will also ask what made Japanese soldiers who entered the Spanish Catholic orphanage not only steal the children's bedding but also go to the trouble of bringing great stones from the courtyard below to smash the wooden spinning and weaving machines in the institution's vocational school, and what pleasure the Japanese soldiers derived from breaking into classrooms and smashing ink bottles against the wall; why the Japanese who didn't want the cooking oil with which refugees prepared their food broke every vessel containing the oil instead of leaving it alone; why in conscripting men for labor they gave the old and weak the heavy burdens to carry and the young men the light ones, then bayoneted any man whose knees buckled under his load.

All these things I either saw or heard from the mouths of hundreds of returning townsfolk who had direct experience.

* * *

During my second stint in Chongqing, the Guomindang government held two kinds of press conferences—military and civil.

The military spokesman, ramrod-backed General Xu Beigen, had a hard row to hoe. There was very little good news from the fronts to talk about, and to report bad news, or stagnancy, wasn't his job. The correspondents joked that this spokesman himself was told nothing, but could only read from prepared texts given him or use a map to make his point with a straight face.

There was not a word from General Xu about war news that was coming from the bases and operations of the Communist-led Chinese forces in supposedly enemy-occupied territory. It was his job to ignore, deny, or conceal.

Foreign newsmen often stayed away from the military press conferences. But they asked for, and trooped to, the civil government press conferences to ask about political problems of the war. Excerpts from that meeting, on February 22, 1944, originally recorded in shorthand by Elsie, convey the atmosphere.[11]

> Theodore White (*Time* Magazine): Can the Minister (Liang Hanchao, Guomindang Minister of Information, conducting the conference) tell us if the blockade of the Communist area is still continuing?
>
> Liang: What do you mean by "blockade?" What is your source of information?
>
> White: In Xi'an four or five times since 1939... I was told it was impossible to go from Xi'an to Yan'an, impossible to send medical supplies, and that military supplies were not sent...This is the blockade I refer to.
>
> Liang: Zhou Enlai and his people go to Yan'an without restrictions. Transportation of the 18th Group Army goes. So the word "blockade" does not... meet the situation.
>
> Stuart Gelder (London *News Chronicle*): How many transports of medical supplies have been allowed to go through since 1940?
>
> Liang: I cannot give the information because the question must be referred to the National Military Council.
>
> Gunther Stein (*Christian Science Monitor*): Does the Minister know of medical supplies from abroad specifically sent to this area which were detained and confiscated?
>
> Liang: To get the details I suggest that you interview General Ho Yingchin (the Minister of War).
>
> Brooks Atkinson (*New York Times*): If the Minister objects to the use of the word "blockade," is there any other word we can use... It is common knowledge that people cannot pass freely to Yan'an.
>
> Liang: The Chinese attitude (to the Guomindang-Communist differences) is that it can be likened to a family dispute...not necessary to publicize... There is a psychological difference between Westerners and Easterners ... in Chinese thought it is important that the man in power say little and do more... In the West you think you should publicize regulations made by your governments... a difference in psychology.

---

[11] The shorthand transcript was quoted by Solomon Adler, the U.S. Treasury representative, in a report to that body.

White: This is a family dispute? But I have heard a Minister say the Communists are a group of gangsters, warlords, etc. That does not sound like a family quarrel... Not a single correspondent has been allowed to send out a full dispatch on the situation in over a year.

Atkinson: What is the status of the (Communist-led) 18th Group Army? Is it an integral part of the national army in the same way as other armies?

Liang: It was originally... but due to cases of insubordination a new situation has arisen and supplies had not been sent them....

White: The Japanese radio says continually that they are fighting the (Communist-led) New Fourth Army, but in Chongqing we are told that the New Fourth Army no longer exists. Which is true?

Wu Guochen (Mayor of Chongqing): If you want to heed the Japanese news, go ahead.

Liang: Elements in China are playing up the situation to serve their own ends. Recently a message carried by *Reynolds News* in England quoted Madame Sun Yat-sen's appeal to Labor in England and America as saying that the reactionary elements in Chongqing are trying to tighten the blockade against the Communist areas, and China is on the brink of conflict. An apparently twisted report, I called on Madame Sun and she denied it, producing the original telegram which reads:

"On the Thirty-Second Anniversary of the founding of the Chinese Republic we must remember that progress toward democracy is like learning to swim. One learns not by talking about it but by getting into the water.... Those serve best who devote all their energies to the fight against aggression. American friends can help democracy by actively supporting all elements actually engaged in fighting Japan. —Madame Sun Yat-sen."

There is nothing like "reactionary elements" in her telegram. And nothing like a demand for lifting the blockade, etc.... I reiterate that I would like to have the opportunity to put the matter before you in the future, and if you will excuse the spokesman, this matter will be regarded as concluded.

Israel Epstein: With regard to your statement that the 18th Group Army was regarded as an army of the National Government until a situation necessitated the stopping of supplies, how long have the supplies been stopped? With regard to the cable sent by Madame Sun Yat-sen in which she says, "American friends can help Chinese democracy by supporting all elements actually engaged in fighting Japan," can we not take it as an implied criticism that the two armies are not equally supported?

Liang: I will answer later as to when the payment of those troops was suspended. The... Communists were collecting taxes on their own responsibility. The moment that was known to the government, payment was suspended...Within the last two weeks there has been no special reason to lay emphasis on the Communist problem....one army corps has been withdrawn from the area.

White: But for months we have been blockaded. We have not been allowed to mention the situation.

Liang: It is to nobody's interest to dwell on this. Why make a mountain out of a molehill?

White: You are trying to make a molehill out of a mountain.

Gelder: If the Chinese government has thousands of troops blockading other Chinese troops, how can they be all-out against Japan?

Liang: In every war you have to both fight at the front and to police the rear.

Gelder: I want to ask if we shall be allowed to go to the Communist areas.

Stein: Will you allow me to send a cable to Yan'an asking for a statement? If and when I get a reply, will you allow me to publish it?

Wu: It is not our system to allow local government to make separate statements.

Liang: I do not wish to say the Communists are trying to undermine the government. If we go that far, how can we settle the question?

Stein: Is it worthwhile to spend money on such a cable (to Yan'an)?

Liang: You must send it by the military telegraph station.

Stein: So there is a blockade.

Wu: Oh no. But don't quote me. I am just talking (laughter).

Unidentified foreign newsman: Are correspondents permitted to go to Yan'an and North Shaanxi.

Liang: So far as my opinion is concerned, I hope all of you may go, but this has to be approved by the military authorities.

Atkinson: Here is a letter signed by some of the correspondents to the Generalissimo (Chiang Kai-shek) asking permission to go to Yan'an.

This press conference was only one of a series, which grew more and more fiery in nature until the final approval of the trip.

In the meantime, Minister Liang Hanchao made another memorable pronouncement. When newsmen repeated that they wanted the truth, he gave them a lesson in philosophy which he said was his special field, and obviously not theirs, otherwise they would know that none of the great philosophers, ancient and modern, Eastern and Western, had even been able to define what *truth* really was!

This became a standing joke in the Press Hostel. So did a statement by Vice-Minister of Information Hollington Tong. He opposed the correspondents going to Yan'an purely out of kindness to them. Not going, they would be disappointed. But they would be even more unhappy if they went and what they wrote was cut out by the government censors, among whom he was one of the chief officers.

*　　*　　*

The reason we of the press finally got to Yan'an and anti-Japanese resistance bases was not just due to our own pressure, which would not have been enough, but that of the allied governments—and particularly the United States. And the reason for that was the rapid crumbling of the already passive military posture of the Guomindang.

In the circumstances of the stalemate on its front with the Japanese, this would not have occurred. But by 1944 the sea-borne links between the far flung parts of Japan's new empire were being severed by increased U.S. naval triumphs. Yet those routes were essential for moving and supplying her occupation forces and importing seized raw materials back to Japan. So she countered by an offensive in China to connect overland routes, mostly by rail, from her northernmost to her southernmost conquered territories on the Asian continent—that is, from Northeast China all the way to the Southeast Asian coastline—and to force the surrender or destruction of the Chiang Kai-shek regime. By that spring, her army was advancing in the direction of Chongqing. In Guiyang to the south, which was directly in the path of the Japanese forces though they never entered it, I saw scenes of the Guomindang's military demoralization and panic before even a shot was fired, which made me realize a single person appearing in a Japanese uniform could have caused the city to be abandoned. Prior to this situation, the Guomindang had been bemused by the prospect held out by General Chennault of the U.S. Air Force—such a believer in the decisiveness of air power—that 500 planes could drive the invaders out of China. This dream naturally attracted Chiang Kai-shek who did not want to risk his own forces in land battles with the Japanese, which he hoarded for civil war. The new offensive by the Japanese, whose easy advance caused the U.S. Air Force to hurriedly abandon its own most advanced base in Guilin, destroying all its own installations on the ground, put an end to the Chennault-Chiang dream. It proved the correctness of the opposite view advocated by General Stilwell, that with good training and leadership, Chinese soldiers could not only fight back on land but provide defense for air bases as well. This was already being demonstrated on the China-Burma border, where troops trained on such principles were very effective in combat. But where were there Chinese forces capable of keeping the war going wherever the enemy penetrated, never yielding? The answer, now apparent to the Allies as well, was the areas led by the Chinese Communist Party, with which contact was necessary for any further conduct of the war with Japan.

It was allied pressure—notably by Stilwell and those who thought like him—which finally caused the Guomindang to authorize the press trip, though it would attempt to control it—and later to accept the dispatch of the U.S. Army observer group (code-named the "Dixie Mission") to Yan'an and the battlefronts it led.

Chapter 16

FROM CHONGQING TO YAN'AN

The real start of the foreign journalists' blockade-breaking journey to the Communist-led areas was their repeated insistence at heated press conferences in Chongqing that the Guomindang authorities should permit them to go there. At first their many requests were refused or ignored. Later, Chiang Kai-shek and his government agreed, but set restrictive conditions: They could only go as part of an officially organized and chaperoned group, in which the foreign newsmen would be outnumbered several fold by reporters from Chinese news media run (or tolerated) by the Chongqing authorities; and all reports of statements by the Communist side would be censored unless accompanied by Guomindang comment or refutations.

But even this grudging and ill-tempered permission could not have been won through the correspondents' pressure alone. In 1944, China's World War II allies wanted that window opened. Though in Europe, victory over Germany was in sight, Japan's forces in China were making fresh advances into areas under Chongqing control, which showed no ability, or inclination, to fight back. Should that front collapse, it would leave the Communist-led forces as the sole hope of anti-Japanese resistance within China. How to verify their claims of effective recovery of vast rural territories behind the Japanese lines? How to make contact with them for joint operations in the anticipated long haul toward victory over Japan? This was of increasing concern to the United States, whose naval triumphs in the Pacific seemed to bring closer the possibility of a landing on the North China coast as well. It was prominent in the mind of General Stilwell, who thought highly of the patriotism and fighting potential of the Chinese people but despised and distrusted Chiang's corrupt officials and battle-shy commanders. Backing the correspondents, he got permission for Colonel Melvin Casberg of the U.S. Army Medical Corps to accompany us. Later, with the backing of the Roosevelt administration, he would send the "Dixie Mission" to Yan'an and the guerrilla fronts—accompanied by his State Department political advisers John Davies and John S. Service, both China-born, Chinese-speaking, and in favor of close cooperation with the Communist forces against Japan.

After the Guomindang, under increasing pressure, agreed to the journalists' trip, it took further steps to control its composition. Elsie, with press credentials from the London *Daily Telegraph*, and several Canadian publications, was excluded on the pretext of a lack of suitable sanitary and other facilities for women. Actually, the motive was political. Xie Baochao, the Guomindang-appointed leader of the tour, at first assured us he was doing everything possible to include Elsie. But behind our backs he boasted to Richard Watts, Jr. of the U.S. Office of War Information in Chongqing:

> Epstein was a fool to expect anyone to help his wife to go. We would never let her go in a hundred years, because we suspect him of wanting to stay in the Border region, and that was certainly the reason he wanted his wife with him.

Absolute nonsense for what we wanted to do—and what the Guomindang feared—was to publicize the facts in the media abroad, not to cut ourselves off from the outside.

The newly-founded Foreign Journalists' Club in Chongqing protested the exclusion of Elsie as sexual discrimination against an assigned journalist. So did the Canadian ambassador, General Victor Odlum, who described to Elsie how he had fumed to Hollington Tong that "a ridiculous regulation" should not "keep the correspondent of the entire Canadian press from going on this trip" and that "women are tough nowadays, not afraid of hardships."

Elsie failed to get back on the list even after she had personally seen Sun Fo, a senior Guomindang elder, and heard him phone angrily to Information Minister Liang—supposedly "his" man—that he should drop the ban. Behind it, seemingly, was someone higher than the level of these officials.

That Elsie had been excluded late, arbitrarily and suddenly, became clear to us who made the trip. At many points en route in Guomindang territory, we were asked—where was the lady reporter they had prepared for? So the final decision must have come too abruptly for them to be notified that she wouldn't come, and from very high up.

Besides Elsie being seen by the Guomindang as shifting the balance of the foreign group too far to the Left, the actually political ban on women also excluded two influential Chinese female reporters who had applied: Peng Zigang of the *Da Gong Bao* and Pu Xixiu of the *Xin Min Bao*, both known to favor full Guomindang-Communist cooperation against Japan. Whose was the ultimate veto, abrupt and deaf to all protests? Indications were that it was imposed by Chiang Kai-shek himself—according to his habit of reaching down to the most minor details.

The Guomindang also "adjusted" the list of male foreign reporters going to Yan'an. Maurice Votaw, an employee of its Information Ministry, was encouraged to obtain journalist's credentials—from the *Baltimore Post*, and the strongly anti-Communist priest Father Cormac Shanahan to be accredited by the Catholic Church magazine *The Tablet*. But both men, as it turned out, would not denounce Yan'an and its areas as the Guomindang hoped. While not abandoning their conservative convictions, they would be impressed by what they saw there.

Among the Chinese newsmen, carefully selected as they were, the Guomindang was also unable to hold the monopoly. Zhao Chaogou of *Xin Min Bao* in Chongqing would produce a favorable serial report on Yan'an. And Xie Shanqiu, representing the violently anti-Red Guomindang army daily, *Sao Dang Bao*, was in fact an underground Communist Party member who would come into the open in the People's Republic.

Despite all its efforts to "fix" the Yan'an journey, the Guomindang would suffer a serious public relations defeat. This was pre-determined by the clear facts of the situation in China in the last year of World War II. Even among the hand-picked Chinese newsmen the Guomindang could not find effective backers of its case.

The take-off point of our journey, after Chongqing, was Xi'an. From there I wrote my initial dispatch to the *New York Times*:

XI'AN—FORTRESS OF BLOCKADE

Xi'an, where our party of foreign correspondents, proceeding to China's Communist areas for the first time in five years has been for last three days, is an important city for the future of China and for coming Allied continental offensive against Japan in Asia. All the more important now that the opening of the road from India to China seems imminent. The military situation has made clear China's desperate need for internal unity. A Communist plenipotentiary sits in the capital waiting to know if it will make negotiations possible. The fact that major decisions must come from Chongqing does not make Xi'an less of a key point. Xi'an is a great political and military fortress the government has been building up since 1957 for "a settlement of the Communist issue"—and whether the Central Government's policy is conciliatory or rigid, it is Xi'an, which will have to give effect to it.

Being a politico-military fortress, Xi'an looks and feels like one. One's movements are not one's private business. Everything is checked, traced and counterchecked. Chongqing by comparison is liberal in the extreme, and the visitor's first exhilaration at leaving the hot depressing dampness of the Yangtze valley for the sun-drenched Shaanxi plateau is almost immediately succeeded by a feeling of being a piece on a chessboard with movements strictly circumscribed by fixed rules and generally not subject to one's own volition.

The welcome the press party received was royal. We were wined and dined daily like visiting potentates. However, since our purpose was not social, we spent the time between the banquets, etc., seeing key men and key places.

General Hu Zhongnan who holds the political-military command in Xi'an, is not here. After the Japanese completed their occupation of the Ping-Han (Beiping-Hankou) Railway he moved to the front with some of his troops—which are seeing action for the first time in this war—to check their advance in the direction of Shanxi. But his chief of staff, Major-General Luo Zikai, who assured us that he spoke in Hu Chungnan's name, declared flatly that the Communists are "doing no fighting."

The police-state features of Xi'an were evident at every step. When we foreign correspondents went to visit the Communist-led Eighth Route Army's [supposedly open and legal.-I.E.] office in the city, we found the entire stretch of the street where it was located empty of people—such was the (Guomindang) surveillance that anyone daring to walk there might be suspected of secret contact with the Communists. We ourselves, coming by rickshaw, were followed by bicyclists who—in a comic effort at disguise—put on wide-brimmed hats when they saw us looking back too often.

The ever-evident control was one sided, but it was in fact porous. Despite all the efforts to isolate it, the Eighth Route Army office proved to be amazingly up-to-date on our doings in the city. "You went to the British missionaries' house yesterday, and talked about this and that?" "Heard you asked the provincial governor some tough questions," and the like.

And the Xi'an anti-Communist fortress seemed less monolithic when, after attending an anti-Red youth rally specially put on for us, the main and most rabid speaker came into our hotel room and said quietly, "What you heard us say today was all nonsense." This must have taken great courage—risking torture and death if an informer had overheard. It took years for me to learn that this young man, named Chen, was an underground Communist (in the People's Republic he would become open and prominent). In Xi'an, he was attached to the office of General Hu Zhongnan, commander of the troops blockading the Communist-led areas. So was Xiong Xianghui, also in his twenties, who in future years, among other posts, would become the new China's *Charge d' affairs* in Britain and, still later a negotiator, under Zhou Enlai, in the secret talks with Henry Kissinger that led in 1972 to the Nixon visit to China which unfroze U.S.-China relations.

As an intended prize anti-Communist witness, the Guomindang exhibited to us in Xi'an a deserter from the Eighth Route Army garrison in the Yan'an areas—apparently genuine but too honest to be of use to his exhibitors. He had, he said, made three attempts to escape from the Communist-led troops, had been caught twice, and succeeded only in the third attempt. Why had he been so anxious to quit? As a soldier he said indignantly, he had wanted to fight, but was made to work. He was referring to the reclamation and cultivation of wasteland in which the troops in the Yan'an area supplied their own needs and those of civil servants and students. When caught, was he locked up? Beaten? No, he said, with a real tone of grievance, "But I was *criticized!*" Hardly a confirmation of the Guomindang allegations about the savagery of China's Reds.

Another propaganda flop was the arranged visit to a "labor camp" where Communists and their sympathizers were supposedly gently educated to repent their past. Most inmates we saw were teenagers or in their early twenties—students seized on their way to Yan'an. Their quarters were newly spruced up, their answers obviously dictated—who knew what strictures awaited any who dared differ? But one young man still managed to give us a peek behind the scenes. Questioned about the regular term of confinement in the camp, he gave the standard reply, "Two years." But when I asked how long he himself had been there, he muttered, "Four years."

The impression, even among the foreign newsmen, including conservative Votaw, was painful. And the doubts aroused were to be subsequently confirmed in Yan'an.

More efforts to pre-indoctrinate us continued further along the Chongqing-prescribed route, meandering for days through other Guomindang-held points before reaching the Yan'an area.

In Dali in southern Shaanxi Province we met a welcoming group, presented as from different sections of society, and stereotypically unanimous in praising local conditions and denouncing the Communists. The "peasant" delegate, in an expensive silk gown—tried to dispel our skepticism by demonstrating, with his walking stick, how he swung the hoe in the fields.

Later, to illustrate how the Guomindang was holding off the Japanese, we were taken to Dongguan on the Yellow River, directly across from the invaders on the other side, with artillery fire occasionally exchanged at near range. There we met General Hu Zhongnan at last, whose chief job was enforcing the anti-Yan'an blockade. Short, slim, nervous, and seeming to seek a resemblance to Napoleon, he spoke only of Dongguan as an anti-Japanese front.

At a meal at his local headquarters, a toast was proposed by his aide-de-camp, Chiang Wei-kuo (Jiang Weiguo), younger son of Chiang Kai-shek. In relation to this, the effort of the Guomindang to project its desired image would become amusingly evident. Chiang Kai-shek, in his puritan, teetotaler mode had decreed that his army officers must not touch alcohol. Therefore the censor in Chongqing, through which our dispatches had to pass, could not allow reference go Chiang's son touching liquor. Only after a tussle with Elsie, left to fight my battles in the capital, did the censor suggest wording that he could pass. It read something like, "On the orders of his commander, Captain Chiang toasted the newsmen."

Face was preserved.

Our next stop, on the east side of the Yellow River after its great northward elbow-bend, was the final one through which we were routed to absorb more anti-Communism before crossing to the Yan'an region. It was the last remaining stronghold in his home Shanxi Province of Yan Xishan, the wily old warlord who had managed to remain its governor ever since the 1911 downfall of China's monarchy. The place was on a huge hill which he Kenanpo (Hill of Overcoming Difficulties). The reference was to the hardships of war which he did not face but evaded. In a pamphlet collection of my dispatches I titled it "The Magic Mountain of General Yan."

The ageing General (who liked to be respectfully called "the Marshal") was adept at holding on to local power. Decades earlier he had made sure no rival could bring troops into his area, with its vast reserves of coal and thriving traditional banking system based on pawn broking, by building a sole-access railway, with a gauge slightly narrower than the national standard, and a substantial arms-manufacturing plant. Before the Japanese invasion he had maneuvered long and skillfully between warlords contending for national supremacy. After Japan's invasion in 1937, when part of Shanxi was held by the enemy and part recovered by the Eighth Route Army, he maneuvered between both so as to survive post-war. In the meantime, alongside twists and turns which involved him win some battles with the Eighth Route Army, he dreamed up a social-administrative outlook based on himself, feudal though dressed up as innovative, which with which he tried to enlighten us.

After four days in Kenanpo, I wrote in a letter to Elsie:

> This is from the Shangri-La that Yan has built himself… On this loess mound live 10,000 people, all in caves—military staff, provincial officials, textile and other workers, and army. They keep themselves by going down into the country and collecting grain and cotton from the farmers, by revenues from the traffic in Japanese goods across one of the Yellow River bridges Henan Province, and four hours of productive work per person per day, gardening or weaving. Besides regular salaries, they have a cooperative-certificate currency given in exchange for labor in their own time, for which they can buy the produces of other people's labor—cloth, shoes, etc.—and some imported goods at fairly low prices…Although up here there are electric lights, trucks (brought up in parts on pack-mules) and other modern things dragged up from everyplace. The surrounding countryside is in utter desolation, and the place itself is, in effect, a medieval baron's eyrie in which the old man presides over his fiefdom. With his entourage he lives on levies on the near countryside and waits until the unsettled times subside and he can go back, as he hopes, to his provincial capital—Taiyuan.
>
> Up here there are no gods but Yan, no photographs but Yan's displayed in schools and official buildings, and no guiding ideas permitted except those of his New Economic System and his "Farmer-Soldier Cooperation System" under which two men work in the fields to keep one soldier. American-trained University professors, doctors, engineers, staff officers and others live in the light of this philosophy, and in addition are not allowed to smoke, drink, or commit a number of other crimes—on pain of gentle advice to commit suicide.
>
> Yan says he has found "the answer to Communism," and that when the time comes he will propagate it everywhere. That answer is: Divide the soil among everybody, tie them to one spot, outlaw them if they leave. Thus the proletariat, from which the Communists draw support, will be "liquidated as a class"—and there will be no footloose wanderers to join "illegal armies." The system will have soldiers a plenty because each two peasants must obligate themselves to keep a third man constantly under arms and provide ev-

erything necessary for his equipment and sustenance.

Old Yan himself is the reputed author of many books up here—we have each been given a heavy load—and just now one of his lieutenants brought a new one with the four subtitles: "Marshal Yam's View of the Universe," "Marshal Yam's Philosophy of Life," "Political Principles of Love and Justice," and "Organization After the Realization of the Soldier-Farmer Union."

The Eighth Route Army is about 15 miles away, across the river to the Northwest. The Japanese are about 20 miles to the Southeast. There is trade with both, the Marshal and the Eighth Route fight sometimes—and there is a clash going on now, but not in this neighborhood. He says that if the Communists capture any of his people they train them for a month and send them back. But if he captures a Communist, he says, he needs to train him for only a week—and sends him back—because he thinks his principles are stronger!

We are set to cross the river into Communist territory tomorrow, and today people here have been warning us—don't leave any papers in your bags, keep them on your person, the Communists will search your stuff thoroughly before letting it in. One fellow who said this, when asked his reason, said, "Well, I once lived in the Foreign Office Hostel in Chungking and they looked through my stuff even there. So just think of what the Communists will do."

The river below us is only forty yards wide. A little upstream it is four times that, then it narrows and flows into a funnel which the local population says is 8 *li* 18 *chang* (about 3 miles) deep! I don't know how deep it is, but it carries an awful lot of water. Yet no good for water power, though, because it is said the silt in the river is so thick it would foul the turbines.

Chapter 17

YAN'AN: AT THE CENTER

We crossed the raging torrent of the Yellow River on a huge, barge-like wooden boat holding about 50 people, with sixteen rowers all sitting on their haunches, several to an oar, straining every muscle, singing a chant hard to forget, once heard. It was a chant that had its roots in the Yellow River Cantata (*Huang He Da He Chang*), a choral masterpiece that sent shivers up our spines when sung by between one and two hundred voices, as we would hear it later.

It took only a few minutes to cross the river into another world. No flags. No banners. No regimented people leaping up and down with joy as though we visitors were Roosevelt and Churchill combined. Just two peasant-looking men—one young and one bearded. They shook our hands, said they were from the rural township (the unit below a county) government and led us up a cliff into a village composed of caves dug in the loess. We were accommodated in one, containing a long kang (a traditional sleeping ledge often heated from below) and stove, fronted by a courtyard with a cow, a donkey, and a lot of chickens.

Early the next day, a soldier in a dusty blue uniform, with straw sandals and a bandage around his big toe, rode in. He introduced himself as Wang Zhen, commander of the garrison along the whole southern boundary of this border region, and told us there would be horses. He was a general, but we might have been a private: so different was he, in mien and appearance, from the tailored-uniformed and white-gloved officers of the Guomindang.

An hour afterwards came the promised horses on which we were to ride westward. And, about the same time, the first Eighth Route Army troops we saw—sweaty, sun-bronzed boys with toothsome smiles, some better uniformed than Wang—who wore no signs of rank. Several were behung with Japanese rifles and the kind of Japanese officers' swords that were given a place of honor in exhibitions of trophies at Division or Army headquarters in other parts of China, but seemed to be on the shoulders of every other man here.

As it turned out they had traveled fast and far to greet us. Because this wasn't the place we were supposed to cross into Yan'an. Our Guomindang escorts later boasted of having purposely changed the landing place to catch the Communists by surprise and force them to take us through places where some supposed "Red secrets" could be uncovered. Subsequently, they claimed, falsely, that opium was grown there.

The Eighth Routers who met us, together with their commander, Wang Zhen, had fought together in Hebei and Shanxi provinces before being transferred to garrison duty in Yan'an. They said, of course, that they had seized their rifles and swords from the Japanese in battle, and turned them round for use against the enemy. They laughed a lot, and you could imagine them going into combat, then coming out—a little browner and sweatier, but with the same grin on their faces, the same obvious care for their weapons, the same bright red rags drawn through their ammunition belts for decoration, and the same exuberant curiosity that made them ask us about many things in the world at large in the first hour.

We did not know then that Wang Zhen, a railway worker before he became a revolutionary warrior, and the 359th Brigade he led, had not only a brilliant battle record stretching back through the Red Army days of the ten-year civil war but were famous throughout the border region for reclaiming a wild, overgrown valley, Nanniwan, and teaching it to produce grain, vegetables, and cotton to take care of food and clothing. This accomplishment we would shortly see for ourselves, and be told that when the brigade moved out, the newly-fruitful lands would be turned over to the people, who already did not to have to pay any of their own crops in taxes to maintain the troops.

Once atop our horses, we were shown that the success of the "production movement," as exemplified by the success and extension of the Nanniwan experience, had sharply changed the reputed "desert" of the Border region, because every once-barren hilltop and terraced slope seemed to be cultivated with millet or wheat or beans or flax or cotton. There was no cotton here at all before the blockade and people dressed in rags for a couple of years, but not any more, because the region supplied half its needs the previous year—with the farmers growing cotton willingly because of tax exemptions for the first couple of harvests, and because wide-reaching publicity taught everyone why the region, and the conduct of the war, required cotton. The marketing and supply co-operatives—with 250,000 members out of a total regional population of 1,500,000—were bound to buy up the whole crop at a fair price—the government standing pledged to take the cotton over if the co-ops couldn't re-sell it. The further spread and local adaptation of the production drive, as we were later to see, also alleviated the material hardships in the Communist-led war bases behind the enemy lines, and was becoming a crucial factor for more victories there.

Work in the fields was done in "labor-exchange teams" in which the farmers organized to jointly till their individual plots—and additionally reclaim waste tract—the crops of which would be evenly divided. So while land was privately owned in the Border region, labor was becoming collective, and, with the reclamation of wasteland collective property was also coming into being. The labor exchange groups speeded sowing and harvesting, and simplified the feeding of the men working in the fields: instead of each man's wife trudging out to bring his lunch, one person from the village could bring it for a whole team. In the meantime, the women were organized into spinning brigades also on the co-op principle. And these savings in labor made it easier to spare men and animals for transport and other jobs if necessary.

The peasants here looked well fed and adequately clothed: some had patches on their clothes but no one was dressed in rags. Instead of running away from the soldiers or staring at them glumly, as those elsewhere in China often did, they engaged them in conversation about the strange beings (us) they were escorting, brought out hot water for the troops to drink and, unasked, took care of the horses whenever we rested. In general, the people behaved as though a member of their own household was on a long journey and needed to be refreshed with drink or cheered up with conversation.

We rode for days, learning all the time. Early on the way, two things happened which illustrated graphically that the Guomindang was still with us, in the persons of Xie Baochao, titular head of our Chinese and foreign reporters' group and some of his henchmen—but also that here they could not run things as they wished, much as they would like to. Early on, Xie declared to Wang Zhen that all the correspondents had been placed under his charge and should not be allowed independent movement. Also, that we foreign reporters on the trip were unscrupulous fools, with no understanding of China and interested solely in writing sensational tales detrimental to Chinese unity to pile up U.S. dollars in our bank accounts. Moreover, he "confided" three of us were Jews—and it was notorious that Jews were out only for money and, being of no nation, could not be expected to understand a national struggle. So his advice was that the Communists should rely on him and let him guide them through this maze.

Contrary to Xie's expectations, however, Wang Zhen told us of this clumsy provocation that same evening, angrily saying that, if it was up to him, he would have shot Xie then and there. Furthermore, Wang had told Xie outright that he, Wang, hadn't fought against Fascists, domestic and Japanese, for so many long years, to be schooled in Fascist ideas by the likes of Xie, whom he considered a *poseur*.

The second occasion was the sudden loud declaration by a Guomindang newsman, from the official Central News Agency, that he had seen opium poppies being grown along our route. Wang Zhen at once proposed that this reporter ride back, accompanied by Zhou Enlai's secretary Chen Jiakang, who had in the meantime joined us, to the area where he claimed to have seen opium poppies, and bring back some samples. He could take all the time he needed. In the meantime, our whole group would go on—he could follow later. The man, sobered at the prospect, refused—and never repeated his story.

Thus both provocations failed, and although Xie would make more difficulties none would make the weather.

* * *

At Kulin, the first country town we reached, we were met by the magistrate, himself a peasant, illiterate a few years before, now able to write if only a simple report. But he knew his county thoroughly, answered every question we asked him in detail, and talked joyfully about the amount of land the peasants had reclaimed and how much richer they were.

He also trotted out a "labor hero:" an old man who had pioneered in reclamation and was helping the resettlement of refugees from the famine in nearby Henan Province. The Border region, which needed people, allotted land to the migrants, supplied them with seeds and implements on long term loan did not tax them during their first three years, and made it a matter of honor and fame for other peasants to help them get on their feet. The labor hero, a tough old man of 60, told how his own life had improved and how he had attended the "Labor Heroes' Conference" in Yan'an last year, learned some new things about the organization of crops and labor, watched a documentary-type movie, shaken Mao Zedong's hand, and been given a suit of clothes and a pair of leather shoes as a prize. He had been landless once, but not any longer, because this was one of the parts of the Border region where the Red Army had divided up the land before 1935.

Though relatively unlettered, he was by no means ill-informed, and asked us about Fascism and Europe, the war in the Soviet Union, When the Second Front would open, and why the Guomindang wouldn't let cotton, medicine, and other necessities into the Region.

The peasant magistrate kidded the peasant labor hero a bit about his new importance (labor heroes became *ipso facto* members of the county government, entitled to attend its meetings and bring up suggestions on their own behalf or that of their fellow villagers. The labor hero joked back that the magistrate had proved good at carrying manure to the fields in the last planting campaign for which all hands had been mobilized—and who had ever heard of a magistrate in the old days doing that kind of work—he never had, though he had lived a long time and knew stories of the area for several times longer than that.

All the days that we rode, we marveled at the new farm tools they had here, hoe-blades and deep plowshares of good white iron or sometimes steel. Several small factories were producing them in the Border region, and its arsenals produced them as a sideline. Even steel dragged all the way from the North China railways (torn up to immobilize the Japanese) was not grudged to agriculture. The production movement got its tools, just as the army did its weapons, through armed struggle against the enemy.

* * *

The next place we got to was Yenchang, where we saw the oil wells and refinery. Three wells were working and they were sinking another, but unable to drill deep enough to get much oil—and they had unluckily lost drilling gear in a failed well. I spoke to the workers at the wellheads and in their club, which was the best building around and was decorated with a Red Star. The trade union chairman was an old seaman from

Singapore who ran their Diesel engines. The organizer had worked in this plant for many years, under American (Standard Oil), Guomindang, and finally Red Army ownership. He said, "Before the Red partisans came we had engineers from Nanjing and workers from Shanghai. They seemed scared to death. I would learn how to run their Diesel engines (they saw I wanted to) and they'd drive us out of the place when they dismantled them. Now I've learned. And we have no professional jealousy among workers because if a skilled man is energetic he can get to be manager of all the wells, no need to be afraid that a local fellow will and leave him out of a job if he learns his secrets."

"Wages are paid in money but fixed in terms of millet (for instance a man may get a *dan* (about 150 lbs.), or 20,000 in Border region currency at this month's rate. Next month, if the price of grain rises it will be worth more. The free market price is standard—there is no controlled market, so the worker can't lose in terms of real wages."

At the small refinery, which had been in ruins before the Border region government re-started it, we saw ingenious improvisations. For instance, when they needed a 2-inch pipe for a condenser and they didn't have one, they fixed a 10-inch pipe inside a 12-inch pipe, both of which they had, and used the space between the two. The manager had been a fitter on a British coastwise steamer. The engineer was educated at St. John's University in Shanghai, and Maurice Votaw, a member of our reporters' group who had taught there was first shocked, then pleased, to recognize in him an old student. They were turning out kerosene, usable gasoline for the 20-odd trucks running around here, and absolutely prime candles—as good as those produced pre-war by the British-owned Asiatic Petroleum Company. The kerosene and candles were big items of trade for the Border region because they, like its salt, were needed outside, and some things could be obtained in exchange. Though those most needed in the Yan'an area were banned by the Guomindang blockade, and because it would cost a merchant his life if he was caught bringing them, the profit was compensation for the risk, which included the cost of bribes.

Earlier, in Chongqing, I had learned things about the Yanchang oilfield which its people themselves did not tell me. In a United front spirit, it had helped the Guomindang, but the latter's press censors had kept the news from going abroad. And the absoluteness of the muzzling, coupled with its mean pettiness, indicated a link with instructions from Chiang Kai-shek himself:

Hollington Tong said to Theodore H. White, *Time* magazine's correspondent in Chongqing, that when the Yumen oilfield in Gansu Province—then China's biggest domestic source of oil—was being inaugurated in 1938, the only drilling machinery in Northwest China was in Yanchang, taken by the Chinese Red Army during the civil war. So, when Guomindang-Communist cooperation against Japan's invasion began, Zhou Enlai was asked by the Minister Weng of the Guomindang government to supply the equipment, to which he responded, "Of course we will hand it over to you. We have been keeping it until China needed it." And he did hand it over.

But when White tried to transmit this in a news report, Tong angrily declared to him:

"This can't go out! Can't you see that the Communists will use it in their propaganda abroad?"

"But Minister Weng himself gave me the facts," White objected.

"The Minister may have, but he had no right to give a newspaperman secret state information. Maybe he wants to take responsibility before Generalissimo Chiang Kai-shek if it goes out. Then it's okay."

Right there, Tong picked up the telephone and called Minister Weng's office. The latter admitted he had given the information, then suddenly asked: "Let me hear White's story. Has he any figures on oil production?"

"Yes," said Tong, "of course he has some."

"Then," said Minister Weng, saving his face and possibly his job, "you'd better kill the message. We can't have figures going out."

*　　*　　*

Rudimentary though industry was in the economic backwater of northern Shaanxi, where the Border region was located, efforts were being made to develop it at several points. I remember a co-operative in which we were insistently questioned about how soap was made in our home countries—and, pleading ignorance, drew looks of pitying contempt. What sort of knowledgeable international journalists were these who couldn't even give helpful tips on soap making?

At a higher technical level, the radio people asked us for the metal foil in our used cigarette packs, which, it turned out, they could use to make condensers.

In fact, whatever could be done was being done. An industrial department, with some highly qualified engineers and scientists who had come from urban China, was looking into local resources and initiating possible applications to suit current and, later, other needs. Although the Region had no aircraft, there was rudimentary aviation school whose students could sometimes be seen wheeling and whirling in the streets with little wooden plane replicas in their spread-out hands. No joke. In the sparse present, there was always a conceived future.

No wonder that, in a letter back to Elsie, I would soon write enthusiastically:

> This Border region is not just a miserable blockaded area with brave people in it but a great nation on a small scale—and it is the rear base of areas many times larger, not on a small scale at all. There are probably more varied activities than in all other parts of China and almost certainly more really active people. And these people are amply sure that they are China, China's future. Not that they say it. But it is apparent in every confident word and action, and smile.

I became ever more convinced then that Yan'an was the shape of things to come in China, and the next decade would prove it.

Self-reliance and self-support were the watchwords. Mao Zedong, a heavy smoker, grew his own tobacco. Zhu De, the commander-in-chief, who liked salads, tended a plot of fine, luscious tomatoes—of which he gave us several boxes when we went back to Chongqing.

Chapter 18

MEETING MAO

Undoubtedly, the most outstanding person in the Chinese Communist Party at the time was Mao Zedong.

Close up, he was the man Edgar Snow had described: pensive, outspoken, readily finding plain words to convey meanings, but not a phrasemonger, displaying flashes of humor. In his personal behavior, Mao was approachable and simple in Yan'an. He would stroll down the dusty paths, apparently unguarded, talking with the people. When photographed with groups, including ours, he did not occupy the center, nor did anyone guide him there—he stood anyplace, sometimes at the edges, sometimes behind the others. Personal interviews with him were not limited by the clock, sometimes lasting for hours as, after answering questions, he liked to turn the tables and question his interviewers about what they knew and thought, or to extend and check his own knowledge.

The several meals we ate with him, together with other leaders, had no banquet ceremony or scale: the seating was at no more than two or three small, square tables, all very effective for conversation, with simple food. When we were leaving Yan'an, Mao came with one or two colleagues to our cave-style guest quarters to say goodbye, and presented each of us with a lithographed portrait which he had signed.

While in Yan'an, we were impressed by how relaxed and at ease he seemed. All the more as his responsibilities were many, and the pressures great. Mao led the Communist Party which headed a dozen resistance bases behind the Japanese lines, with their constant warfare and complex civil organization. He was the key decision-maker in many-faceted relations with the Guomindang—warding off its attacks, avoiding civil war, spurring it to fight better against Japan. He shaped coming policies, both domestic and international, in theoretical writings and inner-Party debates. Yet there could be no greater contrast than that between his manner and that of Chiang Kai-shek in Chongqing, who was formal, strained, jumpy, often monosyllabic and seemingly always tense.

Chiang insisted on personally getting into everything—from second-guessing his own commanders to analyzing, personally, every official the Guomindang authorized to go abroad—together with a physiognomist hidden behind a curtain: observing whether that person's face gave hints of unsuitability or disloyalty. Mao, on the other hand, was at that time clearly good at delegating responsibility. Geographical separateness and difficulties of communication made it impossible to direct in detail the military and political measures in the far-flung resistance bases. Within overall guidelines, which all were required to understand and adhere to, each decided on its own actions, in a dynamic combination of cohesion and initiative.

On June 12, 1944, Mao gave an interview to our Chongqing press corps:

> We have a common aim—to overthrow the Japanese militarists and on a world scale all the Fascists. For it you too have come to Yan'an, in this remote corner and comparatively historically backward corner of China. But here you will witness a strong eagerness for the Communist Party and the Guomindang to fight Japan shoulder to shoulder in resistance to Japan. We are engaged in anti-Japanese resistance.

> The Second Front has just been established in Europe. That great event heralds the defeat of Germany's Hitler [and] finally the defeat of Japan. It is welcomed by all China, and us Chinese Communists.

> After the defeat of Hitlerism and Japan the world will be a happy place. Here in China, the opening of the Second Front helps us to work more successfully. All anti-Japanese forces must unite more firmly, consolidate and in cooperation with the victorious advance in Europe and the Pacific, to all work better for the defeat of Japanese militarism than we did before.

> In this situation you journalists should be concerned about the internal situation in China. Here I'll say a few words to stress the need for unity, and our attitude.

> First, we support Chiang Kai-shek in persistence in advancing Guomindang-Communist cooperation for the common purpose of defeating Japanese fascism and creating an independent and democratic China. This we have adhered to for many years and still do. We must, for it is the common will of the Chinese people.

> China still has defects and they are very great. To sum up, we need democracy. When we have democracy—we Chinese can do our work properly. Resistance to Japan will be strengthened. We will be able to reconstruct China after the victory. If we have unity and democracy now, it will be a guarantee for the future. China needs national unity to continue. But only with democracy can this be guaranteed.

> Our opinions of the national and world situation can be summed up in

what I've said above.

Mao then gave answers to points raised by the visiting reporters:

Q: On the Guomindang-Communist negotiations going on in Chongqing:

A: We hope the negotiations will really solve problems, but up to the present they've yielded no results.

Q: Did the Chinese Party see the Second Front as opening a new world situation, and would it issue a corresponding declaration?

A: The real change came with the success of the Soviet Union's Stalingrad counteroffensive (in November, 1942). The Second Front marks a new stage, a new opportunity, but not the real turning point. The Chinese Communist Party will not issue a special declaration. Our newspapers have already stated our view.

Q: On the editorial in *Jiefang Ribao* (*Liberation Daily*) the other day said that the Second Front in Europe did create a new stage, as the Soviet victory in Stalingrad had done. Both great events were expressions of cooperation of all anti-Fascist powers. Before the Red Army's counteroffensive in November 1942, fascism was on the upgrade while the anti-Fascist forces were defeated and in retreat. But after the November offensive of the Soviet Red Army the retreat of the anti-Fascist forces stopped and they shifted to counterattack, first in North Africa, then in the Pacific.

A: The offensive of the Soviet Army after Stalingrad marked the turning point world-wide. The Second Front in Europe is a big new step in the Allied offensive. Without it we could not defeat the Axis. With it, we can. The Second Front marks a new stage of the offensive significant for Europe, the Pacific and China.

Today, decades later, what strikes one again is that Mao did not take the Western or the Soviet view of the Second Front, as of itself decisive worldwide. He laid stress then as in the future, on the initiative of anti-Fascist forces in each country.

In a similar vein, the editorial, possibly written by Mao Zedong and certainly approved by him, presumed that after victory in Europe, which the Second Front hastened, munitions and manpower of the Allies could be shifted to the Far East. The Second Front thus created a better situation for China, but she had to rely on her own efforts to take advantage of it. If she relied only on external factors, her own problems could not be solved.

To the question (from a Chinese reporter) of what the Communist Party expected others to do and was prepared to do itself, Mao replied:

"We must coordinate resistance to fascism with democracy—only this can increase our strength. China's armies need democracy too—between officers and soldiers, between the army and the people, between upper and lower levels of command, between various armies. If this is achieved, the army will be united like the British, American, or other democratic armies. We must have democracy in all fields, political, economic, cultural and ideological, in publications and artistic expression. Only when culture is integrated with the people can it be enthusiastically accepted by the masses. We should have democracy within parties and in their relations with each other.

"Internationally, we must have democracy within and between countries. We expect foreign countries, and our foreign friends, to take a democratic attitude toward China. Only with democracy can we consolidate unity within China and internationally, to win the war and build a solid relationship after it.

"Only unity based on the peoples can be called democratic unity, or democratic centralism. Such a democratic system is indestructible. In short, democratic unity is what we hope for from the National Government and the Guomindang party, from our countrymen and China's friends abroad, and from the people in the Fascist countries.

"The postwar League of Nations should be built on a democratic basis. In short, in all fields we are for unity built upon democracy."

In my subsequent separate conversation with Mao Zedong which was off the record and of which I did not preserve notes, I passed on to him the greetings of Soong Ching-ling and the China Defense League, of which I was an officer, and asked for his opinion of how we could best help the liberated areas with medical and other relief supplies which the Guomindang was blocking. A list of needs was given to me to send back.

Mao, in his turn, queried me about events abroad. Knowing that I was writing, among other media, for a news agency serving U.S. labor union papers, he asked me who had more members, the American Federation of Labor (AFL), or the Congress of Industrial Organizations (CIO)—then rivals and not yet, as later, merged. I, being inclined to the rapidly-growing CIO said I thought it had more. He said no, and he was right. This showed the extent to which, in his cave in Yan'an, he kept up with matters outside—and how he did his "homework" before discussing anything. He also asked why Earl Browder, then head of the Communist Party of the U.S., had dissolved it into a "political association" to function within the U.S. two-party system. I cited Browder's own reasons, as printed in the press.

"Then what becomes of the principle of an independent political party of the working class?" Mao asked. Though he said no more, he clearly disapproved—months before the French and other Communist parties criticized Browder's move as unprincipled.

*　*　*

One of Mao's most impressive aspects was his ability to express complex strategic ideas in simple, unforgettable words which could engrave their meaning and logic even on the illiterate. This was not a trick of simplification but a talent born of his own clarity of mind, and ability to concisely and graphically convince. Not for nothing had he begun life as a teacher.

An example was his explanation to the troops of the necessity of giving up, at the start of the civil war 1946-49, the numerous middle-sized towns which the Communist-led forces had moved into at the end of World War II in 1945. For those forces, which in the two previous decades had held virtually no such towns, to evacuate them was at first unthinkable. But a simple parable by Mao helped quickly to convince them:

Imagine, he said, that you are waiting for a vehicle to take you someplace. A robber comes along and makes a grab for your bags and bundles. Should you try to hang on to each bag? No. Rather, let the robber pick up all he can and even help him get it all on his back and into both hands. Then, as he staggers away, hit him on the head and capture both him and the baggage.

This, in essence, was the victorious tactic used to smash the Guomindang armies. They were tied down in many places guarding their newly acquired towns, their forces divided and immobile. The Liberation Army, its mobility unencumbered, cut their communications, and concentrated its forces where needed. Ultimately it took back the towns, and captured or wiped out their Guomindang garrisons, one by one and at minimum cost to itself.

Another parable used by Mao to show why one should keep the initiative without encumbrance was his fable about catching fleas. Let the enemy be so foolish as to try and pin down ten fleas (mobile resistance units)—one under each finger. This would enable China's forces to chop off the foe's fingers one by one.

As for supplies, an effective mobile army could capture them piece-meal from the enemy. The Chinese people's arsenals were in the U.S. and Britain and Chiang Kai-shek was the commander of the transport corps that delivered them. Mao had said this happily in the days of the old Chinese Red Army.

Mao's formula of surrounding the large cities from the country-side (the former initially held by the Guomindang and the latter by the Communist-led armies) was another encapsulation of the method needed in China, whose population was then some 90 per cent rural.

Strategically, in the war with Japan Mao had foreseen three stages. First, the superior-armed enemy would advance and the Chinese armies would withdraw or operate only at its flank. Second, a stage of stale-mate with the main forces of both sides immobilizing each other, but China's guerrillas filtering into the enemy rear. Third, China's forces able to move to the counteroffensive.

Politically, the accompanying pattern would be increasing isolation of the enemy as well as the capitulatory forces domestically and interna-tionally, constant mobilization of the masses against the invaders, and finally the strengthening of China's forces to the point where—along-side an increasing number of allies—they could launch a victorious coun-teroffensive.

These concepts, establishing clear patterns in combatant minds, were worth many divisions—they helped prevent pessimism in retreat and stagnation in stalemate—and pointed the way to victory.

On July 21, 1944, I interviewed Zhu De, commander-in-chief of the Communist-led forces, from the formation of the Chinese Red Army in 1927, when they totaled only 2,000 men, through the period of the world-renowned Long March when they numbered 100,000, to the time of our Yan'an visit in 1944 when their successors, the Eighth Route and New Fourth Armies, claimed 470,000 somewhat better-equipped core troops and 2,100,000 auxiliary guerrillas and people's militia, armed with everything from spears and grenades to rifles, machine-guns, land-mines, and weapons of every shape and size, all of which played an important part in warfare behind the Japanese lines, including rural northern China on both sides of the Great Wall, much of central China north and south of the Yangtze, a strip of southern China between Hong Kong and Guangzhou, and a base on Hainan Island.

Of Zhu De I wrote down the following impression:

> He is a stocky, shambling, kindly man of 58 with a head of thick black hair and large, tranquil brown eyes setting off a broad face whose understanding simplicity has reminded American observers of the main characteristics of Abraham Lincoln. Nothing in his appearance suggests the intrepid field leader and strategist of some of the world's boldest and bitterest military campaigns. Rather he looks like everybody's Dad come home after a long, hard, satisfying day at work, leaning back in unbuttoned relaxation and talking and talking with a quiet smile and ripe homespun wisdom about things he knew well from experience so long and intimate that it had become a part of him.

During the course of the interview I asked Zhu De the following questions:

> Q: What to you think of the present military situation in China and possibilities of its improvement?
>
> A: China's war with Japan has continued for seven years but we are still in the stage of trying to wear down the enemy, who is still advancing. Although it is high time for us to prepare the counteroffensive, our strength is still not sufficient. Considering the enemy's position and China's own, we find that Japan is now politically isolated and in an increasingly unfavorable overall situation. She is trying to consolidate her hold on the vast territories she occupied, in expectation of some new international turn. One military aspect of this consolidation is her attempt to establish a complete system of overland communication, cut China off from the Allies militarily and push back the airbases menacing Japan. Economically she tries to support her war in China by using Chinese resources, where our guerrilla activity is not developed. She has succeeded. On the contrary, where we have guerrilla warfare bases she has failed, because we are constantly destroying her communications and production, blocking her trade and stopping her supply of manpower and materials. Generally, the Japanese have had some successes, for example in the Yangtze valley where they can obtain food for their forces. They can also supply some part of their arms needs from the great arsenal in Yangchuan in Shanxi where the old Taiyuan arsenal machinery has been moved to be closer to sources of iron and coal.
>
> After the enemy has connected the Peiping-Canton (Beijing-Guangzhou) railway, attempts at further penetration will take them away from the plains and into the mountain areas where their forces will be dispersed and communications will be difficult. If we mobilize more people and resources—and this is indispensable—we can take advantage of this and smash such penetrations.

As for China, her international situation is immeasurably better than Japan's. But due to the prevailing government policy of trying to fight the Japanese, the Communist and the democratic aspirations of the people at the same time, the people of China cannot be properly mobilized, and the country's potential strength cannot be developed. Economically, the productive and financial power of our people is not being fully used to build a war economy but only for the interests of a small minority. In communications, China has not grasped the possibilities of making up her backward methods by utilizing our great manpower. Consequently, not only have we (China) been unable to advance but our forces on the regular battlefronts are still suffering continuous defeats, which are primarily due to political and economic reasons.

But we have another front—from behind the enemy lines. Here the Eighth Route and New Fourth armies have developed the power of the masses to the utmost degree—the people have been mobilized, armed forces organized, anti-Japanese democratic bases built up. Through seven years of bitter struggle we have built up a new front in the rear of the enemy, and new forces for resistance, and the enemy is constantly compelled to divert forces to cope with it, without it the regular front also could not have remained steady for long years—for instance Luoyang could not have remained so long in Chinese hands without the activity of the Eighth Route Army on the north bank of the Yellow River. It is because similar policies were not adopted on the regular front and because the Eighth Route Army and New Fourth Army and other mobile forces behind the enemy lines have not received the support that their achievements and the national interest demand, that China has been unable to halt the Japanese advance even up to now.

Regarding the possibilities of improving the position, I must say that the only feasible strategy at present continues to be an all-out war of attrition against the enemy, using mobile and guerrilla tactics. The enemy's weak point today is that after occupying tremendous territories he is extremely dispersed, giving us the advantage of mobility and the chance to strike his relatively small and isolated concentrations one by one, thus greatly wearing him down. This is the only suitable strategy for China in her present condition.

We hope that China's condition will improve. On the regular front this can happen only if the political, economic, and military policies are changed, among them the abolition of the semi-feudal, semi-Fascist dictatorship and the establishment of a democratic political contest which makes it possible to arm the people for the development of guerrilla warfare on a large scale. Within the army, a stop should be put to anti-Communist indoctrination so that all troops have one aim—to defeat the enemy. And the political spy system in the army should be abolished. With the above conditions, and with Allied help in equipment to both the regular front and our forces to the enemy's rear, we can achieve consolidation and make possible a simultaneous offensive by both of these forces.

Q: What in your opinion would be the best Allied strategy and form of

Allied help to China?

A: Allied strategy has two phases—from the sea to the continent and a continental advance against the Japanese. This is in line with the Nimitz Plan and the reason for it is that continental warfare must reply on military forces and developed people's strength in China, supplied with Allied arms. Realization of this result calls among other things for rapid and considerable help to the Eighth Route and New Fourth armies so that they can operate in coordination with an ultimate Allied counteroffensive. Without such bases it is impossible to defeat Japan in China. Military, economic, and political reforms by the authorities responsible for the regular front are also absolutely necessary if this object is to be achieved.

Q: Do you not admit that the central government's troops in Burma, when fed and equipped like American troops, have fought extremely well?

A: Of course, but the reason they can be well fed and clothed is because they have been removed from the military and economic framework which fails to feed and clothe the troops on the regular fronts. Also it is because they have been removed from the political framework, which simultaneously maintains strength against the Japanese, these Communists, and the democratic aspirations of the people. They have only one enemy to face. If they are brought back within the old framework, I think that their fighting power will go down. Do not neglect the inner meaning of superficial facts.

Q: How can the Eighth Route and New Fourth armies cooperate with Allied forces?

A: At present the cooperation can only be indirect—by increasingly disturbing the enemy in central and northern China while he is fighting the Allies in Southeast Asia. Also by building landing fields in our bases, better arrangements for rescuing Allied fliers, supplying intelligence about the enemy and provisioning Allied submarines from sections of the coast we control in Hebei, Shandong, Jiangsu, and Guangdong provinces. Later the indirect cooperation can develop into direct coordination—if the Allies land on coasts where we can help them, or if the continental drive from the south materializes and we operate in direct support of it.

Q: What would the Eighth Route and the New Fourth armies need from the Allies?

A: Arms, ammunition, radio materials, medicine, and technical personnel. We would welcome Allied technical advisers. Air force cooperation can at present be confined to transport to bring us needed materials. Tactical cooperation can come in the future.[12]

---

[12] From other conversations, I learned—for instance—that one of the greatest needs was for light portable cannon to pierce enemy blockhouses along the railways, for which bazookas might perhaps be useful.

Zhou Enlai, factual and lively as ever, gave us a typically wide-ranging insider's review of Guomindang-Communist relations during the war with Japan from its onset to the present, in all of which he had been closely involved. The date was October 13, 1944, when we were about to go back to Chongqing after returning to Yan'an. It was barely a week before the sudden removal of General Stilwell from his post as commander of American forces in the China Theater and Chief of Staff to Chiang Kai-shek. For China, it marked the shift away from the possibility of postwar cooperation renewed civil war. For United States foreign policy towards China it ended the trend to back postwar peace within that country to one of backing and supplying Chiang in his civil war, and represented the first step to 22 years of severed relations with new China, the "who lost China" hysteria, and the plague of McCarthyism.

Zhou began with the eve of the China-Japan War when, in the Xi'an Incident of 1936, he was the Yan'an emissary arranging the compromise after patriotic Guomindang generals Zhang Xueliang and Yang Hucheng, tired of the previous ten-year anti-Communist civil war, had detained Chiang Kai-shek in Xi'an to press him to shift to civil peace and united resistance to Japanese encroachment. Chiang, reluctantly promising to comply, was released and resumed his position as head of the state and its army. In July 1937, Japan's all-out armed invasion provoked China's War of Resistance with both her parties pledged to cooperation as her people demanded.

In 1940, with Guomindang violations of cooperation mounting, a 20-point proposal for strengthening mutual unity was carried from Yan'an to Chongqing by Communist leader, Lin Zuhan. Guomindang negotiators would not transmit it upward (to Chiang) until the written points were reduced to twelve, with the remainder described as oral points only.

In August 1944, Zhou published his *Course of the Negotiations*. The talks were re-activated under new circumstances: In the center of China the long-quiescent Guomindang-held front was crumbling under renewed Japanese blows. In the Northern provinces, the Communist-led forces were demonstrating their effectiveness against Japan by winning back ever-larger tracts of rural territory the enemy had earlier occupied. Only on the Burma border where Guomindang troops fought after re-training and re-supply in India—as arranged through General Stilwell—

did they do better against the Japanese, compared to those elsewhere.

But that did not affect the situation in other areas. Reflecting this whole complex of events, and internal and international pressures, was a more mobile political situation in Chongqing itself. One sign was the Guomindang's reluctant permission for our correspondents' group to go to Yan'an, and soon after, for the dispatch there of the U.S. Army observer mission prompted by Stilwell and pressed for by Washington anxious to speed up the victory over Japan. Another was a re-enlivened public discussion of the National situation on an unprecedented degree, despite Guomindang obstruction, in the Political Consultative Conference (PPC), a body in Chongqing which also included, as a minority, some delegates of the Communists and some middle-of-the-road political groups. However, the discussion was hampered, indeed rendered almost impossible, by numerous pitfalls set by the Guomindang.

In the interview, Zhou refuted point-by-point, a statement by the Guomindang Minister of Information Liang Hanchao on July 26, 1944, which gave the false impression that negotiations between the Guomindang and the Communists were going smoothly and relations between the two parties had improved.

Regarding the alleged improvement of relations, Zhou said it was true insofar as negotiations were occurring where previously there were none, but his view was contrary to Liang's opinion that problems were mainly solved: "I can say with full responsibility that not one single concrete problem, no matter how small has been settled. Problems relating to the re-establishment of our radio connections between Yan'an and Chongqing and free use of mail, release of arrested personnel, and stopping rumors and slanderous comments against Chinese Communists have not been settled. And it is almost superfluous to say that none of the major problems relating to the lifting of the blockade and stopping attacks against the Eighth Route and New Fourth armies have been settled.

"Liang's statement that 'there are no serious differences in the viewpoint of the Government and the Communists' is a deliberate attempt to mislead the people here and abroad. In fact, the principles of the two parties show a wide divergence." Zhou went on to say that the Communists, since the Xi'an incident, have maintained that only democracy can strengthen the war and only democracy can provide a basis for a just and correct settlement of the Guomindang-Communist problem. However, the view-point of the ruling authorities of Guomindang and the National Government was different. The Guomindang's insistence on its one-party rule, together with its policy of restricting, weakening, and annihilating others (pretentiously and demagogically insisting that others must obey and support unity without permitting the question whether the kind of unity spoken of is beneficial to the war), contributed to a further stalemate and lack of progress.

Zhou gave further reason why the two parties were so far apart, refuting Liang's statement that the Communist Party, while pledging co-operation, acts to the contrary, declaring that Communists have kept the 1937 pledges while the Guomindang have not carried out the policy of democratic mobilization and the true realization of Sun Yat-sen's Three Principles of the People (Sanmin Zhuyi), which existed as a corollary to the pledges of the Communists.

Finally, Zhou commented that although Liang said that differences between the parties are in the process of being dissolved and has repeatedly said that China certainly should avoid civil war, realities proved otherwise, shown by the fact that many raids on the border region were made last month, such as an attack by the Guomindang 61st army on the Eighth Route Army position in Shaanxi, and an attack on the New Fourth Army in Hubei, which had rescued downed American pilots, and were attacking the enemy to divert them from campaigns on the regular front. Furthermore, Guomindang troops had attacked the guerilla detachments operating in Guangdong. "These incidents," said Zhou, "show that armed clashes still continue and the danger of civil-war is not yet past.

"The Guomindang and the Communists must unite and the existing problems between parties must be solved immediately. For this, it is necessary that the ruling authorities in the Guomindang immediately give up the one-party dictatorship policy—a policy of weakening and exterminating those differing from it, and must at once put democracy into practice, and through democratic procedures reach a fair and just solution in the relations between the parties. Only thus can success be attained and this is the heartfelt hope of the Communist Party."

My interview with Zhou Enlai took place in his cave, its only furnishings a bed, a table, a couple of chairs, and shelves with many books and newspapers. A tiny transmitter was then beginning to send out the first English language New China (Xinhua)-sponsored newscasts. Not only did Zhou give attention to the content, but when I asked how some of the radio equipment was obtained, I was told he had brought it from Chongqing in a personal suitcase. At a time when even medical supplies to the Eighth Route Army and its resistance bases behind the Japanese lines were denied and blocked by the Guomindang authorities, he always took with him, on periodic trips back to Yan'an, medicines and equipment collected by the China Defense League. Sometimes he even carried in own coat pockets many small but important items, such as dental drill-heads and surgical needles.

Chapter 19

BEHIND ENEMY LINES

One of the most enlightening experiences during my visit to Yan'an and other Communist-led areas was a trip behind enemy lines. Following is my dispatch to the *New York Times*, sent from Yan'an on October 9, 1944:

> I and two other members of the group of foreign correspondents visiting Chinese Communist-led areas have just completed a seven-week, thousand-mile horseback tour of the Eighth Route Army's fighting front in Northwest Shanxi during which we spent 17 days, riding and marching 300 miles behind the Japanese lines.
>
> During our brief but incident and observation-packed stay there, we saw two successful Eighth Route Army attacks from distances respectively of 3 miles and 300 yards from the assaulted Japanese strong points; we were in the immediate vicinity of two others which resulted in the demolition of additional forts; were ourselves twice hunted with the enemy forces on our tails—once one mile and once ten miles behind; slept for two nights in the villages within rifle-shot of enemy blockade blockhouses which the people of these villages had in turn blockaded with hundreds of hand-made mines, booby traps and hidden snipers' nests so that the enemy was afraid to sally out unless the way was cleared for him by strong reinforcements from outside; saw portraits of Roosevelt, Churchill, Stalin, Chiang Kai-shek, Marx, Engels, Lenin and Mao flaunted within an hour's walking march of the Japanese, and slogans such as "Back up the Four Power Declaration by smashing Japanese Fascism!" staring them in the face as they peered out through loopholes, and generally gained a substantial idea of the nature, depth and the infinite variety of the people's war which Communist armies and the local population are waging against the invaders of their country throughout North and Central China.
>
> A Guomindang Information Ministry representative and Major Melvin A. Casberg, United States Army Medical Corps accompanied us throughout the tour, and saw the same things.

We crossed the Lishi-Lanxian motor road which the Japanese hold with block-house forts spaced about 3 miles apart along its entire length, on September 8, after four companies of the Eighth Route regulars who were detailed to protect our passage had decided that the best way to do this was to take Mafang fort which they did by sending a squad to cut the ropes which held up the drawbridge—which was the only way across the surrounding moat. Subsequently, a two-hour fight resulted in the surrender of 50 surviving Japanese-uniformed puppets troops who held the strongpoint, with all their arms. One of the captives was a Captain who also commanded Kaifu, the next block house in the chain. Then the Eighth Routers took him along with them to his men to tell them that with Mafang fallen, their position was hopeless and they had better come out quietly—which they did.

With two forts cleared from our path in 24 hours, we were able to cross the blockade by daylight and inspect and photograph one of the captured strong points which stood within the most formidable defense works. It included the outer barbed wire fence and a draw-bridged moat 30 feet across and 40 feet deep, surrounded by another barbed wire barrier and 3 concentric trenches and dug-outs (the Japanese curiously enough call these by the Russian word tochka, meaning dot, which was most likely the designation of similar Soviet works on which Japanese troops came to grief on the Manchurian frontier when they sought to penetrate it at Changhufeng six years ago).

The liberated town below the strongpoint was full of Eighth Routers and Communist local cadres from the neighboring points, dressed in peasant clothing and carrying side-arms, who were working quickly to organize the people who had been outside their control for over 3 years. Since the population of Mafang itself was still afraid to demolish the fort or even to take away its rafters for firewood fearing Japanese retaliation, the peasant associations to which almost everyone in the Eighth Route Army areas belongs, were mobilizing men from other villages to come to do the job, and as we rode on, we saw at least a thousand old and young men in the opposite direction shouldering picks and hoes, laughing and chattering excitedly as though they were going to some entertainment.

When we passed Mafang again seventeen days later (the Japanese had come once in the interim), the blockhouses, the fort walls, barbed wire, moat, trenches and dug-outs had all completely disappeared and there was nothing on the hill over the town except bare earth. The headquarters of the Eighth Sub-Region of the Shanxi-Suiyan border area to which we came the next day is not more than 30 miles from Japanese strongholds in any direction. It conducts the activities of the Eighth

Route brigade which forms a regular garrison and consists partly of veterans of years of bitter fighting in the flat plains of Central Hebei, partly of units of Shaanxi's "new army" and of several guerilla detachments totalling several thousand men operating in the vicinity of big Japanese-held cities such as Taiyuan and Fenyang. In addition to the "Directing Committee" which includes representatives of the army command, of elected local governments, people's associations, and the Communist Party, it issues general directives to over 12,000 armed men and people's militia who differ from guerillas in that they are not divorced from production but are farmers who train in the agricultural off-season and fight whenever necessary in their own localities with labor exchange groups tilling their land for them at such times.

The People's Militia in the whole sub-region number 12,000 (we saw 600 together from four villages alone) and troops and guerillas number about 8,000, making in all 20,000 armed men out of a total population of 4,000,000—a proportion that was similar to two other sub-regions we had traversed earlier. Two-thirds of all these men were armed with weapons captured from the enemy and the whole picture lends a strong corroborative weight to Communist Party's claim that there are 470,000 regulars and 2,300,000 people's militia in all areas under its control. Enemy forces in this area were 5,800 Japanese and 3,820 puppet soldiers, exclusive of a strong garrison in Taiyuan which was flanked by this region and others, distributed through 110 strongpoints like that we inspected. During a month of our stay in Northwest Shanxi, this sub-region alone has destroyed over twenty blockhouses. At its headquarters, we saw six Japanese prisoners captured on August 28 in a lightning attack, the Eighth Routers pouncing on them as they were unsuspectingly eating a bucolic alfresco breakfast outside their blockhouse wall, bereft of any firearms. The significant fact was that all these Japanese except one had been in the army only since June this year, some of them being young recruits and others older men who were previously rejected for physical reasons. They, as well as ten Koreans who came over to the Eighth Route Army, voluntarily told us that it was well-known in the Japanese army, despite their officers', indoctrination, that the Eighth Route Army does not kill prisoners and that they have seen propaganda materials of the Japanese People's Emancipation League not only at the front but also in major garrison points such as Peiping (Beijing) to the north.

At the headquarters of the village, we also saw over a hundred puppet prisoners taken during the past fortnight and a detachment of 40 which had come over of itself and been allowed to keep its arms during their training course preparatory to their incorporation in the guerilla force in the area where they were originally stationed under Japanese command. At the same time, as Japanese garrisons were decreasing and the enemy compelled to entrust more and more strong points to puppet fighters. All indications showed that the puppet forces are disintegrating rapidly. The Eighth Routers' policy toward the puppets plays an important role in this. For instance, we ourselves witnessed how when Mafang puppets declared that they feared to surrender because of certain enemy retaliation against their families in town, the Eighth Routers quickly mobilized donkey carts, and wives and children with their household effects were moved into a safer area immediately behind the marching prisoners.

Leaving the headquarters, we traveled rapidly through villages with hospital units and hidden mountain caves for doctors and the wounded, and a village with an arsenal which produces 10,000 grenades and land mines monthly, until we reached the foothills of a mountain range which overlooks the important city of Fenyang, one of the most strategic points held by the enemy. We watched the Eighth Route regulars and guerillas attack the suburbs of this city for three successive nights, burning the railway station, airfield, buildings, the power station, and a match factory (whose match boxes bore the inspiring legend "Chinese and Japanese must live and die together! America and Britain must be destroyed!"), and taking a fort one and a half miles from the city gate, killing 10 Japanese and many puppets, and capturing 2 Japanese and some puppet soldiers and the entire personnel of the sub-district government which had taken refuge there, plus 2 machine-guns, 70 rifles, and countless cartons of Japanese cigarettes, biscuits, cakes, and canned goods, etc. By forced marches from several directions, we had concentrated a superior force around the city and one of the main objects of the operation was to make the garrison come out to fight which they stubbornly refused to do despite three days' and nights' constant prodding.

The correspondents' group moved every few hours from one village to another, all within equal radius and within plain sight of Fenyang and in each one found the Eighth Route Army's government operating, people laughing and cheering over victories, local organizers assuring us that all spies had been dealt with long ago by fellow villagers, and that enemy agents appeared only in company with Japanese raiding parties. Thus the regular bases where the Eighth Route's undisputed authority reaches extend to the very gates of Fenyang (we slept in one place only a mile from a Japanese fort) and even villages in which forts equally stand frequently have a double governments—one openly puppet and one patriotic that is secret only from the enemy but is known to the people. (The puppet head himself in such places is often delegated to take this post and use it in ways advantageous to the Eighth Route Army).

From one such place, we used captured Japanese Army stationery to write a note to Emperor Hirohito, care of the Japanese Commander at Fenyang, telling in term of facts, what we ourselves saw, and the plight of his army in the area. A local guerilla detachment promised to drop it into an enemy military post-box within the town.

After three days, we dispersed rapidly when our mounted scouts and the secret telephone depots (some using captured wire and some even barbed wire lines concealed in the shrubbery or under ground) brought news of superior enemy forces on the move. We dodged around, often running not away from but in the direction of other enemy strong points already effectively surrounded.

Three days later, we were again operating at Lofan, a point on the Fen River a few miles north of Fenyang where two surrounded strong points had been softened up by nightly megaphone conversations with scouts of the Japanese People's Emancipation League. From three hundred Japanese soldiers and a hundred or so puppets a number of them were wavering but would not come over, so the Eighth Route Army decided to dig a tunnel under them and blow them up. Here we were, under cover, only 300 yards from the blockhouse and hugged the ground as the enemy noticed our movements and proceeded to open fire with rifles, machine-guns, mortars, and 75mm field artillery. The enemy's night firing was erratic and casualties were few but interference was still sufficient to prevent completion of the mission before dawn, and we left without having seen the result of the engagement. But the following evening when we were staying in another village, we heard heavy explosions which confirmed its success, and received news shortly afterwards that the Lofan strongpoint had been demolished and that apart from a couple of prisoners all the enemy were dead.

Our own casualties in all these attacks (in which over a hundred

Japanese and puppet soldiers were killed and much booty was taken), were 12 dead and about 30 wounded, of whom several were members of people's associations who had brought stretchers, scaling ladders and explosives to the scene of battle. All wounded, both our own and the enemy's, were removed by stretcher and evacuated. The amazement of the Japanese at being treated as human beings, and even given morphine by an American doctor, was a sight to watch.

The explanation of how the Eighth Route Army is able to operate in this way lies primarily in its close contact with the people. The militia, guerillas, and regulars coordinate their activities in all actions. The stream of information from village governments, people's associations, and people's militia is constant and we always knew exactly where we were.

Guerilla and militia commanders have repeatedly demonstrated that their knowledge extended not only to the numbers, movements, and habits of inmates of every strongpoint, but also their names, family situation, and relations among themselves, which servants, water-carriers and peddlers dealing with the enemy had transmitted. For instance, we were told how a strongpoint was taken because guerillas learned that the wife of a puppet soldier had been allowed to contact her husband by the Japanese and she persuaded him to drop the drawbridge at night after which they quietly entered the fort, knifed the sentry, and disposed of the rest of the enemy by tossing hand grenades through windows into their sleeping quarters.

By contrast, the enemy's situation with regard to information must be miserable, as our group of foreigners, the first to visit this part of the country for many years, were able to go about unconcealed, talk to people, and even address mass meetings without the Japanese realizing that we were only a couple of miles away. Mutual confidence between the army and the people appears to be complete, and commanders, on arriving at the village, sometimes gave the public an outline of general tasks on which they were engaged and invariably made a detailed report on the results of each action to the entire population, thanking those who had helped and distributing some of the captured arms and supplied to the people's militia and other local organizations.

Add to this the fact that the Eighth Route Army never takes something for nothing, and that one of the primary duties of every Eighth Route unit is not only to train people in self-defense but to screen the retreat of women and children to hills and secret tunnels when the Japanese approach. It is immediately obvious why the people of these areas are convinced that resistance instead of capitulation is not only a vague patriotic duty but the best thing for their own communities.

The nature of Eighth Route Army's present operation was also suggested by our experiences. Despite the fact that it was unequipped to meet any major Japanese concentration, the Eighth Route and its auxiliary armed organizations were constantly on the offensive, outwitting the enemy and striking at its weak spots. This not only causes losses to the enemy, but erodes its prestige and reduces the area of its control while increasing territory and population under the Eighth Route Administration. Similarly, it also does much to prevent enemy retaliation against Communist-led bases—and the people—as the Japanese have to be constantly on guard everywhere and are unable to concentrate locally a force of suitable size. This not only draws on the reserves of the enemy, but also draws on the rolling stock, trucks, gasoline, in quantities that make such retaliation a matter of higher strategic decision.

With the development of land-mine warfare and sniping among the people (we saw hand grenades and mines lying ready alongside frying pans in old kitchen cupboards), even small parties of Japanese simply cannot leave their strong points safely. The Eighth Routers say they are also in preparation for the next stage—a general counteroffensive—when more and more of Japan's forces are engaged by the Allies and the Eighth Route itself with augmented supplies, such a good field-gun, which would blow a strongpoint to pieces in a couple of hours instead of a week or even a month of careful preparation.

Chapter 20

PASSAGE THROUGH INDIA

We foreign correspondents flew back from Yan'an to Chongqing by U.S. military plane, a service established in the autumn of 1944. Leaving China to do more writing abroad was my plan, and a problem in itself. Since there was no commercial international transport in wartime, the only way out was by U.S. Air Force planes shuttling from India over the Himalayan "hump." They would fly back empty after bringing in their supplies, so there was no shortage of space. But for seats one had to get the required military papers. This was quite easy for a regularly commissioned war correspondent in uniform. But it was hard for us as local news people with accreditations limited to Chongqing.

Finally, with the help of the United States Office of War Information (OWI) for which I had worked part time, we enplaned for Kunming, where the U.S. Fourteenth Air Force was headquartered, and we would have to negotiate our further flight—over the Himalayas. At Kunming's airport we ran into Joseph Alsop, then a Captain and aide-de-camp to Air Force General Claire Chennault. Politically, we were not to his taste, all the more because in the recent command conflict we had sided with General Stilwell while Alsop sided with the very pro-Guomindang Chennault. Still, we had recognized Alsop from Stanley Camp, where he had been interned. He demonstrated the quality of his high-bred respect for a woman such as Elsie, and with a few scribbled and spoken words he promptly got us off to Calcutta.

The plane was a big-bellied twin-propeller C-46, built for carrying capacity and not passenger comfort. It was grimly nicknamed "the flying coffin." Its center space was reserved for cargo. For humans it had only a row of narrow jump seats on the side. On the flight Elsie and I were the sole passengers. Flying unpressurized at such a high altitude we literally froze—starting from our bottoms—as we sat directly on cold metal. Nor did it add to our cheer to see, through a window, that one of the engines was dripping oil. Nonetheless we made it that night to the northern Burmese town of Myitkina, recently recaptured from the Japanese, and a dawn take-off took us, the next morning, over the vast, sad muddy expanse of the Ganges and Brahmaputra deltas.

Many tales were told about these C-46s. Not only of how they found it hard to evade Japanese fighters and were prone to crashing in the mountains even without enemy help, but of how and *what* they smuggled into and out of China, with profits for both clients and crew. Gold doorknobs, even gold toilet seats, were substituted for the regular ones on the plane, suitably repainted in olive-drab.

In Calcutta, catching a lift to the hostel for war correspondents, we were lucky to find Stuart Gelder, of the London *News Chronicle*, who helped arrange a night's stay. Soon we got in touch with my *Allied Labor News* colleague, Nikhil Chakravartty, Oxford-educated and a Communist, as was his beautiful wife Renu, later one of the party's representatives in the Parliament of independent India. Nikhil, who then wrote for the party organ, *The People's War*, was subsequently to start his own weekly, *Mainstream*, resembling in some ways the *New York Nation*. Renu remained in the party until her death in 1994. *Mainstream*, a well-informed, thoughtful, and incisive paper is now edited by their son Sumit.

The situation in India was special. The Congress Party, which made support of World War II conditional on advance toward Indian independence, had been outlawed by the British, and its leaders—Gandhi, Nehru, and others—were in jail. But the Communist Party—underground for decades—could exist openly since it called for popular support of the war against Germany and Japan with their defeat as the first objective (a stand reflected in the title of its paper, *People's War*). Utilizing its new legality, it made broad contacts with many sections of society (both Indian and British) and with soldiers and officers of U.S. and British forces sent in wartime, who, as distinct from those of the regular colonial garrisons—sometimes had anti-Fascist or Left-wing backgrounds. This many-sided outreach was facilitated because, besides workers and peasants, the ranks of India's Communists included highly qualified intellectuals, often educated abroad and from families with far-flung social connections.

Such were Nikhil and Renu, and Mohan Kumaramangalam, who was to become a judge in one of independent India's superior courts. In our two months in India, they introduced us not only to the Left-wing activists and the conditions of the working people (as in Calcutta's tragic slums) but to the whole gamut of the wartime united front.

In Calcutta, lodging was arranged for us in the family of an Indian scientist, and we were put in touch, almost daily, with a range of activists. We visited the well-known Chattopadhya family: one of the sisters was Sarojini Naidu, an outstanding leader of the Indian Congress (whom we missed), and another, Suhasini, who was a Communist, we did meet. We interviewed the Muslim League leader Husayn Sahid Suhrawardy, later to be Premier of Pakistan. We were in touch with the editors of the British-run *Statesman* and the pro-Congress *Hindustan Standard*, both in which I wrote extensive articles about China and in particular what I had seen in China's Communist-led areas.

In Delhi, the only place in India where we stayed in a hotel (the Swiss Hotel) another of our ALN correspondents, Sharaf Athar Ali, helped us in many ways.

We were invited by the (British) Indian Army headquarters in the Red Fort, by officers who had already read my pieces in the major dailies, to give views on the war situation in China. This I did with emphasis on the mass nature of the anti-Japanese fight in the Communist-led areas, including guerrilla tactics and mine-laying by the people's militia. This was not an experience that the British colonialists could muster enthusiasm about for India, where they themselves were an occupying force. But they seemed interested in the added trouble that it gave the Japanese in China, tying up forces that could otherwise be shifted against the British on India itself.

In Delhi, too, in the British Ministry of Information (MOI), we met Elsie old friend Dr. Chen Hansheng from her IPR days. Elsie had helped him escape arrest by Chiang Kai-shek's secret police in Guilin. Also there, to my surprise, was none other than Wilfred Pennell, my one-time editor at the *Peking and Tientsin Times*. After being caught and interned by the Japanese, Pennell had been released in an International Red Cross-sponsored prisoner exchange and joined the MOI as a major broadcaster. What side he was on in Britain's struggle against her Axis enemies was not in doubt, but when I spoke of "the anti-Fascist war," he looked unhappy—though what remained of his early adherence to Mosley and the British Union of Fascists was hard to tell. Perhaps not much. Post-war he would be prominent in Hong Kong as an editor of the *South China Morning Post* and write a memoir, *A Lifetime With the Chinese*, admiring many of the achievements of the new China and in particular, Zhou Enlai, whom he admired. He would live to a ripe old age and retire to Spain, where he died.

In Delhi, also, I was able to negotiate permission to take unhindered to England, our destination after India, not only my notes but also a trophy: a revolver captured from the Japanese and presented to me in Yan'an by Zhu De, with an accompanying note, which helped me show I came by it legitimately.

Bombay, our last stop in India, from which we were to sail to Britain, was another scene. Mohan Kumarangalam took us to see P. C. Joshi, then head of the Indian Communist Party, in its headquarters. It was a sort of commune, with leaders and workers living and eating together. Seemingly loved by all, the small, bespectacled but volcanically indefatigable Joshi talked with machine-gun rapidity moving from subject to subject, domestic, foreign, political, economic and cultural—the latter a lifelong love. He was interested in all we had to say about China, and questioned me on how folk culture was harnessed to national and social objectives in Yan'an, as in the famous *yang-ge* dance and skits.

After these Bombay contacts, the Chinese Communist Party's People's Publishing House collected my Liberated Areas dispatches to the *New York Times* and printed them, with some woodcuts I had brought from Yan'an and captioned, in a pamphlet of a hundred or so pages which they titled *I Visit Yenan, Eye Witness Account of the Communist-led Liberated Areas in North-West China*. It had a wide distribution and, after three decades during which I lost my own copy, I had the pleasure of meeting an American ex-serviceman, the late I. Chevat, who had kept an original ever since buying it in wartime India. Chevat supplied me with a photocopy. Years later he was president of the New York Chapter of the U.S.-China People's Friendship Association.

In India I also met once more two Burmese revolutionaries, Maung Thein Pe and Maung Tin Shwe, who had come to me in Chongqing in 1942 or so with an introduction from Edgar Snow and a request to put them in touch with the Yan'an delegation there, which I had done.

Mohan also arranged that Elsie and I would be house guests of Mrs. Phiroza ("Pipsie") Wadia, a Parsee who lived in a stratosphere of wealth and social position on exclusive Malabar Hill, but nevertheless was a friend of the Left (her husband, whose chief interest was horseracing, did not interfere). At the Wadia house—a frequent guest had been Nehru— we met the gaunt but sartorially immaculate Mohammed Ali Jinnah, leader of the Muslim League and future founder of Pakistan. He was very secular, not at all strict in religious observance, and had married into the Parsee community.

And among prominent Parsees to whom Mrs. Wadia introduced us one was India's top industrialist, the mustached and sporting J. R. D. Tata. Another was the youthfully and handsome pioneer nuclear scientist Homi Baba who would sadly die in a plane crash at the end of the decade. A third was a Wadia cousin prominent as a film producer. Parsee talent shone in many fields.

With Jinnah, I had an interview, the notes of which are unfortunately lost. Tata invited us to his seashore residence, to talk informally about China with some members of his Board of Directors. Our stress, as I recall, was on three things: China would fight until victory whether or not Chiang Kai-shek stayed the course. Her future would be progressive, with the Communists playing a key part. Her postwar development would create prospects for trade and collaboration with Indian partners—including the Tatas if they took the opportunity in time.

A further evidence of the breadth of the Wadias' acquaintance was that we met, in the same milieu, a former royal princess of Turkey, married to a son of the multi-millionaire Nizam (Prince) of Hyderabad. She too was friendly to the Left. And, incidentally, so beautiful that Elsie mocked me for having been struck dumb, unusual for my talkative self, and swore (falsely and teasingly), that she had later heard me whispering breathlessly in my sleep: "Princess, Princess."

Though our stay in India was so short—only two months—the memories of it were indelible. It was a beautiful country, but it was also a sad one, sadder even than bleeding, scarred China.

Despite a seething independence movement, there was, in the ambience and in the eyes of the people, a passivity, a seeming acceptance of fate, an inner tragedy, as distinct from China where people could summon smiles in the face of the worst adversity and where vitality was everywhere apparent—and especially so in the vibrant and awakened liberated areas: war-scarred, bleeding, but with the buoyant joy of defiance against overweening odds and confidence that they were laying the basis of a new China in a new world.

We left Indian convinced that her season of change would come, in her own time and her own way, but inevitably.

*　　*　　*

From Bombay we journeyed to England aboard the *Dunedin Castle*, sailing in convoy through still enemy-infested seas. It took weeks, during which I began writing my book, *The Unfinished Revolution in China*.

The look-out for submarines was constant, with passengers taking turns along with the crew at various points on deck, fore, aft, port, and starboard. The convoying warships—a couple of destroyers—had put a few naval men aboard our ship to drop depth charges and man a couple of guns—both anti-aircraft and surface. Elsie and I were both on the sub watch schedule (I, too often sitting at the typewriter, got a sharp rebuke to appear for duty on time). Elsie, meanwhile, went above and beyond the call of duty: she convinced the anti-aircraft gunners to let her go up in the cockloft and fire practice rounds on the large machine-gun—just in case the regular operator was shot, she could take over!

All this was not just a drill. We did drop depth charges. And, when nearing Gibraltar, we saw sunken hulks sticking out of the water—a reminder of what might be avoided with proper vigilance.

Among the civilian passengers, men and women were segregated for more efficient use of space. But, through friendly arrangements, married couples could have an hour or two together while cabin-mates stayed discreetly out of the way.

We were let ashore en route only once—at Aden. There we saw the great stone cisterns supposedly built by King Solomon—a reminder of the eternal importance, in Arab lands, of fresh water. On one street we dropped into a small bookstore and found—and bought—a Moscow-published English-language translation of Leontieff's *Political Economy*—recommended by the shopkeeper who said it sold well. Marxism was spreading during World War II, even here.

One of my cabin-mates was a young Englishman with an impeccable accent. He had been a commando in various places—and had become a thorough thug. His favorite possession was a Gurkha Kukri, a huge, vicious-looking curved knife, which he would lovingly fondle, running his finger over its razor-sharp curved inner blade and repeating endlessly how neatly and silently it could, if properly handled, slice off a head. Listening to him, he had become fascinated with the act of killing—not any particular hatred for the enemy. His rage, in fact, seemed to be directed at all colored people—who were called "wogs"—and the like. What had crushed the Orient's ancient glory and blocked its dawning future was colonialism and its racial prejudice—clearly the target of the next world-wide struggle.

Chapter 21

ENGLAND, 1945

Going to England was my first experience with Westerners on their home soil, and not as the privileged ruling stratum in a colonial or semi-colonial setting. We arrived there in the spring of 1945, toward the end of the war in Europe, with Nazi bombs still falling on London.

From my early concepts of imperial Britain, I expected monumental grandeur in its capital, but saw none when I got there. Wholly concerned with the war, and with talking about China, I was very much the non-tourist. No time or urge to see the sights—the Tower, London Bridge, Windsor Castle, Hampton Court, Westminster Abbey, St. Paul's Cathedral, nor any of the famous art galleries or any of London's famous museums.

Through the windows of the train from the coast to London, the scene was mostly drab, backyard-like clutter beside the track. The great city, when we got there, was dirty-gray. Its buildings, long unscrubbed and streaked by smoke, showing neither whiteness of marble nor fullness of color, most unlike my imagined metropolis. The true greatness of the people's steadfast courage under the grim reality of war, I would take time to feel.

Elsie's mother, meeting us in London, took us to book a room in the Imperial Hotel in Russell Square, near the British Museum and London University. Like all else, it was war-shabby. Many windows which had lost their glass to bombs were boarded up. At the registration desk, the clerk asked for evidence that Elsie and I were married. With head held high, Elsie's mother declared, "This is my daughter!" which settled the matter.

Lodged on an upper floor, we slept until jolted awake by a distant but powerful explosion. A V-2 rocket had hit Smithfield Market, causing some of the worst casualties that late in the war.

For our first London breakfast a frowsy young waitress slapped down two leathery omelets. "Dried eggs" she drawled, "They're aw-f-u-ul!" I rather liked her bluntness. Things were what they were, and one put up with them, didn't pretty them up, and did what one had to do. A firm basis for living through, and winning, long wars.

Concerning dehydrated products, I would soon hear a wartime joke: British troops were wading ashore under fire in Normandy. Close by was a landing craft from which tiny men, flat as if cut from cardboard, were disembarking in droves. "Gor, what's that?" one soldier said to another. "Dehydrated Yanks," said his mate. "Yanks with the piss taken out of them!"

Not that the British didn't want help from their U.S. allies. But their high pay, unlimited Post-Exchange supplies and bumptious vigor not yet wearied by war, plus the real (or fancied) appeal to many British girls and women, was resented. The Americans, ran the complaint, were "Overpaid, Over-sexed, and Over Here!"

Indeed the British, on the low side of unequal rewards and elements of foreign occupation, showed some signs of feeling, in their own homeland, just as "natives" in their colonies felt toward them.

I quickly came to appreciate the English at home much more than I had their compatriots in the East, so often given to superior airs. I was impressed by the wartime spirit of equality, the wholesome if unimaginative food in the government-run "British Restaurants" available to all at rock-bottom prices. Lunch was a shilling and sixpence (in U.S. money about a dime), though money then was not so inflated. Also cheap were the "utility" clothing and shoes, plain in appearance but eminently durable. Decades later I would still be using items that just wouldn't wear out.

Some of the down-to-earth equality would in time disappear—after all Britain's was a class society and despite the wartime community feeling would remain so. But its pre-war rigidity was much shaken.

From London we went to Elsie's home area, the North Riding of Yorkshire. Her younger brother, Richard, still farmed the last of the family land (on which he was a tenant of older brother Francis, a banker.) We went by train. With fuel supplies controlled, private motoring was virtually nonexistent.

Elsie remarked that the countryside was less green and lush than before, because so much grassland was ploughed up in wartime to ensure grain supplies.

Elsie's brother Richard, university-trained in agriculture, was both a working and a scientific farmer. He took most seriously the mission of producing more food in the nation's crisis. Up and booted at dawn, he would stump in, already tired, to lunch, rouse himself to do the honors with a glass of sherry, eat heartily, move to an armchair with his newspaper, and doze off. Often I would embark or comment on events major and minor, but would receive no response: he was asleep. Waking an hour or so later he would pull himself up and stump back to the fields and cow pens, until sunset.

In the Orient, I had never seen Englishmen doing manual work. Here I found that they did so, much harder than I had ever done. Once when Richard's wife, Rachel, and Elsie were putting away the meal and I was ensconced in a chair, his four-year-old daughter, Daphne, suddenly piped up, "Uncle Eppy sits, and sits and sits and sits!" It cleared my mind. In China, even though poor as foreigners go, we had had at least one servant (compared to several in wealthier households) and many home chores were done for us.

Banker-brother Francis, now in uniform as an officer in the anti-aircraft defense, came to the farm for only a day. Unlike Elsie's mother and Richard he did not take me in stride. His favorite sister's marriage to someone like me, a Jewish scribbler, didn't sit well with him. Wasn't it bad enough that his younger sister, Rosamond, had married Christopher Caffrey, an Irish Catholic aircraft worker? Francis kept his distance, albeit politely.

Towards Elsie, close to him in age, whom he respected and who knew how to hold her own, he could not disclose much of his full displeasure. But toward Rosamond, twelve years younger than Elsie, he did so, not inviting her to his home and hardly acknowledging Chris at all, not even to the extent of taking him out to lunch. He did ask me, as a formal gesture, to eat with him at his London club, White's. But there were spots of awkwardness: How would I like my steak, I remember the waiter asking me. "Rare," I said. "What on earth does that mean?" harrumphed Francis, and when I explained, he said, "Hmm, an Americanism. We say 'underdone.'" He always kept me at arm's length, and Chris, a very good man and a well-read one, at more than arm's length.

Francis was to rise high in Barclay's Bank, to head its Paris branch and a directorship. He knew France, her language and literature. He had a sense of humor. But towards whatever and whoever did not conform to his concepts, he could be all stiffness. That mellowed only much later, under the impact of tragedy: the death of his son in skiing accident.

Meta, his Scottish wife, was warm, with no airs.

It was in 1945 that I also first met Rosamond Caffrey, Elsie's younger sister, who, for a half-century to come, would be a loved relative and friend. Insouciant and brave, Ros turned up carrying in her arms her daughter Gill, then her only child, destined to be the eldest of eight and, at this writing, already a grandmother.

At the war's end, Ros was just 28, a university-trained hospital dietitian, thanks to her father's belief, rare for his time and class, that even daughters of "country" families should have a profession enabling them to earn their own living. In marrying Chris Caffrey she had also shown great grit, not only because of the opposition of her family, including her mother, but also because Chris was not a well man, suffering from osteomyelitis. This, however, did not keep him from his job. He was strong in his skills, his Labor Party affiliation, and his Catholicism, a combination bred in Manchester's largely Irish working-class suburb of Salford where he grew up. Because the British aircraft industry in which he worked was scattered about, he was employed in another part of the country, and he and Ros had no fixed abode: they lived and moved in a caravan (motor-towed trailer) until four of their children were born. This family, which grew and kept to its chosen road against great odds, became and remain, very dear to me as they were to Elsie.

In Yorkshire I met some of Elsie's friends among her father's former tenants. Though they called her "Miss Elsie" they had grown up together and there was no other formality. With them we went to cattle fairs and other rural gatherings. Elsie, trained in dairying at Reading, was an acknowledged good judge of bulls and cows—and completely in her element.

All in all, involvement in Elsie's class-segmented family gave me much palpable knowledge of the shifts in British society, both then and later on.

* * *

After several weeks in England, I began to speak and write much about the situation in China, especially my still-fresh experience of the Communist-led resistance behind the Japanese lines.

I did so mainly under the auspices of the China Campaign Committee, a pioneer British organization helping and publicizing wartime

China. My correspondence to them dated back to my China Defense League work in Hong Kong in 1938-1939. The honorary secretary and active leader was Dorothy Woodman, of the British Union for Democratic Control, wife of Kingsley Martin, editor of the Left-liberal weekly *New Statesman and Nation*. The national organizer was Arthur Clegg, a Communist teacher and poet, and ever after a personal friend.[13]

To keep Left-wing opinion in Britain informed of the news I brought with me, I wrote in the *Labor Monthly* in 1945:

> The Japanese [have launched] their first major strategic offensive since 1939 whose rapid success in occupying all of America's advanced air bases in China has proved to the hilt the degeneration of the Guomindang military machine to the point of worthlessness.[14]
>
> The Guomindang armies have not always been worthless. We remember the heroic stand at Shanghai, the victory of Taierhzhuang, the slow retreat to Hankow [Wuhan], and other achievements of the period of greatest national unity in 1937-38. In many cases the troops that distinguished themselves at that time such as those of General Tang Enbo, were the same ones that six years later disintegrated at the first attack of the enemy in Henan in 1944 and fled across the province as an unruly rabble so hated by the people it was supposed to defend that the peasants disarmed its stragglers and beat its wounded to death with flails. Why? In the meantime the province had suffered from misrule and famine. Masses of refugees fled from it to the Yan'an region and liberated areas. Here they found something that they had previously thought existed only in propaganda—Chinese forces, sustained by Chinese resources, well fed, with high morale and not only fighting Japan but winning battles and recovering territory.

I also spoke, invited through Arthur Clegg, to a small group of top leaders of the British Communist Party, including R. Palme Dutt (editor of the *Labor Monthly*), Ted Bramley, and others. Despite their strong sympathy, they were only sketchily informed of details of life and struggle in China's liberated areas and listened with keen interest. I also wrote more than once in *Reynolds News*, the newspaper of the British Cooperative Party, both on the general situation in China and on the important

---

[13] Clegg, many years later, wrote a most informative book, *Aid China: Memories of a Forgotten Campaign*, about the work of the Committee. It was published in English by New World Press, Beijing, in many years after the war.

[14] This refers to "Operation Ichigo" the last major Japanese offensive operation in parts of China where it faced the Guomindang-led armies.

role of cooperatives in the economy of the liberated areas.

With the Cooperative Party, whose 1945 national conference at Scarborough in Yorkshire which we were invited to attend, we had the common ground of Elsie's long work for, and my active interest in, wartime China's pioneer industrial cooperatives. Scarborough, I knew from hearsay, was a famed seaside resort. But how different, I found its cold sea, iron-gray sky and break wall of hotels, also gray, from the open golden sands, warm sea and sunny skies of Beidaihe in North China, beloved from my childhood.

With the Yorkshire resort, Elsie's family had a historic connection. One of her ancestors—on the Fairfax side—had been in command of Scarborough Castle in England's Civil War of mid-1600's, first holding it for Parliament against the King, then turning his coat and handing it over to the Royalists, not an honorable memory.

It was in England, that I gave my earliest public speeches abroad. The very first was sponsored by the China Campaign Committee in London's Caxton Hall, where the memorabilia I had brought from Yan'an were also exhibited. I described what I had seen and experienced in both the Guomindang and Communist-led areas of China.

Then, as at other times, Guomindang representatives turned up to try and discredit me and my reporting. George Yeh (Ye Gongchao), later to become "Foreign Minister" in Taiwan, who was in charge of the Chiang Kai-shek regime's publicity in Britain, got up to deny that there were political concentration camps in Guomindang-held territory. Could I specify even one? I named and described four, leaving him scowling and silent.

Another time, speaking before the Women's Cooperative Guild in London, I noticed one listener, younger and more dapper than the rest, busily bent over a shorthand pad on her knee, as if making sure she got my every word down. In the break, I told the Chairman, who asked her for whom she was recording. For the Chinese Embassy, she answered after a pause. Could she hand over her notes? No, she pleaded; she had to type them out for her employers but would send a carbon. How the Embassy might misreport the content there was no telling. In any case, her verbatim record (which I long kept in my papers) could help parry distortions.

H. Vere Redman, an author on Japan then doing wartime work for the British Ministry of Information, expressed great interest in my account of the many Japanese prisoners who, after capture by the Eighth Route Army, had been successfully convinced—through good treatment and a class-brotherhood approach—of the injustice of Japan's war. Joining the Japanese People's Emancipation League in Yan'an, they went with the Chinese guerrillas to the front lines and exhorted their countrymen to come to the same conclusions that they had. Other forces (Chinese and foreign) fighting Japan had taken few prisoners and in even fewer cases (if any) turned them into fellow-fighters. How it was done interested the British military, as it had the American, but they could not follow suit.

In a BBC broadcast I said to a much wider public:

> "We call the parts of China where the Japanese have not yet penetrated 'Free China.' How many people know that there is also a 'Liberated China' behind the Japanese lines and won back from the enemy, and that it consists of fifteen separate anti-Japanese bases with a population of 90 million—a fifth of the people of China, very little less than the total in what remains of Free China (the customary name for unoccupied areas ruled by the Guomindang) and twice the number of people in the British Isles. After five and a half months in Liberated China, I am convinced that these bases can be important to the impending offensive against Japan.

> "How is it that we did not know about these forces before? For over five years the movement of supplies and persons from Free China to Liberated China was forbidden and rigorously suppressed by the Guomindang.

> "Finally, as a result of pressure on the Guomindang leadership, a group of foreign reporters, of whom I was one, were able to go the liberated areas and see for ourselves. We spent two months on horseback and rode a thousand miles through areas in the rear of the enemy. We marched and lived with the patriot troops and people and saw them fight—not only fight, but win victories.

> "The Japanese army had tried for years to exterminate these forces but we saw them kill Japanese occupation troops, blow up their airfields, burn their factories, and drive them out of their garrison strong points.

> "The Japanese had come to rob the people. But we saw Chinese fighters using captured Japanese arms and equipment, and their arms factories using machines captured from the Japanese to make trench-mortars and rifles out of rails from enemy-held railroads, and cartridges out of copper from great heaps of Japanese telephone wire that lay in their dumps. Radios and telephones captured from the enemy link Chinese guerrillas near and far. During our travels we and our escort troops ate captured Japanese rations and smoked captured Japanese cigarettes.

> "The Japanese had come to spread poisonous Fascist nonsense and the

doctrine of submission to the Master Race. But we saw on the walls of every ruined village portraits of the leaders of the United Nations and such slogans as: 'Welcome the Allied landing in Europe!' (Referring to the Normandy landing). It spells the death of Fascism in the West and speeds the counteroffensive against Fascism in Asia. 'Strike the enemy harder. Enlarge our liberated bases. Prepare to take part in the Allied counteroffensive. Work harder. Raise more food. Support the army. Feed and clothe the liberated people. Save the harvest from the enemy.'

"We were not the only ones who saw these slogans. The Japanese too saw them—posted within three or four hundred yards of their garrison posts and sometimes written, at night, on the very walls of their barracks.

"Slogans alone can make men start fighting but they can't keep them fighting for seven years. What made these people persist in the face of Japanese reprisals as ghastly as anything in Europe?

"Strange as it may sound, we found the people of these war-ravaged areas better clothed and fed than those of the much richer and more peaceful parts of the country. This was possible because peasants' rents had been drastically reduced. The tax for the upkeep of the army is assessed in such a way that the poorest peasant pays 5 per cent or less while the landlord pays about 30 per cent of his rent income. Power is in the hands of the common people—whose common lot for centuries past had been impoverishment and misery.

"No wonder the peasants work hard. And the laws are enforced not by officials appointed from above and subject to corruption but by representatives elected on the spot and subject to removal and control."

I also spoke, in a conference room within the British Parliament, to a group of Labor Party M.P.'s chaired by Emmanuel Shinwell, whose main constituency were coal miners.

And the upper end of the social scale, on the introduction of Lord Listowel, active in the China Campaign Committee, I went to see Air Marshal Sir Philip Chetwode, a retired, bushily-mustached old warrior who was chairman of the British Red Cross. My purpose was to see if his organization would give medical aid equally to areas under the two political parties in China instead of just to that under the Guomindang. He was quite sympathetic until I mentioned that such aid—besides its humanitarianism—would show the British public's concern for Chinese unity. At that idea Sir Philip shot bolt upright and expostulated:

"By Jove there are *five hundred million* people in China. It would be *terrible* if they all united."

In Greece, in early 1945, when the anti-Fascist war was not yet over, the British general, Robert Scobie, was already helping Greece's extreme Right-wing turn on and kill the most active fighters in that country's anti-Fascist resistance. This the Chinese knew and Mao Zedong, speaking in April, warned that in China the same kind of thing was being prepared—as the Guomindang "had long been making, and was stepping up, preparations to unleash civil war as soon as the forces of a certain Allied country have cleared a considerable part of the Chinese mainland of the Japanese aggressors."[15]

Mao, of course, was referring to the United States, and what the Guomindang hoped was that Allied countries will do in China what the British Government has been doing in Greece: applauding the butchery perpetrated by Scobie and the reactionary Greek government. Mao's view of the Guomindang was that it was poised to plunge China again into the maelstrom of civil war, as in 1927-37.

Also, at this time, I learned something of the nature and limits of the freedom of the major press in the West in such circumstances. As a fresh arrival from China, I was asked to do an article on the current situation there, by the venerable and respected *Times* of London. In it I drew a parallel between certain wartime events and those of 1927 when the Guomindang had had, as I wrote, "Massacred its Leftist allies" and "suppressed the anti-feudal movement in favor of the landlords." This was a statement of historic Chinese political fact which was incomplete only because it failed to mention the foreign imperialist factor sufficiently. But it didn't suit the Times which proposed rewriting it to read:

After arriving in the Yangtze valley, *the Guomindang reasserted the essentially Chinese character of the revolution as against Russian inspiration and made terms with the more stable elements of Chinese society.*

The editorial additions (italicized above) by me were the complete opposite of actual history. Because it was precisely the Chinese elements of the revolution which suffered from the compromise with foreign domination. But as the article was only signed "A Correspondent" and I thought it not worth jeopardizing what it said about more timely matters, I did not fight this insertion.

As it happened, the article was never published because the war with Japan, which was its main context, had quickly ended after Hiroshima

[15] Mao, *Selected Works*, p225. In "On Coalition Govt" Apr 24, 1945—under the head "The Danger of Civil War."

and Nagasaki. But the *Times* did send me the final proof, to show what they had intended to print, had not events interfered. It contained, in addition to the first "correction" a further editorial gloss, which had not been shown to me before despite our agreement.

The passage concerning the origin of the 1927 Guomindang-Communist split now read:

> Unfortunately the disorders reached a pitch at which orderly government because impossible. The Guomindang then made its peace with the more stable elements of Chinese society as against the Russian-inspired movement organized by Borodin, the excesses of which had excited great opposition among all peaceful citizens. Many Chinese secret societies joined in the massacre of Leftists, and those Communists who survived went into a temporary enclave (where) the Communist creed assumed an essentially Chinese form, compromising with Marxist principles.

It was a good thing that the article died although that would not prevent the same version of events from being peddled again and again. But note the terms of the swindle. "Russian inspiration" as one factor in that revolution—which it had been though not in the *Times* interpretation—was replaced by *"the Russian-inspired movement organized by Borodin"* as if the revolution had no roots in Chinese history. Now the Guomindang had *"made terms with the more stable elements,"* not for the needs of the domestic and foreign rulers but under the pressure of *"all peaceful citizens"* who could no longer tolerate the *"disorders."* The people, this implied, had risen against the Left (and slaughtered the people!)

Where were the gangsters called in to massacre workers and active trade unionists in Shanghai? And where were their Chinese banker patrons and the foreign authorities of Shanghai's "International Settlement" (its then chairman an American) and local French concession, both of whom gave the armed suppressers passage through their territory so they could attack the workers from the rear? In the *Times* version of history they did not exist.

Non-existent too, in that version, were the overwhelming majority of Chinese, the hundreds of millions toiling and exploited on the land and in the towns.

Finally, to justify the subsequent course of the article which praised the current war efforts of the Chinese Communists, the emendation carefully explained that, after a little curative bleeding in the old medical tradition, their redness had paled and they too had become "national."

What had the Chinese peasants and workers been when they continued to oppose imperialism after Chiang Kai-shek compromised with it? Russians, by the definition of the *Times* editor who last doctored the manuscript.

I do not recount this story out of any special animus against the British press or the Times of London, which, particularly during the later war years, had a better score of fairness and fact-facing than some other big papers (diehard Tories even took to reviling it as "the threepenny edition of the *Daily Worker*," the organ of the British Communist Party).

But what all this goes to show is that establishment papers, liberal or otherwise, editorially end up on the same side in class issues, some slowly and shame-facedly, and others with no pretense of moderation or scruple.

What was happening, in fact, was that with the anti-Fascist World War II ending, the line-up was altering to one for an anti-Communist World War III, or, as it turned out, the "Cold War." The example of Britain's General Scobie turning his guns on the Communist-led Greek guerrillas—World War II allies—would be followed repeatedly, in China and elsewhere. For these actions, the propaganda drums were rumbling, while plans were being hatched.

Chapter 22

FROM THE NEW DEAL TO
"WHO LOST CHINA"

Our stay in the United States, from 1945 to 1951, fell into two phases, with the watershed at around 1947.

In the first phase, the post-World War II changes in U.S. policy toward China were already clearly in view, still unfolding gradually, in a complex situation in both countries.

Within China, tensions between the Guomindang and Communists were high. However, the two parties were negotiating to avoid all-out civil war. And the U.S. was acting as mediator through General George C. Marshall (later to be Secretary of State). He was specially sent by President Harry S. Truman, a man of much more limited horizons than his predecessor, President Roosevelt, who had died in April 1945, several months before the end of the war in the Pacific.

Internationally, Washington and Moscow were engaged in summit-level negotiations on a range of world issues, which included the policies of both toward China.

Within the U.S., public opposition to its government's support of Chiang Kai-shek was still not gagged. In this situation, Elsie and I could air our views, not without hostile attention but with no undue hindrance.

In the second phase, the Marshall "mediation" collapsed. Its net effect had been to win time for Chiang Kai-shek to position his forces, partially equipped by the U.S. and largely moved by U.S. air and sea transport, for his civil war. That war broke out in mid-1946. Contrary to Chiang's and Washington's hopes, it ended in 1949 with the military and political defeat of Chiang on the Chinese mainland. Beaten, he fled with his battered forces to the island of Taiwan, again aided by the U.S.

Ruefully, U.S. Secretary of State Dean Acheson had to admit, in his Letter of Transmittal to the official 1,046-page "White Paper" (U.S. Relations with China, August 1949):

> ...(the) result of the civil war in China was beyond the control of the government of the United States... It was the product of internal Chinese

under pressure from Chiang Kai-shek, the U.S. State Department's China staff was being decimated in a campaign begun by the showily boastful but China-ignorant new ambassador, Patrick Hurley. And Jack Service was paying the price—ruin of name and career for having been right, as was later proved, about the basics of the Chinese situation. Only in later years would Service be recognized as one of the most clear-eyed U.S. experts on China.

For me and Elsie, that first American morning was not only tarnished but proved salutary, because it gave sobering warning of things to come—the "those who lost China" outcries in Congress and in major media, and other precursors of McCarthyism on a national scale.

It also pre-ordained that the book I had come to write would only place us at complete odds with Washington's developing policy. The background was that, in China, the Communist-led forces, and their increasing supporters throughout society, were refusing to knuckle under to the virtual American-Chiang Kai-shek alliance against them, with its flagrant utilization of surrendered, but still not disarmed, Japanese troops.

Nor were they overawed, as anticipated, by America's unveiling of its atomic bomb, with its immense killing power. While denouncing the trend to civil war, and advocating a future, fair peace within China, the Communists refused to capitulate to any combination of threats, actual or potential, to avoid a facedown if indeed it proved inevitable.

We in the U.S. chose to help, then and for years to come, with a new organization of progressive and liberal Americans opposing pro-Chiang U.S. intervention in China—the Committee for a Democratic Far Eastern Policy. Expectedly, this subjected us to unfriendly scrutiny by the U.S. authorities.

Indeed, during our first week in New York, we had our first whiff of FBI surveillance, though then targeting the Left-wing American journalist and author Agnes Smedley. Agnes, our old friend, already long away from her beloved China, came to hear our more recent experience. We had just moved to a Riverside Drive apartment lent to me by an acquaintance away on vacation. Within half an hour, the doorbell rang. A solidly-built man said he had come to check on the refrigerator. From the manner in which his wandering eyes observed everything in the room on the way to the kitchen, we suspected a different aim.

With Agnes we talked so late, and she stayed with us overnight.

Before leaving the next morning, working woman that she was, she scrubbed out the kitchen and the garbage pail—jobs she obviously thought wouldn't be done properly by impractical intellectuals.

What the intruder had in fact been up to would be proved to me and Elsie some thirty five years later. A researcher on Smedley in the by-then declassified FBI files came across the agent's report. It mentioned that Agnes had "slept over at Epstein's," with no word, if I recall, of Elsie's being there as well. An example of the insinuations used to spice up the meager findings of surveillance reports.

But despite such disturbing signs, the prevailing social climate we found in America, even with the tide in the Pacific War turning, was still that of the preceding Roosevelt New Deal. In it, rank-and-file Americans had fought for and won many improvements in their outlook and lives, and had come to see the Left as friends and allies, despite tides to the contrary.

An example. While moving from another brief lodging, a cold-water walk-up on New York's worker-inhabited Avenue C, we had piled up along the sidewalk, awaiting a taxi, the threadbare old bags we had brought from China. A passer-by, thinking we were too poor to pay the rent and being forced out, called to others on the street: "An eviction! Let's carry the stuff back upstairs!" As between tenant and landlord, they automatically sided with the tenant, a conditioned reflex developed in the American people's fights against the effects of the pre-war economic depression.

When the FBI began to eye us, this time personally, the same spirit surfaced. Neighbors warned us, voluntarily and unasked, that even this was risky as the Cold War clouds gathered.

The surveillance intensified alongside our increased activity for the Committee for a Democratic Far Eastern Policy. Sometimes the watch seemed deliberately obvious, perhaps to scare us into desisting, sometimes more clandestine. It continued throughout our U.S. stay.

The Committee itself had its triumphs and vicissitudes. It went public in 1945 in a leaflet calling for the return of U.S. troops from China as soon as the Japanese were defeated, and warning against the misuse of American arms and personnel as a political, military, and logistic prop for Chiang Kai-shek's grab for total power. American soldiers in China were also worried by this trend. With the Japanese surrender, many sent petitions for immediate repatriation to their bases. Some paraded in the streets of Shanghai and other Chinese cities with shouts of "We wanna go home!" at times intersecting with marching Chinese students demanding "Yanks go home!" Asked by the Committee to comment on such news from our own China background, by speaking and in print, we gladly complied.

The rapidly-growing list of the Committee's officers, sponsors and other public supporters, reflected the considerable spread of anti-interventionist public sentiment in the U.S. Chosen as chairman was my acquaintance of Wuhan and Taierzhuang days: Brigadier General Evans F. Carlson, who was one of the examples of how Americans, imbued with their country's early democratic and revolutionary values, were drawn to China's Revolution. Repelled by the clear all-out U.S. official support for Chiang Kai-shek, Carlson minced no words and, in November 1946, declared:

> It is my considered opinion that future generations will regard the betrayal of the Chinese people by the American Government in the Truman Administration as one of the greatest errors ever made in American diplomacy.

Along with the stinging anti-imperialist statements of General Smedley Butler before the war, and the wartime attitudes of General Stilwell, those of General Carlson show that the higher ranks of the U.S. military could, and did, include men very different from self-worshipping or swashbuckling types like Generals MacArthur or Patton. And that they could hold principle above ambition or career.

On the Committee letterhead, besides Carlson, were such media figures of the time as Edgar Snow and Helen Snow, Richard Watts, Jr., Leland Stowe, and Freda Kirchwey and Michael Straight, chief editors, respectively, of America's chief liberal weeklies, *The Nation* and, at that time, *The New Republic*. Senior scholarly authorities included Professor L. Carrington Goodrich of Columbia University and Nobel Prize winner Linus Pauling; political notables including former vice-president Henry Wallace, New Deal administrator Rexford Tugwell, and a half-dozen Senators and Congressmen. African-American leaders such as Dr. W.E.B. DuBois and actor Paul Robeson were also included. Several large labor unions (mainly C.I.O.) were represented by national-level leaders. From the world of entertainment came many screenwriters and actors, among them Ronald Reagan, then head of the Screen Actors

Guild.[17]

I was listed a Committee consultant. So were other former newsmen in China, Edgar Snow, Hugh Deane, Richard Watts, Jr., and also Harrison Forman and Gunther Stein who had been with me on the blockade-breaking 1944 trip to Yan'an.

Soon the Committee's active ranks were enlivened by young World War II veterans who began flocking home across the Pacific, from China, Japan, the Philippines, India, and Korea. Some formed affiliated sections dealing with their particular areas. From their personal experience they argued for continued adherence to anti-Fascist aims and knowledgeably called for support of people's struggles against reactionary postwar developments in those countries.

Elsie, a Committee employee and staunch activist, for some years edited its news publication, *Far East Spotlight.*

In addition to their many publications and press releases, the Committee and its war-veteran affiliates sent out speakers, locally and countrywide, and organized national and regional conferences on key issues. I spoke often, and, besides Committee publications, wrote about China, Asia, and other international matters for U.S. and Canadian papers and for Allied Labor News to be carried in scores of trade union weeklies.

In 1947 my book, *The Unfinished Revolution in China* was published by Little, Brown in Boston.

The Committee's executive director, and dynamo of energy and courage, was Maud Russell, who had a long record of YMCA work in China. Arriving in China right after the end of World War I and not returning to live in the U.S. until the early 1940s, she had witnessed the famous May Fourth anti-feudal and anti-imperialist movement of 1919, the revolutionary movement of 1925-27 and its betrayal by Chiang Kai-shek, the temporary capture of a provincial capital, Changsha, in 1930 by the Chinese Red Army, and much of China's War of Resistance against Japanese invasion which began in 1937. In between, she had worked for years among the impoverished working women of China's main metropolis, Shanghai. Increasingly and firmly, Maud sided with the oppressed and exploited majority of the people in their developing revolution against foreign and domestic overlords. The same stand, one must

---

[17] This was the only time my name appeared on the same letterhead as that of any U.S. President. But about Reagan it must be noted that he was no genuine backer of progressive causes but already, as afterwards publicly revealed, an FBI informer.

say, was taken by the majority of American YWCA personnel sent to China. Unlike the YMCA, a part of which was geared to the foreign communities, and which was joined by many Chinese men for advantageous business relationships, the YWCA volunteers for China were placed under, not above—or even on equal terms with—the Chinese YMCA organization. Their assignment, to social and educational work mainly among working women, largely in the industrial sectors which had some dedicated and selfless Chinese leaders, generated quite a different set of sympathies. After retiring back to the United States, many members of that generation of American YWCA Secretaries, became supporters, listed or unlisted, of the Committee for a Democratic Far Eastern Policy. Among them were Rose Terlin, Talitha Gerlach, Lily Haas, and others. Ida Pruitt, who became head of the American Committee for Promotion of the Chinese Industrial Cooperatives (Indusco), though not a YWCA functionary, was a very similar type of social worker.

Maud Russell was truly outstanding—sturdy, agile, a defiant forelock of sandy hair streaked with gray topping her frank-eyed face, she was equal to any emergency. Speaking around the country, she drove her own car—or rather succession of them used up in immense mileage—filled with papers and books for distribution. To save time for her talks, and liaison with local supporters, she drove long hours nonstop. Her ancestors had crossed the continent in covered wagons in the pioneering 1840s and she showed the same grit and endurance.

The FBI Maud could face and outface. Once, in New York, one of its agents came to question her on the Committee's doings. Name some of its supporters, the agent pressed her. "Can't you read? It's all on our letterhead," Maud snapped. "My name is Russell too, we may even be related," the agent said to lower the tension. "Really? Maybe you come from those Russells who dropped off halfway on our hard road to California," Maud countered. To her the quitter was among the lowest forms of life.

Memorable, too, was her self-devised counterstrategy, in later and rockier days of the Committee, to summons for questioning by Red-hunting Congressional committees in Washington. Out-of-towners so "invited" were given a *per diem* of $25 to cover food and board while in the capital. Maud would stay with friends or supporters for free. But for more *per diems* she would try to draw out the sessions by delaying excuses, such as feeling unwell. Then with the maximum possible such funds in her pocket she would go back to New York and burst triumphantly into the office: "Look! Enough money for a new issue of *Spotlight!*"

She herself took no pay. Even so, our Committee's resources were pitifully smaller than those of the then-called "China Lobby," financed by the Guomindang to expand its influence in the United States. But what it lacked in cash, the organization made up in diligence and enthusiasm.

During our time in New York, the renowned former warlord and "Christian General" Feng Yuxiang—a man of huge physique and booming energy—was among our Committee-sponsored speakers. Historically, he had expelled the remaining members of the Manchu monarchy (including ex-emperor Pu Yi, who had already abdicated the throne) from the Forbidden City in 1924, had sided with China's Revolution of 1925-27 (when he had accepted Communists to work in his army, including the young Deng Xiaoping.) But he had veered Right after Chiang Kai-shek's sanguinary betrayal, though taking no part in Chiang's massacres. After the Japanese seizure of Manchuria in 1931, Feng advocated, and once regionally led, armed resistance to the Japanese, in direct contrast with Chiang's passiveness. During the eight-year (1937-45) nationwide war against Japan's invasion, Chiang gave Feng no military command but tried to keep him quiet in a sinecure advisorship. But Feng favored an effective cooperation between the Guomindang and the Communists, and, following V-J Day in 1945, spoke out against Chiang's renewal of civil war, and U.S. support of it. He did so not only in China, but on a visit to America despite efforts by Washington, first to entice him into a "moderate" (actually pro-Chiang) position, then by threats of reprisal, including cutting short his stay, when he persistently refused.

Vivid in my mind still is Feng's street oration in New York's garment district with Agnes Smedley, from a truck that moved slowly through the throng of workers out on their lunch hour. Agnes, eloquent and incisive as usual, was listened to attentively. The marvel was that Feng, speaking in deep-toned Chinese in his parade-ground voice, attracted so much attention. Even with no interpreter, the strength and sincerity of the massive old soldier protesting against foreign backing of civil war in his own country won seemingly instant understanding and sympathy from the crowd.

Faced with Feng's outspokenness, the U.S. government, which had wanted to flatter him into becoming a "third force" obstacle against the approaching Communist victory, shifted to harassing him through the Immigration Service. He came to us for advice and we found him a good defending lawyer, Ira Gollobin of the U.S. Committee for Protection of the Foreign Born.

Ultimately, Feng left the U.S., accepting an invitation to go to China's liberated areas. In 1948, on his roundabout way home, he died, as did one of his daughters, in a fire during a film showing on a Soviet ship in the Black Sea. His wife, Li Dequan, a former YWCA secretary and a progressive as so many of them were, survived and reached China. After the proclamation of the People's Republic, she became its Minister of Health, serving for decades until her own death. Known for energy in her job and for opposition for tobacco smoking, Li would often press Mao Zedong, even at Cabinet meetings, to drop his lifelong habit. Since she was an editorial board member of our magazine, *China Reconstructs*, I, then a constant pipe smoker, was also admonished whenever we met.[18]

Though rough times and smooth, the Committee would survive until after the founding of the People's Republic, when it advocated prompt U.S. recognition, friendship, and trade with the new China.

During the Korean War (1950-53), the McCarthyite pressure on the Committee rose to high pitch. Finally, directly harassed by the U.S. government, the Committee had to dissolve. But Maud kept going. Right up to 1989 she put out her own paper, *Far East Reporter,* and kept driving across the country annually, lecturing and distributing publications. Memorable to us was a trip with her on one coast-to-coast tour. We spoke in Pennsylvania in Pittsburgh and York; in Ohio in Cleveland and Columbus; in Minnesota in Duluth, and Hibbing on the Mesabi Iron Range; in Utah in Salt Lake City and an open-cut copper mining town; in California in San Francisco, Los Angeles, and Asilomar on the Monterey peninsula at a specially-convened conference.

In 1949 we met the founding of the People's Republic of China with enthusiasm. On the cover of the current issue of *Spotlight on the Far East* the Committee printed China's new five-star flag, the first time I believe that it was reproduced in full color in the United States.

[18] Almost half a century later I would often meet, as a fellow member of the Chinese People's Political Consultative Conference, the robust daughter of the pair, Dr. Feng Lida, in the uniform of the medial corps People's Liberation Army, with the rank of Major General.

Elsie and I also celebrated privately. In a recording booth in Times Square I sang the rousing *March of the Volunteers* which I had heard so many years before in Tianjin, inspiring China's fighters in the war against Japan's aggression, and which was now designated as her national anthem.

* * *

The great gulf between the political systems of understanding in the United States with regard to China was considerable when Elsie and I arrived there in 1945. By 1951, when we returned to China, we felt a sense of accomplishment that at least some understanding of the new China had made a difference in popular thought. There was, in America, a tendency, even if superficial, of favoring unity rather than civil war.

In this atmosphere, we made our small contribution to musical contacts between the budding new China and the United States. The China Aid Council was able to arrange the first performance in America of the stirring *Yellow River Cantata* by composer Xian Xinghai. It is a rousing symphonic and choral work which powerfully conveys the depths of the common people's suffering under Japanese invasion and their indomitable will to fight back. Hearing it first in Yan'an in 1944, it had greatly struck our foreign correspondents' group as an expression of the vigor we felt at every turn there. Feeling strongly that it should be heard abroad I had been given a score copied by hand. While still in England, on Elsie's and my way to the States, I worked with Chinese writer Ye Junjian, my old colleague from Hong Kong, to translate the libretto into English. In New York, the China Aid Council succeeded in presenting a recital by the Westminster Choir in Trenton, New Jersey, under the patronage of Charles Edison, governor of that state, and Clare Boothe Luce, wife of press magnate Henry Luce of *Time* and *Life* magazines. Since both Edison and in particular the Luces were on the Right in American politics, the occasion was symbolic of the fact that while the Guomindang was failing in national resistance, the Communist-led forces were enlarging their intensity and scope, and that cooperation between the two parties was the only way to carry China forward. For Elsie and me the Trenton performance marked the first—and last—time we rode in a gubernatorial motorcade with multi-motorcycle escort.

Previously, while weekending in rural Massachusetts with Elsie's former employers, Edward and Alice Carter of the Institute of Pacific Relations, we had shown our Yan'an score to their friend, the Russian-American composer Sergei Koussevitzky, conductor of the prestigious Tanglewood Music Festival, hoping that he might present it there. But the old Russian émigré; perhaps with prejudice against anything from a Communist area, said after a glance at the score that the orchestration was too elementary. The CAC enlisted a sympathizing composer, Wallingford Riegger, to help with an accompaniment for more instruments than were available in Yan'an—which was used with success at Trenton. It was the first time the *Yellow River Cantata* was heard in the United States. As for the Yan'an score, I later presented it to the Chinese Musicians' Union, along with the U.S.-published Riegger version, the libretto as translated in London, and the program printed for the Trenton performance.

Other activities in America in the earlier post-war years when we were still "respectable" were my confrontational debates with Right-wing opponents like Joseph Alsop in Philadelphia under the sponsorship of the Foreign Policy Association, and with Freda Utley and others on New York and national radio (on which Elsie also spoke separately). To this period, too belongs my first and last experience on the fledgling American television industry in the mid-1940s, at the invitation of Henry Cassirer of CBS: where I was dehydrated and almost roasted by the as yet uncontrolled heat of the bright lights.

We went to teach the *Yang-ge* (a traditional peasant harvest dance, which in China's liberated areas was combined with songs for political and social education) to labor union and other progressive summer camps in the Catskill Mountains of New York State. With its joyous, swaying rhythms easily learned, it helped everyone to identify in feeling with China's newly emancipated rural folk.

* * *

From 1949 on, however, Elsie and I were increasingly followed about and even harassed.

Though this was generally unpleasant, I remember one bit of surveillance, which, quite by accident, I rather enjoyed. Leaving an evening meeting on New York's West 23rd St, I soon discovered someone trudging along behind me. At the time we lived on West 123rd St., a hundred blocks uptown. I had of course intended to take the subway but, to my chagrin, found that I hadn't any money in my pocket. So I proceeded to walk the entire way, as at that age I could.

But my "tail," an older and heavier man, found it hard. I quickened my pace, past subway stations at which he must have wished I would catch a train. If he knew my reason, he might even have been tempted to offer me the fare and hopped on after me. As it turned out, I walked all the way, and so did he! In discomfort because he huffed along in a formal business suit, necktie and all, the way J. Edgar Hoover wanted his agents to dress.

Speaking of J. Edgar Hoover, I know at least one occasion when my name was called to his personal attention. In the archives of Stanford University (ironically the Hoover Institution but of course named for President Herbert Hoover), I found in a file bearing my name, a copy of a declassified letter to the FBI chief from Alfre Kohlberg, an active American backer of the Guomindang "China Lobby," asking that I be deported. Kohlberg was a businessman said to have made a pre-Liberation pile out of importing embroidery then done in China by little boys whose eyesight was quickly ruined by such work. So diligent was he in avenging himself on the Chinese Revolution that, despite his wealth, he personally attended and took shorthand notes at our meetings. To FBI Chief Hoover, Kohlberg wrote that I was a danger to the United States and shouldn't be allowed there. That may have been one spur for keeping a watch on me.

Our names also kept appearing in anti-Communist literature: In *Counterattack*, the sheet put out by "retired" FBI agents, one mention in it was enough to prompt the firing of major film stars and screenwriters by intimidated Hollywood studios. In the voluminous printed proceedings of the Senate Internal Security Committee, victims they grilled were repeatedly asked if they knew Israel Epstein and/or Elsie Chomeley if so why, when, where, and how, etc. And we were vilified in books of the anti-Red diatribe variety by John T. Flynn and others.[19]

In this atmosphere, the Immigration authorities began to close in on us. A Mr. Morse, who had first appeared in the *Allied Labor News* office in the guise of a friendly visitor, turned up in a new role—as the interrogator before whom I was summoned in a hearing prior to pos-

---

[19] An example were the extensive quotations in the bulky *Amerasia Papers* by J. Kubek, devoted to incriminating John S. Service and other U.S. officials alleged to have helped "lose China."

sible deportation. With the Committee itself struggling to survive, our remaining in the U.S. with mouths gagged and our friends burdened with defending us as well as themselves seemed to make no sense. So we decided to head back to China, transformed by the Revolution's victory where, perhaps, we might be helpful.

One day I overheard on a crowded New York subway car, two young strap-hangers wedged in beside me, chatting about various things including the physical charms of their respective girlfriends. Soon, they got on to a more serious subject—Korea. One of the men was going to be sent there. This might mean they'd never see each other again, said the other. "The Chinese are in there now—there are 500 million of those people!" That youngster showed a better sense of the realities involved than President Truman, his Secretary of State Dean Acheson, and General Douglas MacArthur, who commanded the U.S. forces in Korea.

In November 1950 came a rare opportunity for direct contact. Soon after the entry of the Chinese People's Volunteers into the Korean War, a delegation—the first and last for some 20 years—came from Beijing to the United Nations in New York. In the delegation were people who had known me well in Hong Kong and in Chongqing, including Qiao Guanhua, who much later would be the China's Minister of Foreign Affairs. Seeking him out I transmitted my request, which resulted in an invitation from Soong Ching-ling to come and work on an English-language magazine she was founding and named *China Reconstructs*.

Elsie, with British passport, was the first to leave the U.S., initially for her home in England, and spending a couple of months in Paris. There, under Dr. Michael Sachs, an American department chief who in wartime had been in China and sympathized with our views, she worked for the International Children's Fund. I, with my passport and visa problems in intervening countries, left the U.S. in March 1951, meeting Elsie in Poland, whence we proceeded further.

My departure from America was voluntary. Besides, where could a stateless person be deported to? Deportation would have been bad since it carried a ban on revisiting the U.S. But I did leave in the nick of time. For, although the Immigration Department was doubtless glad to see me go, a Congressional committee wanted to keep me in the country for one of its inquisitions—and were furious upon hearing the news that that I had been allowed to depart.

Chapter 23

POLAND

We had decided to return to China, but how? For Elsie with her British citizenship, she could go to England and on from there. For me, things were more complicated. With the news of my invitation from the People's Republic, which could be checked with Poland's embassy in Beijing, I asked the Polish Consulate-General in New York for a passport from the new, postwar Poland, on the basis of my Warsaw birth. Now that there were Left-wing states as well as movements and parties, I thought, there should be no difficulty. But there was.

"We're a government now," Polish Consul-General Galiewicz reminded me, so there were no short cuts, only long citizenship procedures. Personally, he was sympathetic. Himself Jewish and a survivor of the Holocaust, he showed me a concentration camp number tattooed on his forearm—remarking that he was probably the world's sole Consul-General so branded. Though unable to make out a passport, he would, on the basis of the verified invitation from China, stamp a transit visa on any other travel document I could obtain.

Luckily, in the U.S., a stateless person could swear out, before any roadside notary, an affidavit of his own identity. While not a travel paper in itself, this could serve as one when anyone visaed it—which Galiewicz did. With no further formality, it would take me to Poland, and, with a Chinese visa issued there, to Beijing. With it, I booked a passage from New York on the liner *Batory*, pride of Poland's renascent merchant marine. At the dockside, for a warm sendoff, were some close friends including my attorney Ira Gollobin.

On the voyage, I met interesting fellow-passengers: Poles going back to re-settle in the homeland, plus one, an old veteran of the U.S. Army in World War I, coming temporarily to visit a sister unseen for decades. When I mislaid a key to my locked suitcase, he taught me how to open it with a bent paperclip—I did not ask whether he had learned this technique to solve personal forgetfulness or for past pilfering. There was a middle-aged Hungarian, inclined to the Left but still a Catholic, who told me indignantly that his priest in Canada had required him to undergo periods of fasts, and abstention from sex with his wife, to protest Hungary's detention of Cardinal Mindzenty, who had served the Fascists. There was a young former Soviet soldier, originally a peasant, who had been captured by the Nazis, then emigrated to Canada where he worked as an unskilled laborer when could find work at all; and finally chose to go home to the U.S.S.R., even though ex-prisoners of war faced severe investigation there on suspicion of capitulation or treason and were frequently sent to punishment camps. When we reached Poland, at the port of Gdynia, he would be met by a towering Soviet officer in full uniform, in whose car they would drive off, for where I don't know.

At Southampton in England, Elsie and I were briefly reunited. The *Batory* anchored outside, not in, the port. It wasn't easy for Elsie to come out to the ship, and on board, but with her usual determined energy she overcame the hurdles. My heart leaped as I glimpsed her on a launch coming across the choppy water. She stood like a figurehead at its prow, her hair, the color of ripe wheat, streaming in the wind.

On board, amid brief intimacies in my cabin, she told me of things since our parting. In an hour she was gone. Hurrying, she had left behind a glove, which I kissed and put away.

In Warsaw I found a room at the Hotel Bristol. Pre-war it had been a top-grade fashionable hostelry, and subsequently, under Nazi occupation, headquarters for the invaders, which was probably why it escaped the destruction of most of the city's buildings by the Germans. Now pretty worn, it still retained signs of past distinction. One sign was the ancient elevator, with its ornamental wrought iron doors. On the move it grunted and clanked, but it had style, like an old dandy from a former age.

Registering at the reception desk, I learned my first lesson, that in a Socialist country of the time what was important was not you were but who was your host. "Who is taking care of you?" I was asked. "I'm taking care of myself," was my reply. This won me a doubting and sidelong glance. I might not have been checked in at all, and had to face wider questioning if I hadn't mentioned that I was going, that same day, to the Chinese embassy. There my travel affidavit was promptly visaed, which made everything legal and proper.

When I produced U.S. dollars to pay my room bill, Zloty, the white-haired desk clerk perhaps pitying my young ignorance, told me that I could get a much better exchange rate on the street. I didn't, being unwilling to break the financial discipline and regulations of a Socialist land. The old man, to his credit, showed no sign of wanting to handle, or profit from, the exchange transaction. Nor did he raise the point again, perhaps deciding to leave a young fool to his folly, or doubting whether I, in my enthusiasm, would say to some governmental friend that I had rejected an illegal suggestion—and from whom? Or was it all a trap, set to catch patrons of the black market? I would never know.

Soon, noticing that I was short on funds, the old man usefully suggested a place where I could get meals suited to my purse. Breakfast of bread and butter, a glass of good milk, and two peeled soft-boiled eggs, was available cheaply at any of the city's many "milk bars"—set up, among other things, to wean Poles away from vodka bars—a difficult task. A cheap substitute for coffee, if you were willing to forget how real coffee tasted, was called Enrilo—made of some sort of roasted grain, like Postum, an American coffee substitute also made from grain but more gritty. All of this helped me to avoid bankruptcy en route to China. Even so, I couldn't have done it if I had not gone promptly to the Polish publishers and the Hungarian and East German embassies to see what I could get in terms of author's royalties from translations of my book, *The Unfinished Revolution in China*, well received in those countries. Payments for two versions: *Revolucia w Chinach Trwa* in Poland, and *Kina Forradalma* in Hungary, did come through. But East German compensation was delayed until after I arrived in Beijing—when I negotiated to get it not in money but in kind: a Contax camera, a portable typewriter, and an accordion.

An early visit in Warsaw was to the Society for Cultural Relations with Foreign Countries. I had been advised to go there by Polish friends in New York, news correspondents Wionczek and Gall and an official of the Polish cultural service whose name I've forgotten. At the Society I was received by a balding man named Rubach, who listened with apparent belief and respect to my tale of having known these people—as well as Poland's chief delegate to the United Nations, Julius Katz-Suchy, and her ambassador to the United States, the noted economist Oscar Lange. Yet, he finally said, pityingly, "But…haven't you got even a little piece of paper?" The Society, as such, couldn't help me see Poland unless there was a document, even a "little" one. This, too, was my first encounter with such matters.

However, the Society did help me within its procedural limits. I was told where there were interesting exhibitions (wystava), of which Warsaw was full. And I was given some fine books—albums of reproductions of outstanding Polish paintings and of the work of Poland's medieval woodcarver Wit Stwoscz, perhaps the world's greatest master of that art. Rubach, personally helpful, found the Polish translator of my book, named Dzialek, after which the two showed me around a bit—apparently with the approval of the Society.

Rubach and Dzialek were interesting products of a complex time. Rotund, jocund Rubach, a literary type, told me how he wrote and published without fear of criticism. Any opinion he expressed, he fortified with a quotation from Marx, Engels, Lenin, or Stalin—from his private card index suiting almost every occasion. Of any other influence other than them, his ordinary conversation gave no inkling.

Dzialek, thin and intense, owed his good English to a great deal of reading plus service in a Polish unit that had warred alongside British and U.S. forces (General Patton's command) in Western Europe. A Polish patriot to the bone, he could not bear to mention anything in which Poland did not excel. During our time together he followed keenly the *Tour de France* bicycle race, in which the Polish team ultimately came in third. Swallowing his disappointment that they were not first, of which there had been some hope, he said, with head held high, "We *won* third place."

A good friend I made was Stanislaw Brodski—an outstanding journalist of *Trybuna Ludu*, then Poland's main paper. I had met him first in New York when he came from Poland to report on key meetings of the United Nations, where I was also an accredited correspondent for *Allied Labor News*. Later I would once more have the pleasure of Brodski's company—when we went with the same reporters' group from Beijing to the signing of the Korean War armistice at Panmunjom.

A much earlier friend I knew from anti-Japanese war days in China was Stanislaw Flato, who had come there in 1939 with a group of medical doctors—he was a doctor himself—after the defeat of the anti-Fascist International Brigade in Spain in which they had previously worked. Flato was an old Communist who under the pre-war reactionary Polish regime had served time in a brutal concentration camp. By 1952, in the new Poland, he held a military position so high up that, in order to see a foreigner like me, he had to get personal permission from Poland's army chief, Konstantin Rokossovsky, who, though a Pole, had been a famed Marshal in the Soviet Army in World War II. Unable to meet me due to scheduling concerns, Flato sent another former International Brigade doctor who had been in China, and who was currently chief medical chief of the Polish Port of Gdynia. Both men would have a tough time in Poland's subsequent political purges after 1951. Flato, after rehabilitation, would transfer to the diplomatic service and return to China as to be Minister-Counselor of the Polish Embassy in Beijing, where we saw each other often in renewed friendship. But such were the political ups and downs in Eastern Europe. After further service in the Polish Foreign Office in Warsaw, he was discharged because he was Jewish—in the wave of anti-Semitism there in the 1960s, when most, if not all, Jews were dismissed from Polish government posts of any significance.

American progressives were then quite numerous in Warsaw, partly due to the dawning menace of McCarthyism in their homeland. Beatrice Johnson, a ranking member of the Communist Party of the United States was working in Polish Radio, where she introduced me to do some script work and writing, mainly on new China, work which helped me with social status as well as with expenses. Solidly-built Boleslay ("Bill") Gebert, for many years a prominent organizer of steel workers in the U.S., had become editor of *Glos Pracy* ("Voice of Labor"), the daily newspaper of the Polish trade unions, for which he appointed me correspondent in China before I returned there, though I actually never did the job. Gebert, in his later years, was appointed Poland's ambassador to Turkey, though it was hard to imagine this old strike leader as a diplomat. Also in Warsaw was Maxim Lieber, a Left Wing literary agent who had helped arrange the East European translations of my book. And, more prominently, the noted Polish-born mathematician Professor Leopold Infeld with his wife and children and sister-in-law Margaret Schlauch, an authority on Europe's medieval culture.

Infeld was Jewish. Amid the later local upsurge of anti-Jewish prejudice, China's Premier Zhou Enlai came on an official visit to Warsaw. At a reception in his honor, he asked for Infeld, whose scientific and progressive reputation he knew. When Infeld, standing apart from the throng in a far corner was pointed out to him, Zhou walked across the hall to shake his hand, in an unmistakable gesture of disapproval of anti-Semitism in a Socialist country.

Poland, newly a Socialist state, was also traditionally Catholic. Only in Warsaw could one encounter a phenomenon such as the co-existence of two major boulevards, one named for Pope Pius XI, and the other for Stalin.

On May Day 1951 in Warsaw, I witnessed my first international workers' day procession in the Socialist camp. From a sidewalk, I watched the surging river of some half million people, with red flags flying, taking hours to pass. Not long afterwards I watched the Catholic parade on the festival of Corpus Christi, also of several hundred thousand people under religious banners with priests in charge in the streets and no police to be seen. How many of the marchers were the same? A question that could occur only in 1951 Poland. And only in Poland could one see young soldiers in an army led by a Communist party piously taking off their caps as they passed a church, not just on foot but when seated in a bus!

I asked myself, why was the faith so much stronger in Poland—and in Ireland—than in Catholic countries like France and Italy? Why was there such an extensive secular and anti-clerical tradition in those countries while in Poland and Ireland there was no comparable trend, and, also in marked contrast, so little irreverent humor about priests, monks, and the like?

The answer, I think, is that while in France and Italy, the Catholic Church was for long centuries bound up closely with officialdom and the ruling class, and therefore a target of criticism by the ruled and the free-thinking. In Poland (as in Ireland) the rulers were foreign and of different creeds. For most Poles, when large parts of the country were ruled by Tsarist Russia, where the official church was Eastern Orthodox, and Germany (Protestant Lutheran) in Prussia, to be Catholic was closely tied to patriotism and the fight for national independence.

In the post-World War II new Poland, the policy toward the church was sensible, one example being the different treatment of the upper and lower clergy regarding the ownership of rural land. Church estates, like those of lay landlords, were divided among their former peasant tenants. But village priests, mostly from peasant families, were allotted their share in the land reform. This led many of them to sympathize with the new society and government.

Welcomed by Poles of all classes was the restoration in Warsaw, which had been almost obliterated by the Germans, of reminders of the centuries in which their country had been an independent kingdom (before its partition, in the eighteenth century between Tsarist Russia, Prussia, and Austria.) By 1951 the capital's "old town" district, *Stare Miasto*, had been fully rebuilt in its original beautiful style of rose-colored walls and frequent verdigris-green copper roofs, with only the work on the onetime royal palace, the *Zamek*, still awaiting its eventual completion.

In other parts of the once-ruined capital, extensive apartment blocks had been built for the population. An early one was in the Muranow district, site of the one-time Jewish quarter which had been leveled to rubble after the murderous Nazi suppression of the heroic Warsaw Ghetto Uprising. Here now stood a bronze monument to the Ghetto fighters, and nearby lived Beatrice Johnson with her young daughter. Brodski lived in another new apartment district, Mokotow, also built on former ruins.

Elsie's arrival in April brought me joy. Together, while awaiting a ship to China, we visited many historic sites in Warsaw and elsewhere in Poland.

In the National Military Museum we saw, besides relics and records of Poland's seventeenth century role in defending Europe against Ottoman Turkish invasion, many more of her repeated armed struggles for national independence after partition, and of the unforgettable participation by her patriots in battles of other peoples for freedom and progress over two centuries: Kosciuszo and Pulaski were generals in the American revolution, and Dombrowski commanded the army of the Paris Commune in 1870.

At the Lazienki Palace in Warsaw's outskirts we found, unexpectedly, a relic of Chinese cultural influence in eighteenth century Poland: a building with Chinese and imitation-Chinese decor.

On a trip to the resort of Zakopanie in the Carpathain Mountains we spent attentive hours in the memorial cottage in the village of Poronino where Lenin once lived and worked, in exile from Tsarist Russia—that part of Poland was Austrian during the partition.

I discovered again and again that Poland was a state, not just a part of the international Left that was in power. My departure for China, with an appropriate visa, was set—but there would be no ship available for weeks. In the meantime, I had several times to extend my stay in Poland, which involved going to the Warsaw police station for several temporary extensions, and be shouted at by an official who thought that was the proper tone to take with applicants.

Leaving Poland, I again declined the helpful offer of the Chinese embassy to see me off, which may have smoothed many details. Almost an instinct with me was the independent journalist's aversion to sponsorship by officials, even the most friendly. Though I had long believed that a journalist should be committed to a cause, my feeling was that this should be by one's own volition and that one should be judged by one's writings, not who one's sponsors were.

Poland, to me, was tragic, lovable, and contradictory—all three. Though repeatedly trampled on, the country had produced giants like Copernicus and Curie in science and Chopin in music. To its lasting honor, its sons and daughters had fought and died, with passion and devotion, not only for the emancipation of their own land but in many revolutions elsewhere. Yet in the country's periods of independence it had oppressed its own minorities—Jews and Ukrainians, and as early as the Napoleonic period, Polish troops had been used—by France—to suppress black ex-slave fighters for independence of far-off Haiti. But in history's balance, Poland and her people's contributions to freedom and progress will, I believe, have a bright place.

Chapter 24

RETURN TO CHINA

Our sea voyage, from the Polish seaport of Gdynia to Tianjin, the Chinese port where I grew up, took 49 days. We passed through the Baltic and North Seas via the Kiel Canal, where cows grazed on green pastures a few feet from our gunwales, on to the English Channel. Then we skirted the Atlantic coast of Europe, and crossed the Mediterranean (twice, in and out, through the Dardanelles) into the Black Sea in a de-tour to Romania to pick up fuel oil with which no Western-controlled port would supply us. Further, through the Suez Canal, we entered the Red Sea and Indian and Pacific Oceans. On the last stage of our journey we hugged the China coast through to the East China Sea, the Yellow Sea and, nestled in the Bohai Gulf, Tianjin.

The route and duration of this odyssey, no luxury cruise to put it mildly, was determined by the Cold War. So, also, were the conditions on board. Our aging passenger-freighter, originally of the Danish Moller Line, which had plied the pre-war China coast, was newly-bought by a joint company of the new China and the new Poland. Previously named after one of ship owner Moller's daughters, it was now called *Przyazn Narodow* (Friendship of the Peoples). But from governments along our route, we experienced no friendship. Not only were we denied fuel, but even water and provisions.

Nonetheless, we did not feel isolated or beleaguered. In the geo-politics of the time our starting point, destination, and the vessel on which we were traveling were all part of the newborn and then huge Socialist world. For us, the resulting hope seemed far larger than the difficulties attending such a new, vast and complex enterprise.

The Polish crew, though young and enthusiastic, were almost to-tally inexperienced, some on their first ocean voyage. One blond lad inquisitively opened an engine fuel hatch and was scorched by burning oil down the front of his body—he had to be left in a hospital at Istanbul.

The middle-aged captain, by contrast, was an old mariner, from the remnant of Poland's pre-war merchant fleet which had escaped from

Hitler's invasion to England. With Poles of his skills so few, and even fewer returning to their homeland after World War II, he was almost a national treasure. He alone was allowed ashore by port authorities en route, for necessary navigational contacts. Each time, in view of his long time in the West, there was some doubt whether he would come back aboard. Yet he always did, with a careful selection of nails, screws, hinges, door handles, and other household hardware—for the residence he said he was building in his home port, Gdynia. Its dimensions, he explained, would be based both on fact and foresight. Soviet captains had told him that their rules for home-building allowed more floor space than was the rule for Polish captains. But, he said with a wink, wasn't the current watchword in Poland "The Soviet Union's today is our tomorrow?" So he was planning the size of his house foundation on that assumption: the extra superstructure could be added later.

The ship's political officer, Lewandowski, half the captain's age, did not argue with the latter's self-centered outlook, but amicably played chess with him not trying too hard to win. His job, after all, was to keep the captain on the ship and in good humor, not to irk him.

Personally, young Lewandowski was a strong Socialist and internationalist. Sailing past the immense military cemeteries on the bloody World War I battlefield of Gallipolli on the Bosphorus, he showed no interest in my comments on the campaign. To him the essence was, as he burst out, "All those young lives, on both sides, wasted for their exploiters, on both sides."

Nature's climate combined with that of politics to challenge us. Being short of drinking water, we put up canvas troughs to catch the rare rain. In the Red Sea, the heat not only wilted us, it convinced the potatoes we had stocked up in Poland that Spring had arrived, so they sprouted and became unfit to eat.

To cool ourselves, an on-deck swimming pool was cleverly improvised from tarpaulins, with sea water pumped up. To keep busy, we joined the crew in re-painting the ship's metalwork and life-preservers for Poland's National Day. Luckily, also, we had brought books and our typewriters. I spent much time writing drafts for upcoming book projects.

Our final days at sea took us close to the ongoing Korean War. Almost within sight of Tianjin, we were overflown by U.S. warplanes. Some were huge bombers passing deafeningly above, at almost mast-height, apparently to frighten us as well as observe, and doubtless photograph, our canvas-swathed deck cargo (which consisted mostly of vehicles). In return, we snapped our own cameras at them.

Off Tianjin, we anchored at Dagu (Taku) Bar, site of the former Chinese Imperial Army fortifications. From it, fourteen years earlier, I had departed while reinforcements landed for the Japanese invaders. Already then, I was confident that they could not crush a China awakening to the danger of her national existence. But I would not have dreamt of returning, not only after they were beaten, but to a China victorious in her long revolution. Now a People's Republic cadre from Tianjin came out in a motor launch to welcome us. After a day, he said, we would entrain for Beijing.

Strikingly different were the longshoremen who boarded us to unload cargo, not the ragged, haggard, bowed porters of the past. "Going to Beijing?" one said. "Then you'll be seeing Chairman Mao!" When I replied that we hoped to, at the next National Day celebration, other men gathered around. In all my years in Guomindang China, I had never heard any ordinary Chinese worker wonder, or care, whether I had seen, or would see, Chiang Kai-shek. Obviously, these workers thought of Mao Zedong as their own.

On the train to Beijing, there was no longer the old stark contrast between the capacious, well-appointed first-class cars in the rear, catering to foreigners and the rich, and the filthy third-class cars close to the smoke emitting engine, jam-packed with the poor. Now there were only two grades of cars: "hard" and "soft," both kept very clean. A fellow passenger was a young Chinese Air Force pilot recovering from a wound on the Korean front. He ate with a pair of metal chopsticks, which, he said, were made from a downed American plane.

The countryside we passed through was familiar to me in location, yet different in many features. Where there had been alkali-white tracts, covered more with sparse scrub than with crops, irrigation channels were now many, as were emerald-green paddies of rice. The soil itself, I was told, was being washed clean. The fields, owned no longer by landlords but by the tillers, were clearly well cared for.

In Tianjin's major department store, I saw buyers of a new type— workers and peasants in their working clothes. Time was when anyone so dressed would not be served, but pushed out of doors. Also in Tianjin, the old administrative buildings of the former foreign concessions, massively constructed to overawe the Chinese population, had been turned over to Chinese public institutions (the handsome rose-marble former French concession municipality was earmarked for a library). The old foreign-type buildings I had known in semi-colonial Tianjin (a conglomeration of British, continental European, and U.S. styles of the late nineteenth century), were still there, but put to new uses. Once, the Chinese venturing among them had been made to feel like intruders. Now their spirit in these streets was that which I had seen in Yan'an in 1944, geared not to the humiliating past and current hardships but to present victories and the beckoning future.

We took the train to Beijing, where we were met by Chen Hansheng, who handed us one of Soong Ching-ling's calling cards on which she had written, "Welcome home" in her familiar, firm script. Thoughtful and timely, nothing could have warmed us more.

In Beijing I found resplendent palaces and temples once built for emperors now thrown open not only for foreign tourists but, for the first time, to the working folk whose forebears had paid for them and built them with bitter labor and consummate skill. Tai Miao, the old Memorial Temple of the Imperial Ancestors, had become the Workers' Palace of Culture.

Though still dusty and often unpaved, Beijing's streets now seemed almost surgically clean and free of litter and garbage (among the first jobs of the People's Liberation Army, and the most impressive to the townsfolk, had been to clear up the dumps and clear the centuries-old sewers which had been blocked and disused throughout living memory). On one of my earliest days there, I threw away an empty cigarette pack as I walked along, something I had done without a thought in New York. But, looking back, I saw it was the only such discard on the well-swept road. Retracing my steps, I picked it up.

Spitting in the streets, a notorious practice in old China, was being combated in Beijing by an ingenious—and effective—campaign. Red-scarved pre-teen "Young Pioneers," armed with chalk, would draw a white circle around every fresh gob seen by their sharp eyes, then keep the spitter standing by it while they lectured him. To be publicly scolded by children was a woeful loss of face for an adult in patriarchal China, much more of a moral blow than a fine or bawling-out by police. The police, if nearby, simply insisted that the kids should be heard.

Also striking was the apparent end of the ceaseless cheating and haggling in the shops that had prevailed before. In post-Revolutionary

Beijing, we found prices clearly displayed and fixed, with no bargaining, and an astonishing level of honesty among the store workers. For example, one of the most popular bicycles for those able to afford it had been the British "Phillips" brand, which was counterfeited again and again to snare the unwary. Now I found, in the shops, all versions were clearly labeled for what they were: "Real Phillips" if so; "Fake Phillips" for the better copies; "Fake Fake Phillips" for the lowest type. For each category, the prices were similar from shop to shop.

Almost unbelievably, China had succeeded in curbing the astronomical inflation of the pre-1949 years. Part of the reason was the ongoing rebuilding of its own war wounds, but also the strain of the war in Korea. The Chinese government's economic methods, including backing the currency with state-held reserves of foodstuffs and clothing materials, of which a market supply was guaranteed, were thoughtfully conceived. But none, however ingenious, could have achieved this result without the fact, apparent to all working people, that the guiding concern was for their daily needs—and the consequent mass support.

The currency, in its face value, was still many-zeroed. My pay, in terms of figures, made me, as never before or after, a "millionaire." But the real devaluation had stopped, and the next step would be to lop off the zeroes: 10,000 *yuan* of the previous issue could be exchanged for one new *yuan* in the banks—with no loss of anything except those zeroes—the purchasing value was stable.

In matters large and small, China seemed to be recoiling from the stains of the old with determination. Passive, depressed moods were giving place to buoyancy and activity. Plain people, ceasing to submit to "fate" were happily and earnestly remolding it. *Meiyou banfa* (No way out), once a common expression, was being replaced by *You banfa* (There is a way).

Along with this new feeling that all difficulties could be overcome was a sober realization that the striking changes already observable were "only the first steps of a new Long March." The country was still impoverished. Urban and rural productivity on a scale formerly undreamed of was needed to create a prosperous life for all. That arduous task required everyone to work, work ever better, and respect all others who worked, in whatever capacity.

Tongzhi (Comrade), the form of address expressing this awareness, was succeeding old terminology which had previously reflected differing status and rank. One said "Comrade" to hotel attendants and rickshaw pullers (who still existed). They, in turn, called you "Comrade." It was a strikingly warming contrast with the past, a sense of "we" more than "I" in everyday life.

Obstacles to overcome were still formidable. Strong forces at home and abroad remained neither willing nor able to reconcile themselves to the idea that the Chinese had now "stood up," in Mao Zedong's ringing words. Remnant Chiang Kai-shek troops were still active in parts of the mainland, to say nothing of their restoration-hungry refuge in Taiwan. War was raging in nearby Korea, with U.S. leaders from President Truman down, and field commanders from General MacArthur down, threatening openly to use their atomic arsenal, then possessed by the U.S. alone: the Soviet Union had only in 1950 made its first test, followed by Britain in 1952, and China was still years behind.

As early as November, 1950, Truman told the press that nuclear bombing of Korea was "under consideration." MacArthur urged that the North Korean and Chinese forces be stopped behind a death-dealing nuclear war belt of radioactive cobalt across the peninsula, and that Chiang Kai-shek should be helped to retake the mainland. General Mark Clark, succeeding MacArthur in Korea, continued for two more years to advocate a double nuclear strike. In the Pentagon and U.S. Congress many similar demands were on record. A repeatedly-expressed aim was the "rolling back" of China's Communist Revolution.

Under President Dwight Eisenhower, who succeeded Truman in 1952, there was less preparation for an imminent nuclear strike—partly due to the alarmed opposition by America's allies—specifically Britain. But the threats continued to be voiced.

We, on coming to China, found that the U.S. possession and brandishing of nuclear weapons were widely known. But we sensed no fear among our co-workers or Beijing's people in general. They were too busy building China's new life. In fact, ever since 1945 when Mao Zedong had called the atom bomb a "paper tiger," there had been no trembling before it in the new forces of China. Contrary to distortions, Mao did not deny the bomb's destructiveness. What he stressed was that man, not weaponry, was the decisive factor in history, and that in the end, the bomb would not destroy the people but the people would destroy the bomb (prevent its use and ultimately abolish it), as he told Anna Louise Strong.

Soong Ching-ling was now vice-chairwoman of the new People's Government, and wanted us to help launch *China Reconstructs*, her newly-planned English language magazine. Chen Hansheng soon took us to see her and Zhou Enlai and his wife Ding Yingchao. Together, we discussed not only plans for the magazine but the situation of old friends abroad, such as Edgar Snow and others, whom they fondly remembered and for whose welfare, in that era of McCarthyism, they were deeply concerned.

Perhaps second only in importance to the founding of People's Republic of China in the minds of the Chinese people was the halting, on the line of the 38th parallel, of the U.S. forces in Korea, in which Chinese units, fighting as volunteers, played such a key part. This was undoubtedly the greatest restorative element of the Chinese people's national self-respect. The triumph of their revolution, despite the U.S. backing of the Chiang Kai-shek regime, had put an end to the century of their nation's defeats and humiliations. The success in Korea, in direct combat with the U.S. war machine, was also the defeat of plans for a "roll back" of the Chinese Revolution from the direction of the West.

On July 27, 1953, in my only trip out of China in this period, I was one of the newsmen covering the conclusion of the Korean armistice agreement, in the Korean village of Panmujom. There I witnessed the first time in the history of the United States that its representatives signed an end to hostilities without victory.

Our group of foreign journalists from Beijing, on which I represented the U.S. radical weekly the *National Guardian*, traveled by a road then still under constant air attack. On the way, we found Pyongyang, the capital of North Korea, with virtually every surface structure flattened to debris (government functionaries met us in premises, including a huge public hall, it had built deep underground.) In Sariwon, another town we passed through, only the stark high-spired skeleton of a gutted Christian church still stood above the surrounding buildings reduced to rubble by air attacks. "Bomb them back into the Stone Age," had been among the stated aims pursued for three years by the U.S. military. But the North Korean army and the supporting Chinese volunteers had unfalteringly fought on.

And among the devastation, besides their unbroken spirit, there were signs of continuing, though bizarrely war-distorted, "normalcy." Surplus electricity still flowed abundantly from a hydroelectric station on the Yalu, the river separating Korea and China, which was expended in lights burning outdoors in the daytime as well as brightening underground bunkers at night. At army posts along the way, we were given pound after pound of sturgeon caviar, which could not be canned or exported because of the hostilities, wrapped in old newspapers, as free wayside-lunch fare.

After the armistice, we saw Korean and Chinese troops with their equipment pulling back from the new demilitarized zone (as required of both sides). On our way back after the formal armistice signing, reconstruction had already begun—Chinese volunteers were repairing bombed bridges.

A day or two earlier, in the town of Kaesong near the ceasefire line, the Volunteer headquarters had asked us to dinner. Walking up to the main table, we toasted their commander, Peng Dehuai, on the successful cessation of the fighting. "Don't thank me, thank Karl Marx," he responded. Years later, I was told, it was held against him that he had not mentioned Chairman Mao. This would happen after he had criticized, in a letter to the Party Central Committee—which was the proper procedure—the results of the "Great Leap Forward" on China's economy. Demoted from his post as Minister of Defense, and in increasing disfavor from then on, he was finally harassed to death in the Cultural Revolution before later being posthumously cleared of all charges.

Among the sacrifices made by China in Korea was that of Mao Zedong's son, Mao Anying, killed by a U.S. bomb.

He was the last of several members of Mao's family, including his first wife Yang Kaihui, two brothers, and other close relatives, to be slain in the struggles for the victory and consolidation of China's Revolution. Mao Anying had enlisted with the encouragement of Mao Zedong who, after the shock of his firstborn's death, decided that his body should rest forever on Korean soil.

*   *   *

On the publicity front, in the Korean War, the U.S. (and, nominally, the United Nations) side suffered repeated setbacks because its press officers misinformed or stonewalled Western journalists, while the Chinese-Korean side supplied timely facts which proved accurate.

This was done largely through two foreign correspondents accredited to that side, the Englishman Alan Winnington of the London *Daily Worker* and the Australian, Wilfred Burchett, of the British *Daily Express*. In constant contact with the newsmen of the opposing camp on the "neutral" ground of the site of the long-drawn armistice talks during which the fighting also continued, they gained the latter's' respect, first grudgingly, then on a personal basis, for never misleading them. It was a feat seldom equaled in the annals of wartime journalism, based on what which even the obviously uncomfortable U.S. spokesmen finally had to admit were true unvarnished facts.

* * *

In those early post-Liberation days, we and our colleagues engaged in foreign-language publicity work for China, regardless of rank or age, worked, learned, and played in close togetherness. Many were the nights when we toiled together from dusk to dawn, interrupted only by snacks of noodles, to get out urgent copy. The atmosphere on the revolutionary side was like that described in *The Field Full of Folk* by the famed nineteenth century British Socialist and populist William Morris in his utopian *Dream of John Ball*.

Joining in physical labor together, in the pre-industrial conditions of the time, we took our two-week muscle-wrenching but heart-warming turn in carrying heavy loads of earth in baskets slung from shoulder poles, and pushing and pulling wheelbarrows filled with stones uphill to help build a major Beijing water conservancy project—the Shisanling (Ming Tombs) dam and reservoir.

I have a color slide of Elsie setting off from the door of our house to her half-month's work on the project, a towel at her belt, a pack with her bedding and a change of clothing on her back, a picture of the pick-and-shovel laborer. But despite her years (she was 53), Elsie proved a pace-setter, even among those a decade or two younger. So did another middle-aged British colleague on our magazine, Nan Green, a veteran of the International Brigade in Spain where her husband, a musician and fellow-Communist, had been killed in battle. China and Spain, the anti-Fascist fronts of the 1930s were still palpably linked in the minds of contemporaries. For her work Elsie was chosen by her fellow workers as a model builder of that reservoir. The next stint, of equal length, was mine—with a passing grade but no honors. The sweat we shed as

44

45

46

47 | 50
48 | 51
49 | 52

53
54

55
56

57
58
59

64 | 65
66

67

68

69

70

71

72

73

74

75

76

77 | 78
79 | 80

81

82

83

84

85

86

87

88 | 89
---
90 | 91

92

93

94

willing and eager volunteers, moved by the same spirit as our colleagues and the entire liberated people, linked us deeply. Later we joined other work groups in transplanting rice, harvesting wheat, afforesting bare hills, or digging a canal. All this made us, as nothing else could, forever part of this land, shaped, tilled, and watered by the toil of so many generations, and now in a state of active rebirth. Whenever we saw new watercourses, roads, or tree-belts, we felt that we, too, had helped create them. Such a feeling is hard to describe by any who have not worked truly mutually, not for monetary wealth, but for a common aim.

That spirit of the 1950s affected children as well as adults. I remember how Nancy Hodes, an American pre-teen expressed it in her own terms when asked how the U.S., from which she had come, compared with China, where she had recently started school. Her answer, "There we can eat ice cream and chocolate. Here we can serve the people and not try to be famous."

Such was the mentality then in the air, inherited from wartime liberated areas. It inspired tremendous efforts, both useful and creative. Later it would be misapplied in over-estimates of what could be materially achieved at the time, and be distorted by competing boasts of having achieved the impossible, the more so the better, as in the nationwide campaign to smelt record-breaking amounts of steel in small furnaces during the Great Leap Forward, or, in agriculture, the competitive reports of harvesting crops of unbelievable density and size.

Our recreation, too, was a shared activity. With our co-workers we would pile into a truck (standing room only) to go to skate on the Forbidden City moat in winter or swim in a lake or public pool in summer. Simple sports, ping-pong and badminton, not requiring much space, could be played during work-breaks on office premises. Collectively, and at no charge, we attended films and cultural performances (for which our trade union booked seats). We organized song and dance evenings in our workplaces (I finally learned to play the accordion, but badly). To the extent of our capabilities, we donated funds and belongings for support of the Resist the United States and Aid Korea campaign. Practically all our Chinese co-workers volunteered for front-line service; the few who were chosen were widely envied.

Another development, however, came as an unwelcome shock. It was the unveiling of erosion, in the revolutionary structure itself, of the post-Liberation spirit of simplicity and integrity so welcomed by the people in contrast to the spate of corruption and larceny, petty and grand, in old China. Cynical foreign commentators had for some time predicted such decay. To be honest, in the poor boondocks of China, they jeered, was easy—but just wait until the Communists took over Shanghai with its socially complex population of several million.

Urban technicians and Western-educated intellectuals, they also predicted, would flee. Facts proved them wrong—the bulk stayed, wanting to help the nation in its newly-won independence.

Moreover, the cynics prophesied, the rural-minded Communists would break their necks on the knotty administrative and economic problems of the big cities, which had become miasmas of speculation and vice under foreign control and Chinese reactionary rule. Thus, the "values of the free world" were to be saved from the "Red menace"—by corruption! But that, too, did not happen in these early years. In Shanghai, it was the social atmosphere that changed, not its new authorities.

The Communist Party did not deny the risks. It had long cautioned against them. In 1944 in Yan'an, five years before the nationwide victory, I heard much discussion of issues raised in a play by progressive writer Guo Muoruo about how the leaders of the Taiping Rebellion in the mid nineteenth century had degenerated after claiming victory throughout a considerable part of China. And in the late 1940s, on the eve of the takeover of the big cities, Mao Zedong had warned that revolutionaries who had hitherto fearlessly faced the enemy's shot and shell on the battlefields, might be felled spiritually by the "sugar-coated bullets" of the moneyed classes in the big cities.

An ominous example of this occurred soon after we had arrived in Tianjin. Two new senior officials there, Liu Jingshan and Zhang Zishan, both veteran Communists and participants in the Long March with good past records, military and political, were found to be at the center of a corrupt network, embezzling large sums of money through the channels that opened automatically with power. Some thought that the two men's former services should lighten their punishment. But Mao Zedong insisted that they suffer the maximum penalty: death, precisely because their change had been so enormous. On this, I thought Mao would convince the people that, unlike the Guomindang, the Communist Party would not condone, much less breed, betrayal of public trust by its own officials.

The Liu-Zhang case precipitated a nationwide movement, briefly called the *San Fan, Wu Fan* ("Three Againsts, Five Againsts") in which we, alongside our Chinese colleagues, took part.

The "Three Againsts" targeted corruption, waste, and bureaucracy among public servants. On New Year's Day 1952, Mao Zedong personally initiated this campaign, to "vigorously and resolutely cleanse our society of the filth and poison left over from the old."

The "Five Againsts," launched a month later, took aim at private industrialists and traders guilty of bribery, tax evasion, theft of state property, cheating on government contracts, and stealing confidential official information for private gain.

In both campaigns, the death penalty was rare. In the "Three Againsts" it was virtually limited to the executions of Liu and Zhang; in the "Five Againsts" to the executions of sellers of fake or contaminated medical supplies for casualties in Korea—which rightly aroused nationwide fury. Severity toward chief offenders was combined with leniency toward the secondary offenders and those who demonstrated repentance, in varying degrees from reduced penalties to none at all. The primary purpose was not revenge but prevention through public education.

The objectives were that government personnel, regardless of position, should not violate public property. Private enterprises should not cheat, or, in particular, defraud or undermine the state. At that time the enterprises of Chinese "national capitalists" were still not only legal but protected, even encouraged, to help lift up the country's economy. The policy toward them was quite different from that toward properties formerly owned by the Guomindang state or personally by its bureaucrats, which were nationalized; or those owned by foreign imperialism, which could be frozen or taken over if they or their governments acted to subvert the People's Republic of China. But using the private sector to bribe public functionaries or reverse the country's Socialist direction would not be tolerated. As Zhou Enlai then explained, the "national bourgeoisie" has its two sides: the opportunity to serve the new society with legitimate profit, and the temptation to corrode and plunder it.

In the two movements, everyone in public service, or in the private sector dealing with the government, was required to make a self-examination report for possible transgressions, and to listen to the response of those listening. Whoever did so honestly would incur lighter penalties or no penalty at all. Liars, however, could not expect mitigation.

The spirit was positive and popular—the substitution of a new social morality for the despised old. People even criticized themselves for such things as using office stationery for a personal letter. Many and true, in those days, were the stories of visitors to China about how hard it was to lose anything there. Even worn socks discarded in a hotel waste bin could bring someone running up to say, "You've left something behind!" This reputation spread far and wide. In later years, Elsie, after money was stolen from a shoulder bag she left carelessly unzipped while shopping in London, was told by the British police when she reported the theft, "You should be more careful. Don't think you're still in China."

The era of post-Liberation cleansing and self-cleansing from dishonesty is fondly remembered, as is the feeling of togetherness in those early years, as not only possible, but attainable.

Though this was the prevalent attitude among us, there remained still shades of difference, sometimes illustrated in small detail. During the early days in Beijing, I still wore my American clothes, neckties and all. My new colleagues, however, were all dressed in the blue cotton outfits later erroneously called "Mao suits" abroad (in fact they owe their origins to Dr. Sun Yat-sen, decades earlier). The virtual uniform, with no outward symbol of inequality of rank or wealth, was in most cases proudly worn, as a sign of oneness with, and service to, China's common people. Besides, it was convenient—it was a loose fitting garment which was comfortable however one moved; its four jacket pockets capacious enough for anything one wanted to carry around, its style everywhere acceptable. I, for one, was anxious to change to this style as soon as possible.

But not everybody was. While still in my Western attire, I suddenly found a newly-uniformed young colleague furtively unbuttoning his collar to reveal a handsome silk tie inside. Though his work showed no reason to doubt his general welcome to the revolution, he was sartorially nostalgic for his days as a dapper young blade in Shanghai. And on another level there was the use of uniformity as a protective disguise. Those who wore the grimiest and most patched blue or gray cottons, I was told early in Beijing, had often been the most expensively dressed in the past, and wanted it forgotten. More ordinary people, even when threadbare, were neat.

Most importantly, thrift and simplicity had become the genuinely preferred values. Even children did not like to wear anything freshly bought. Clothes handed down from older siblings, or remade from those of adults, were more acceptable among their schoolmates: "Couldn't you sew on a patch or two? These don't look simple and hard-working," was a typical child's line.

As for income in the early 1950s, public servants in China were not on wages but on the "supply system." In clothing, one got a set in winter, two each summer. Food budgets were reckoned on the price of raw produce. Housing and essential furniture came with the job. Even so, distinctions of rank could be discerned by the informed. One friend who sat down on our newly provided bed, announced the judgment apparently registered by her buttocks from the thickness of the bed mat that we were treated as cadres of such-and-such a grade. A "basic conclusion," we joked.

Canteen fare was adequate and well-cooked. The dishes for personnel with major responsibilities were more varied, but no one minded. But when they moved from the common dining hall to a screened-off section, there was criticism—weren't they getting too clubby—talking not with everyone but among themselves? That, after all, they could do in their offices, so why eat separately and limit informal exchanges of views with the rank-and-file?

In foreign relations, China's positions were clear cut. With the governments of the Western "great powers" there was no normal diplomatic contact—because of the latter's non-recognition of the new state. But goodwill among peoples was impressively symbolized at the Conference for Peace in the Asian and Pacific Regions held in Beijing in 1952. Delegates came from scores of countries. I attended as a news correspondent. Elsie worked on its English-language technical staff. Slightly later, we both worked for China's National Trade Union Congress. Here again we were in our element, I as a long-time writer for the labor press, and both of us were union members: I of the American Newspaper Guild, and Elsie of the U.S. Union of Office and Professional Workers.

One thing China definitely did not do, contrary to the long-current Western media myth, was to purposely retreat into "self-isolation" behind a "bamboo curtain" in international relations and trade. On the contrary, as expressed repeatedly before and after the Asian-Pacific Conference, she stood in principle for peaceful normal diplomatic and commercial links with all countries—including those fighting her in Korea

259

and enforcing the Western embargo against her—on the basis of equality and mutual respect for sovereignty.

In July 1952, at the very height of the U.S. blockade, Zhang Hanfu, China's vice-minister of Foreign Affairs, praised the expansion of Sino-British trade through a £10 million contract, citing the British government's support of a U.S. led anti-China embargo as the main obstacle to further growth. This was during the war in Korea, where British units were a part of the force fighting against the Chinese volunteers. Soon after that war, Labor Party leader and ex-Prime Minister Clement Attlee, led a group to Beijing, which also helped improve interchange, political and economic. In old China, no foreign figures of that rank had ever come: it took the Revolution to bring them.

Full diplomatic relations were established, from the beginning of the People's Republic, with the Soviet Union, with which a mutually defensive alliance was signed in 1950, and with its associated Socialist states. Soon afterward came normal ties with newly-independent India and Northern Europe's neutral countries.

Moreover, at the Conference for Peace in the Asian and Pacific Regions, the charge was made and documented that the United States was using bacteriological weapons, both in Korea and across the border within China. At the time, despite the presentation of much evidence and affirmation by an international group of eminent scientists, that charge was denounced as false, impossible, malicious, and so on by the U.S. government and its press. Today, historians with access to U.S. documents at that time a closely guarded secret, have greatly clarified the issue—biological weapons identical with those employed in Korea were indeed produced and packaged on a large scale by the U.S. military, many being modeled on those pioneered by the notorious Japanese biological weapons units and their experiments on captives (in return for handing over its test records and results the Japanese culprits were given immunity from War Crimes prosecution by the U.S.).

But between the Chinese and Japanese peoples, too, new relations were already emerging. We saw this on an early trip to the Marco Polo Bridge, where Japanese friends now came to pledge their efforts against Fascism. Japanese delegates to the Conference expressed determination that both peoples should live in harmony. Again we were reminded of Yan'an and the liberated areas, where, already during the war, members of the Japanese Emancipation League, risked, and sometimes gave their lives at the front to persuade their fellow-countrymen still in the ranks of the Japanese Imperial Army to stop warring against China.

In general, the essence of the new China was showing itself daily, despite the difficulties of reconstruction and renewal. And this despite the tirades in the West—particularly in the U.S.—about China having ceased to exist as an entity and become a possession and tool of the Soviet Union. In this period China's people were slandered as "Blue Ants" if they built; and "Red Hordes" if they fought. Nothing, however, could stop the awareness in those early post-Liberation years that in China, new hope had been born, nationally and internationally. And this time there had been a special effect: speeding the independence of the former colonies of the Western powers.

Within a few years most had broken their chains and raised their own national flags. Regardless of the usually non-Communist, even sometimes anti-Communist leadership of these new states, the majority would recall the stimulus to their own freedom from colonialism given by China's revolutionary struggle. This would be shown later by the historic gathering of such countries in Bandung, Indonesia in 1955. And still later, in 1972, by the virtually unanimous vote of their delegations to restore China's place in the United Nations and on its Security Council, which, in fact, marked the end of virtual U.S. control of that body.

In these years, the Chinese people, led by their Communist party, ending the country's century-old vassalage to the "unequal treaties" that, through repeated defeats and sell-outs had reduced it to a semi-colony (or, in Sun Yat-sen's phrase, a "proto-colony," by which he bitterly meant everyone's prey). Not only had it straightened its back in the international arena, but internally, so had its vast working population, the overwhelming majority of them peasants, who had suffered from every form of class oppression.

The next task was envisioned as the building of a Socialist society through stages and by methods appropriate to China's conditions, a complex search and process that, through experience, and trial and error, was to last the rest of the twentieth century.

Chapter 25

BASIC TRANSFORMATIONS

In general, the period of 1949-56, for the majority of the Chinese people and their friends in many countries, was one of those in which "bliss was it in that dawn to be alive, and to be young was very heaven," as the English poet Wordsworth had written, in his own years of young hope, of the impact of the French Revolution in Europe.

In material construction, the period was divided into two phases: 1950-52, or rebuilding from the ravages of long-drawn wars; and 1953-56, China's First Five-Year Plan, with Socialist transformation of the economy.

Already in the first phase, there were totally new breakthroughs. Symbolically striking was the building in 1952 of the first railroad in Sichuan, China's most populous province, linking its major economic center, Chongqing, with the provincial capital, Chengdu. As a concept on paper, it was old—dating back to the closing years of the Chinese monarchy. Then, local investors had already projected it. Indeed, their stormy protests against the construction rights being turned over to foreign companies had helped ignite the 1911 Revolution, which made China a republic. Subsequently, however, it was not built. Even during the war with Japan in 1937-45, when Chongqing became China's provisional capital, not an inch of rail existed in the city or the province. Working there for some years, the only pathetic sign of it I saw was a once-optimistically begun Chongqing station, orphaned, connected to nothing. But in new China's infancy amid a host of pressing problems, it would be energetically begun and completed. On July 1, 1952, its first regular trains ran.

Also, never in China's long history had the Yangtze River been bridged, though plans had been drawn by American engineering firms for China's old governments. Only after Liberation was the task successfully undertaken by China with Soviet technical aid. I reported on it in mid-construction, beside the city of Nanjing, crawling over its uncompleted steel skeleton. Elsie, in 1957, attended its grand opening to traffic by rail and road.

During the rebuilding phase, the People's Republic of China received foreign aid only from the Soviet Union and the bloc countries it had formed in Europe after World War II. This aid included the building of 156 major industrial projects, virtually in all branches which in old China had been completely blank. It laid the initial foundation for an integrated national system of modern industries. On this basis, China announced the target of "surpassing Britain in 15 years," referring mainly to the total output of steel in absolute figures, not per capita.

How far the publicity for this aim was heard was illustrated by our adopted daughter, Ai Songya (Sonia, nicknamed Meimei), in 1958, when she was only a six-year-old kindergartener in Beijing. At that age, we took her on a visit to England, via the U.S.S.R. Waking at gray dawn, in a Moscow hotel, she looked out of the window at the street below asked, "Why aren't there any people?" And promptly gave herself the answer: "I know, they went to work early to catch up with Britain."

Socially, the key process of the rebuilding years was the completion of the land reform plan, which gave soil to till to every one of China's hundreds of millions of peasants. Not only to men but also to women who had never previously had the right to own land. In family relations, this went hand-in-hand with the new Marriage Law, codifying the fundamental equality of women and men. Throughout the economy, land reform was the basis for a step-by-step transition to co-operative farming. And it ensured the support of the peasants, then 90 percent of all Chinese, for a subsequent gradual nationalization of urban industries. In peace, it was a further development of the strategy of "surrounding the cities from the countryside" which had won the civil war for China's Communists, with the difference that now it would not cut off the cities but help them to become China's locomotive of industrial advancement.

Simultaneously, with the deep changes in the economic and social sectors, mass campaigns were launched in the field of culture, often on the initiative of Mao Zedong, to whom it was a special concern. In 1951 came the criticism of a widely shown and hitherto favorably reviewed film, *The Life of Wu Xun*. It presented Wu (1838-1896), who had fawned clownishly on the rich and powerful to get funds for free schools for the poor, as a high-minded pioneer in popular education. Mao angrily called Wu an advocate of slave education. What, Mao asked, did Wu really teach and stand for? Had Wu, by a single word or act, helped the death-defying courageous progressive movements of his time against the international and domestic oppression of China, the root of mass poverty and illiteracy? Wasn't the teaching in his free schools simply a spreading of the old education, to breed devoted tools for the old rulers? How could he be lauded in the new society, even by Communists? The discussion reached very widely, as film attendance, previously affordable mainly to the urban middle class and elite, was rapidly expanding, with lavish state support to the poor and the peasants—among whom ideas conveyed by films now had direct effect, positive or negative.

Three years later came a discussion concerning the eighteenth century novel, *Hong Lou Meng,* known as "A Dream of Red Mansions," and arguably the pinnacle of the Chinese literary tradition. The work was not only familiar to generations of readers, but carried with it the special mantle of national treasure. Long prevalent had been the view of it as a masterly depiction of all aspects of classical Chinese scenes, mannerisms, individual traits, and the complex relationships of its immense (over 400) range of characters. The current chief exponent of this tradition was the veteran scholar Yu Pingbu. Now, in the post-Revolutionary cultural milieu, the work was boldly challenged by Li Xifan, a young critic, who saw it as a *bona fide* example of the decay of feudal society as a whole. But Li, who was not of the established school, and considered a "nobody," had difficulty presenting his argment. Mao backed the views of these "nobodies," ignored by the bigwigs "as is their habit," he said indignantly. A critical movement against the old scholarly monopoly was started by Mao's open letter to the top leadership of the Communist Party, asserting the right of the "nobodies" to be widely published.

In the same year, again with Mao as the chief promoter, an attack was launched on the literary group gathered around Hu Feng, hitherto regarded as a veteran Left-winger. Hu Feng's complaints against the "sameness" of writings produced after 1949 were branded as seeking freedom of expression for counterrevolutionaries, to whom the group was declared to belong, with some members sent to prison.[20]

---

[20] In 1980, a quarter century later, the verdict on "the Hu Feng counter-revolutionary clique" was reversed as a misjudgement. The official "History of the Chinese Communist Party 1949-1990," while not totally negating the cultural campaigns of the 1950s, described many of the polemics then published as "over-simplified and crude."

Unlike the movements against corruption, which Elsie and I understood, supported, and joined, we did not closely follow or take part in those in the cultural sphere—neither of us was sufficiently fluent or well-read in Chinese to follow all the detailed references and arguments. But we did not essentially doubt the charges, accepting the word of the Party, which had led in the creation of the new China in place of the old.

Internationally and domestically, of major importance in 1956, was the impact of the 20th Congress of the Soviet Communist Party. Its spear point was the speech in which that party's then chief, Nikita Khruschev, denounced Stalin, who had died in 1953 and, by implication, the whole period during Stalin's supremacy in the U.S.S.R. and the world Communist movement. The speech stunned and confused members of many Communist Parties, totally unprepared for the sudden turnabout. Even their leaders, invited as guests for the Congress had not been given any hint in advance, nor been allowed hear or read Khrushchev's speech. All they got in Moscow was an oral summary by minor Soviet officials. To most, the wording became available only after leakage, through intelligence sources, to the Western press. Harry Pollitt, head of the British Communist Party, who had been invited to the Congress, voiced hurt resentment when he afterwards came to Beijing, to British party members and sympathizers working there. And also to the Chinese party, which had likewise been treated in cavalier fashion.

Basically, the Chinese leadership considered that taking the lid off Stalin's serious faults was a good thing, in order to prevent their repetition. What it thought wrong was the crude method chosen by Khrushchev, which led to wholesale condemnation of Stalin and the Soviet Union during his ascendancy. After all, that was when the first Socialist state was industrialized, and played its heroic and decisive part in winning the world anti-Fascist war. Even more wrong was abandonment of faith in socialism on account of faults in the first practical efforts to build it. This would be throwing the baby out with the bath water.

Undoubtedly, China's reasoned opinions on the Congress, and on the Polish-Soviet dispute and Hungarian revolt that it precipitated, helped to steady the shaken ranks of the world Communist parties and the people of the then Socialist camp. They certainly increased the prestige of the Chinese Communist Party.

An impressive sidelight to me—*multum in parvo*—was the strong approval with which my aged paternal aunts, Sonya, Emma, and Anna, retired schoolteachers in Moscow, reacted to the Chinese statements on these matters, *On the Historical Experience of the Dictatorship of the Proletariat* and *More On the Historical Experience of the Dictatorship of the Proletariat*, then freshly published in the Soviet Union. The three aunts, whom I met for the first time in my life on my earliest visit to the U.S.S.R. in 1958, were by no means just simple old ladies. They had lived through decades of that crucial experience, with its ups and downs. In early youth, attracted by the October 1917 Socialist revolution in Russia, they had moved there permanently from their home in the Polish-Lithuanian borderland. Since then they had witnessed the civil war and its hard-won victory, the tremendous national constructive effort darkened by terror under Stalin: in it their brother, Sender, who had come with them, disappeared; and Sonya's husband spent 17 years in prison camps from which he was released only to die of cancer soon after. Aunt Anna's husband gave his life in the defense of Moscow against Hitler's invaders. The aunts themselves, and the rest of the family were saved from the menace of Nazi racial murder by the Soviet government's mass evacuation of Jewish women, children, and the elderly from the threatened capital.

After World War II, they faced new dangers, including renascent official anti-Semitism in the U.S.S.R. itself. Still, they remained patriots of the Soviet Union, and did not, like many, seek to leave. So their endorsement of the points made from Beijing carried much weight. "You have wise-thinking heads there in China," tiny Aunt Emma summed up.

Of deep interest then to Soviet and East European Communists and sympathizers was Mao Zedong's speech, made in February 1957, and released some months later, entitled "On the Correct Handling of Contradictions Among the People"—a new concept within socialism. So were Mao's broad-minded instructions to "let a hundred flowers bloom" simultaneously in art and literature, and "let a hundred schools of thought contend" in science, technology, and research, with no officially-backed monopoly of any school (such as had been imposed in various fields, from genetics to linguistics, in the U.S.S.R.).

Its central theme was that differences of opinion and advocacy under socialism should not be lumped together as antagonistic (between the people and its enemies) and be eliminated by suppression, for there was a very broad range of existing contradictions, such as those within and between the workers, peasants, intellectuals, co-operating national bourgeoisie, and between the state, collective groups and individuals, leaders and led, and so on, which were essentially non-antagonistic. Though they might involve matters of right and wrong, they should be settled by debate and education, and not by suppression, as had become the way in the Soviet Union.

Broadly speaking, in 1956 and through much of 1957, the Chinese Communist Party itself was summarizing what had been accomplished in previous years—the laying down of the framework of a Socialist society—and what had to be done, or avoided, particularly in light of the shortcomings of the Soviet Union's theory and practice as revealed by the 20th Soviet Congress. Among Soviet attitudes it considered wrong was great-nation chauvinism with regard to other Socialist countries and authoritative paternalism instead of equality toward other Communist parties. But the leading role of the Soviet Union in the whole movement was not then questioned, what was desired was its improvement in fulfilling it.

In September 1956, the Eighth Congress of the Chinese Communist Party declared that the Socialist transformation of the country's society had been basically accomplished, and that henceforth the main task would not be the struggle between classes (though that would remain a factor) but the rapid material and cultural growth, made possible by the new society.

I was among those involved in "polishing" the English translations of the reports, speeches, and resolutions. Their tone, like the nationwide feeling at the time, was one of calm triumph and confidence.

It was in apparent harmony with the key ideas of China's Eighth Party Congress, and lessons drawn from the Soviet 20th Party Congress, that Mao Zedong launched the policies of "Letting a hundred flowers bloom," and "letting a hundred schools of thought contend," based on common acceptance of the Socialist system.

From this perspective, a general invitation was issued by the Communist Party for critical comment from society at large of defects in policy and action. Much was carried in openly-displayed posters, or given space in the major media. In it, some unexpected notes of hostility did crop up, beyond the bounds of constructive criticism. These were first published, then cited as evidence that counterrevolutionary moods, such as had resulted in the armed rebellion in Hungary, were a menace in China as well.

Proceeding from this estimate, a nationwide "anti-Rightist" movement was abruptly launched, and long continued. Virtually canceling the concepts of non-antagonistic contradictions and calm debate, friendly parties, such as the Democratic League, were denounced and paralyzed, and their newspapers closed or taken over. Intellectuals in general increasingly became a target, with denunciations and demotions of such prominent figures as the sociologist Fei Xiaotong and the leading economist and advocate of population control, Ma Yinchu, who were dismissed from their academic posts. Many thousands labeled ("hatted" as the phrase then went) as "Rightists" were sent to "reform through labor" in the countryside. Many were imprisoned.

While antagonistic elements undoubtedly existed, the campaign was greatly exaggerated and, in some respects, a precursor of the future Cultural Revolution. Only decades later, when the latter was declared ended, were the oppressive "hats" worn by the vast majority of designated Rightists removed and their wearers rehabilitated.

To those "hatted," often unexpectedly to themselves, the earliest hint of things to come, was an attack on a wall poster, which, if followed by others, was a sure indication of deepening trouble. In one instance, I remember seeing my old friend and colleague Feng Yidai, prominent in the Democratic League, reading the first such omen directed at himself, hung on the office corridor wall. Normally warmly talkative, he now stood strained and wordless. As silent were most of yesterday's cordial friends as they passed by.

I knew Feng from the anti-Japanese war years, in Hong Kong and Chongqing. There he had been a participant as essayist and translator in the Left literary movement, as well as a material backer, as he had a job in a bank with good pay, which he generously drew on and did not hesitate to risk. After Liberation, he readily gave it up to come to Beijing to help in foreign language publicity for China. His support of, and joy in, the Chinese Revolution, was undoubted. Now he suddenly found himself dubbed a Rightist, a political pariah—and years would pass until his rehabilitation. Hardest to bear, for people like him, was not the loss of position and pay but the feeling of being discarded by the cause to which they had been, and were, so devoted.

Feng was not a Communist Party member. The latter, if named as

"Rightist" or "right deviationist" could be expelled as well as demoted. The togetherness of Communists and progressives of the early 1950s was seriously breached, in our workplaces, and in society at large.

The often indiscriminate application of the "Rightist" label was a precursor of physical and psychological maltreatment, which, during the Cultural Revolution, resulted in deaths and suicides. Fortunately, in a key contrast to the Soviet purges of the Stalin period, executions of oppositionists and critics were rare in China. As Mao Zedong said, a head, once chopped off, could not be grown back in cases of error. Indeed, many victims of the Chinese political struggles were ultimately restored to work, respect, and honor.

*   *   *

It was during Zhou Enlai's visits to Burma and India in 1954 which marked the advent, through joint effort, of the Five Principles of Peaceful Coexistence, as applied to relations between states with different social systems (and, ultimately, to relations between Socialist states as well— the latter through China's efforts in subsequent decades).

In 1955 I was at first scheduled to go, as a correspondent for the *National Guardian* in New York, to the epochal Asian-African Conference in Bandung, Indonesia, the first in the modern history of the two continents in which their representatives met without the presence of colonial powers. Dearly as I would have liked to cover this event, I had other work keeping me in Beijing. Otherwise I probably would have died, with other journalists, in the catastrophic crash of the Indian airliner *Kashmir Princess*, a result of sabotage by Guomindang agents in Hong Kong who thought the plane would be carrying Zhou Enlai, and not just members of press, to Bandung. Among my friends who perished were Shen Jiantu of the Xinhua News Agency, whom I had met in Yan'an in 1944 and who had afterwards worked as a fellow-correspondent of *Allied Labor News*, and Fritz Jensen from Austria, a multi-talented medic, journalist, and author, who had come to China in the late 1930s with other foreign veterans of the International Bridge in Spain. They, and other Chinese and foreign newsmen aboard at ill-fated flight, are commemorated by a collective monument in the Cemetery for Revolutionary Martyrs in Beijing. Having narrowly escaped their fate, I am alive to write these lines. But I am still sorry to have missed Bandung—

a major landmark in history.

Bandung marked a historic diplomatic victory for the People's Republic of China. It was achieved by Zhou Enlai, whom enemies of the People's Republic had conspired to kill before he got there, and to isolate after he did, and who overcame initial misunderstandings and thus laid the basis for extended and lasting fraternity with many countries of Asia, Africa, and Latin America.

Having shown that it could defend its own borders, and the Chinese Revolution from "rollback," the People's Republic gained greatly in prestige not only among its own nationals but among other newly independent countries in Asia and those still struggling to throw off the colonial yoke or remnants of it.

Chapter 26

TIBET

I visited Tibet in 1955, 1965, 1976 and 1985, each visit lasting two or three months. Of all the transformations I saw in China, those on "the roof of the world" were the most dramatic. A leap over a thousand years from theocracy, serfdom, and slavery to the building of Socialism.[21]

In 1955, my first journey from Chengdu, capital of Sichuan Province, to Lhasa took a grinding 12 days in a jeep and truck convoy. Even that seemed a marvel of speed. The new 1,400 mile-long highway (then only a year old) was still bone-shaking rough. Zooming at times to mountain passes over 17,000 feet above sea level. Plunging, deep, at others, into the abyss-like canyons of several great rivers of China and Asia: the Jinsha, head of the Yangtze; the Langcang, which becomes the Mekong in Laos, Thailand, Cambodia, and Vietnam; and the Yalutsangpo, which becomes the Brahmaputra, in India.

Landscapes along the way were splendid beyond compare. Colors shone unbelievably bright in the transparent ultra-violet suffused air. In the intensely blue skies, dazzlingly white cloud formations appeared in ever-changing patterns, ranging from monumental masses to the sheerest gossamer.

The road, besides its bumps, was blocked by frequent landslides, and drivers and passengers alike had to pile out to help maintenance workers clear the road. Yet the advance it represented was already epoch-making. The only previous transport was by yak or mule caravan—where six months was considered good time for the trip. A People's Liberation Army unit, no slow marchers, took pride in its record of "only" 104 days.

My second, 1965, trip to Tibet was by a Chinese civil airliner. The flight from Chengdu to Lhasa took two and a half hours. It was easy to forget how recently this atmospherically perverse route had been pioneered, first by veteran military test pilots. Now passenger and cargo flights were

---

[21] The process is reported in detail in my book, *Tibet Transformed*, New World Press, Beijing, 1983, based on hundreds of on-the-spot interviews, recorded in thousands of pages of notes.

routine and frequent. Most of the 2,000 delegates and other visitors coming from all over China for the official founding of the Tibet Autonomous Region were flown in within a few days.

By my third visit, in 1976, there were two regular air routes, from Chengdu and Lanzhou in Gansu Province. We flew in by one and out by the other, over some of the most spectacular and impassable mountains and deserts on Earth. The aircraft were big, the scheduled flights almost daily occurrences. Passengers, Han Chinese and Tibetan, were casual as on a suburban bus. On our plane were geologists and meteorologists, construction personnel, middle-aged skilled workers, and trainees in their twenties. Tibetan students from colleges in China's interior provinces, officials on business or on leave.

By the time of my fourth journey, in 1985, one could also fly to Lhasa directly from Beijing; or from Kathmandu, in Lhasa's first international air link with Nepal. On my first two visits I was still one of the very few travelers of foreign origin to reach Tibet in decades, even centuries. Now tourists from abroad came in hundreds, mounting in following years to tens of thousands, flying in on the latest jumbo jets.

* * *

Travel within Tibet is still overland. Old Tibet had no tracks for carts, much less motorways. The only wheels then turning were prayer wheels—copper contrivances, often artistically made, moved by hand or by the water in fast-running streams, stuffed with sacred texts—each twirl would credit the worshiper with multiple incantations. In subsequent decades, several major highways were built, three to other parts of China and one to Kathmandu. Their grading, embankments, and traffic capacity improved constantly. Inside Tibet, virtually all counties were linked by road. Vehicles, rapidly increasing, were largely of Chinese make. Hauling material for road construction and repair, I happily saw swarms of "Iron Ox" tractors manufactured in Tianjin, my childhood home.

Freight convoys, each consisting of scores of trucks, labored their way over the "roof of the world"—where an internal combustion engine is even less adaptable to such altitudes than the human heart and lungs. Researchers were working not only on high-altitude medicine for humans, but on getting engines to breathe more easily on the world's oxygen-starved rooftop.

Long lines of heavy trucks from other parts of China were loaded to the brim with industrial goods to supply Tibet: driving in full, but driving out empty. The same was true of cargo aircraft. Hard to explain for those who continually pursue the line of "Beijing's exploitation."

China's aid to the Tibet Autonomous Region has been many-sided: administrative expenses are largely covered by the National treasury; tax rates are only a fraction of those in China's inner provinces. Subsidies to long-distance transport of goods keep prices in Tibet the same as at their points of origin. The central government has footed all costs of personnel sent for research and development in Tibet, and for students sent from Tibet to schools and colleges elsewhere in China. Much of the industrial equipment has been allotted gratis; while farm machinery was supplied at low prices. But prices paid for the produce of Tibet's peasants and herdsmen have been raised several times. All these measures proceeded from the formal equality of China's nationalities specified in her Constitution. Their aim—the creation of actual equality—which can come only with extensive development of production, education, and other fields.

Needed for really expanding Tibet's economy was a railroad. But its building has faced many obstacles, not the least of which were the physical challenges: impossibly high mountains, broad, turbulent rivers, frequent landslides, and permafrost (frozen soil) which is hard and weight-bearing in winter but in summer turns into a thin crust that can crumble to submerge heavy vehicles in the treacherous morasses below.

Economically, a lack of fuel resources along the far-flung route, and also lack of trade in the interim expanses with little or even no population, deterred rail development. By 1979, nevertheless, a railhead had moved closer to Tibet—in the north to Golmud, in neighboring Qinghai Province. From the south, several other routes have been surveyed. In 2001 came the news that the northern route had been chosen: trains from Golmud would reach Lhasa by the year 2006. I hope to make the rail journey, a long-held wish.

In the meantime, highway transport has been facilitated by the construction of an oil pipeline. Previously, the trucks had to carry their own fuel for their return trip. But only rail can move the huge machinery needed for harnessing the power-generating potential of some of the biggest and fastest-flowing rivers on Earth, and for the transport and processing of Tibet's rich mineral resources.

*   *   *

During my first trip to Tibet in 1955, in contrast to the democratic and Socialist changes in the rest of China, the region's capital was still deeply feudal—comparable to Europe in the eleventh century. Medieval and flamboyant, the Potala Palace of the Dalai Lamas, with its sunlit roofs of sheet gold, its vaults for stored wealth, and its dank, scorpion-infested dungeons for offenders and opponents, towered above almost unbelievable squalor. A third of the city's population were beggars and vagrants. Beyond the bounds of the great lamaseries and park-encircled ruling-class mansions, I saw them huddling in rotting hovels or in tiny, ragged tents, doomed to starvation, contesting with feral dogs for filthy morsels amid excrement and fetid pools. Mounted aristocrat-officials clothed in brilliant brocade and choice wool, followed by retinues varying with their rank, trotted in pomp through the streets.

Ragged, grime-besmeared, and with eyes down (for it was brutally punishable insolence to look above a noble's or high cleric's knees), serfs and slaves toiled for them in the dust. High and low, the belief had for centuries been enforced on the Tibetans that everyone's status was predetermined by fate, as a reward for virtues or penalty for faults in one's past incarnations. Hence it was deemed senseless for the rich (even though compassion was abstractly preached) to have qualms about sitting on the necks of the poor, and both criminal and blasphemous for the poor not to patiently bear the yoke.

"Shangri-La" the old Tibet was definitely not. That fancied place never existed. The origin of the never-never-land of James Hilton's novel was the desire to mentally escape, if only for the soothing hours it took to read it, from the depression-and-war-torn Western world of the early decades of the twentieth century.

In the early 1950s, when I first saw Tibet, it was moving forward in its own real mid-century way, amid sharp contradictions. The five-star flag of the new China already flew over Lhasa. The newly-constructed highways converged on it. The first modern hospital and lay primary school had been built. But in its regional inner administration, in return for their undertakings in the 17-Article Agreement signed in Beijing in 1951 to sever ties with imperialism and not to obstruct future social reform (both ultimately dishonored), the old Tibetan local power structure of upper clergy and lay aristocrats still held sway.

A striking embodiment of this was what I saw on October 1, 1955, at a celebration of the sixth anniversary of the founding of the People's Republic of China, held on the open ground fronting the Potala. A giant portrait of Mao Zedong was flanked by those of the Dalai and Panchen Lamas, both then pledged to the 1951 Agreement. I had met them both, slim and young, a year before, at a reception in Beijing where they were attending China's newly-inaugurated National People's Congress. There I asked them to autograph my invitation, unknowingly extending it first to the Panchen Lama. "I am the Dalai Lama," said the Dalai Lama, snatching it to sign first. No mistaking his assertion of precedence even in so informal a matter. Modest he wasn't. And, though still young, he was by no means simple.

On the reviewing stand at the Lhasa ceremony in 1955 were China's central government cadres in plain blue cloth uniforms, and members of the Kashag—the old feudal clerical-lay local council under the Dalai Lama, clad in robes of gold brocade. While scarlet banners fluttered overhead, the not yet reorganized Lhasa police loped through the throng, their rifles left behind for the day but their rawhide whips slowly swinging. I did not see them lash anyone, hardly the date and occasion. Yet nothing illustrated more vividly the smoldering contradictions of those years between the larger entity, the country committed to socialism, of which Tibet was a constituent part, and the still-extant local rule by serf owners. Between the people and the Revolutionary red flag stood the feudal whip. Something had to explode, and in 1959 it did.

In that year, the serf-owning local regime itself, by launching an armed revolt, tore up the 1951 Agreement. Accordingly, the steps the central authorities undertook to help the people had to be done via the feudal local authorities or with their consent, while the latter's ultimately frustrated reform.

For example, the central government had introduced the innovation, for Tibet, of wages for work on public projects—initially the road system. But many of the serfs and slaves engaged had their wages seized by masters or headman. The serfs and slaves themselves were others' property. By their masters' logic, so were their earnings.

Modern schools were beginning to be built. But the teaching of natural science was resisted by local powers as "contrary to the faith" (while religious instruction was compulsory). And, in history and social science, nothing could be taught in the schools about the exploitation of working people—in a social order in which their labor was appropriated in a most naked way without even the intermediacy of money: serfs could work as many as 300 days a year for lamaseries or nobles, as their *ulag* obligation, akin to the *corvee* system of feudal Europe.

Through the 1950s, the old Dalai Lama-led local authorities continued their customary methods of oppressive rule. They still subjected Tibet's common people to not only ruinous exactions but to some of the most brutal atrocities sanctioned by medieval law and practice. In 1965, when the memories and evidence were still fresh, we met, interviewed, and photographed former serfs and slaves who had had their hands or feet chopped off, leg tendons severed, or even eyes gouged out for alleged, often quite petty offences and defiance: herders who were charged with losing a sheep from their master's flock, and servants who had "insolently" denied small thefts of which they had been accused, and so on.

Moreover, such horrors were not denied but coolly described by Tibetan separatist self-exiles, publishing in English, who even found apologies for them.

One wrote:

> During the hearing of a case, (it) was resorted to when there was no other way of getting at the truth. As a lad I used to watch unfeelingly while two law officials would interrogate (the accused) during the intervals in the lashing session.

The same author recalled such penalties as "…taking out the eyeballs, amputation of tongue or hand, throwing the criminal alive into water or off a precipice," and further found it possible to comment, "The Decrees (traditional Tibetan legal code) were formulated at a certain period of history; nevertheless, the system sufficed even in the 1950s. Tibet's self-sufficiency as a nation never ceases to be a source of pride to me."[22]

Another émigré, nostalgic for the old order, herself a member of two of its leading families, wrote that a special caste in that society, the *Ragyapa*, had among its duties "putting out the eyes or chopping off the limbs of the few criminals punished in this manner" as well as "providing the monks with human skulls and thigh-bones for special rites."[23]

On the essence of pre-1959 Tibetan society, one may cite the conclu-

---

[22] Dawa Norbu, *Red Star Over Tibet* (London 1974). pp. 76-80.

[23] Rinchen Dolma Taring, *Daughter of Tibet* (London 1970), p. 9.

sion of a prominent American academic from information supplied by Tibetan separatists themselves in their Indian sanctuary:

> Tibet was characterized by a form of institutionalized inequality that can be called pervasive serfdom... Demographically, with the exception of aristocratic families... the rest of the key population were serfs... There were no "free" peasants.[24]

The policy of the Chinese Communist Party, as conceived and practiced by Mao Zedong and Zhou Enlai, was to give the feudal elite leeway until, as was inevitable, the most hardcore elite elements would expose itself to an increasingly aware majority of the commonalty through overt rebellion. And when that happened, to strike down the old social order with the help of the oppressed majority. This, in fact, was done in 1959, with the basics similar to the changes in the rest of China, with some distinctions drawn even among the old ruling groups.

In Tibet's reform, the estates of serf owners and Ngapo Ngawang Jigme (an ex-member of the former slaveholders who did not rebel), were not confiscated but bought. Among them were former high officials of the Dalai Lama-led local government, like Ngapo Ngawang Jigme who held various high posts at the central level and served, in later years, as chairman of the Tibet Autonomous Region.

Notables, clerical and lay, who were given positions at the national or new local level, included not only those accepting reforms but participants in the rebellion, who had served terms of imprisonment and changed their views; one was Lhalu Tsewang Dorje who had been commander-in-chief of the rebel forces. Ultimately, such aristocrats worked alongside Tibetans who had been former zealots of their class.

In 1965 I met and talked to many of the new leading figures in Tibet, who had risen from the most downtrodden strata of the old society with nothing even remotely resembling human rights. They belonged, one might say, to three generations:

The first, stemming from the earliest contact of China's Communist-led revolution among the Tibetans, had joined the Chinese Red Army in the

[24] Melvyn C. Goldstein. *Serfdom and Mobility* in the *Journal of Asian Studies* of the University of Michigan, May 1972. The author had been married to the daughter of Surkhang Wangching-Galei, an ex-Galon, or Council Member under the Dalai Lama and a leading plotter of the 1959 rebellion.

mid-1930s, when its Long March took it through provinces with large Tibetan minorities, though it did not enter Tibet itself. As impoverished, illiterate teenagers, they had volunteered to join a force that called and proved itself to be an army of the poor, and which, though composed of ethnic Han Chinese, did not despise or discriminate against minorities, but stayed with them despite all hardships and perils. Among them were Sanggye Yeshi (also called Tian Bao), a novice monk; Shinrob Dondrup (Yang Dongsheng), a serf herdsman, and others, thousands, from all areas of Tibet. Educated in the Communist army, they fought in its ranks for twenty years: against Chiang Kai-shek, against the Japanese invaders, and in the War of Liberation after 1945. They fought on many fronts, including the taking of Tianjin and Shanghai. Following the victory of the Revolution in 1949, they worked in civil administration, particularly in national minority autonomous areas such as Inner Mongolia.

Finally they returned to their Tibetan roots. By the 1960s, Tian Bao was the chairman of the Tibet Autonomous Region, Yang Dongsheng the head of the Regional People's Congress, and Tashi Wangchuk the governor of Qinghai Province, which has a large Tibetan minority. All were members of the National People's Congress and other leading Communist Party bodies. Of the old Red Army generation they were by then among the few survivors—a large number had perished in battle.

The second generation of Tibetan cadres arose, also in surrounding provinces, during the march of the People's Liberation Army into Tibet itself in the early 1950s. In social origin and motivation they were much like the first group, though in numbers much greater. Among them I met and interviewed Lobsang Tsechen, originally a carpenter, who in the 1960s became a vice-chairman of the Tibet Autonomous Region; Zhen Ying, of peasant origin, who became the vice-Party secretary of Xigatse prefecture; Dorje Ben, a former "masterless man" (which unfortunately meant he could be mistreated by any superior without the protection of his "owner") who became vice-head of the Lokha (Shan Nan) prefecture; and an industrial administrator, Shirob Watsa, assistant director of the important Auto Vehicle Repair Works of the Tibet Autonomous Region, who as a young man had had his knees shattered by order of his serf owner (after the democratic reform in Tibet they had been surgically repaired so that he could walk, but still with a bad limp).

The third generation, rooted in the Tibetan Autonomous Region itself, dated from the time of the 1959 serf owner rebellion and its suppression. I met Basang, a former female slave who had risen to membership of the Tibet Committee of the Chinese Communist Party and the nationwide Communist Party Central Committee; Raigdi, originally a serf herdsman who also attained this Party status and was, by 2001, chairman of the People's Congress of the Tibet Autonomous Region; Tsering Lhamo, a vital, remarkable woman, who began as an organizer of a collective of fellow ex-slaves who took over the estate of their former master, and after many years became vice-head of the entire Tibetan Autonomous Region.

Such people were not suddenly elevated but went from rung to rung of the new order in Tibet, with opportunities of education which it afforded side by side with their work. They were impressive examples of the abilities and human dignity latent in the ranks of the former downtrodden.

I interviewed, among many others, including Ngawang Gyatso, who as a serf boy had been threatened with strangulation by reactionaries for daring to go to a new school and wear a Young Pioneer red scarf. He was in charge one of Lhasa's districts; Champa Gyatso, a former serf tailor who headed a rural county; Tsering Phuntso, a Lhasa police officer who had been a slave.

I also talked with Tibetan members of the People's Liberation Army ranging in rank from privates to generals. To Tibetan mountaineers—one a young woman, Puntsog, who had scaled the world's highest peak—Qolmolongma—known in the West as Mount Everest; Tsedan Chomo, a gifted singer famed in China and abroad for her performances of Tibetan songs, and scores of people with similar transformations in their lives.

Above the township (formerly commune) level, the Tibetan cadres in the early 1980s numbered 36,000—over 60 per cent of the total population. Among the region's qualified medical personnel, more than half were Tibetans. Among teachers in the 6,000 primary schools in Tibet (thirty years earlier there had been less than ten schools), about nine-tenths were Tibetans; among the 1,370 middle-school teachers, over a third; and among technicians of all kinds a rising proportion. The 1990s brought a further increase in all categories.

In the disestablishment of the monastery-owned estates, the reform in Tibet did what had already been done in England in the sixteenth century under Henry VIII, except that the land and livestock were distributed to the serfs and not to the aristocracy. And that in Tibet, unlike England, there were no enclosures driving peasants off the land to become vagrants and beggars.

As for moves toward Tibet's secession from China in modern times, history reveals their implanting and fostering from abroad, mainly by the British Empire after its eighteenth century conquest of India. Britain's probing into Chinese territory from the land side, via Tibet, was long coordinated with its naval invasions (from the Opium Wars on) along China's far-off eastern coast.

Following World War II, and especially after the start of the Cold War, came a change in the main foreign patrons and manipulators of separatist trends. The United States, seeking supremacy in Asia in succession to the declining power of Britain, now reached for the distant roof of the world. By 1947, George Merrell, then U.S. *Charge d'Affaires* in New Delhi, was urging that Washington take action on "the inestimable strategic importance" of Tibet in Asia—all important in the new nuclear age. Sounding this note, Merrell argued that the "conservative and religious" Tibetans, under "firm control" by their local government (theocratic and based on serfdom, which he did not specify) could, if backed by the U.S. for separation from China, "resist possible Soviet or Communist infiltration into the Tibetan plateau which, in an age of rocket warfare, might prove to be the most important territory in Asia." Media articles in the U.S. touted the same view as did several books.[25]

In 1948, the explorers and publicists Lowell Thomas, Sr. and Lowell Thomas, Jr.—briefed in advance by the U.S. ambassador to India, Loy Henderson, and General Willoughby, chief of Intelligence under General Douglas MacArthur—made their way to Lhasa. There, officials of the Kashag directly inquired: "If the Communists strike Tibet, will America help? And to what extent?" Needed from the U.S., they said, were weapons and instruction, specifically, for guerrilla warfare.[26]

Clearly, the U.S. government had already been in contact with the separatists for some years, when, in the middle and late 1950s, it secretly flew selected groups for training to Camp Hale in Colorado, then air dropped them, with arms and communications gear, into Tibetan-inhabited areas. Two Camp Hale-trained parachutists, with their U.S.-supplied radio equip-

---

[25] See Knaus, John Kenneth, *Orphans of the Cold War, Public Affairs,* New York, 1999; and de Riencourt, Amaury, *Roof of the World-Key to Asia,* 1950

[26] Thomas, Lowell, Jr., *Out of This World,* New York, 1950.

ment, accompanied the Dalai Lama on his 1959 flight to India.[27]

The connivance flowed from the Cold War urge to "roll back" the 1949 victory of the Chinese Communist Revolution, with no real concern for the Tibetans, including the secessionists. The latter themselves had now begun to complain publicly that Washington viewed them only as pawns to be used in some wider plan. That most of the secessionists were promptly exposed and caught showed the hostility to such ventures among a population newly freed from serfdom. How, otherwise, could the 1959 rebellion have been quelled with such speed in this mountain land, where guerrilla warfare might have been waged endlessly in any popular cause?

*　*　*

The new Lhasa I saw rising on my second trip, in 1965, was the fruit born of the post-1959 upsurge. The Potala, still there and resplendent, was no longer such a subject of mystery and awe. In the Museum of the Tibetan Revolution, built nearby, the past misery of nine out of ten Tibetans was shown as due to very worldly reasons. The furs, jewels, and utensils of pure gold belonging to the Dalai Lamas, brought out for public display from the chambers and vaults of the great palace, matched those of the Tsars of old Russia who had 160 million subjects to sweat while the Potala had less than a million under its direct sway. Here, too, one learned that "fate" was not irresistible but reversible. The people had thrown off the oppressors who had robbed them of the products of their labor. Tibet's grain crop had increased by almost half, its livestock by over a third. New structures in Lhasa, built in the Tibetan style, included the headquarters of the Tibetan Autonomous Region and the People's Palace of Culture, with 1,200 seats in its main hall—not bad for such a small city which by then also had other new theaters and halls. Performances and cultural functions held there were packed with men and women who had only recently lived in cattle-sheds. Nearby, a new state-owned department store was filled with goods ranging from needles and thread to transistor radios, sewing ma-

[27] Knaus wrote on p.168: "A small group of officials in Washington, including the president, had been following the Dalai Lama's journey through messages sent by CIA-trained radio operators dropped the previous summer." (that is, several months before the rebellion in Lhasa, though during its preparatory phase, in the Kham area.)

chines, and bicycles. Many were bought by people who were *themselves* bought and sold prior to 1959.

Lhasa had miles and miles of new, electrically lit, asphalt-paved streets with underground drains (not an inch of either had existed before my first visit in 1955). A pipe-laying team was installing the first mains for running water. No more stinking ditches or refuse-filled pools.

New, too, was the airline terminal. And the long-distance bus station from which, in later years, one could travel in motor coaches specially made for the high plateau: well-heated and outfitted with its own oxygen supply.

Since Liberation, Lhasa had gained more than ten times as much space in dwellings, factories, schools, hospitals, and theaters as it had during its previous 1,300 years as a city. Electricity had been available only to the Potala and a few aristocrats, and even that was supplied erratically. By 1965, nine-tenths of the city's homes were lit. By my third visit in 1976, Tibet had several medium-sized hydro-electric power stations for urban use, plus a great many smaller substations in the remote countryside supplying electricity to small villages and communities. Since the region was poor in mineral fuels, much attention was paid to alternative sources. Geo-thermal energy was being tapped both for power-generation and for hot-houses growing hitherto unavailable crops. Solar power, latent in Tibet's 3,000 hours of annual sunlight, was increasingly utilized.

In 1955, Lhasa had no machines. Spinning, weaving, printing, and metal work existed—but all were done by hand. By 1965 the city had had a truck-repair station and a cement works, and by 1976 was turning out simple farm machinery, tractor parts, small turbine generators, and electric motors for rural power. Tibet had 178 factories, thrice as many as a decade earlier. Industrial workers, virtually non-existent in 1955, numbered some 25,000 in 1965, and 65,000 in 1976. By the middle of the 1980s, 41 new projects were under way in industry urban construction, education, medicine, culture, education, tourism, and sports. State aid, besides funds and materials, included some 50,000 construction personnel temporarily in the region, all due to go home when their work was done. In the 1990s, the central government built an additional 63 projects in Tibet, investing 2.38 billion yuan (U.S. $290 million).

Preserved and developing were the best cultural achievements of Tibet's warm, brave, talented, and hard-working people over the centuries—in architecture, medicine, arts and crafts, beautiful and vigorous songs, dances, operas and dramas, and literature.

In old Tibet, 95 per cent of the people were illiterate. Today, school children learn to read and write in their own tongue, with a word-fund expanded to meet new needs, but shedding its servile vocabulary for compulsory fawning on feudal superiors and contemptuous treatment of inferiors. That more could have been done in stimulating the building of a new Tibetan-language culture is not an unfair criticism, however, the accomplishments already made are not small.

Today, Tibet is an organic part of a multi-ethnic China, its woe and weal linked to those of its other areas and peoples. Within this larger entity, Tibet has distinctive features—historical, social, linguistic, and cultural.

Secession is not a rational conclusion from these peculiarities. The Tibetan separatism of modern times has, from its start, been linked not with the needs of Tibet's progress and people but with the ambitions and heritage of imperialism aimed at the break-up and subjugation of all China, Tibet included. At no point was the separation of Tibet, or any part of it, agreed to by any Chinese government. Nor did any foreign government formally challenge the legal status of Tibet as part of China even while engaged in undermining it by military invasion, by spy craft, or by diplomatic threat. In 1912, Britain went so far as to threaten not to recognize the new Republican government of China if Tibet had seats in its Parliament.

There have also been errors affecting the whole of China as well as specific ones relating to minority nationalities—the Tibetans among them.

Country-wide, for some years, the Leftist urge to undue speed of economic advance strayed from the requirement adhered to by the Chinese Communist Party up to the mid-1950s: that social change be accompanied by year-by-year improvement of the working people's living standards. Politically, the same path toward the Left led, particularly in the Cultural Revolution years of the 1960s and 70s, to ignoring the difference between antagonistic and non-antagonistic contradictions, between those with inveterate foes of the people's progress, and those between different sections of the people.

In the case of national minority regions, such Leftist actions sometimes even confused mere dissimilarities between ethnic groups with basic class antagonisms (which were assumed to play the key role even when they no longer did). Methods and tactics suited only to the Han areas were sometimes unduly copied.

In agriculture, Tibet's grain crops were reported to have more than tripled between 1952 and 1980, and livestock 2.5 times. But mass living standards, though they increased greatly between the suppression of the rebellion in 1959 and the founding of the Autonomous Region in 1965, did not improve correspondingly afterwards, despite continued output growth. This was not the result of colonial or class exploitation of the Tibetans. Very significant funds were put into the region and no profits taken out. The cause lay, rather, in imbalance between the efforts made and the actual possibilities and needs of the region, including assortment of food grains and other products, disproportions between input—including labor—and economic effect, including created purchasing power.

Regional autonomy, provided by China's constitution, was also not consistently carried out. The number of Tibetan functionaries—political and technical—did increase greatly. But this, for years, was not accompanied by policy adaptations to local circumstances. Tibet's new officials tended to be judged, and to judge themselves, by how closely they followed models outside the region. That, in turn hampered the creative initiatives that their closeness to their own people and local realities should have generated, within the framework of regional autonomy and Socialist principle.

All these defects, from the 1980s on, were noted and being corrected. If there was retreat, it was not toward Tibet's old society but to the policies of the early post-rebellion and post-reform periods, which I found Tibetans remembering as "the golden age" of democratic and Socialist advance. Some older thinking did re-surface amid the confusion, but there was also an overcoming of imbalances, shortages, and strains brought about by past efforts to do too much too fast. This brought about progress which strengthened unity and support.

New flare-ups of separatism did occur, fed and backed, as for decades past, from abroad. The channels used were multiple. Secret infiltration of agents continued and increased. Some tourists fanned the sparks, intentionally or because they were misled by the unceasing harangues of Western media. The Dalai Lama traded his religious status into political capital in innumerable statements and travels abroad, or at times in talks, through intermediaries, with China's central leadership in Beijing or emissaries sent openly to Tibet. In the West, sweetened by praise as a world-level religious luminary, with nary a word about his serf-state antecedents, was advertised as the political leader of his people, received "unofficially" by foreign heads of state, and, as a built-up climax, given the Nobel Peace Prize.

Although, as before, no foreign government recognized any Tibetan claim for independence, not a few were involved in ways ranging from direct, though covert, intervention to fostering and encouraging media attacks on China on the "Tibetan issue."

Among foreigners there was then, and persists, a belt of promoter-worshippers of old Tibet as a kind of Shangri-la. It ranges from foreign officials, still dreaming of Tibet as a diplomatic-military outpost, to intoxicated mystics including a vocal Hollywood group. The latter have been the target of recent sarcasm by Americans authors whom no on can accuse of being "one-sidedly" pro-China. How would these film stars have liked living as serfs in the old days? They asked. Barbed, too, were the comments about the film *Seven Years in Tibet*. Intended as a super-bomb of international propaganda for Tibetan separatism, but waylaid by the discovery that Heinrich Harrer, its Austrian protagonist and author of the book on which it was based, had long hidden his own documented Nazi past.

Among Tibetans, according to my experience and many accounts by others, nostalgia for Tibet's pre-Liberation past hardly extends beyond the ranks of ex-aristocrats and high clerics who fled abroad—the chief beneficiaries of the old serf society.

* * *

Tibet's transition from past to present and future, even more than that of all China's, is a complex road with many detours. Under present circumstances, the "threat to Tibetan culture," so loudly proclaimed by the Dalai Lama and many foreign echoers, came not so much from inside China as from the influence of Western lifestyles. This manifests itself as a general rootlessness, and applies not only to Tibet itself but much more to the new generation of Tibetan exiles.

These young expatriates are largely more fluent in the language of their sojourn than in their own language, which in Tibet is the primary one with Mandarin Chinese as a second.

Policies of contempt and exploitation toward ethnic minorities, which were the rule in pre-Liberation China, have been replaced by those of legal equality, with the nation's majority obligated to actively help the minorities and their autonomous areas to real equality in economic and cultural development. A great deal has been done in this effort and spirit. However, though the old mental concepts have repeatedly been denounced by the leaders of the Chinese Revolution and government, their vestiges in society

285

sometimes reappear.

After the oppressive theocratic system in Tibet had been done away with for the benefit of the oppressed and with their participation and support, there was a Left variant of Han supremacy—in the form of insistence that the most progressive thing for Tibetans to do was to carbon-copy what were considered the model pattern of advance in the Han areas. Some Tibetans themselves came to believe this, but in fact it resulted in arbitrary action that impinged on the faith and hearts of the people—as ultra-Leftists did—in other circumstances in other parts of China as well.

And in the later period, when that fanatical Cultural Revolution ended and commercial considerations came to the fore, the feeling of many Tibetans were insulted from another direction by private touting of some of their customs as spectacle for sensation-hunting tourists. One example was of "sky burial" in which a corpse of the deceased person is fragmented for complete consumption by vultures, leaving no trace. To the Tibetans this was an honored return of the body to nature. Happily, the luring of morbid Peeping Toms to view it as something gruesomely "thrilling" has now for some years been forbidden.

Overall, the Tibetans are better off within the family of China's peoples than they would be with an "independence," which would not be real at all, but merely make them a satellite. Without doubt, such a Tibet would be played with as an international probe against China, to be manipulated or discarded as the atmosphere changed. Global geo-political strategists in the West might even place Tibet in the role of a forward post for a U.S.-dominated net of bases extending from Europe through Central Asia to impinge on China's heartland. But the only real losses from such intermittent deliriums, and the inevitable bleak awakenings would be the tranquility and welfare of Tibet and the Tibetans.

*   *   *

Elsie accompanied me during my third trip to Tibet, so intrepidly, that on the copy of my book *Tibet Transformed* I gave her, I wrote: "To dear you, without whom there wouldn't have been any book, and whom the Roof of the World couldn't daunt but damn near killed."

Indeed, it almost did, for Elsie was already in her seventies, her heart was giving her trouble, and she was barely recovered from a fall when she slipped on the ice running to catch a bus as she carried medicine for a sick friend. She had turned and broken her ankle so badly that her foot pointed the wrong way and, freshly out of a cast, she was limping on a stick. But she was determined to go to Tibet just the same.

Once there, she hid—as much as she could—the altitude's effect on her. In this she was abetted by an accompanying young doctor who saw and respected her iron resolve, and was willing to assume the responsibility for seeing her through. For Elsie to have gone in for a mere hospital check would have meant being promptly packed off by its solicitous specialists ("make sure that nothing happens to a foreign expert") straight back to sea level. As it was she gasped, inhaled oxygen, took medicine from our youthful medic's kit, and made recovery after recovery. Thus, for six weeks, she thumped merrily along, leaning on a stick thick and long as a Boy Scout stave for which she had discarded her slender cane.

Chapter 27

IN THE CULTURAL REVOLUTION

The Great Proletariat Cultural Revolution was slow in getting to me. I had taken the children to the seaside at Beidaihe. Elsie was on a home visit to Britain. Only from a letter from her, based on foreign news agency dispatches, did I learn that the young Red Guards were in Beijing's streets. Elsie seemed puzzled, with some alarm at what she read in the papers. I replied reassuringly, that Western news sensationalized every event in "Red China." Continuance of the Revolution by young people born under socialism, meanwhile, could be healthy. If limits were initially overstepped, as they were apt to do in mass movements, adjustments would come. As often, I tended to rationalization after the fact.

Used to China's political campaigns, and their frequently sudden starts, I did not realize the unprecedented sweep of this one, or dream of its unprecedented climax beyond all control. It would demand the ultimate surrender and denunciatory self-denial not only of those who had ruled China's old society but of those who had sided with, or, in many cases, led in, its overthrow. The majority of Communist Party functionaries, high and low, would themselves become its targets. From intellectuals, particularly, it would demand the scrapping of all that they had, or could have learned, from previous culture, within which anyone over age 30 in 1966 (or over age 13 in 1949), had been taught. Karl Marx, and indeed even Mao Zedong, had said it should be critically absorbed, separating the useful from the dross. The Cultural Revolution tended to reject all.

My own strongest motive was not to tumble off the train of revolution when "the locomotive of history took a sharp turn," as Lenin once put it. Nor to be like the old woman with bound feet dragging and nagging behind the bold vanguard, in Mao Zedong's homely Chinese simile. To move in step with revolution had been my choice since boyhood. I resolved not to be left behind, dejected and rejected.

Important in this regard was the example of the *dazibao* ("big character poster") put up by American friends, Joan Hinton and her husband Sid Engst. They urged that revolutionary-minded foreign workers in China be accepted as participants in the campaign, as a new development in world revolutionary practice. Such foreigners were to be treated "not like bourgeois experts but like class brothers... permitted and encouraged to join in physical labor, be assisted in their ideological remolding...(and) have contact with workers and peasants." Their offspring, too, "should be treated the same as Chinese children with the same strict demands." There would be no more special treatment such as higher living standards compared to the Chinese, which prevented foreigners who wanted to be revolutionaries from grasping Chairman Mao's thought, and isolated them from their Chinese class brothers and the undermining push toward proletarian internationalism.

I was the first to respond positively and publicly, followed by others. On September 8, 1966, Mao Zedong put the supreme seal on the Hinton-Engst initiative by his instruction:

"Revolutionary foreigners and their children must be treated exactly the same as Chinese, no differences should be allowed... All those who wish to must be treated this way without exception. Please discuss and decide how this it to be done."

To relay and implement this endorsement, Chen Yi, Minister of Foreign Affairs, called in a group of signers and initial supporters of the original poster. He stressed to us that adhesion must be entirely voluntary, no external pressure should be applied.

We then formed a Red Guard-type group of foreigners (including those naturalized as Chinese) named the "Bethune-Yan'an Rebel Regiment of Mao Zedong Thought."

"Bethune" symbolized the commitment to world revolution, like the noted Canadian doctor, Norman Bethune, who died while serving the Communist Army wounded and who was famously eulogized as a model of Communist internationalism by Mao Zedong; "Yan'an" symbolized the Chinese Revolution's road to victory; "Rebel," a usual adjective in the names of Red Guard units, was in line with Mao's dictum that it was "right to rebel" against revisionism, bureaucratism, and other tendencies to "take the capitalist road" as the Soviet Union was accused of doing.

Half or more of us foreign-born workers in Beijing joined the

Regiment, usually in its components in our places of work. Like all Red Guards, we dressed in blue or gray cotton cloth, wore red armbands and attended meetings (our own or those we were increasingly invited to attend or speak at). I accepted almost every invitation by a Chinese Red Guard unit, regarding all as revolutionaries regardless of how they saw each other.

What I did not foresee was the rapid advance into ruinous factionalism. In general, the Cultural Revolution marked my failure as a prophet. Earlier, when everything in China seemed to be moving smoothly, Mao Zedong had warned against complacent disregard of three dire possibilities:

1. Outbreak of the Third World War
2. Natural calamities causing China-wide famine
3. A split in the Central Committee of the Chinese Communist Party.

My reactions were, roughly: Another world war? Possible, as capitalism had already bred two; and the Socialist camp—which would never start one—might fail to prevent it; A general famine? Improbable, since crop failures in some areas were generally offset by good harvests in others; A split in the Central Committee? Impossible, since there was unity from 1935 on, when Mao had assumed leadership, in contrast with many the fissions in the Soviet Union's leadership and in other Socialist areas. Yet a split did explode, and soon, in the Cultural Revolution, which I failed to see looming despite many previous political movements which seemed to me not forerunners of fission but barriers to it.

Nor can I pretend to theoretical perception with regard to the Cultural Revolution's basic concept of the danger of capitalism being restored through the bureaucratization and corruption of "power holders in the Communist Party" in Socialist countries. Such a process had worried Mao Zedong at least since the late 1950s, as occurring in the Soviet Union.

In my thinking, however, history had shown that revolutions which abolished a previous social order were decisive. Feudalism had not returned to France after her great Revolution of 1789-93, even though, on the political surface, it was followed by the restoration of monarchy, and two Napoleonic empires. Despite those zigzags of form of rule, it was capitalism that grew in France, while feudalism had been supplanted for good. Nor had the old social order returned in England, in the political countercurrents, which followed her Revolution. After the Commonwealth led by Oliver Cromwell, which had toppled and beheaded King Charles I, the monarchy had revived, preserving the titled aristocracy (some still possessing large landed estates). But all this was under the new, capitalist economic system, which prevailed from then on.

Much less could I really believe in the return to capitalism in the Soviet Union. The U.S.S.R. was the child of Russia's victorious October Socialist Revolution, strengthened by the heroic and decisive Soviet role in the worldwide defeat of reactionary fascism. Admittedly, the Socialist system there had flaws, but I could see no capitalist comeback.

Yet capitalism has undeniably returned to Russia and the European countries once in the orbit of the former U.S.S.R. Or perhaps not "returned" because in most of those countries it had never been fully dominant, and their revolutions, which swept away feudal remnants, could open the way to capitalism as well as to socialism and communism.

It was just such a danger that Mao perceived and wanted forestalled. To resist it, he tried to rallying, in succession, all the elements in society which he saw as having no roots in the past: the young people born under the Red Flag, the workers who had known and had fought exploitation by capitalists, and more by now their vast majority who were too young to have done so. And, finally, the People's Liberation Army.

In my own feelings and thoughts, there was also a lurking regret that I had not been born soon enough to have witnessed and perhaps taken some part in what I saw as the greatest, most spectacular world event of the previous generation, the Russian October Revolution. The fanfare drama of China's Cultural Revolution, with its huge rallies and street marches seemed for a time to fill this gap in a new age. Though I had witnessed truly world-changing events in China, it was mainly as a sympathetic observer, not in its ranks of struggle and action. This shadow I would call, self-mockingly, my "Miniver Cheevy complex," after a fictional character—the broody young man in a humdrum small town in Midwest America who expressed sorrow that he had not lived in an earlier period of great events and heroic deeds—vividly created by Sherwood Anderson, the acclaimed writer of modern American short stories.

It is not my intention here to retrace or try to analyze the decade of the Cultural Revolution either chronologically or in great detail, as many have done and will do; but to present my personal experiences in which I tried, and had a chance, to participate.

I assumed that all Red Guard groups were equally revolutionary and well intentioned, and factional rivalry was secondary. Many asked me to attend or address their meetings, hoping to show, at least symbolically, that my foreign face denoted foreign revolutionary sympathy. I mostly complied, making at least 20 speeches in the capital. In the educational world, the venues ranged from Beijing University and specialized colleges including the Iron and Steel, Foreign Trade, and Physical Culture Institutes, and national-level units run by the army such as its Rear Services Institute and Radio School, as well as various middle schools. Among non-student "rebel" groups they included those at the Foreign Ministry, the First Machine-Building Ministry, the People's Bank, the Import-Export Ministry, and other government offices and undertakings. I also addressed large outdoor rallies in Beijing geared to current national events, and a citywide rally held at Nankai University in nearby Tianjin.

Most of these affairs were organized not by the work units, but by one or more of the contesting Red Guard detachments. My choice of invitations to accept was mainly first come, first served. I can remember only one I refused: to accompany a group planning to drag Liu Shaoqi, one of the highest-ranking politburo members, and accused of being the "number one capitalist-roader," physically out of the government area where he still lived. On street marches and at meetings I did join in shouting slogans against him, and against Deng Xiaoping. But I did not believe he should be seized by mass action. For this reservation I myself was threatened with censure by the inviters. Now, only when requests came directly through Red Guard factions to which I (and Elsie) belonged in our own workplaces did I make appearances.

In the Bethune-Yan'an Regiment, I was for a time the virtual head, in a committee that included Chilean, Belgian, and Sri Lankan experts. This was after the arrest of Sidney Rittenberg, the American who for a time was in the "rebel" leadership of China's international broadcasting station. He had given signs of being in the confidence of the nation-wide Culture Revolution Committee, which practically replaced the top levels of the Party and government, and particularly of Mao's wife, Jiang

Qing, who first appeared to find him of use, then threw him aside.

In the rhetoric of the Cultural Revolution there was a competition for ferocity of wording, but in fact, there was a well-understood gradation. When one faction in our workplace used the slogan, "Down with Chen Yi" (the then Foreign Minister), they were clearly demanding his overthrow or dismissal. But when another shouted "Bombard Chen Yi," or even "Fry him in oil," which sounded more violent, they were only asking that he be criticized and rebuked. In general, the relation of bombast to action was often like that of John L. Lewis, longtime leader of the United Mine Workers in the U.S., who once famously roared to his supporters to "Tear opponents limb from limb!" then added, in a much lower tone, "Figuratively speaking." Except that in the Cultural Revolution, with loudspeakers on both sides, the sound-level was always far greater than even John L. Lewis could muster, or even imagine.

*   *   *

Civil strife without two flags is fiercer when both sides fly the same flag, or claim the exclusive right to it. All factions professed the same goals: "defense of Mao Zedong Thought," and opposition to all revisionism. Precisely because each claimed to be totally correct and denounced its opponent as totally wrong, there could be no compromise: one or other had to be knocked down. Even though Mao Zedong called for debate, not force, and Zhou Enlai worked himself to the bone for this mode, more and more violence developed. First, primarily, was violence against individuals. Then growing to clashes between large groups, some with deadly weapons and many causalities, were islets of civil war.

Of rational debate most traces were soon lost. What remained, between contending groups, were only charges, countercharges, and attempts to out-shout each other. Listening to each others' arguments for possibly valid points was unknown. For persons caught to be "debated" with, the only options were to admit guilty error or, if brave enough, to remain silent—never to give a reasoned reply.

*   *   *

The stated aim of the Cultural Revolution was to uproot capitalist tendencies. The method recommended by Mao Zedong was the widest possible mass unity and action to strengthen socialism. Instead, the epidemic of divisive factionalism not only slowed material progress but crumbled, instead of strengthening, Socialist and communist conviction as the motive for action.

Growing, moreover, was another evil factor. Increasingly, the struggle was not only for a view, but for power, independently of principle.

As factionalism hardened, each initially-small group frantically sought allies outside. It was not as before, where, preferably among related work units, groups could share experiences with possibility of mutual benefits. But everything now depended on whether the prospects had already been enlisted by the other side. So "rebel" organizations, swelled to citywide, provincewide, and even nationwide in scope. The sole test became "whoever is not with us is against us."

Proliferating were the personal ambitions of budding faction heads, often claiming a natural right to dominance as born representatives of the oppressed classes. But the crowning cynical vice was manipulation from high levels in the national Culture Revolution Committee itself. Jiang Qing did not scruple at telling rival agglomerations they were the genuine revolutionaries, waiting for them to smash or checkmate each other, then elevating someone, from their ranks or outside, whose only loyalty was to her own clique.

* * *

The quotations from Chairman Mao, whether from the "Little Red Book" or elsewhere, whether genuinely applicable or not, were prime bludgeons in the factional fights. The quote might be out of context, but anyone saying so risked being branded as unrevolutionary, or even a counterrevolutionary pettifogger. Lin Biao preached that one word of Chairman Mao's outweighed 10,000 of anyone else's. Mao himself ridiculed this hyperbole, but who else would dare to do so? So it was safest and wisest, if slammed by a quote, to slam back with another, since all were "supreme directives" and absolute truths regardless of time and place. But woe to any quoter who had even one comma in the wrong spot, or a stroke missing from one of the characters. That could be, and often was, seized upon as a sign of hatred for the revolution and the Chairman, to be probed to its black depths: ideological, historical, or even genealogical, going back three generations. As for any effort to get anything clear about one's pre-Liberation experience, it could plunge one into a dilemma not unlike one in which my daughter had put me when she was only six: "Daddy," she had asked, "did you ever see Chiang Kai-shek?" "Yes," I said. "Then why didn't you catch him?" While I explained that the circumstances weren't then right, doubt spread over her face. "Did he see you?" she asked. Again, I said yes. "Then why didn't he catch *you?*" she probed, her doubt turning into suspicion.

* * *

Sometimes, arguments and accusations reached heights of absurdity. A much-copied big character poster asserted that the red lights to stop traffic were an obvious capitalist scheme to discredit the Red road to revolution, which under proletarian rule should invariably signal "forward," not "stop." Also denounced as a conspiracy was the rule that vehicles keep to the right side of the road—because left was alone the proper line of advance.

Such "reasoning" reminded me of a story told by my friend, the Soviet newsman Yakshamin, about his boyhood in a Mordvinian-minority village which often changed hands between the Red and White armies during Russia's civil war. A Red political officer, taking a liking to the boy and gave him a book to read when he was older. It was Marx's *Kapital.* The semi-literate village elders advised: Hide it from the Reds, who hated capitalism. Leave it in plain view for the Whites, who were for it.

With the same uninformed "logic," The Japanese, during their occupation of Hong Kong, decided that the internees in Stanley camp could not bring in any English book with a red cover or the word "Red" in its title.

* * *

Aside from its eccentricities, however, the original thrust of the Cultural Revolution contained, and even enhanced, some good qualities long taught by the Communist Party. The absence of greed. Faith in an ever-better future. The spirit of service to the people. The prevalence of mutual aid, rarity of theft, and readiness of all ranks of society, and particularly of the youth, to volunteer despite fatigue and peril. After the Tangshan earthquake disaster of 1976, millions of people lived and worked for months encamped in tents in the street of Beijing.

Nor should it be assumed that the Cultural Revolution was a time of no material advances. During it the Yangtze was bridged. Equally independently, China produced its first hydrogen bomb and launched its first satellite. There was argument, afterwards, as to whether these historic "firsts" in peaceful construction and national defense were speeded by the movement or achieved despite it. Though, it must be said, China's economy teetered on the brink of collapse, the enthusiasm these projects evoked were very real.

*   *   *

Nor, specifically, must one forget that the happenings of the Cultural Revolution were in part conditioned by the heavy risks of war, emanating from the Soviet Union as well as the United States and at times from the two together. Both Washington and Moscow were talking of a joint missile strike at China's incomparably smaller store of nuclear weapons, which she had unilaterally pledged never to be the first to use. In that period, huge amounts of labor, energy, and funds were expended in construction, beneath Beijing and other Chinese cities, of deep tunnel systems, unmatched worldwide in their extent, to shelter and disperse the populations in case of nuclear attack. No less was the effort to place industries underground, or move them, camouflaged, to distant parts of the country.

All this, however, does not change the fact that China's Cultural Revolution was not the answer to the problem of consolidating and advancing her Socialist system and its transition to a future communist society. Despite that key motive in many minds and especially in Mao Zedong's, facts proved the movement to be misconceived in theory and destructive in practice. Grave indeed was the loss in formal education, which was supposed to be transformed root and branch. It left young children out of school for several years (even small children could and did negate their teachers by chalking "Bourgeois Authority" or the like on their backs). Teenagers in middle school beat and sometimes even killed their teachers (early on, in Beijing, Zhou Enlai denounced a notorious example as plain Fascism, and a public exhibition condemned, but could not altogether halt, such abuses). Universities essentially stopped for ten years, but not before professors, like the historian Qian Buozan, were manhandled and disgraced (he and his wife committed suicide) or sent off for "re-education" at hard rural labor camps. Even after studies were nominally resumed, examinations usually were not, and an entrant who purposely turned in an empty paper was hailed as progressive model in the national press. The gaps in education and training would take half a generation to fill.

For a time the railroads charged no fares, and huge multitudes of adolescent boys and girls traveled up and down the country to revolutionary sites, as reinforcements to local Red Guards, or to Beijing where several rallies were held, each with an audience of a million, to hail and be reviewed by Mao Zedong, who himself wore a Red Guard armband. The enthusiasm was real. So, especially at first, was mass intimacy with the leadership. I saw from close by how Mao, Zhou Enlai, and others came down from the Tiananmen rostrum and sat down on the flagstones in the square surrounded by the rejoicing youngsters.

Negatively however, the Cultural Revolution produced deafness to political and ideological appeals. Its over-use and constant crescendo of slogans had the opposite effect.

*　　*　　*

One may ask how Mao Zedong, proved to have led so effectively in the long struggle for the creation and early shaping of the People's Republic, could have so misjudged its later situation. His previous impressive record of successes may have made him think that he alone could lead the way forward through socialism to communism, setting the course and sweeping away the obstructions in his own lifetime. That same record of triumphs accounted for the overwhelming popular confidence that he could do so. But in fact his once unparalleled ability to travel to the grassroots and see and weigh matters firsthand had shrunk due to increasing age and infirmity. With precious little time left, he had perhaps become impatient, and with a narrowing range of travel and contact, was even trustful of those few beyond his immediate entourage.

So, not too long after launching the Cultural Revolution, Mao began to lose control. And the 1971 failed coup and treacherous flight by

Lin Biao, his groomed successor, was a particularly crushing blow. Then the conduct of the movement fell into the hands of the scheming and unscrupulous Gang of Four who, headed by Jiang Qing, were not supporting him as they claimed, but plotting to seize all power when he died.

* * *

Rose Smith, an elderly but feisty journalist of pure working class origin and a founding member of the British Communist Party, worked in the official *Xinhua* (New China) News Agency, and for a time with us at *China Reconstructs*. In the arguments in the international movement she leaned toward China's side. But the rampant factionalism among Red Guard groups cut her to the heart. Whenever she could, she preached unity.

Enlisting Elsie, the two of them had once saved a man who was about to be kidnapped, "debated with," and possibly beaten up by a rival group. Seeing him surrounded by assailants, the two tall women moved on either side of him, like protective walls, and marched him to safety.

Chapter 28

IN DURANCE VILE—THE PRISON YEARS

Soon came the exclusion of all foreigners from even a shadow of participation in the Cultural Revolution, but the worst was yet to come.

The imputations against me were that I was a member of a cabal seeking to dominate China's foreign publicity, and that I was an international spy. The spy suspicion was also hung on Elsie.

Those working close to us, I would later learn, would be deemed "guilty be association." Zhang Yan, deputy Editor-in-Chief of *China Reconstructs* was especially harshly grilled, confined to a cowshed, and beaten severely until several of his ribs were cracked. He refused to even acknowledge the accusation that I was a spy. Tian Aiqing, a reporter, was also harried on my account. Incredibly, Zhang Yan later headed the magazine and his former tormentors now became his subordinates, though he showed no bias against them.

In 1968 the Cultural Revolution turned to what was called the "cleansing of class ranks," in which countless people were arrested, many never dreaming it could happen to them.

So it was with Elsie and me. For almost two years we had supported and been involved in the movement. In our workplace we were members of a major Chinese faction. I had become one of the leaders in the "Bethune-Yan'an Rebel Regiment" composed of those two wanted to take part. True, two of its other activists, both old timers in China, had already been detained. But the case of Briton David Crook of the Beijing Foreign Languages Institute, seized by one faction when he tried to mollify a campus fracas, seemed to be a fortuitous one in the struggle between two "rebel" groups. And that of the ambitious Sidney Rittenberg, an American highly placed in Beijing radio, took place in a milieu far above ours.

Nor did I take alarm at a public assertion by Kang Sheng that at least one foreigner (often seen on Cultural Revolution platforms), was an agent or spy. I should have done so. Kang was a member of the Political Bureau of the party and of the nationwide Cultural Revolution

Committee, top man in China's national security system, and a patron of what would come to be known as the Gang of Four. I, for one, never thought that Kang could be targeting those whose participation in the movement had been welcomed by Chairman Mao himself as motivated by revolutionary internationalism.

Hence it was as a crushing "unexpectation," a term invented by Elsie, that the blow fell on us both, on March 18, 1968. Ironically, it was the same date as our escape from Hong Kong 26 years earlier. Shortly after midnight, when we had barely fallen asleep, a quiet knock came at the door. Outside were two young colleagues, ex-army men who had recently joined our magazine after a post-demobilization foreign-language course, who said almost diffidently, "There's someone who wants to talk to Eppy." At such an hour, that should have given us pause. But "Making Revolution" night and day was a common sign of zeal then, so I said, "Bring them up." No, said the young men, still politely. They wanted to talk in the office—across the courtyard.

As I dressed, doubt assailed me, because the lads belonged to an opposing faction. It grew when, going downstairs, one preceded and the other closely followed me down the stairs. Elsie, standing tall in her bathrobe on the upper landing, seemed concerned. I said, "Don't worry, I'll be back soon." But the worst we could think of was that I was being taken away for awhile to be "debated with," which meant being encircled and having to listen to accusations with any reply shouted down.

It was far worse than that, and I would not see Elsie again, nor know anything about her whereabouts, for nearly five years.

Within minutes, I was jostled, in the dark courtyard, into a waiting Jeep, which started off. I asked the uniformed pair seated on either side of me where we were going. They did not answer.

Elsie was taken an hour after me, lured with the explanation that I wanted to see her. The one thing I did not expect was that she too would be arrested. What happened to the children I did not know either. In fact, for them there was at least some forethought. They were taken to top floor rooms in a good hotel, the Qianmen. There they were lodged and fed in comfort but in strict isolation; the rooms blocked off, the windows papered over. Nearby were the children of two other foreign detainees—Rittenberg and Michael Shapiro (a senior foreign expert of Xinhua News Agency, originally sent by the British Communist Party, who was picked up the same night we were). In theory, the children were to be kept unaware of each others' presence. In practice, all being normal kids with curiosity and poking fingers, they soon managed to catch forbidden sight of each other, though they could not communicate.

Our children were also lucky enough to have with them our housekeeper Li Mama (Li came from her married name, her own was Dong Shaozhen), who had looked after the children from infancy. She insisted on staying with them—at considerable risk—and wrangled permission to go back to the apartment for their clothes and their schoolbooks. Though hardly literate herself she saw that they did every lesson.

The children emerged six months later, pale and obese, and were soon sent to a farm where, again by someone's forethought, they were taught to drive tractors and didn't have too hard a time, growing tall and husky, with much schooling lost but much experience gained. But Li Mama was exiled from Beijing and joined an adopted daughter elsewhere. Though of poor peasant origin, she had been briefly married-off to a minor landlord who had died decades before. Now she was expelled from the capital as a "class alien."

On that dark night I was initially taken to an army camp in the Western outskirts of Beijing, beyond the Summer Palace. There a Public Security Bureau arrest warrant was handed to me: sign now, no questions.

I stayed at the camp for about two weeks, where I was able to read newspapers and buy cigarettes. They would get them for me, said the officer who had booked me. I was kept in a barrack room with a bed and desk, and the door left unlocked, but with an unarmed soldier seated athwart it, yet showing no malice. At first he willingly helped me read the paper. Later, perhaps told off, he was more silent, but still not hostile. He would follow me to the toilet, or to the outdoor clothesline when I went to sun my bedclothes, being allowed to do so alongside those of the troops. My food was the same as theirs. There was no interrogation. Life was quiet except for the gnawing questions in my mind which belied my seemingly calm appearance, and the endless waiting.

Next, I was whisked back into the city and a very different scene. I was placed in a cell, musty and small, no bigger than 10' x 6' in an old city jail. There was a bucket in the corner. They tiny window was barred and set too high to see through. The thick door was slammed behind me with a jangling of latches and bolts, and I was alone. Before I could get to the bucket, I was suddenly and explosively sick on the floor. The door opened and, with nothing said, I was handed a broom and dustpan, then a mop, to clean up the mess.

My first questioning, a few days later, was by an official, perhaps a warden, and a young man with a briefcase. A lawyer or prosecutor I thought at first, until I realized I had seen him before as a sub-editor of another English-language magazine. "What am I charged with?" I asked. "Don't try to worm anything out of us!" he snapped. "You know perfectly what you've done, or you wouldn't be in this place. Make up your mind to spill the beans. It's your only way. To pretend you are here wrongly is to insult the Proletarian Headquarters, adding to your crimes." After that Kafkaesque encounter I was marched back to my cell.

How well I came to know it. Grimy, dull-green walls halfway up, grimy grayish white above that. A dim light burned, never turned off. Someone's tiny diagonal scratch marks on one wall: twenty, thirty, forty. If he was here for that many days, so might I be. The door opened once each day for carrying the contents of the bucket to a common dumping place. There were three servings of food a day: cornmeal gruel, corn muffins, and soup made of stale turnips. Once every two weeks, there was a ten minute exercise break in the yard. With no one else in sight, evidently it was done by turns.

There was nothing to read. Only the wall to stare at. Damp spots gradually seen as a pattern, two faces, one in profile, one half turned, which I gave names—they had to be fantastic—"Algernon" and "Marmaduke." Looking at the extended back of my hand I suddenly found the knuckle on one finger wrinkled into a face, narrowed eyes, flat nose, and wide curved mouth, with and expression mocking but not unkind. I named it Milo.

What had happened to me, and why? For years I had been eager to help China's Revolution. Personally long known to its leaders, editor of one of its publications, I had followed its stated logic at every turn. Right up to campaigns against "revisionism" culminating in the Cultural Revolution in which I unquestioningly marched calling for the downfall of Liu Shaoqi and Deng Xiaoping. As a figure in the "Bethune-Yan'an" group I had often been asked to sit on the rostrum of this or that group, all flying the banner of Mao Zedong Thought which I myself accepted as the acme of Marxism in our era. Yet here I was, suddenly, in jail, a jail of the revolution, *not* of the reaction, which I could have understood. I was a little Jew in a lock-up. How familiar did that sound? I railed at myself at a moment of self-inflicted bitter irony.

But this fatalist gloom did not last. Endlessly I wrestled in my mind with some "whys." Mao Zedong in one of his writings advocated always asking "why" but I had done it too seldom, or switched off the question too soon. Why had so many longtime revolutionaries, in the Soviet Union and Eastern Europe, ended as felons, with an executioner's bullet or hangman's noose? Was it true that the class struggle by its objective laws, independent of human will and even perhaps of self-knowledge, turned friends into enemies as well as foes into friends? I must think, think, think, I told myself.

But my objective was unchanging. To stay in the revolutionary ranks, to live or die if need be as a revolutionary, was who I was. Not simply to be freed from my cage but to get out without being bundled across the frontier labeled as a traitor or spy, which I thought would be the worst fate, an anathema for life and beyond, a permanent excommunication from the ranks to which I wanted to belong: that of the world's revolutionaries, and leaving behind "a stink for ten thousand years" as the old Chinese figurative expression has it.

I had no thought of leaving China as a way out. Never, I vowed to myself, would I renounce what I had so long honored, before the hostile press at some border crossing, and end up "dining and whining" at capitalist tables, which was what I called the performance of "penitent" deserters from the Red Banner. I would rather die.

But, in marked contrast to my calmly taken decision after the surrender of Hong Kong to the Japanese—to kill myself if faced with the choice of being tortured to death or informing on my friends and becoming a propagandist for the invaders—I did not plan on suicide, though at deep lows in my mood the fleeting thought did occur. Whatever happened to me, I insisted to myself, our cause would go on, and I must live and not to hurt but help it, in the best case if I was welcomed back, in the worst even if not.

History, the Chinese people, China's Revolution, and the Communist Party of China were basically just, I was convinced, and would do me justice. Whether I would live to that day was uncertain, but not the main thing. Though storm-tossed, this mainstream of thought was to keep me, like many others, sane in those shut-away years.

After some three weeks in the city jail came another move, to the more modern, concrete-built Qincheng prison, again in Beijing's outskirts. It was then little known, an elite place where top officials of the Guomindang listed as war criminals had long been kept and re-educated. Now senior Communist Party cadres targeted in the Cultural Revolution were among those held here, and treated worse than the old public enemies had been. Its current procedure was not trial or sentence but incommunicado confinement "for investigation," with family and friends uninformed of inmates' whereabouts. To me, through my years there, its name was never mentioned. What I was told, often and bluntly, was, simply: "It isn't easy get into this place, and it's harder to get out of."

That I would be sure to stay out of circulation for a long time may have been why, the escorts, on the ride of almost two hours, seemed little concerned about my looking out, which I did eagerly but as inconspicuously as possible to avoid rebuke.

It was already April, and roadside trees and wheat fields were turning their first mild, shy pastel green. I drank in this familiar fresh, tender and short-lived color—each year's brief and caressing respite between the winter's bare brown and the sultry summer's heavy, solid green. It denoted nature's annual rebirth in North China.

But I also glimpsed the glaring new dazibao of denunciation: "Down with Yang Chengwu" and "Down with Fu Zhongbi." Yang, a Long March hero, was the People's Liberation Army's chief of staff, Fu a vice-commander of its Beijing garrison. To me, deprived of newspapers or anything else to read since transfer to the town jail, all this was an enigma. Why so many "Down withs" one after the other?

Finally, as we turned off on a byroad toward a craggy hill, I saw, hidden partially behind it, a walled-in group of barrack-like buildings, each uniform and several stories high—the Qincheng prison complex. Admitted through the barred gate—by which time I now knew this was a jail—we drove to a basement door, where I was checked in. Standing opposite a middle aged, tired-looking officer seated at a desk, I was ordered to strip. My personal possessions were catalogued and sealed in a bag: pen, notebook, keys, and a metal pipe-reamer (which I had to convince them was merely a smoking accessory), leather belt, wallet, and money. The black prison uniform I was issued did not fit in any direction. From then on, I was informed, I must no longer use my name but only my "number," which began with 68 (for 1968) followed by three others, already in the hundreds for the year reflecting the order of my entry.

Then I was taken up three flights of stairs encased in wire mesh, a copy of a Soviet prison, I guessed, remembering that in a prison of the GPU, the Russian secret police, the former revolutionary terrorist and later agent of British intervention, Boris Savinkov, had jumped over a banister to his death in a deep stairwell, leading to precautions against a repetition of such self-destruction of evidence. On the third floor, turning into a corridor-block of cells itself shut off by a steel gate, I was escorted to my cell.

Compared to its predecessor it was luxurious, about double in area and height, bare, but airy and sanitized. Under the large window, set too high to see through, and facing the door, was a board bed on trestles, and in one corner a flush toilet and small washstand once standard in Chinese trains. The door had a peephole for the guards to observe the inmate, and a trapdoor, rather like those sometimes contrived for the comings and goings of the family cat, but used here for passing in food. All was clean. The cell was all white—except that on one wall there was a smudged imprint, apparently of a bloodstained palm. Had the previous occupant attempted suicide? Or been badly beaten? Or had it been put there deliberately, to intimidate?

Through the peephole, I often saw only the peering eye of the guard on duty. But at times, unobstructed, it revealed, through the outer window it faced, a tiny cameo from the surrounding country—gorgeous especially in the Fall, when a persimmon tree gleamed golden in the sun.

On arrival, I had been told the routine. The trapdoor, besides food, was for written material required by the interrogators, to be passed out. Through it, too, before bedtime, I had to put out my glasses for the night, presumably so I could not slyly slash my wrists or jugular with the lenses. After several months, apparently deemed non-suicidal, I was allowed to keep them. If ill, or needing anything that was permitted, I had to shout: "Number so and so reporting!" and someone would come. If medicine was supplied, I had to swallow the prescribed number of pills as a guard counted the ups and downs of my Adam's apple.

The overhead light in the cell, protected by wire netting, was on day and night. At first it was glaringly bright, and only later then dimmed. It never kept me awake. Bedtime and naptime were obligatory. In China, still close to farm habits, the midday nap was held sacred both for the free and the captive. When in bed I had to lie on my side, facing the peephole. Both hands had to be in plain view, atop the blanket or sheet, presumably also to forestall suicide.

The food was simple, still corn muffins or gruel, with a bit of fermented bean curd (rich in vitamins) and, very occasionally, a few slivers of meat. And once a year or so, and on festivals, I was told, we were given an apple. To stimulate hope or perhaps move to repentance through memories of home. These rations may have been set before the Cultural Revolution, with some nutritional advice. For the taste buds, the only fare was the vegetables, which in season were exceptionally fine, needing no extra flavoring. They were grown right on site and served within hours. Partly due to this fact, I think, my physical condition stayed fair throughout.

*   *   *

Psychologically, the first few nights at Qincheng were the worst. I myself was not berated or pushed around, or even beaten. But from surrounding cells I heard thuds, as of someone being hit or knocked down, and curt commands like, "On your knees!" From further away, through the windows, came a young woman's high-pitched and incessant wailing, "I want to go home!"

After those first days came a long silence, almost as though the earlier sounds had been orchestrated to shake up newcomers. Only in the summer, when all windows were opened, did I hear, from sufficiently nearby interrogation rooms, the irate tones of the questioners and the often weepy responses of the questioned, though the words were indistinct.

By rapidly-acquired instinct, my ears perked up at the tinkle of keys at the belts of guards striding along the corridor to fetch someone for interrogation, and the clang of thrown bolts as cells were opened or re-locked. Were they coming for me next?

There was no radio, but outdoor loudspeakers did, however, broadcast news daily to other parts of the prison. Listening hard, I could sometimes catch bits of the content, as well as the slogans. One day, the usually trio of "Down with imperialism! Down with revisionism! Down with China's Khruschev!" (referring to Liu Shaoqi) was supplemented by a fourth phrase, "Down with the traitor and scab Liu Shaoqi!" I knew it was a new watershed, not just with names named but with charges specified, and no reply possible, only the burial of the target in eternal disgrace. Actually, the determination was made by, or rather dictated to, a plenary session of the Central Committee. Reluctantly, I thought of the old rhyme from *Alice in Wonderland*: "I'll be judge, I'll be jury, said cunning old Fury, I'll try the whole case and condemn you to death!"

Never did I see another inmate from our block, or recognize anyone's voice. Even the outdoor exercise pens were partitioned for individuals, as were the showers.

Among the worst lacks of my lonely imprisonment, was having nothing at all to read for the first four months. Such deprivation may be a prime cause, for the literate at least, of going mad in solitary confinement. The only print I saw was on my paper package of the prison-issue toothpowder, fortunately varied by a colored design. This I propped up on the wall-ledge, as my sole literature and art.

Then the official newspaper, *People's Daily* (*Renmin Ribao*) began to arrive, first cell-by cell for a half-hour's perusal, and after a year in copies to keep. I read every word, repeatedly, which was good for my Chinese. Only after another year, in 1970, was I issued the four-volume set of the *Selected Works of Mao Zedong*. With a warning that I must prove deserving by using them to help me realize my crimes, not simply as reading matter. Once I left my glasses on top of the stacked set. Observed through the peephole, I got a roaring reprimand from the guard on duty, plus an angry lecture from someone in greater authority that must have been specially called to handle the "disrespectful and hostile" act.

Still later, the theoretical monthly *Hongqi* (*Red Flag*) was added to my permitted reading. And I was allowed to keep issued publications indefinitely.

* * *

In September 1971, all accumulated newspapers and copies of *Hongqi* were abruptly recalled from my cell—and undoubtedly others. The next day's *People's Daily* suddenly called upon everyone to learn and sing the *Internationale*, with special attention to the passage which, in the English version, reads, "We want no condescending saviors, To rule us from the judgment hall, We workers ask not for their favors, Let us consult with all."

The reason, though we did not know it then, was the downfall of Lin Biao.

I had in fact, wondered why Lin was not in the daily headlines or news as he used to be. In a "thought ventilating" interrogation, I expressed concern. Was Lin Biao ill? If so, was Chairman Mao more burdened without his designated heir and closest helper beside him? At first there was no comment, then an explosive, "Lin Biao is a rotten egg!" Either way it was a bombshell. Only much later would I learn of his demise, in an air crash in Mongolia, en route to the Soviet Union after a failed coup against Mao. For years the slogan had been, "May Chairman Mao live forever! May Vice-Chairman Lin be forever healthy!" Any aspersion on Lin, as on Mao, had been a crime.

I was not a fan of Lin Biao, and I had the flash of doubt when the Ninth Congress of the Communist Party of China, in 1969, not only proclaimed his future succession to Chairman Mao, by then taken for granted, but wrote it into the party constitution, which was unheard of. Seeing a newspaper photograph of the Congress hall, and all hands going up to approve the change, I had felt that some things were going beyond the bounds of the normal. But was there some overriding necessity, like making sure by all means things did not go badly? It turned that my first reaction had been much more rational than my attempts to reason it away.

After Lin Biao fell, my reading expanded further. Suddenly I was asked, "What books would you like to have?" I said *Anti-Duhring* by Engels and *Materialism and Empirio-Criticism* by Lenin. I had them in English at home, and first asked for those to be sent over. But the copies that came were newly-bought Chinese translations. This made my reading slower but more detailed than it would have been in English, and hence more thorough.

My habit was to mark and annotate the books as I read, but how to do it in my cell? Pen and paper were supplied only for writing confessions and self-criticisms, to be returned when done, including all sheets cancelled or left blank. So I found another way to mark passages, with bits of toilet paper which stuck to the margins when moistened, but could be peeled off when dry to avoid inspection. Fortunately there was no check on the books. I still have them, with those markers.

In *Anti-Duhring*, Engels not only thoroughly demolished the arguments of his selected opponent but, by positive statement, gave a famously lucid exposition of Marxism. Even before the main text, a passage in the preface leaped out to sear, and rejoice, my heart. Along with the statement that he had "finished" Duhring theoretically, Engels wrote of the ethics of responsible polemic, and of what should be one's attitude toward an opponent defeated in debate:

> I owe it to my adversary not to improve anything in my work (in a new edition) when he is unable to improve his... I must observe the rules of decency in literary warfare all the more strictly in his regard because of the despicable injustice that has since been done to him by the University of Berlin... which so abuses itself as to deprive Herr Duhring, in circumstances which are well known, of his academic freedom...

The "circumstances" were the university's administrative revenge for Duhring's criticisms of some of its procedures, Duhring's personal misfortune of being blind, and the fact that, while he was dismissed, a professorship was given to an undeserving candidate who was liked by Count Bismarck, political leader of Prussia.

What a contrast to the abusive fury with which opponents in "literary warfare" were denounced in the Cultural Revolution, branded virtually as criminals from birth, spewed with such rhetoric as "we will smash their dog heads," denied the right to defend their views, frequently uprooted from work, home and family and sent off to corrective labor or jail, even though official killing, as happened in the U.S.S.R. under Stalin, was rare.

The example set by Engels, a founder of Marxism, of how uncompromising defense of its principles could, and should, be combined with Marxist fairness and humaneness, strengthened my faith in Marxism.

In interrogations roughly from the fall of Lin Biao onward, there was less bullying and more stress on understanding: "You've read the papers. What do you think both of the national and the international news?" There were also fewer demands for written testimony than in the years before. Between 1968 and 1971 I had written 1,500 or more pages of "My crimes of this or that." These titles were pretty nearly obligatory. If I titled something, "My trips abroad" or "My acquaintance with so and so," the comment was likely to be: "Who cares where you went, or who you knew, it's your crimes you have to confess!" That I produced only incriminating headings without incriminating content irritated them to no end. Once I was asked to write an autobiography which I did over months in hundreds of painstaking pages, only to be mocked: "Born in Warsaw, raised in Tianjin, worked here, traveled there. Who wants that garbage again? Get to the substance, your crimes!"

Each time I was summoned, I had to read some quotations from Mao Zedong's works posted as slogans on the wall. Once it was an injunction to quit the camp of Chiang Kai-shek and take the side of the people. I said it didn't apply—I had never been Chiang's man, even if I had not served the people as well as I might. The reply was that I still did not understand my own misdeeds or essence. Another of my disavowals was met with an analysis: "You can't think of any evil you've done? No wonder, in your mind it must have seemed good. The root is your stubborn reactionary attitude. That's what you must change. Go back and think some more."

And after several sessions when, I could produce nothing new, came the ominous reply: "We've better use for our time than to fritter it away with you. When do you want us to come back to hear you again? In a month, you say? Knowing you, we think that's too soon. How about ten years?"

Generally, the interrogations were in a bare room with anywhere from three to ten people sitting at a long table, slightly raised. Down below sat the inmate on a solid, glazed ceramic cylinder—round, slippery and heavy—to prevent its being picked up as a weapon.

Sometimes I was taken to what I mentally called "the room of dire threats." It was small and stuffy. Besides the customary poster: "Confess and be treated leniently, resist and be dealt with severely," there would be something more menacing: "Don't take a granite-hard head with you to see God," plainly hinting at the death penalty threat. Though I was never beaten, a grim-faced young officer attached to the interrogation team flourished a black-gloved fist within an inch of my head saying: "Better come clean before it's too late. We've seen many more stubborn and prouder than you. But when taken to be shot their legs melt under them and they have to be dragged like sacks." When I first saw this tall soldier, with dark rings of fatigue under his eyes, I had felt sympathy. Why should people like him be put to so much trouble with cases like mine? An unbelievable reaction? Only to those who have never been held prisoner by what they firmly believe to be their own side.

The worst threats, under these circumstances, hurt less than sneering rejection. As when I addressed a questioner as "Comrade" and he shot back: "Who's your comrade?" Or when I said that, whatever my misdeeds, I was happy to have done some work for the cause, and was shouted down with: "Don't you dare, ever again, to insult the revolutionary people by putting yourself in the same bracket!"

In the interrogation process, I soon came to see that abrupt changes of mood as prepared in advance—were a part of the method. Sometimes the tone was level, even coaxing. Then, without apparent cause, faces would harden and redden, and shouts thunder. If seated, I would suddenly be ordered to stand, if looking in front of me, to bow my head. All this was in conformity with the two constantly stressed alternatives, "Frankness brings leniency; resistance—severity."

In one historic episode, Chen Chunying, a magazine colleague brought in to help in the questioning, stormed at me: "You're a longtime imperialist agent! No use denying it. The proof is *in our filing cabinets*!" But years afterwards, when I asked him what proof existed, he answered. "I really don't know. It's what they told me to say. I didn't dare ask them to explain."

High dudgeon and stress were only part of the picture. Most prison time is monotony, the same cycle again and again, and every change is welcome. Clippers for finger and toenails could be had from the guard about once a month. Monthly, likewise, were the shave-haircuts, by clippers run simultaneously over the face and scalp, with about the same growth of hair and beard. Showers, once or twice a month, were hurried, no nonsense affairs. Managed so that no one saw anyone else before, during, or after. Nor did I even see my own face.

What made it possible to live through years of solitary confinement? First, conviction and confidence in the future. Second, routines, both imposed like meals and bedtime and self-devised to keep busy. Physically, I did *Taijiquan* exercises, happily learned earlier in China, and dry-land "swimming"—bent at the waist I practiced the crawl, turning my head to breathe, though unfortunately unable to kick my feet. Mentally, I not only recalled my whole history to cope with my "case" but "re-read," in memory, major books that had influenced me, and even reviewed my very poor secondary-school math (for weeks I tried, and failed, to remember how to extract a square root). For entertainment I told myself jokes—largely Jewish—and hummed songs and melodies, as quietly as possible, risking reminders from over alert guards that laughter, like singing or weeping, was not allowed, and regarded as flights from facing one's own crimes into frivolity or self-pity.

I played mental games. One, purposeless, was recalling all the names staring with "Macs" I had known or heard, from MacAdam to MacWhirter. Another was philological exploration, seeking root-relations between English words with French, German and Russian ones, like knife-caniff, knee-genoux-koleno, cow-kuh-korova. I long puzzled why dolicho (Greek) and daleko (Russian) were so similar, and why in some tongues closer in origin, some likenesses that should exist, didn't. I joyfully realized ptero, ptitza and ptashka—Greek and Russian for "bird" were linked in sound—and that the English word was also faintly so. Once one gets going the brain-game field is virtually limitless. I did not play mental chess or bridge, since I was hopeless in both games in real life. Yet this hopelessness was itself grist for humor. On bridge I remembered, with a grin that I carefully kept turned away from the peephole, joking to myself that it turned my friends into foes and my foes into friends. On chess I recalled boasting of being the world's best teacher in the field. The proof that after I explained the moves to a complete novice, I won our first game and he the second.

*　　*　　*

Without human company, I found pleasure in two small living creatures, a fly and a lizard.

With "Fly Friday" named by me for the day it appeared, I had a love-hate relationship: love for the creature's quick vitality, hate because it would light on the rim of the toilet, then of the mug from which I drank. At such times I would attempt murder with a towel or newspaper, but never succeed, through my inadequacy of malice or speed or because the country's flies had become so expert at deft evasion after years of pursuit by hundreds of millions of Chinese with fly swatters. What finally doomed Fly Friday was technology, applied by a nameless and silent convict with an insecticide sprayer. Sadly and reverently I picked up my friend's corpse and consigned it to the waters—of the flush toilet:

De mortuis nil nisi bonum.

"Lizard" was an even briefer companion, with a favorite spot on the ceiling where his useful and entertaining hunt for mosquitoes and midges won my admiring affection. Then a convict cleaner, sent to remove dirt from the overhead light with a long-handled brush, sent him hurtling down to the floor. In outraged panic, he scurried under the door to the corridor, from which, to my regret, he never returned.

The animals gone, I turned to plants. From the exercise pen in summer, when the eyes of the guard walking high on the brick dividing wall were directed elsewhere, I would quickly pick a blade of grass or a tiny wildflower, stow it in my blouse and smuggle it to my cell, to be secretly looked at cherished, till, faded, it was water-buried like Fly Friday. These were small triumphs of contact with life, though not human life.

*   *   *

What was most lacking was work. Other than keeping clothes, bedding and the cell clean, none was allowed me. I appealed for permission to sweep the corridors, which I could hear being done by other inmates outside the door, but only ordinary prisoners could do that, not "isolatees." Also refused was my offer to teach English, Russian, or both to warders and guards. "Don't even *think* of such things until you've settled your problem," was the invariable response to requests of that kind.

My anxious questions about my family met with the same put-down. My thoughts about them were constant, over the whole range of fond memories of Elise and the children. In newspaper photographs of pigtailed little girls, one would suddenly turn into our Meimei at that age. And Didi would flash across my mind intently stalking grasshoppers, or grinning with delight at some funny thought. "Yingele" I once muttered through gathering tears, involuntarily breaking into the affectionate Yiddish word for little boys which my mother applied to me at that age—which I had not heard or thought of for some forty years. Where were the children now?

*   *   *

The regular warders, mainly middle-aged and trained before the Cultural Revolution, were professionally taciturn but not abusive. They did their job without shoving, hitting, yelling, or sneering.

The cell-block guards were mostly young soldiers, rotated every few months. From their dialects (some of which I didn't understand) they seemed to come from widely different parts of China. They differed, too, in character. Some were quiet, others enjoying their small authority. Most, or all, I am sure, didn't know my name or anything else about me, just that I was an enemy with a number, to be watched and kept in order. Except for keeping their eyes to the peephole they didn't bother me. But once or twice I was loudly shouted at, and made to stand for a couple of hours at a time, with no purpose I could discern other than reminding me that I had better behave. Ruefully, I remembered the story of a father who whacked all his sons every Saturday to instill discipline: "What have they done wrong?" a friend asked. "I wouldn't know, but they do," said the father, continuing the serial spanking.

On the other hand, there were deeds of kindness. When I was moved from one building to another, a guard helped me, wordlessly, to carry my gear, apparently out of respect or sympathy for my age. Was it genuine? Was it planned? Was he expressing compassion for a person he believed innocent?

*　　*　　*

Not allowed to participate in any public celebration, I devised observances on my own. Each May Day, standing at attention, I sang the *Internationale*, half audibly in English, Russian, and Chinese. Also, I would pace my cell as if in a march, humming the Warsaw March, *Whirlwinds of Danger*, familiar to me from my father's reminiscences of demonstrations in Russia's (including Poland's) 1905 Revolution. Or the American workers' song "Joe Hill," or slogans I had marched with in New York: "One two three four, we don't want another war. Five six seven eight, we don't want a Fascist state!"

When I learned of Anna Louise Strong's death in 1970, I stood silent and recalled her appearance and voice, her history of struggle and Elsie's and my hundreds of Tuesdays helping her put out her printed *Letter from China*, for over a decade. When Edgar Snow died in 1972 I mourned similarly, remembering our forty years of friendship. I stood silent again for Gong Peng, who had for so long been hounded but had been visited, on her death-bed, by Zhou Enlai.

*   *   *

My treatment improved further through 1972. The questioning became less severe. Pressure for an early confession, though it did not cease, became gentler. In contrast with the past, and again for no reason that I could cite, I was told that I had made progress and might not remain in jail for too long.

A clear indication of light at the end of the tunnel was a visit from the children. Meimei, whom I had last seen at sixteen, was now eighteen, looking well and bigger and more substantial, yet of course familiar at a glance. But Didi I would never have recognized if I met him on the street. I had left him as a compact, round-faced twelve-year old. Now he stood perhaps a foot taller, having shot up, like a telescope quickly pulled out to full length, a lanky, well-built and handsome young man, with a profile that was almost aquiline. Glad at the reunion, we were photographed together. Meimei was still in the cadre school, in a neighboring rural county, and had traveled to Beijing especially to see me. Didi had returned earlier to enter a middle school in the city. The talk with the children was animated until I said (as I had been told to) that to win leniency I had only to face my faults with full frankness, which I was determined to do. At this their faces turned blank, as though they either did not believe me or thought I had no guilt to explain, so why pretend?

On a second occasion, Didi came by himself with the news that they had been to see Elsie.

The prison food, in the meantime, had become suddenly better, more plentiful and less roughly served. "I don't want so much," I protested, being used to leaner rations and believing in the virtues of austerity, besides which the suddenly richer fare gave me indigestion. "Don't question the wise policy of our Party and government," I was reproved. Quickly I grew in girth and weight, to my all-time record. Chen Chunying turned up again with a tailor from *Hong Du*, one of Beijing's best outfitters, who whistled when he measured my waist, saying it would be hard to buy a belt to go around me. I joked that it might be better to put me in a stretching machine, to alter my profile.

*   *   *

Later I heard from my father, and from Elsie's sister Ros, what they had been doing while we were in jail. Dad had written Soong Ching-ling and Premier Zhou Enlai but had received no answer. Whether his letters had even been delivered is uncertain. However, at least one, addressed to me, via Zhou's office, was received and, whoever opened it, had authority from him to pass it to our magazine to get it to me. It said Mother was in decline and that seeing me again might be the sole hope. I was desperate, burst into loud tears for the first time in my adult life, and asked to be allowed to phone, with a monitor if necessary. I pleaded to go to New York with the Chinese mission to the United Nations (in which China's seat had just been restored) returning after seeing Mother in the hospital. The interrogators listened, but the answer was "No." However, I was permitted to write, and from then on did, to Dad, and Mother, while she still lived. Also approved, and promptly acted on, was my request that *China Reconstructs* remit money from my savings, converted to foreign exchange, to my parents. This was a very unusual thing to happen at the time and could only be mediated at the top level. It was a comfort to me, and Dad, although whether Mother knew of it was unclear.

Contact thus established, and having already been told that Elsie was in custody, I asked that she, with her own affectionate bonds with my parents, be permitted to add a postscript to my letter. Approved again. This confirmed to me that Elsie was indeed near. And when she saw my handwriting, she would know that I too was close, though I could not write her directly.

All of these factors proved to be a result of Zhou Enlai's concern for us. Even though I, unlike some other people in trouble, never asked him to intervene in my case because I knew how he worked night and day on larger issues, though I was not yet aware that he himself was in danger in his political life.

It was only in 2001, two decades after it was written, that I saw a copy of Dad's letter to Zhou Enlai, preserved in the papers of Elsie's sister Rosamond, and sent to me by her eldest daughter:

> I am the father of Israel Epstein (Eppy) whom I understand you knew well.
>
> Until the beginning of 1968 my wife and I received letters from our only son with inquiries about the health of his ailing mother suffering for years from acute high blood pressure and severe arthritis. Since March 1968

we have had no word from him or our daughter-in-law. Later I read in the press, with astonishment, that they had been arrested and were forbidden to send or receive mail, cable and telephone messages.

My wife is over 80 years old (I will be 86 next January).

I know that my son would never forgive me if I were to ask your intervention on his and his wife's behalf.

It is on behalf of his sick mother that I appeal to you personally to kindly approach the authorities in charge of my son's isolation to permit him to send us a few words in his own handwriting.

I do hope this appeal will evoke you kind consideration, for which I thank you in advance.

There is no doubt that it was this letter that prompted the granting of the specific permissions it requested. The Premier was plainly warm-heartedly responsive and the time (it was written in August 1971 and must have reached him after the fall of Lin Biao in September) was more favorable. Also to be noted is the fact that, despite the turmoil of the Cultural Revolution, a letter sent through the post could come directly to the Premier's attention, showing Zhou's insistence, despite the tremendous volume of his mail, on being informed of what letters had come in and from whom.

As for my father, his conduct had been truly heroic. He heard of my plight first when a friend phoned him about an item in the *New York Times*, the second thunderbolt from this source, after 1942 when it reported me killed in Hong Kong. Dad immediately made sure to be near the telephone, so that he could answer all calls and spare Mother the shock—for with blood pressure already sky high and mind confused with initial Alzheimers—the truth might have come as a fatal blow. He also trained friends to stay away from the subject with her. As for letters, he would produce old ones and pretend to read (which she could no longer do for herself) some reassuring content. Already in 1966, when he turned eighty, he had retired to stay at home and tend to Mother. Doing the housework, dressing her for visitors, turning her in bed as she became less mobile, all this he did lovingly and indomitably, carrying a burden both mental and physical, as he was tiny and thin, and she larger and heavier. She died in 1972, and still did not know of my trouble, or of course, news of my release which was still a year away.

*   *   *

In 1972, like Mahomet to the mountain, Nixon came to China.

That he had been a lifelong anti-Communist was history's ironic but reasoned choice. On the one hand there were the international realities. Despite more than a decade's contrary efforts by the United States, and especially its politicians of Nixon's persuasion, the People's Republic of China stood firm as a rock, while steps taken to strangle it from without had led to U.S. to defeats, partial in Korea and total in Vietnam. On the other hand there were the internal demands of American politics. No liberal or "pink" could come to nationally mutually advantageous terms with the new China without accusations of being "soft on Communism," only a proven Right-winger like Nixon could, and did. I swallowed hard. To me, an old labor-union journalist, Nixon meant the anti-worker Mundt-Nixon Bill. And being a one-time target of McCarthyites, could I forget Nixon's identification with that reactionary frenzy, including his mud-slinging election campaign against the progressive Helen Gahagan Douglas, whom I had met and liked while in the U.S., when they ran for Congress in California? Still, there it was. And, both in the United States and in China, Nixon was given credit for helping build the bridge between the two nations.

Previously, Edgar Snow had revisited China, and, as a signal that Sino-U.S. relations could improve, been invited to stand with Chairman Mao on the rostrum of Tiananmen on National Day, October 1, 1970. It was to Snow that Mao said Nixon was welcome to visit Beijing, either officially or privately. Seeing Snow's grimace at the mention of Nixon, Mao explained that state-to-state relations could be turned around only by those in control of the states involved, while sympathizers could influence opinion, it was by power-holders that binding decisions had to be taken.

In the prison, the reappearance in China of Snow, and somewhat later (but still before Nixon), the presence of old American friends in China—John S. Service, Max and Grace Granich, and others—were cited by my interrogators as a lesson to me: "Look where they are. Look where you are. You could be there with them if you only confessed your crimes." But how to confess criminal actions I was not aware of myself was beyond me.

Snow had mentioned personally to Mao Zedong that I (as well as Elsie) was in jail and he didn't understand why. Mao replied that he didn't know and would look into it, but whether this affected our treatment and eventual release is hard to say. Our whole plight seemed not an individual but a blanket affair. Later I was to learn that a review of abuses did begin in the months preceding my eventual release from prison. In 1972, the wife of ex-vice-Minister of Railways Liu Jianzhang had written to Mao about the ill-treatment in prison of her husband, whose innocence she asserted. Chairman Mao had given these instructions: "Let the Premier attend to this. Who authorized such Fascist-type interrogation? It must be abolished all along the line."

In mid-December 1972, Zhou Enlai, transmitting this wording, ordered the Ministry of Public Security and other concerned departments to:

> 1. Transfer Liu Jianzhang under bond from jail to an outside hospital as required by his physical condition... and inform his wife and children that they may see him.
> 2. Send the entire record of Liu's case to Li Xiannian and Ji Dengkui for their comment.
> 3. Get the Ministry of Public Security and Beijing Garrison Headquarters, before the year's end, to make a thorough re-check on the treatment of prisoners in Beijing jails in accordance with my (Zhou's) suggestion to the State Council. Every case of maltreatment and beating falling under Chairman Mao's description of "Fascist-type interrogation" should be reported, and such practices again declared abolished. This should be announced to prisoners. Violators should be punished by law. Prisoners should be allowed to make charges.

Elsie and I did not hear of this in prison, perhaps because we were let out in January 1973, less than a month after it was issued. Others, not released until later, did have it read out to them, and complaints were made, though lingering fears kept their number below what it might have been.

Chapter 29

THE MONTHS AFTER OUR RELEASE

After our release, it took weeks to get re-accustomed to freedom. Physically, our legs were temporarily impaired by long periods of non-use—muscles would stiffen or cramp from climbing upstairs (three floors to our flat, four to the office) or a block's walk outside. Mentally, we talked in circles about our experience in jail. Elsie saw the mental pressures applied as all wrong. I argued that, while misdirected when used on the innocent, they could break down resistance by the guilty—thus protecting socialism—and benefit both by limiting punishments and opening the doors of useful citizenship to those who came clean. Also we argued about our way of life. Elsie wanted to discard all fixtures and papers belonging to the past—we must start anew. I was more conservative and spent weeks re-arranging the mess—especially old papers—which she wanted me to "chuck out and be done with."

In those first months, back in our home and at our jobs in Beijing, Elsie did her habitual bit of spirited *pro bono publico*. To the administrators of our publishing organization she wrote:

> In the East Building (our residence) we have a hot water supply from about 4:30 p.m. to about 5:30 p.m. every Tuesday and Saturday... and only in working hours. This means that comrades who live there have to go without baths or take working time in order to do so. Some comrades have told us that this is because the working hours for the boiler room must for some reason be the same as in the office. This does not seem any more rational that making the mealtimes hours of the cooks the same as those of the office...

This shows how difficult living conditions were in those days even for us with foreign-privileges. But it was not for the privileges she was fighting but—as usual with her—for fair sharing:

> A second point is that whereas hot water is supplied to the East building twice a week, none at all is supplied to the West building (for showers for the Chinese workers). I was told that this was because there is not enough coal. If so, my suggestion is that the allowance of coal for providing hot water be equally divided. Let the East building have hot water once a week

instead of twice, and the West building once a week also. And adjust the hours so that hot water is supplied at a more convenient time.

In fact, things returned quickly to normal. Neither of us nursed hostile grudges. Our letters to friends abroad were as full as ever of enthusiasm about constructive developments in China.

Elsie wrote:

> Ep, Didi and I set off for Henan Province to see the nationally famous Red Flag Canal, a man-made river which waters a whole county formerly wild and poverty-stricken. It's very dramatic, like putting a circulatory system into a man born without one, and, and perhaps the most dramatic part of all was the way the water was brought from a river in the Taihang mountains and carried along channels blasted on the sides of mountains, often through iron-hard rock. And like a man who has suddenly been given blood to course through his body, the countryside has sprung to life—covered with emerald-green wheat fields and dotted with young fruit trees.

Soon, too, Elsie was doing something new which she liked—teaching English to young people working at China Reconstructs magazine, and, knowing little about such work, always asking the more experienced to help. One thing she knew: the old bookish method in China—rote memorization of vocabulary and grammar rules—did not lead to living communication. So she asked a colleague:

> If you can tell me of your experience with the direct method, what you think of it and what were the results it would be a great help, and I am anxious to find a good way to help the young…
>
> I much prefer reaching to language polishing, because you are really close to people.

Her interest in society and politics, worldwide, as well as in China, was unabated, indeed had been sharpened by her long isolation:

> I've just read a book about the (French) student and workers' struggle in 1968… That whole movement was tremendous and I now understand it better. It seems it was touch and go for the old order and scared the daylights out of them…
>
> Yesterday evening we discussed with some visiting American friends what will be the outcome of the Watergate scandal and the possibility of Nixon being impeached. I don't believe he will be. He'll make a number of deals, right and left. But he is sitting on the brink of a volcano… Wonder how Tricky Dick can wriggle out of this one! As Ep says, how long can he hang on by the skin of his Kissinger?

With regard to conditions in the Soviet Union, she could not ignore some of the revelations but had no use for the motives of writers such as Solzhenitsyn (recommended to her by friends). In February 1974 she wrote of him to our friend Talitha Gerlach:

> I have read his books and his speech on receiving the Nobel prize… He is a reactionary who hates socialism… wants to hold back the wheel of history.

Keen as ever on things agricultural she was writing to old connections about purchases of new devices for Sid and Joan (Hinton) Engst working on a commune in Beijing. Sid was a hereditary dairy farmer from upper New York State, educated at Cornell. Joan, trained as an atomic physicist, preferred working with cows in China to making weapons for the U.S. military. Elsie asked her own farmer sister-in-law in England to find information "about modern milking machines with both electric and vacuum pulsation, and also what kind of connection each machine has at the point where the milk tube connects with the pipe to the dairy."

A year later, when we traveled to America and England, we brought for Sid and Joan a dry-ice frozen canister containing semen from a prize-winning bull. We nearly lost it at Frankfurt airport where we bumped into a full anti-terrorist alert—with carbine-toting cyclists patrolling the indoor area of the air terminal and examiners unscrewing even camera lenses to see if explosive devices were concealed in the film chamber. Luckily, when we said "sperm" the German examiners first huddled in consultation, then did not insist on opening the canister. One of them might have been the son of a farmer.

Just before our travels, we did one of the then-still customary stints of manual labor, which we always enjoyed:

> Ep and I are going off to lao dong (labor)—digging the foundations for a new block of flats for workers in our Bureau (foreign language publishers). Generally there is much construction in all directions—apartments, offices, roads, drainage, etc.

She did not mention that I was also helping dig an underground shelter in the comprehensive system interconnected to facilitate the evacuation of Beijing residents in case of nuclear attack—the slogan then was "dig tunnels deep, store grain."

Meanwhile our son Didi was both studying and working:

> Didi is in a technical training school learning to make machines for the

metallurgical industry. At the moment the whole school, students and teachers, are all off in the countryside learning from the peasants, for a half-year. He is very happy and comes home four days each month.

Preparing for our trip abroad, Elsie applied for a Chinese driving license, recognized as an international license for tourist driving in England, etc. Though she had driven since her teens, with her old licenses long lapsed this had its snags:

> They generally don't give licenses to anyone over 60. I had to explain all the difficulties of travel in England without a car... on my last visit I had spent one whole week out of four on trains and buses.

Actually, her old experience did not serve her so well when she did drive again. In England, the rules of the road had changed greatly. More so were the newer, sleeker, faster cars which prowled the motorways. Using a secondhand automobile her farmer brother had temporarily bought for our use, we almost got propelled into space by a speeding Jaguar running into us from behind.

Chapter 30

I LOSE ELSIE

Elsie died on Sept. 24, 1984, a few days before her 79th birthday. She died alone.

The evening before, at the hospital, she had been clear-minded, tranquil, even cheerful. At 5 a.m. they phoned me that she was sinking fast. Rushing over, I found her gone.

Our forty one years together—as one flesh, of one mind, had abruptly ended. So inseparable had we become that by our friends and fellow workers, "Elsie and Eppy" had been used almost as a single word.

Now we were sundered. I from the daily grace note of my existence for forty and more years, from the age of 26, when we came together, to 69 when she left me.

At her last glimmer, the nurse said, Elsie had called for me. To my lifelong regret, I was not there, to hold her hand, to close and kiss her blue eyes. Seeing her dead, I sobbed uncontrollably. Back at home, for two days and nights I read her favorite authors, William Blake and William Morris, early openers of her mind and heart to social justice and progress. I heard again, in vivid recollection, her voice reading them aloud to me. And I leafed through many of her old and recent letters.

After her cremation I gathered myself to do what she would have wanted—keep on with our work. Within a week I entrained for Wuhan, to speak, as scheduled, at a memorial meeting for our friend, Agnes Smedley.

Agnes, always outspoken, alternately deadly serious or boisterously humorous, lived once more for me—and Elsie and all we had fought for lived again. After returning, I had no more tears—except when sorrow stabbed without warning and they surged in my eyes and throat.

* * *

That we might not live out our entire lives together was expected. At the start, Elsie had been reluctant to marry me, arguing that, nine

324

years older, she would age earlier, be a burden, die first, and leave me isolated. Afterwards, with good health surviving perils and hardships, we were hardly conscious of the age gap. So we changed the prospect— we would age together, Elsie mused, like two old trees by a riverside. Then cancer shattered her sturdy physique but never her blithe spirit.

*   *   *

Beauty shone from Elsie, at all times of her life.

I recall how in 1944, when she was in her thirties, a colleague saw her from the diagonally opposite end of a smoke-filled party in the Chongqing Press Hostel, and suddenly said "Isn't she beautiful!"

In 1984, when Elsie was in her eightieth year, "You're beautiful!" were the words that burst out of our friend the Chilean painter Jose Venturelli, when, after a long absence abroad, he saw her in hospital in Beijing in her last weeks, her welcoming wan smile lighting up not only her face but, seemingly, the whole room.

Robust herself, Elsie had previously been reluctant to admit the possibility, or genuineness, of illness. When I came down with anything her response was "Cheer up!" or "Up and at 'em!" which generally had the desired tonic effect. It was in wonder, not fear, that she mentioned one day that she felt a weight in one breast, and yielded, only reluctantly to my insistence that she go for a hospital check. It revealed a sizeable lump. A radical mastectomy was ordered. A day before it, she went with me to the exhibition in Beijing on the tenth anniversary of the death of Edgar Snow—animatedly exchanging memories of Ed with mutual friends. After the operation, the doctor told me that the prognosis was not good, and that her lymph glands were badly affected. But Elsie was quickly on her feet. She would spin off on her bicycle for radiation and chemotherapy, which did not seem to distress her at the start. We traveled to the maritime province of Fujian where she outpaced me and others in climbing high hills. A few months later we vacationed at Beidaihe by the seaside. Though she was worn with further treatments, we swam as usual and took long walks.

Bone pains, the physical devastation of repeated chemotherapy, and the bed-ridden months, came later.

By the time she found it hard to read, we were fortunate to have books on tape mailed by friends in New York. We listened to, enjoyed and discussed a wide range—from Brecht's *Mother Courage* to Luigi Barzini's *The Italians*.

Elsie toward the last was not in pain (radiation had halted a brief agony in her bones). When a new grandchild was brought in to see her, her smile shone like a sunburst.

Family, friends, and colleagues came to visit regularly. Her sister Rosamond flew in from England with her husband. Visitors coming to cheer her often said she cheered them.

To the last, she was interested in the news near and far, and the causes she had espoused. Gladdening her last bed-bound months was the resumption of activities by the Chinese Industrial Cooperatives, for which she had worked long and hard in wartime. "I want to do something," she said, accepting nomination to their promotion committee in anticipation of being able to.

Dr. Wu Weiran, a surgeon of world note, entrusted with the health of China's key leaders, was a good friend—to us and other "old China hands"—foreigners who had cast their lot with China's Revolution. No health matter was too minor to catch his attention, none so serious that he did not extend aid and inspire courage.

After she died, hundreds who had known Elsie through long years attended the pre-cremation farewell in Beijing's Revolutionary Cemetery. As is the modern Chinese custom, her portrait was carried by the eldest child, in this case by Songya, our daughter, her drawn tearless face masking the sorrow which in our younger son, Songping (Robin was the English name Elsie chose for him though he seldom used it), sent his whole tall frame into spasms—he was the gentler, his sister the stronger of the pair.

We had no offspring born of our own union, remedial surgery having failed. But children, all children, were Elsie's objects of love. She helped a Beijing primary school whose pupils came often to her bedside, always joyfully received. A cascade of craft-made flowers which they prepared was placed, at her request, where she could always see them from her bed. A scarlet silk Young Pioneer scarf they presented to her was ultimately immured—as a flash of youth and promise of a better world—in the urn with her ashes in a wall at Babaoshan, Beijing's cemetery for revolutionary heroes. Another part of Elsie's ashes were carried by her sister Ros to England to be buried, beside their parents, in the churchyard of their ancestral village of Brandsby.

Elsie's sympathy for the oppressed, unfortunate, or unsuccessful in competitive society—generalized in her politics—was expressed a personal scale in spontaneous readiness to help lame dogs over stiles—sometimes regardless of merit or lack of it. Of her habitual thought for others before herself I wrote in recollection of a previous health emergency:

> *With medics clattering around you*
> *To revive your threatened life*
> *You said: "Please be quieter*
> *And don't disturb*
> *The patient next door*

Of her internationalism I wrote:

> *For the Chinese people*
> *for forty years*
> *you gave your heart's blood*
> *When you yourself fought death*
> *Into your veins the blood*
> *of China's sons and daughters*
> *flowed unstinted*

In Elsie, the best of East and West mingled in one stream. I want nothing better than to live like my Elsie, be as devoted as she was, face perils, illness and death with her smiling fortitude.

Chapter 31

EVENSONG

In the twilight of my days, I am often asked if I regret my choices in life. In the place and time in which history found me, I can think of nothing better and more meaningful than to have witnessed and linked myself with the Revolution of the Chinese people, one fifth of all humanity, with their weight in the fortunes of the entire world.

In this process, as in all else, there have been joys, pains, and sorrows. But the overall road has been upward, contributing to progress nationally and internationally.

Published in the United States in 1947, was my book *The Unfinished Revolution in China*. In a sense, that Revolution was soon completed—in 1949 with the establishment of the People's Republic. But that was only one stage, albeit a huge and decisive one. In the longer stretch, it was the doorway to future stages, likewise parts and extensions, of China's continuous, unfinished Revolution.

As with nations and societies, so it is with individual lives. All end physically but retain their influence as active or passive parts of larger currents. In a sense, all human activity, individual or collective, is an unfinished Revolution, consisting of stages, which may themselves be major historical watersheds.

For China's people, their Revolution of the twentieth century has laid the foundations for unprecedented growth and progress as we witness the first years of the twenty-first century. It has raised the life span from under 40 in 1949 to over 70, and halved infant mortality from among the world's highest to the level in some moderately developed countries. From the last two decades of the previous century, China's economy, the basis of this progress, has grown annually at a rate of 8% or more, fastest among the world's nations at the time. Her steel production, now about 200 million tons a year, puts her far in the world's lead, a feat all the more extraordinary because, in 1949, production was less than 1 million tons.

In astronautics, China has now joined an elite club: in October

2003 sending up their own astronaut in a domestically-designed and built rocket. Only the former Soviet Union and the United States can claim such a feat.

China's agriculture, while its growth has been much slower than that of its heavy industry, has been producing enough grain to feed its ever-growing population, plus a surplus for adequate storage. This in spite of the regular cycle of partial natural calamities, such as flooding or drought, and sometimes both in alternating areas. To deal with such vagaries of nature, immense works of civil engineering, including the worlds biggest dam spanning the Yangtze River, will provide power and contribute to the re-direction of flow in other waterways, from the moisture-rich south to the relatively dry north.

In the meantime, there has been a significant shift of rural population to urban areas, which are now home or workplace to 40% or more of the population. Today, most families have members in both categories, with one or more young folk in short or long-term jobs in cities and towns. Once flooded with migrant workers, now hundreds and perhaps thousands of high ride residence buildings area home to seasonal or permanent rural employees. These migrants are being helped to legalize their residence status, join trade unions, and overcome bureaucratic difficulties in getting schooling for their children. So far, China has managed to avoid the pattern of towering metropolises ringed by teeming slums so distressingly familiar in Latin America and Third World areas elsewhere. One test for the country's leadership and Socialist direction is to continue to keep things from going that way.

In the meantime, the situation, as always in speedy growth, is one of unevenness with corresponding stresses, social and personal. With the shrinkage of traditional neighborhoods, there is more aloneness—a family in a high-rise apartment is not necessarily acquainted with the one next door, though efforts are made by voluntary residents' committees to create a community. Architecturally, as well as socially, the erasure of the traditional Beijing habitat has at times been too drastic. Apart from some key historic landmarks, and ordinary signboards in Chinese, one might be in a modern city anywhere else in the world, and Beijing's distinctiveness may seem lost. But some of the nostalgia for the "good old days," especially in the local English-language press, I, who knew the old as well as the new, feel to be misplaced, elitist and even repellant. "Good" for whom? Of course, a capital's historical ambience is in many respects inevitably determined by the decisions of the former rulers. But, the Revolution must not fade back into the past, for it too is part of tradition—its freshest and most vital. As an older Chinese saying goes: "When drinking water, don't forget the well-diggers."

*   *   *

Silenced during the Cultural Revolution, Soong Ching-ling responded to the overthrow of the Gang of Four with a great new spurt of writing and other activities despite her age (she was by then over 80) and poor state of health. As always, she was rock-firm in principle and very modest personally. At one point, she wrote me about an allegation that she would not let anybody touch a word she wrote. On the contrary, she insisted that all good suggestions for improvement were most welcome to her—and this was the fact.

One could not tell that she had suffered through so many dire personal shocks, including the desecration of her parents' grave and the lurid exhumation of their bodies, which Red Guards perpetrated on the grounds that they were also the parents-in-law of Chiang Kai-shek. She wrote often for our magazine. In Shanghai, where she spent a good deal of time, she breathed new life into the work of the China Welfare Institute, semi-paralyzed in the turbulent years. From a mainly local undertaking, it developed into a nationwide organization active in women's and children's care in other parts of the country, especially in poor and distant areas, such as Guizhou Province and the Ningxia Autonomous Region. Notable was the development of children's and young people's exchanges with Taiwan, a contribution to the movement for national reunification.

Remarkable was her strong interest in new technologies and extra-curricular education for children from a very young age. In the Children's Cultural Palace in Shanghai, she showed Elsie and me, as early as the 1970s, the computer room, well equipped for that time. More importantly, during one of his visits to the city, she made sure that Deng Xiaoping saw the equipment and talked to the boys and girls there—which he did, impressed and encouraging. Since that time, some of the pupils there have become high-level experts in the computer field.

Moreover, in these years, the China Welfare Institute initiated numerous exchanges of visits of children—including juvenile theatrical and musical performance groups—between China and other countries, stimulating mutual appreciation and understanding at an age when impressions are deep and apt to initiate lifetime interest—good seeds for knowledge and friendship between people and countries.

Soong Ching-ling died of leukemia on May 29, 1981. On June 1, Children's Day in China and other Socialist countries, I had the sad privilege, with others of her old friends, of participating in a farewell vigil.

That same evening I wrote *Thoughts After Standing Guard at Soong Ching Ling's Bier*:

> She lay tranquil among the roses, serene as she had always been in life. Her serenity had nothing to do with the kind born of retreat from the world and its battles. It is hard to name any major struggle of the past seven decades in which she did not engage herself, to which she did not contribute with her effort and valor. In these struggles she never took shelter behind the backs of others. It was her instinct and habit boldly to step into the forefront to assist and shield others. Perhaps it was this serenity—of a fighter confident in the triumph of her cause—that made her seemingly impervious to the ravages of age and of illness. At almost ninety, she looked in death as in life, smoothly youthful and unfaded.
>
> Indeed, she looked more as if asleep, as if resting for a moment with eyes closed. To open them again, to speak again in her soft, clear voice; to write again in her firm, vigorous hand; to fight, and above all, work again with the decisiveness and speed that marked her to her last days.
>
> I could not think to say to her, "Rest in peace!" as she lay there amid the roses, draped in the Red Flag. I could say only, "Work on, fight on, peerless comrade!"
>
> That is what she is certain to do, in the hearts of those who knew her; in the hearts of the thousands of children who passed by her bier this June 1—their day; in the hearts of many yet unborn, whom her flame will continue to inspire, and in the hearts of generations to come.

I again expressed my feelings for her in a poem published in our magazine in 1984 when her statue was unveiled in the cemetery where she was buried in Shanghai:

> *Shanghai girl, sparking, serene,*
> *How wondrously you grew.*
> *Schooled abroad, lifelong for China.*
> *Regard in comfort, choosing struggle,*
> *Staunch backer of frontline fighters,*
> *Sharer of the underground's perils.*
> *Your all for the people, the Revolution,*
> *the children, the future*

Under the dawning star.

Modest, how high you stood.
Low-voiced, yet heard worldwide,
Gentle, yet iron strong,
Graceful, by no storms bent.

More imperishable than your statue's marble
Your spirit's unquenchable fire.
Pure, changeless, fearless, tireless.
Igniting new hearts
To adorn new centuries.

*   *   *

1979 was the year in which Hu Yaobang, then in charge of the propaganda department of the Chinese Communist Party Central Committee, and a bold pioneer of reform in many fields, broadened the editorial staff of many publications in China. In the field of foreign publicity, one of his breakthroughs was to offer leading roles to persons of foreign origin and experience, as often fitted to know how best to write for readers abroad.

His actual instruction of March 13, 1979 read: "For a long time our comrades have ignored the opinions of our foreign experts. We should basically consider the amount of authority they should have."

In this spirit, in May, 1979, I was appointed editor-in-chief of *China Reconstructs*, in full charge of its professional work. I wasn't the only one to whom such ample responsibility was offered, but I alone accepted; the others being wary, for the Cultural Revolution in which prominence often meant vulnerability to denunciation and overthrow, was still too recent in memory. On the staircase leading from the room where the announcement was made, I heard various comments, some encouragingly friendly, but one jeering: "Epstein must want to go back to jail."

I regarded the appointment as an honor. Though it was not an essential change to my everyday pre-Cultural Revolution work as "executive editor," in which experience in journalism and record of friendship for the Chinese Revolution was given weight by Soong Ching-ling and others on and around the magazine.

Returning to the magazine, after prison, was not immediate. For more than two years I worked in the book department of the Foreign

Languages Press. There my function was mainly to improve the English, and to teach the younger comrades—something new to me. One thing I learned was that they knew much more about English grammar than I did. A young man said about a sentence we encountered, "That's in the nominative absolute." I didn't know what he meant, and still don't. But to him it seemed absolutely clear.

*　*　*

Before his death in 1972, I shared warm reunions with Edgar Snow. As journalists, we traveled to Switzerland in the early 1960s and I accompanied him his journey to China in the middle of that decade, which resulted in his book, *The Other Side of the River*. In that work he argued for recognition of and good relations with China on the part of the United States, for which Beijing was ready.

But Snow was ignored in Washington: not only did he no longer have access to the White House as in Roosevelt's day, but he was cavalierly snubbed by the then Secretary of State, Dean Rusk. Ironically, on the eve of Nixon's historic appearance in Beijing, the President wrote a letter to the dying Edgar Snow, full of flattery for his pioneering of renewed U.S.-China relations. Snow, remembering Nixon's long negative previous record in this regard, did not answer. However, had he been physically able, he would certainly have been prominent in the large journalistic group which accompanied Nixon to Beijing. For a rapprochement between the U.S. and China was the aim Ed had long worked for.

The improvements in U.S.-China relations moved forward, inevitably but slowly, to their next logical step: the formal establishment of diplomatic ties in 1979. It was a dramatic and watershed reversal of policy, and the once U.S.-backed Guomindang regime now on Taiwan found itself in a diplomatically precarious position.

Among contacts renewed on my trips to America was Hugh Deane, who had become a leading member of the New York Chapter of the U.S.-China People's Friendship Association, with other chapters in cities all across the country. In California I stayed with old friends Bill and Sylvia Powell in San Francisco, and in Los Angeles I had visits with my first cousin Beba and her family. I saw much of Richard Young (Yang Mengdong), a Chinese-American who as a wartime officer in the U.S.

Army had been General Stilwell's *aide-de-camp*. Young's wife, Helen, who while living in China did extensive research on women participants in the Long March, later published one of the best books on the subject.[28]

When the Cultural Revolution was fading, I joined in the spontaneous days-long memorial for Zhou Enlai, who had died on January 8, 1976. Tiananmen Square was flilled with wreaths bearing white flowers (white is the color of mourning in China) made of paper, silk, or, when sent from factories, even metal. Innumerable poems, some by professional writers, most by ordinary people, were posted in or near the Square. But the Gang of Four had not yet been toppled, and soon the order was given for the Square to be suddenly cleared of all these tributes, causing great indignation and many scuffles and arrests. The popular outpouring was officially condemned as counterrevolutionary. Beijing residents who made copies of the poems on the spot were ordered to give them up. Those who had taken photographs had to hand over their film—I could not even keep mine. People who wore black armbands were admonished to take them off—many didn't. Years later, collections of the poems were published and the mass demonstration was fondly remembered.

*   *   *

The events culminating in June 4, 1989, when public disturbances were suppressed by the People's Liberation Army were tragic and perhaps avoidable. Their causes were due to a broad variety of dissatisfactions internally, and a growing amount of incendiary stimuli from outside the country.

The crisis began in April and exploded in June. International attention was concentrated on Beijing largely through two unrelated coincidences. The first was the striking amount of student memorial activity for Hu Yaobang (which in many ways paralleled the spontaneous outpouring of grief for Zhou Enlai) who had died on April 15. The second was the visit by the then top Soviet leader, Mikhail Gorbachev, to China

---

[28] *Choosing Revolution, Women Soldiers on the Long March*, published by the University of Illinois Press in 2001.

in mid-May. The latter's arrival in Beijing—at last restoring once-strained Sino-Soviet ties—attracted a much larger number of the world's media. The world would be watching.

On April 26, the *People's Daily* ran an editorial condemning the demonstration (one thought to be patriotic) as counterrevolutionary. This had an irritating effect on the students, who thought they were the target, although the editorial statedly took aim at "instigators" using public sympathy for Hu to advance their own grievances. The demonstrations continued to spread and grow exponentially.

At that time, I was writing my biography of Soong Ching-ling, walking daily to her former residence adjacent to Beijing's Houhai area, which, for atmosphere and tranquility, was the best place to work. Each morning and each evening, I saw what was going on in the streets. The demonstrations, at first comprising many students marching together, were soon joined by groups of speedy motorcyclists often carrying slogans or flags. Another change was the increasing use of two-way radios, then rarely in private use. These, I was told by a student, were brought in from Hong Kong.

New, too, was the rapid mushrooming in Tiananmen Square of a veritable tent city in which thousands of demonstrators were encamped. They were more visible and audible than they would be elsewhere in the capital. With extensive, worldwide press coverage broadcast live globally, even Gorbachev's visit had seemed a footnote to this growing dilemma, where foreign reported constantly talked of "something happening" in China.

At first, the Chinese government did not physically interfere. On the contrary, it provided sanitary and other essential facilities. During this phase, the foreign press commented that few governments would have done so much under similar circumstances.

Of the Tiananmen crises much has been studied and analyzed. One thought I have always had was that if Zhou Enlai was still living, the violent end of June, 1989 could have been avoided. Zhou's manner and his ability to relax mounting contradictions had been repeatedly demonstrated. As would, I belive, his ability to have reached out to various generations of Chinese students and citizens in a way no other twentieth century Chinese figure could.

In 1989, things were different. The insulting baiting to which the then premier, Li Peng, was subjected by student delegates clad in pajamas on April 29 would have been inconceivable, much less even tolerated by public opinion, with Zhou in the post.

After June 4, there was an easy, obviously-assisted exodus of some well-known student participants to the United States, together with the ostentatious offer by U.S. authorities of what amounted to permanent residence to students and visiting scholars already in America, whether they asked for it or not. To have refused would have put them out of favor with U.S. authorities.

At the same time, Western specialists, students, and other residents in China were advised by their embassies to leave the country. Most did so, some for many months, others for years, some never to return.

That there were foreign governments fishing in troubled waters was well known, and outward signs, often taken for granted, were only the tip of the iceberg, as previous covert operations against China have shown. We can get a glimpse from the frank and even boastful memoirs of former government agents and their handlers. Here it only needs to be mentioned that the secret operations branch of the U.S. Central Intelligence Agency was authorized, from 1948, to carry out:

> ...any covert activities relating to propaganda, preventive direct... including assistance to underground resistance groups in support of indigenous anti-communist elements... so planned and constructed that... if uncovered the U.S. government can plausibly disclaim any responsibility for them.

It is difficult to believe that with this mindset, there would not be an eager grasping on the part of Western government operatives, of opportunities presented to them by China in 1989. This has occurred before. And no doubt will again.[29]

*　　*　　*

---

[29] Several examples are given by Professor A. Tom Grunfeld in a 2003 review article in *Critical Asian Studies*, Routledge (USA) entitled *"God We Had Fun": The CIA in China and Sino-American Relations*. Books cited include *China Spy: The Story of Hugh Francis Redmond* by Maury Allen (Yonkers, N.Y. Gazette Press, Inc. 1998); *Raiders of the China Coast: CIA Covert Operations during the Korean War*, by Frank Holober (Annapolis, Md.: Naval Institute Press, 1999); *Orphans of the Cold War: America and the Tibetan Struggle for Survival* by John Kenneth Knaus (New York, N.Y.: Public Affairs, 1999) and two other books on under-cover doings in Tibet.

In 1984 I was invited to join the Chinese People's Political Consultative Conference (CPPCC). This was the body in which Mao Zedong had proclaimed the founding of the People's Republic of China, and for its first five years, was its supreme assembly. After 1954 when the Constitution was adopted, the National People's Congress became the country's highest executive and legislative organ. The CPPCC remained as a kind of broad united front advisory "brain trust" for proposals to the government—in a combination unique to China. For this, it was well-qualified by its recruitment from many professions. During the Cultural Revolution, its members being largely intellectuals, then denigrated as a "stinking" category fit only for re-education, it was prevented even from meeting. Following its subsequent resumption, it went through several stages. In the first, it was devoted almost entirely to the political rehabilitation of its membership. Since then, it has functioned mainly as an advisory pool representing a wide range of knowledge—including both that existing before Liberation, and acquired afterwards in the great expansion of education. Politically it inherited from the first CPPCC, and from higher organs of the liberated areas earlier, the principle that the Communist Party, which leads, should not take up more than one-third of its number. The rest includes the democratic parties which had supported the Communist Party in the Revolution and individuals who had subsequently taken or come around to that position—including some once prominent in the military and civil ranks of the former regime.

This may be taken as a realization of Zhou Enlai's remark to me and Elsie as early as 1944 that a coalition government in China would certainly come about—with or without him—meaning Chiang Kai-shek.

The story of my inclusion in the CPPCC was curious, and typical of the times. Early in 1966, Liao Mengxing, an old friend and co-worker from the China Defense League days of the 1930s, who was already a member, phoned to congratulate me on my forthcoming entry into the organization. In May, when the Cultural Revolution began, I still had no formal notice. Then the CPPCC itself was suspended. The next I heard of my nomination was a decade later. And not until 1984 was I seated, first as a member of the National Committee of about two thousand, and, soon afterwards, of its Standing Committee of about two hundred. (The CPPCC exists on many levels down through the provincial and county, and for the whole country, then numbered 300,000, is now up to half a million). It has become richer in knowledge and experience as well. And younger. There seem to be fewer graying or bald heads while there seem to be more black-haired heads of the fortyish and younger generation.

My own suggestions to the CPPCC, either made in writing or orally, have included:

Dismissal of proved corrupt officials and their disqualification from further service, regardless of whether the sums involved made them liable under criminal law; Penalization of makers of fake medicines and intentional profiteers from them; Constant support of requests by many members that the CPPCC should take an active part in supervision against administrative malfeasance arising from bribery and other forms of corruption.

At a number of sessions, both jointly with others and alone, I urged that the National People's Congress be asked to adopt a Cooperative Law. China, unlike most other countries, does not have one, even though her Constitution, over many years, listed a co-op sector as one component of the economy. Collectivization of all farming (culminating hastily in the communes) had been promoted, then abandoned. But cooperatives for special services, such as transport and marketing, could still be very useful—as proved in many countries.

In China's society as a whole, corruption has unfortunately grown with the increase of the role of the market economy, which has powerfully stimulated material advances but also given rise to abuses. In the relatively poor but honest 1950s, the memory of Guomindang corruption and misgovernment was still so vivid that it stimulated scrupulous honesty by the widespread spontaneous impulse to get rid of it, like washing the dirt off one's hands.

In recent years, regrettably, some social evils of the old society have re-appeared in new guise. Prostitution in old China was mainly induced by poverty—daughters had even been sold by their despairing parents rather than have them starve in the frequent famines. Now it began to recur among folk who had enough to eat but wanted more to spend, including some college students aspiring to live among the rich and high-flying consumers. This is something quite distinct from the greater freedom in gender relations, resulting from the overall advance of Chinese women in terms of equality.

In China, as elsewhere, a "glass ceiling" for women seems to have developed. They have difficulty in finding ordinary jobs, especially in the private sector, for the usual profit-conscious reasons—they marry, get pregnant, stay away to take care of the children, and the like.

All this does not, of course, change the key fact that the Chinese Revolution has lifted women from an abyss of semi-serfdom to legally defined rights of citizenship, apportionment of rural land, freedom of choice in marriage, paid leave for childbirth and other provisions to guard their equality.

Women make up only about 10 per cent of the CPPCC membership. This is far from "holding up half the sky" as Mao Zedong said they do and should. Also, of the 10 percent, many are concentrated in the section from the Women's Federation, and in groups such as the medical or cultural areas. In earlier years, there were more women in the higher echelons, as was the case in the Communist Party—a heritage of the revolutionary years. For some years, the CPPCC was headed by Deng Yingchao, widow of Zhou Enlai and herself a member of the Party Central Committee.

A year or so after Elsie's death, I had a chance to chat with Deng Xiaoping, then 81. That evening, during a televised meeting, he was in high spirits. He asked how long I was jailed in the Cultural Revolution, and when I answered, "Almost five years," he remarked, "Less than me, I had six" (referring to his purge from leadership and the period of disgrace, exile, and house arrest). Deng then lit my cigarette and we smoked together. This brought me a censorious phone call from Deng Yingchao the next day: "You and Deng Xiaoping are setting a bad example for the youth, smoking on television!" Deng Yingchao then took the occasion to once again recall our slipping away from the Japanese in Tianjin some four decades earlier.

In the CPPCC, there was a general appreciation of the immense progress the country had made plus sharpened awareness of the pockets of poverty and backwardness inherited or regurgitated from the past. City-bred members who went on inspections of distant and impecunious rural areas were sometimes deeply shocked by the conditions they saw there and, on the positive side, made all kinds of suggestions for improvement. Clearly understood were the twin aspects of modern China, its rapid progress and the amount of effort and time needed to overcome its consequent, and often widening, gaps between peak and lag.

Some old revolutionary traditions have faded, others persisted or been revived. When natural calamities strike, the army is still there promptly to help the people. Newer are youth volunteer movements. Though only beginning, trends to go to the Western parts of the country are in sharp contrast to tendencies, especially since the 1980s, of "swallows flying southeast" to richer climates. Personally affecting me was the decision of a woman editor in her forties, with a responsible job in a top Beijing publishing house that put out the Chinese translation of one of my books, to leave to work for some years in Tibet.

As in the Third World, especially between its developing and underdeveloped parts, and also between the older and younger generations in all countries, there are different degrees of the "digital gap," ranging all the way from difficulty of access of computers to their availability, but coming too late in life to adjust. By contrast, there are dramatic leaps across time and space. Already 20 or so years ago, I saw computers in use in Tibet, in the Tibetan language.

In the years following 1978, and after, under the direct guidance of Deng Xiaoping, major attention was focused on economic construction—increasing national productive forces—with spectacular results which put China in the world's front rank in its rate of development. From the late 1990s, the role of her Communist Party was defined by Deng's successor, Jiang Zemin, by what were called the "Three Represents"—listed as the China's most advanced productive forces, foremost thinking, and the most widespread welfare of her population.

Very visibly, both the retiring leadership in its last period, and its new successors, have done much for the peoples' physical welfare. In Beijing, outdoor fitness equipment, mushrooming in a great many other places, is used enthusiastically and free of charge by the young from toddlers upward, all the way to elderly men and women well into their eighties and beyond. There is something for everyone, including handicapped ancients like myself. A general passion for exercise is visibly improving the appearance of many urban Chinese—backs are straighter, and the scholar and clerk are no longer so easily differentiated by their stoop, traditionally recognized, and even encouraged, as a sign of learning. All these changes have shown their effect in the record number of gold medals won by Chinese athletes in the Athens Olympic games of 2004 and their fruits in the 2008 Beijing Olympics, among performers and huge new numbers of fans both in China and around the world..

Another trend is renewed activity by the country's labor unions.

Vigorous in the formative and young years of the People's Republic, they lost strength in the years of the immutable "eight standards" for workers when wages, housing and other benefits for workers depended on their administrative classification into eight legally defined grades in seniority and skill under that system virtually all urban residents were entitled to jobs—which certainly gave much essential protection. But the unions, under those circumstances, gradually lost their function— the degree of authority they continued to enjoy for years—work-safety measures having been under their control—gradually faded and the broad benefits they conferred dwindled largely to matters like securing blocks of tickets, free to members, to showings of films, etc. and arranging holiday outings. It would seem that, under those circumstances, unions lost much of their necessity. But with the unprecedented growth of the economy, and the development of private or corporate enterprises, including many financed in part or wholly by foreign companies, they are clearly required again—and the new national leadership in China is attentive to this need, as reflected on the 2003 Congress of the All-China Federation of Trade Unions.

A marked advance was the attention paid to the farming areas with their relatively undeveloped medical facilities. In this period, people recalled the rural cooperative medical insurance that had spread in previous decades but been half forgotten—and began to talk and act on their revival.

In these respects, as in others in China, there were excessive swings of the pendulum. When facilities were universally available, even though rudimentary, there was a tendency to denigrate high quality as purely elitist. When quality and modernity were the main stress, the mass factors tended to slip from attention. Now, there is dawning new appreciation of the merits of "walking on two legs" as it was once termed. What has become possible is a higher level of application of this concept, with more scientific means and understanding to back it. In need of attention is the financial cost of illness, which may be prohibitive for ordinary people in severe cases. This is particularly the case when hospitals and clinics rush to get the latest medical machines which can be very expensive, with the cost passed on to patients, fewer of whom can pay what is required. Today, the prices of some medicines have been reduced by government action, but more need to be—and some such steps are under consideration. The new leadership of the Communist

Party and government, which took office in 2003, appears more sensitive, and active, in this respect. At this writing, it is launching a nation-wide informational campaign against the spread of AIDS.

*   *   *

Early in the twenty-first century, China was both the point of origin, and the site of victory over the health scourge called SARS (Severe Acute Respiratory Syndrome). Many are the examples of heroism in this battle, especially among the nation's doctors and nurses, some of whom gave their lives. Notable, too, was the behavior of the new generation of leaders. They put a vigorous end to bureaucratic tendencies to gloss over inconvenient facts with uncompromising demotions and replacements of those responsible. At the same time, China's soft-spoken new Premier, Wen Jiabao, appeared in designated danger areas without a face mask, which practically everybody else there was required to wear. This had a steadying effect on panicky tendencies. Efforts to ensure the supply of food, medicines, and other necessities were energetic and generally successful. At centers of infection, new isolation hospitals were rapidly built.

I myself was then in a hospital for a post-surgical check. So strict were the precautions against SARS that parts of its interior were quarantined in relation to other wards. To pass between them one had to don protective gear. On a wider scale, the movement of people in and out of Beijing as a whole was suspended for several months.

*   *   *

At the end of the day, I remain a Marxist. Repeatedly pronounced "dead" almost from its very beginning in the mid nineteenth century—Marxism has repeatedly come alive in theory and been sought as a guide to practice in the periods since.

Marxism is not prophecy but a method of analysis. Its essence is the inevitable succession of social systems, applicable to capitalism as to all previous forms, culminating in socialism and finally communism with the development of production as the basis and all forms of organization and thought as the superstructure which it makes possible and indeed inevitable. These changes vary with the situation and degree of development of each country and depend on the recognition of the people of their possibility and necessity. There is no time table.

It is a remarkable fact that even among those who do not accept his conclusions Marx is widely regarded as the foremost thinker of the first millennium.

Such was the opinion of the British Broadcasting Corporation, the magazine The Economist and some other media. A common theme was that even if Marx did not predict the experience of the first Socialist countries, he certainly understood capitalism.

*　　*　　*

There is a Chinese expression *nao-hai*, which means, literally, "brain-ocean." Nothing, in any other language I know of, conveys better the immense and complex working of the human mind, from its deepest depths to its highest tides, its quietest to its stormiest. The ever-practical Chinese, do not assume the existence of an abstract element such as the soul. Despite many popular superstitions about the spirit world, the function of thought, like every other human attribute, was attributed to a physical organ—though in more ancient tradition this was located as the heart, the seat of both understanding and conscience.

One's "brain-ocean" can be seen as recording experience, and individually reacting to wider stimuli at all levels, as the geographical ocean reflects the color-moods of the sky above it and the dank cold or boiling volcanic heat at its bedrock base.

INDEX

NOTES TO PHOTOGRAPHS

1. As a reporter with the *Peking and Tientsin Times*, 1934.
2. My grandfather David Epstein (*second left*), grandmother Haya-Kraina Baver (*third right*) and father Lazar Epstein (*fourth left*) in 1905.
3. My father Lazar (*third left, rear*) with the Jewish Labor Alliance members in Minsk, 1905.
4. With my mother Sonya Epstein in Harbin, 1919.
5. With my father at Beidaihe, 1920.
6. With my mother.
7. With my classmates in Tianjin, 1930.
8. As a youngster.
9. With my parents.
10. My first wife, Edith Bihovsky.
11. With my second wife, Elsie Fairfax-Cholmeley, 1946.
12. Visiting two aunts and a cousin in Moscow, 1963.
13. With my sister-in-law Rosamond and household helper Li Mama.
14. As a correspondent with United Press, covering the battle of Taierzhuang. With filmmaker Joris Ivens and his assistant John Ferno alongside a disabled Japanese tank.
15. On the train to Taierzhuang, 1937. *Right to left*: Chinese American photographer Jack Yang, Joris Ivens, John Ferno, myself, and renowned Hungarian photographer Robert Capa.
16. In Nanjing with fellow journalist Tilman Durdin (*right*) of the *New York Times*, 1937.
17. With Communist Party representative Bo Gu at the gate of Eighth Route Army Nanjing office, 1937.
18. With my UP colleague Wang Gongda in Wuhan, 1938.
19. Myself (*center*) reporting on the Japanese aerial bombing of Guangzhou (1938).
20. In Guangzhou, 1938.
21. Anti-Japanese resistance militia in Zhongshan County, Guangdong Province, 1938.
22. Anti-Japanese propaganda poster in Guangzhou, 1938.
23. Soong Ching-ling with the Central Committee of the China Defense League in Hong Kong (1938). *Left to right*: myself, Deng Wenzhao, Liao Mengxing, Soong Ching-ling, Norman France, Hilda Selwyn-Clarke, and Liao Chengzhi.
24. Soong Ching-ling (*fourth from right*), Edith Epstein (*fifth from right*) and Morris

Cohen visiting the wounded at a Guangzhou military hospital, 1938.

25. The Hong Kong office of the China Defense League, at 21 Seymour Road.

26. With other noted Chinese and foreign journalists in Hong Kong: Ye Qianyu, Edgar Snow, Jin Zhonghua, Zhang Guangyu, Ding Cong.

27. My co-workers at the *Hong Kong Daily Press*.

28. Upon Hong Kong's Japanese occupaton in 1942, I was confined in a Japanese detention camp. I escaped in March 1942.

29. With the staff of *Jiuwang Ribao* (*National Salvation Daily*) in Guilin.

30. With other members of the China Defense League in Chongqing: Anna Wang, Chen Jiakang (assistant to Zhou Enlai), novelist Mao Dun (*third from left*), Zhang Hanfu, and American journalists Hugh Deane, Graham Peck, and Jack Belden.

31. Wearing an Eighth Route Army uniform, Yan'an, 1944.

32. Mao Zedong (*back row, right*) meeting our journalist group in Yan'an.

33. Mass rally in Yan'an after the opening of the "Second Front" in World War II, 1944.

34. Mao Zedong (*third left, front*) and other leaders of the Central Communist Party meeting with visiting Chinese and foreign journalists, 1944. Right to left, first row: Zhou Enlai, Yang Shangkun, myself (*fourth right*), and Zhu De (*fifth right*).

35. With Zhu De and Zhou Enlai, 1944. Front row, myself (*first left*), Zhu De (*middle*), Zhou Enlai (*third right*), He Long (*second right*) and Lin Biao (*first right*).

36. Inspecting a Japanese sword captured by the Eighth Route Army.

37. With colleague Harrison Forman in Eighth Route Army uniform in northwest Shaanxi, 1944.

38. Interviewing Lin Feng, a leader of the Chinese Communist Party.

39. Soong Ching-ling inspecting an international aid shipment of pharmaceuticals and medical equipment for the Eighth Route Army.

40. At the typewriter preparing my book *From Opium War to Liberation*, 1956.

41. Talking about China to overseas Chinese students in the U.S. in 1948.

42. In Monterey, California, 1949.

43. Elsie and I were guests at a dinner given by patriotic general (and former warlord) Feng Yuxiang in New York.

44. With the staff of *China Reconstructs* in Beijing, 1951.

45. Elsie working with Chen Hansheng, Editorial Director of *China Reconstructs*.

46. Soong Ching-ling, Zhou Enlai, Chen Yi and Deng Yingchao with editorial staff at *China Reconstructs*' 10th Anniversary in 1962. Rear: Soong Ching-ling (*fifth left*), Chen Yi (*sixth left*), Deng Yingchao (*fourth left*). Front: Zhou Enlai (*first left*) and myself (*second left*).

47. Soong Ching-ling and Chen Yi with myself, Elsie, and Ione Kramer, 1962.

48. With Soong Ching-ling, George Hatem (*second right, front*), Rewi Alley (*third right, front*) and other Chinese and foreign friends.

49. Elsie and I with Soong Ching-ling, Liao Chengzhi, and Edgar Snow.

50. State leaders at the celebration of the 10th anniversary of *China Reconstructs* with editorial staff. Rear: Soong Ching-ling (*fifth left*), Chen Yi (*sixth left*), Deng Yingchao (*fourth left*), Zhou Enlai (*first left*) and myself (*second left*).

51. Zhou Enlai (*second from left*), myself (*second from right*), and Manya Reiss (Ayerora), from the Xinhua News Agency.

52. Mao Zedong with foreign experts, 1964. Left to right: Sidney Rittenberg, myself, Anna Louise Strong, Frank Coe, and Sol Adler.

53. Mao Zedong with translators and editors of the English version of *Selections from Mao Zedong* (1964). Tang Mingzao (*first left*), myself (*third left*), Frank Coe (*first right*), and Sol Adler (*fourth right*).

54. With Edgar Snow and Rewi Alley in Beijing, 1964.

55. In Switzerland in 1961 while covering the Geneva International Conference on Laos. With Edgar Snow (*back row, second from right*), and Chinese diplomat Qiao Guanhua (*back row, first from right*).

56. Reporting from the site of the Sanmenxia Dam on the Yellow River, late 1950s.

57. Visiting Dazhai, touted as China's model village in the 1960s. Chen Yonggui, the village leader, is at center.

58. Conducting an interview in the countryside, June 1965.

59. Reading from Mao Zedong's quotations at the beginning of the Cultural Revolution.

60. Writing my book, *Tibet Transformed* in an outdoor shelter after the Tangshan earthquake, 1976.

61. With Tibetan friends.

62. Tibetans in Gyangze, 1976.

63. Visiting Tibet at age 70.

64. In front of the old *Peking and Tientsin Times* office on a visit to Tianjin in the 1980s.

65. Standing on the bank of the Yellow River.

66. With children on the bank of the Yellow River, site of former guerilla resistance bases.

67. An interview with American media about China (1995)

68. At a promotion meeting of *China Reconstructs*.

69. The 40th anniversary of *China Today* (*China Reconstructs*) (1992).

70. With children in the Soong Ching-ling Kindergarten founded by the China Welfare Institute.

71. With my present wife, Huang Wanbi, and Lu Ping (*front*), vice-chairman of the China Welfare Institute, and Sufei, widow of Ma Haide (*rear*) (2003).

72. At the Memorial for Soong Ching-ling, May 29 1981.

73. Attending a meeting of the Standing Committee of the Chinese People's Politi-

cal Consultative Conference (CPPCC), March, 1991.

74. With other Foreign-born members of the CPPCC.

75. In America, with John W. (Bill) Powell (*first right*), former editor-in-chief of the Shanghai *China Weekly Review*, who suffered persecution during the McCarthy era.

76. With Mrs. Hellen Rosen (*left*) and hugh Deane (*center*) of the American-Chinese Friendship Association.

77. Revisiting Yan'an with American journalists in March 1985.

78. I hosted Dr. Charles Grossman and Dr. Herbert Abrams, and their wives, at my home.

79. Calling on old friends Joan Hinton (*right*) and her husband Erwin (Sid) Engst (*left*).

80. Visiting my aged primary school teacher, Helen Yates, in California.

81. With former chairman of the Edgar Snow Foundation, Dr. E. Grey Dymond (*left*).

82. Visiting Jack Shapiro and his wife Marie in England. Jack's elder brother Michael was an expert at the Xinhua News Agency for many years.

83. With Elsie, George Hatem, Rewi Alley, B.K. Basu, and family on holiday at Beidaihe.

84. In 2004 Ambassador of Moldova, Dr. Victor Borscvici, presented me with an honorary doctorate on behalf of Moldova.

85. On my 70th birthday, I sharing a toast with Deng Xiaoping at the Great Hall of the People, 1985.

86. In 2003 I presented former President Jiang Zemin with my newly-published *Selections of News Works*, a compilation of my articles and news reports on China.

87. With former Premier Zhu Rongji.

88. President Hu Jintao visited me during Spring Festival, 2004.

89. Premier Wen Jiabao visited me at home.

90. With my children, Ai Songya (*left*), and Ai Songping (*right*).

91. With Elsie and my first wife, Edith, in Beijing.

92. With Songya and her family in the U.S.

93. My extended family.

94. Atop the Great Wall.